ARCHETYPAL
DIMENSIONS
OF THE
PSYCHE

A C. G. JUNG FOUNDATION BOOK
Published in association with Daimon Verlag,
Einsiedeln, Switzerland

The C. G. Jung Foundation for Analytical Psychology is dedicated to helping men and women grow in conscious awareness of the psychological realities in themselves and society, find healing and meaning in their lives and greater depth in their relationships, and live in response to their discovered sense of purpose. It welcomes the public to attend its lectures, seminars, films, symposia, and workshops and offers a wide selection of books for sale through its bookstore. The Foundation also publishes *Quadrant,* a semiannual journal, and books on Analytical Psychology and related subjects. For information about Foundation programs or membership, please write to the C. G. Jung Foundation, 28 East 39th Street, New York, NY 10016.

ARCHETYPAL
DIMENSIONS
OF THE
PSYCHE

Marie-Louise von Franz

SHAMBHALA
BOSTON & LONDON
1999

SHAMBHALA PUBLICATIONS, INC.

HORTICULTURAL HALL
300 Massachusetts Avenue
Boston, Massachusetts 02115
http://www.shambhala.com

Originally published by Daimon Verlag, CH-8840 Einsiedeln, Switzerland,
under the title *Archetypische Dimensionen der Seele,* © 1994 by Daimon Verlag.
Pages ix–x constitute a continuation of this copyright page.

9 8 7 6 5 4 3 2 1

FIRST PAPERBACK EDITION

Printed in the United States of America

⊛ This edition is printed on acid-free paper that meets the
American National Standards Institute Z39.48 Standard.

Distributed in the United States by Random House, Inc., and
in Canada by Random House of Canada Ltd

The Library of Congress Catalogues the hardcover edition
of this book as follows:

Franz, Marie-Luise von, 1915–
[Archetypische Dimensionen der Seele. English]
Archetypal dimensions of the psyche / Marie-Louise von Franz.—
1st ed.
p. cm.
"A C.G. Jung Foundation book."
Includes bibliographical references and index.
ISBN 1-57062-133-0 (alk. paper)
ISBN 1-57062-426-7 (pbk.)
1. Archetype (Psychology)   2. Jungian psychology.   I. Title.
BF175.5.A72F7313   1997   96-38919
150.19′54—dc21   CIP

CONTENTS

FOREWORD

■■
■■

THIS FOURTH VOLUME of the selected writings of Marie-Louise von Franz concludes our project of making available in book form for the first time this author's widely dispersed shorter works. Following *Dreams, Psyche and Matter,* and *Psychotherapy,* this volume consists primarily of articles, essays, and lectures from the years 1969 to 1985 addressing the workings and contents of the archetypal realm, i.e., unconscious collective forces acting in relation to past, present, and future developments in ways often not readily evident.

The works comprising this series were not originally conceived as chapters of a book, having been prepared for disparate occasions, often a lecture. They have now been reworked, edited, and arranged thematically, but this, nevertheless, does not preclude a certain amount of repetition.

For those readers unfamiliar with Jungian terminology, a glossary is located at the end of the first volume, *Dreams* (Boston and London: Shambhala Publications, 1991). A bibliography and an index are located at the back of this fourth volume, and the "Sources" section in the front lists the original publication locations of material previously appearing elsewhere in print.

As we conclude our series of the selected writings of Marie-Louise von Franz, we would like to thank the author for her tremendous contribution, not only in formulating these works in the first place, but also in helping when it was most needed to compile the present collection, and this at a time in her life when every effort has been difficult for her. We would also like to thank Dr. René Malamud of Zurich, who originally conceived the idea of this series and helped it to become a reality. May these books and the ideas they carry lead to much reflection and stimulation.

ROBERT HINSHAW
Daimon Verlag
Einsiedeln, Switzerland

SOURCES

■■

"Antichrist or Merlin?: A Problem Inherited from the Middle Ages."
    Book Forum 5, no. 2 (1980): 234–43. Copyright © Marie-Louise
    von Franz.
"The Problem of Evil in Fairy Tales." From *Evil,* edited by the Cura-
    torium of the C. G. Jung Institute Zurich (Evanston, Ill.: North-
    western University Press, Studies in Jungian Thought, 1967).

The following chapters were translated by Michael H. Kohn.
The translations are copyright © 1996 by Shambhala Publications, Inc.:

"The Bremen Town Musicians from the Point of View of Depth Psy-
    chology" ("Die Bremer Stadtmusikanten in tiefenpsychologischer
    Sicht")
"The Cosmic Man as Image of the Goal of the Individuation Process
    and Human Development" ("Der kosmische Mensch als Zielbild
    des Individuationsprozesses und der Menschheitsentwicklung")
"The Discovery of Meaning in the Individuation Process" ("Die Sinn-
    findung im Individuationsprozess")
"Highlights of the Historical Dimension of Analysis" ("Streiflichter auf
    die geschichtliche Dimension der Analyse")
"Individuation and Social Relationship in Jungian Psychology." Based
    on a lecture given at Loyola Campus of Concordia University
    in Montreal on March 19, 1975. Another version appeared (as
    "Individuation and Social Contact in Jungian Psychology") in
    Harvest 21 (1975): 12–27 (published by the Analytical Psychology
    Club of London).
"The Individuation Process" ("Der Individuationsprozess"). Another

version of this essay was published as "The Process of Individuation" in *Man and His Symbols,* ed. C. G. Jung (New York: Doubleday, 1968).

"In the Black Woman's Castle: An Interpretation of a Fairy Tale" ("Bei der schwartzen Frau: Deutungsversuch eines Märchens")

"Jung's Discovery of the Self" ("Die Selbsterfahrung bei C. G. Jung")

"Nike and the Waters of the Styx" ("Nike und die Gewässer der Styx")

"The Self-Affirmation of Man and Woman: A General Problematic Illustrated by Fairy Tales" ("Die Selbstbehauptung von Mann und Frau: Eine allgemeinmenschliche Problematik durch Märchentexte illustriert")

"The Transformed Berserk: Unification of Psychic Opposites." This was the keynote address at the Eighth Conference of the International Transpersonal Association on Individual Transformation and Universal Responsibility, August 27–September 2, 1983, in Davos, Switzerland. Another version of it appeared in *"ReVision* 8, no. 1 (summer/fall 1985).

"The Unknown Visitor in Fairy Tales and Dreams" ("Der unbekannte Besucher in Märchen und Träumen")

HIGHLIGHTS OF THE HISTORICAL DIMENSION OF ANALYSIS

■■
■■

SIGMUND FREUD MUST RECEIVE the credit for being the first to point out the psychic significance of childhood experiences for the etiology of neuroses. After behavioral research proved the receptivity of animals in the early juvenile stage to external influences, this view was reinforced yet further. Nonetheless, many healthy as well as pathological psychic tendencies cannot be traced back to experiences of early childhood. This fact has brought many researchers to seek the causes even in prenatal experiences, but this leads to endless speculation. In contrast to this attempt at a biographical-historical explanation, numerous psychological schools are looking for the explanation for the more deep-seated characteristics of the individual in the social milieu, which in my opinion might actually be a suitable way to illuminate certain of the problems involved. A further source was discovered by C. G. Jung: the influence on the child, not of the conscious social behavior of the parents, but of *the parents' unconscious*. In Jung's view, the *unconscious atmosphere* of the family milieu is even more influential than the conscious pedagogical behavior of the parents. But we must go still a step beyond that: many people (not all, as we shall see later) are consciously or unconsciously ruled by something that has been aptly described by the term *zeitgeist*.

The zeitgeist is a curious phenomenon. On the one hand it is the sum of collective, shared outlooks, feelings, and ideas of a generation or a historical period—for example, the zeitgeist of the Renaissance or the zeitgeist of the Enlightenment. This kind of zeitgeist takes shape predominantly in centers of culture and urban agglomerations, while often in geographically more remote parts of the country and culturally less interesting social strata, older forms of outlooks and traditions persist strongly. In a certain sense, only very few people are "modern"; in every population nearly *all* historical strata are represented—a fact that psychotherapy must take account of.

In my town of Küsnacht in the vicinity of Zurich, I have even encountered a downright "stone-ager." I went into his junk shop and bought a saw and a sawhorse for my vacation cottage. In so doing, I passed a couple of deprecatory remarks about electricity and that sort of "modern nonsense." He immediately took me by the sleeve and tugged me into the yard behind his house, insisting that I sit down with him, and said, "You understand me—yes, you understand! That's why I'm going to tell you how I live. I work a few months in a factory until I've gotten enough money together. Then I buy dried meat and wine and go off high into the mountains. I make myself a bed of brush in a cave and I live there. When there are no people around, I wander naked over the glaciers. Yes, and Christianity! Isn't that the greatest of nonsense?! To believe that God lives in a building, in a church! God is in the flowers, in crystals, in the clouds, and in the rain! *That's* where God is!" I assured him of my complete sympathy but wondered to myself what the wife of such a man might have to say. Then I coincidentally ran into her too. She was an illiterate woman from Sicily—just as archaic as he was! When I told Jung about this encounter, he smiled and said, "There we have a stone-age Swiss! He should be put in a provincial museum with a sign saying, 'Here's a Swiss from Neolithic times. You can interview him!'" A narrow-minded psychologist might have considered the man mad, but that would have been inaccurate. After all, he lived in a quite well-adjusted manner, just in another historical period.

In Switzerland, a part of the population—mainly rural—lives in the Middle Ages, and most ordinary middle-class folk have an outlook that belongs to the nineteenth century. Radio and television apparently do little to alter this. But it is not only individual groups within a people that live in different historical periods. The individual too, as we might discover by taking a core of his depths, carries within him, stored in his unconscious, the entire historical past of his people, even of humanity as a whole. For example, up until today, I have never analyzed an Italian, man or woman, in whom motifs from classical antiquity did not appear in a fully living condition in dreams. For example, I remember the initial dream of a fifty-two-year-old psychologist. He saw clouds grouping in the sky and a magically beautiful youth with winged shoes descending toward him. He awoke strangely shaken. I was very frightened, because the youth was obviously Hermes, the conductor of souls, and in fact it soon came out that the man's health was in ruins. The analysis would become his guide into death. He was, like most intellectual Italians, an armchair Communist, but on his deathbed he found his way back to the Church. But why Hermes and not an angel of death? Because ancient times are still that much alive in Italy.

Or let me give you an example from my own life. Twenty years ago I bought a remote piece of property on the edge of a forest and built myself a house without electricity, telephone, or any other gadgetry of modern civilization. Many of my acquaintances tried to frighten me, saying that the house was too isolated and dangerous. The first night alone in the new house, I had the following dream. Out the window I saw a procession of people approaching and thought, "Oh God, another disturbance already!" Then I saw that the people were all peasants in medieval garb and that it was a ceremonial wedding procession with the bride and groom at the head of it. I thought, "I really must receive these people." As I was on my way to the cellar to get some wine, I woke up. Jung interpreted this to mean that through my return to the land, the spirits of my peasant ancestors had been reawakened. It was a return to inner historical roots.

But that was not the end of it. A few nights after that, I had another dream. It was evening and I became aware that there were people at my door. I went to see who it was, and there was a gang of young people dressed up as Shrovetide carnival goblins, with animal and ghost masks on. Gradually, however, they seemed to turn more and more into real ghosts. I began to get an eerie feeling, and I went back into the house and closed the door. Then I saw a light blue glow coming in through the window. I went to the window and saw that my house was as though under water, but it was bright, glimmering water in which it was possible to breathe. In contrast to reality, the trees came right up to the house. In them were romping blissfully happy, large silver-gray monkeys with dark, lemurine faces and long tails. I awoke invigorated and refreshed, as though I had been watching these monkeys all night long.

As you can see, in this case I went back beyond even the pagan masks to animal ancestral spirits! You can imagine how much my "monkey soul" was enjoying life in nature, while my urban ego consciousness was reacting rather fearfully, needing to acclimate itself to the situation.

Thus, as a psychologist, one always has to be acquainted with the entire historical background of a person so as to understand him or her better. I remember the analysis of an educated Korean man. I had oriented myself as best as possible to the Korean culture, but what showed up in his dreams? Motifs that I was initially completely unable to understand. The dreamer also could not understand them, because his only orientation was to the Buddhist past of his country. But these were motifs of Tungusic shamanism! In point of fact the Koreans are ethnic Tunguses, and in the pre-Buddhist period, their religion and therapeutic art was shamanism. Thanks to the books of Mircea Eliade, Nioradze, Findeisen, and others, the two of us were able to come to understand these dream motifs.

One case that left a particularly strong impression was that of a Catholic, well-educated Mexican. Although I liked him from the beginning, I had the uncomfortable feeling that I didn't understand him, and I suspected that he also was not getting much out of what I was saying to him. Then without warning, seemingly without connection with his outer life, he had the following dream: In the fork of a tree lay a large obsidian stone, which suddenly came to life, jumped down out of the tree, and rolled menacingly toward the dreamer. The dreamer was panic-stricken and ran for his life, with the stone hard on his heels. Then the dreamer saw some workers, who had dug out a rectangular hole in the ground. They called to him that he should get into the middle of the hole and stay still. He did this, whereupon the obsidian stone grew smaller and smaller, until it lay "tamely" at the dreamer's feet, no larger than a fist.

When I heard this dream, I involuntarily exclaimed, "But for God's sake, what have you got to do with Tezcatlipoca?" Coincidentally, I happened to know that obsidian was one of the main symbols for this primeval Aztec god. Then it came out that the dreamer was three-quarters Aztec, which until this point he had never mentioned, because in Mexico racial prejudices still exist. Now it was clear to me why we had had such a difficult time understanding one another: the Native Americans think in an imagic and mythological fashion, but from the heart; our rational abstract thinking is entirely alien to them. I reoriented myself, and then we understood each other. After this dream, a deep wound opened in the dreamer—sadness and resentment over the brutality of the pseudo-"Christian" Cortés and his gold-crazed band of adventurers, but also a burning interest in the old Aztec gods. Thus he found his spiritual roots again and also began to work creatively on old Aztec texts. His neurosis was cured, and he became much more himself. He could now also better understand the Christian truth, that is to say, as an archetypal parallel to the Aztec religious myths. Although Cortés's crimes go back approximately four hundred years, this historical episode stood immediately behind the psychic disorientation that had caused the dreamer to undertake analysis. The still-living archetypal divine image of the god Tezcatlipoca literally stalked him, and by facing him and becoming involved in an encounter with him, he rediscovered the point of connection to his ancestral spirits and to his cultural and religious roots.

Here we encounter on a concrete level one of C. G. Jung's most significant discoveries, his concept of the collective unconscious and its archetypes. For Jung, archetypes are inherited, inborn, structural dispositions with respect to the species-specific modes of behavior of human beings. One aspect of these modes is that of an action: they express themselves in typical actions, similar in all human beings, and thus are instinctive (as Eibl-Eibesfeld, among others, has proved, all the peoples of the earth express themselves through similar gestures of greeting, child rearing, courtship, etc.). But beyond this action level, these "instincts" also have a form of expression that can only be perceived inwardly within the psyche, that is, in feelings, emotions, mythical fantasy images, and "mythical" primal ideas, which take a similar form in all human beings. This last aspect Jung referred to as archetypal. The archetypes are the primal elements of the mind and of the various cultures. Whenever this profound collective stratum is activated in an individual, it can become either a source of creative structuring and new spiritual realizations, or if something goes wrong, it can become a source of pathological states and actions.

All of the greater religions of the world that are still intact contain and display in their imagery the great archetypes of the collective unconscious—the primal images of the Savior-Hero, the Great Mother, the Heavenly Father of the Spirit, the helpful animal, the creator of evil, the world tree, the center of the world, the beyond and the realm of the dead, and so on. Often such primal notions are so similar in different cultures that cultural researchers invent absurd theories of migration in order to explain the similarity. Though of course there actually have been migrations and exchanges of religious motifs, we psychologists are skeptical about overly wild speculations in this area, because in our work we have the daily experience that such primal images can be spontaneously activated and manifested in the unconscious of a person, even in the unconscious of an individual whose consciousness is totally remote from such images. For example, though as a Mexican the dreamer mentioned above did have a very vague acquaintance with the existence of an old god named Tezcatlipoca, he never even remotely thought of him, and after the dream, he first had to read extensively about him in books before the god's image began to become more comprehensible to him.

One might well ask at this point why it should be necessary for a person to be in contact with his or her historical-spiritual roots. In Zurich we have the opportunity to analyze many Americans who come to the Jung Institute and thus to observe the symptoms and results of a hiatus in culture (emigration of their forebears) and a loss of roots. In that case we are dealing with people whose consciousness is structured similarly to ours; but when we bore into the depths, we find something that resembles a gap in the steps—no continuity! A cultivated white man—and beneath that a primitive shadow, of which the Americans on the average have far less sense than we do. The effect of this is a certain restlessness and suggestibility, an uncritical susceptibility to currents of fashion, and a tendency toward extreme reactions. Of course this also has a positive side, which expresses itself in the average American's sense of enterprise and openness to the world. When one analyzes such people, sooner or later through their dreams the story of their ancestors up till the time of their emigration to the United States comes up for discussion. At that point most of the analysands spontaneously feel the need to take a "sentimental journey" to the country of their ancestors. Renewed connection with the country of their forefathers usually contributes to a better self-understanding on the part of these analysands.

Emigration or periods of living in another culture on the whole have quite peculiar psychological consequences. The English are familiar with the notion of "going native," by which they mean the unconscious influence upon colonists and colonial officials, and the like, who are infected by the African mentality. The influence is initially negative, taking the form of tardiness, uncleanliness, a tendency to make up fantastic stories, and so on, all attributes of which the whites routinely accuse the natives. This unconscious negative influence can, however, be transformed into something positive if the person in question does not look down upon the other culture but rather opens himself respectfully to it and takes its views and traits seriously. Then it has an enriching effect rather than an undermining one. This is, of course, true everywhere, not only in Africa.

I had the opportunity to analyze a man who spent the first twelve years of his life in Hong Kong. It was astonishing to what extent he had unconsciously become Chinese. When, during the analysis, he began consciously to study Chinese wisdom, hitherto unimagined horizons opened up. As Jung once remarked, the Americans have unconsciously assimilated into themselves a great deal from the black population and from the Native Americans, even those who have no blood connection with them. Today, many years after Jung made this remark, the Americans are starting to become aware of this, and many are now consciously trying to open themselves to these cultural influences. However, such influences still are studied far too little. Nonetheless, it is indisputable that the country and people to which one belongs and their historical development are a prominent factor in the psyche of individuals. We are up to our ears not only in our biographical past but also in our collective historical past, whether or not we like it or have even noticed it.

Indeed, from a psychological point of view, history can become a true devouring monster which can completely paralyze us. The past, into which the flow of historical events ineluctably disappears, is an enormous force. For this reason, the people of India represent time as the monstrous goddess Kali (from *kala,* blue-black, death, and time), or in Tibet as Maha-Kala (great time, the great black one), or in our own culture as Father Time, a crippled, saturnine old man who devours everything. Just as in members of old, cultivated families a *fin de race* quality can be observed, a kind of skeptical fatigue that no longer wants to begin anything new, too much cultural past also can weigh down an entire people. For instance, I have often noticed with Italian intellectuals that ancient and medieval culture weighs on them so heavily that they sometimes lack a certain naiveté that is necessary to begin anything really new. (Of course, this is something that can be overcome through understanding.) As a result of an ambitious perfectionism that requires them to show their *cultura,* express themselves with linguistic refinement, and back up each statement with countless references and footnotes, they produce things that have lost all their clout, finely chiseled artworks devoid of power and impact. The past is like a strong sucking force that draws you into it and petrifies you if you are no longer going forward or are standing still. I believe that many people have become sympathizers of Communism and anarchism because they seem to promise a *tabula rasa* for a new beginning. They project a naive and powerful quality onto the lower social classes and hope for a creative renewal from them. Of course, this is a mistake, a projection. They must work out the *tabula rasa* and the creative new beginning within themselves; for when such transformations are left to the external collective level, they usually take a negative turn.

But why is any transformation necessary at all? Why does the zeitgeist change in a culture over the course of centuries? In the Jungian view, this is connected with a peculiar contrariety within human nature, namely, a certain opposition between consciousness and the unconscious. I mentioned above that collective unconscious factors have a double aspect: on the one hand, they express themselves as "instincts" or "drives"—as behavioral forms such as sexuality, status seeking, child rearing, and territoriality; on the other, they manifest as a peculiarly human religiomythic fantasy world. In this last, Jung saw the primal element of the mind, whose form of expression is the *symbolic* gesture and the *symbolic* image. On the archaic level, for example, this is the many "magical" ideas that grow up around instinctive actions.[1] Jung observed in Africa, for instance, that the natives living at the foot of Mount Elgon spit in their hands every morning and then held up their open palms to the rising sun. When he asked them about the meaning of this action, they could only say, "We have always done that that way." They strictly denied praying to the sun. In fact, saliva has the significance everywhere of a "soul substance," and the *oriens,* the *aurora consurgens,* signifies the appearance of the deity. From our psychological point of view, the archetypal gesture of the Elgonyi means something like "O God, we give you our soul as an offering!" However, they were completely unconscious of what they were doing. They knew as little about it as we know why we hide eggs at Easter or at Christmastime put up lights on a tree that we carry into our living room.

The instinctive world of the primitive, as Jung pointed out, is by no means simple; rather it is a complex interplay of the action of physiological instincts with taboos, rites, and tribal teachings, which impose formal restrictions on the instinct, prevent all instincts from being acted out in an unbridled, one-sided manner, and place them at the service of higher purposes, that is, spiritual activities, which on this level are all part of religion. Thus instinct and mind are ultimately not opposites but rather interact as part of a finely tuned psychic equilibrium. However, all forms of religion have a tendency to become fixated in a rigid form in which the original balance between spiritual form and physiological form turns into a conflict—the spiritual forms rigidify into mere formalisms and poison or suppress the instincts, which then take revenge through an increasing tendency toward unbridled acting out. This seemingly unfavorable development has repeated itself countless times in the course of the history of all peoples. According to Jung, it is not simply a meaningless catastrophe; rather its hidden meaning is that it spurs the development of human consciousness on toward greater differentiation. There is indeed no decline of energy without an opposite pole, and therefore nature continually creates conflictual tensions, which in all probability have the sense of producing a more differentiated third factor as a solution. Whenever the harmony between religious form and instinctual nature is disturbed by the rigidification of the former, a psychic emergency situation arises. In the past this was usually depicted by the myth of the disappearance of the favorable gods and the ascendancy of the harmful ones; or in the myth that as a result of human hubris or blasphemy, the gods had become remote altogether; or (for example, in China) the myth that heaven and earth were no longer in harmony. At such times new religious symbols that reconcile or unite the opposites are always constellated in the collective unconscious—usually the image of a "cosmic person," who as healer and savior once again unites the upper and lower aspects of creation.

The cause of this transformation process, which can be shown to occur again and again in the spiritual history of peoples and which we have only briefly outlined here, is to be found first of all in the tendency of spiritual forms to rigidify. This is connected with the fact that it is the nature of human consciousness to wish to, or even to have to, formulate and pin things down in a clear and unambiguous fashion. By contrast, the unconscious psychic life tends toward more fluid and less precise modes of behavior. That is the reason why, in individuals as well as in whole cultures, consciousness and the unconscious can fall into opposition. When this happens, we speak of neurosis in individuals and in cultures, of a spiritual crisis. (Obviously we find ourselves today in the midst of that kind of a situation once more!) This means, as Jung pointed out, that today many individuals have purely facultative neuroses. If they lived in other times, they would be normal, not psychically disturbed; but they are deeply shaken by the prevailing historical crisis of our time and are made uncertain by it. Thus we cannot find the causes of this ailment in the personal history of such a person; rather we must find a solution with him—we do it with the help of his dreams—for the problem of the times. All the same, as we said, these collective crises guarantee the necessity of a further development of human consciousness—on the individual and on the collective levels. They are motivating causes, underlying creative spiritual renewals.

Because this is a universal human, typical psychological process, it has also taken symbolic form in folklore and myths—in the myth of the old or sick king, who is to be replaced or to be healed by the water of life. The old sick king is a symbol for the rigidified spiritual forms of culture referred to above, which are no longer in harmony with the sphere of the instincts nor with the *unconscious* spiritual tendencies of the collective unconscious. The renewal is usually brought about in the myth by a hero, who is often a simple man or a simpleton altogether. His naive genuineness is capable of bringing the creative transformation to completion. This myth is to be found among all the peoples of the earth, and its existence shows how important this kind of historical-psychological transformation is.

If we turn our attention, with the help of dreams, to the processes taking place in the collective unconscious, we are able up to a point to predict certain historical or spiritual developments. It is also on attending to these processes that prophecy is ultimately based. And it is in keeping with the mythological rules that the prophets of the Old Testament were often scorned, indeed even regarded as simpletons or madmen. Thus Elisha was referred to as mad (2 Kings 9:11) just as was Jeremiah (Jeremiah 29:26), and in Hosea 9:7, the following is presented as the *vox populi:* "The prophet is a fool, the spiritual man is mad." When the people saw the rapture of Saul, they said, "What has happened to the son of Kish? Is Saul also among the prophets?" meaning that such behavior was by no means fitting for a king.[2] But the prophet sees into the depths and in this way he foretells future spiritual developments through images. Thus the Church saw in the visions of the Son of Man in the Book of Daniel and the Book of Enoch (60:10) a portent of the coming of Christ, to give only one example.

If the hypothesis is true that spiritual transformations can be read in advance in the collective unconscious, then the question naturally arises where we stand now with our modern crisis. C. G. Jung, in his works "Answer to Job" and *Aion,* made an attempt to answer this question. Repeating what is said there in very broad outline, the problem could be depicted as follows: In the Old Testament, the image of God is whole in the sense that

Yahweh contains both good and evil within himself: "I form the light and create darkness: I make peace and create evil: I the Lord do all these things" (Isaiah 45:7). With the advent of Christianity, in this regard a major transformation set in. Not only did God become man in Christ, he became more and more only the righteous, the good God. Satan, on the other hand, as is said, "fell like a lightning bolt from Heaven." From now on it is he who is the creator of evil. In the first Christian millennium, we find a constant struggle to suppress evil and help the good to triumph. Then, in the year 1000, most people expected the Final Judgment, the vanquishing of evil and the end of the world. Before that, however, as Christ himself prophesied, the Antichrist would appear and establish a short-lived dominion of evil. When in the year 1000 the world did not end, a psychological transformation occurred, which was characterized by the fact that the problem of evil once more entered into people's field of vision or even became manifest in all kinds of anti-Christian movements.

The return of pagan spiritual traditions to the West by way of the Arabs at the same time brought about a revaluation of nature and—in the Renaissance—even the world. This led—without going into the details, since these are things that are much discussed nowadays—to the completely worldly orientation of the modern natural sciences as well as to the rationalism of the Enlightenment. Though this rationalism was initially used by the Church against those whose beliefs differed from its own, today it has cast doubt on those very beliefs themselves. National Socialism and Communism were large movements that caused—and still cause—the disintegration of Christian belief for large numbers of people to become evident. In Jung's view, however, there exists today in the collective unconscious a clear tendency to understand the poles of good and evil, which have split too far apart, in their human psychological relativity and to reconcile them again within an integral image of God. This reconciliation, however, obviously can come about only through an intermediary, and this is, according to Jung, the hitherto neglected *feminine principle.* Jung's serious criticism of the Old Testament religion—as well as Protestantism again today—is that it is a purely masculine religion. Starting with Eve's prominent role in the story of the Fall of Man, the tendency to associate woman with evil has constantly manifested. Prophethood and the priesthood are denied her. Even still today, in the Orthodox synagogue a woman may not shake hands with a rabbi and is allowed to participate in services only from behind a grillwork screen! In the relatively late wisdom books of the Old Testament, at last a feminine figure appears, the personified "Wisdom of God," who is praised as a pagan tree and a fertility goddess: "I was exalted like a cedar in Libanus, and as a cypress tree upon the mountains of Hermon. . . . I am the mother of fair love: . . . [I] am given to all my children" (Ecclesiastes 24:13ff.).

This figure of Sapientia Dei has been interpreted *inter alia* as the anima of Christ, as a feminine element in the configuration of his symbolism. In the Middle Ages she was also regarded as a kind of world soul that bound together all things. And not least important, according to the view of the Catholic Church she was a prefiguration of Mary. It is surely no coincidence that it was in Ephesus that Mary was later raised to the status of "God bearer"; Ephesus was *the* city of the cult of Artemis Ephesia, the great mother of the gods. At least in the Catholic world, a certain feminine psychic element has persisted in the form of the veneration of Mary. But the feminine principle seeks more the reconciliation than the polarization of the opposites, which is why in fact the Mother of God is considered a mediator. When seen in the light of this historical background, it becomes much easier to understand why the psychologist C. G. Jung extolled the celebrated *Declaratio Assumptionis Mariae* of Pope Pius XII as the greatest spiritual deed of our century. Of course there is not much in the *Declaratio* that had not already long been assumed in the custom of the folk. Nevertheless, the *Declaratio* is quite remarkable, because it recognizes and accommodates a very modern tendency of the collective unconscious: the Mother of God being raised to heaven along with her body, which was not sinlessly received, also indirectly betokens a much broader acceptance of the human body and with it of matter as a whole. This takes the wind out of the sails of anti-Christian materialism, for it is clearly a tendency in the unconscious of people today no longer to exclude their bodies and their sexuality from the wholeness of their development and self-realization the way medieval man, with his ascetic exercises, did.

It was interesting to see how individuals reacted to the *Declaratio*. Most of them, including myself, paid almost no attention to the newspaper articles. Many people thought that this was a thoroughly outdated issue—but not their unconscious. A whole series of dream reactions to the *Declaratio* were brought to me in my analytic practice. For example, a Protestant woman who on the conscious level had paid no heed to the news, had the following dream: She was going over the Limmat Bridge to a familiar place in Zurich. There a huge crowd of people had gathered. People were saying, "Mary's ascension is going to take place here." She mixed in with the crowd and began staring along with everybody else at a wooden platform where the event was supposed to take place. There a marvelously beautiful black woman appeared, naked. She raised her hands and slowly floated up toward heaven.

That the Virgin Mary appeared as a black woman need not surprise anyone. There are, after all, black madonnas in many places. As I see it, in the dream this only serves to give special stress to the primeval chthonic element. In reality the woman had difficulty accepting her femininity on a bodily level. She frequently escaped from it into masculine mind realms. Thus the dream emphasizes that the feminine body is also spiritual and indeed even has a sacred function.

For the psychologist it is interesting to see what happened after the *Declaratio* in the Church—a campaign against the celibacy of priests and another to allow women to assume ecclesiastical offices. Although the writings advocating these causes hardly ever call upon the *Declaratio* as an argument, from a psychological point of view, these campaigns were a direct consequence or continuation of the spiritual direction expressed in the *Declaratio*.

Not least important in this context is the wave of women's movements, which have taken on particularly large proportions in North America. It is by no means my intention here to evaluate all these movements positively or negatively; I am only mentioning them as a psychological *symptom*. I personally do not believe that women in the parts of the world populated by the white race are more oppressed now or have been more oppressed recently than they were long ago. So these movements are being triggered unconsciously by an *archetypal constellation* in the collective unconscious; however, this constellation itself results from a very long-standing neglect of the feminine principle.

The reader will have noticed that I frequently say "feminine principle" and not "woman." In fact the latter refers to something different from what I am talking about. As Jung pointed out, men also possess feminine psychic components, which Jung called the man's anima. If a man suppresses his feminine features, the consequence is that he unconsciously becomes "feminine." This takes the form of irrational moods, sudden accesses of sentimentality, fascination with pornography, hysterical qualities, and so on. If on the other hand he consciously acknowledges and develops his feminine traits, then he will cling less rigidly to principles, become generally more "human," emotionally warmer, and become more open toward the irrational, artistic side of life. The historical period of courtly love showed what beautiful cultural forms can arise through the acknowledgment of the anima. Unfortunately this period was replaced by the period of witch hunts and renewed suppression of the feminine principle.

That recognition of the feminine principle is even more important for women than for men goes without saying. In the absence of it, women must become masculine in order to prevail, or else they remain unable to overcome a deep-seated lack of self-confidence. For the moment it is not my intention to evaluate the movements referred to above; rather at this point I am concerned with showing what a transformation of this kind in the zeitgeist is like and with indicating that such changes are probably based on profound transformational processes in the collective unconscious.

These processes cover very long time spans, even centuries. Thus the current coming to the fore of the feminine principle in Christian cultures has a very long prehistory. Again and again the feminine principle has welled forth in order to compensate for the one-sided intellectuality and patriarchal tone of prevailing cultural outlooks. Today, however, it seems to be thrusting its way into the foreground on a particularly big scale, because behind it an even more profound problem is being activated—the problem of evil. For up till now in the Christian world this problem has purely been suppressed or treated as insignificant. But now worldwide terrorism, an enormous increase in crimes, and the total absence of rights of the individual that has come to prevail in many countries confront us. Christ's prophecy of the inevitable coming of the Antichrist seems to be coming true. This prophecy was psychologically possible because the Christian "program" has hitherto contained a one-sided emphasis on God's righteousness and goodness. In such cases, according to our psychological experience, sooner or later a backlash *must* occur. The feminine principle of which we have been speaking is the only possible mediator between the opposites.

When we read the papers or listen to the radio these days, we hear endless, quite seriously researched reports about why terrorism is on the rise or why women are suddenly seeking more recognition, but insight into the true deeper dimensions of these problems, which would require a knowledge of history, is rare. This is because the average reader or listener of today still knows nothing or next to nothing about the existence of the unconscious in people, to say nothing of the collective unconscious. The collective unconscious manifests itself in a century-spanning historical dimension, as we saw, for example, in the case of the Tezcatlipoca dream of our Mexican friend. If more and more people came to know the collective unconscious from their own experience, I believe history—primarily our spiritual and intellectual history—

could be seen in terms of quite other dimensions than they presently are. But we are still far away from that.

The difficulty lies in the fact that the basic processes take place in the unconscious, and the unconscious really is, as its name says, not conscious. Thus, although the woman who dreamed about the black Virgin Mary had feminist tendencies in her consciousness, she knew nothing of the historical roots of this problem and, as we mentioned, had had no thoughts at all about the *Declaratio Assumptionis*. For her Protestant consciousness that was at best an antiquated concern. It is therefore of the greatest importance that we become more educated about history, and it should not be merely a matter of learning who conquered whom and which countries changed hands—that is no more than a continuation of the natural-historical pattern of eat and be eaten. Rather such education should involve living knowledge of our religious history, of Christian mythology as Jung formulated it. Our Mexican dreamed not of Cortés nor of the racial persecution of the Indians, but of Tezcatlipoca, the still-living archetypal image of the primal god of his people.

History proves, as Arnold Toynbee has particularly impressively shown, that peoples and human groups that lose their religious mythology are soon destroyed. Their mythology provides a meaning for life that makes them feel a harmonious part of the entire cosmos. This, for example, is the great significance of creation myths. If you would like to become more acquainted with these matters, read, for example, the excellent book of Marcel Griaule, *Dieux d'eaux,* in which the old blind wise man Ogotomeli presents the rich, complex world system of the Dogon, which gives its cosmic religious meaning to everything, even the most ordinary everyday actions and instruments of the tribe. Also, many peoples, for example, the Polynesians, enumerate in their tales all their previous kings in interminably long lists as a way of preserving their connection to the past. According to the Zuni Indians, the gods told their emissary, the storyteller Kaiklo: "As a woman who has children is loved because she keeps the chain of her clan unbroken, so will you, who tirelessly listen to us (as we recount our myths), be loved by the gods and honored by human beings, because you keep the creation stories intact and everything that we make known." In ancient Egypt, whenever the king showed himself to the people in a procession, the standard bearers carried the standards of his fourteen last predecessors behind him, representing their *kas*—their immortal, virility-charged souls—in order to show that the entire past, as it were, stood behind him and sanctioned his deeds.

Whenever this kind of historico-religious mythology of a people is destroyed, the people lose their feeling of belonging to a meaningful whole and become disoriented. Thus today we see how many North American Indian tribes are forced to combat alcoholism and declines in their birth rates—decline altogether. Their mythology is destroyed and with it their feeling of the meaning of their existence. For such people the only goal that remains is that of acquiring material goods in this world—or dying out. The young people leave, the old fall into a state of resignation, and the tribe disintegrates. Wherever our modern technological rationalism comes into contact with peoples still living undisturbedly within the terms of their mythology, we can see this sad picture. The "department store" then becomes the modern temple.

In Bali I once had a conversation with an aristocratic-looking Balinese woman who had married an Italian. She had lived for a short time in Rome and was now living with her husband in Bali again. I said, "You must be happy to be living in your homeland again." "Oh no," she replied, "I really long to go back to Rome." "What did you like about Rome?" I asked her. "Oh," she said, "the big, rich department stores." So not the Forum and not the Vatican! But don't laugh at this woman—among us too there are more and more people for whom the banks and the department stores are the real holy places. This is a flawed neurotic development from which a great number of people and entire social groups suffer. Many have lost all spiritual values that transcend material reality. We also have lost considerable parts of our spiritual mythology and thus we too, as history teaches, are menaced by a concrete historical decline. As Jung pointed out, it is the official representatives of the churches, among others, who are to blame for this. "Christianity has fallen asleep" and has neglected to relate to the stirrings of growth in the unconscious psyche.

Today when neurotic patients come to us for treatment, they are very often only partially suffering from personal problems. Many people come these days because they are suffering from the meaninglessness and hopelessness of our times. Today there exists a collective melancholy or ill-humor, a malaise that has taken hold of whole groups. Here there is a resemblance to the time of the fall of the Roman Empire. The more primitive people make it easier for themselves by distracting themselves with *panem et circenses* or by finding some external scapegoat on whom they can discharge their rage/despair, which of course leads nowhere. However, others suffer deeply from the apparent meaninglessness of their existence. With these the caregiver has to descend with open eyes into the unconscious so as to bring back the answer of the psyche that already lies waiting in the depths.

I would like to relate to you the dream of an American that more than clearly illustrates this crisis of our times. For the psychologists among you, let me remark that the dreamer is neither psychotic nor endangered by psychosis. His dream is as follows:

I am walking along the so-called Palisades from which one can look out over New York City. I am walking with an unknown woman (the anima) and a man who is guiding us. New York has been reduced to rubble; fires are everywhere. People are fleeing in all directions. The Hudson River has overflowed its banks. At twilight fireballs from heaven land. It is the end of the world, the complete destruction of our entire civilization. The cause of this was a race of giants that had come from outer space. I saw them scooping up people and devouring them. Our guide explained to us that these giants had come from different planets where they lived in peace together. Actually *they* had devised life on earth and "cultivated" our civilization the way one raises vegetables in a garden. Now they had come for the harvest, because a special event was about to happen.

I was saved because I had slightly high blood pressure, but I had been chosen to go through a horrible ordeal. I saw before me a gigantic golden throne, radiant like the sun. On it sat the king and queen of the giants. They were the perpetrators of the destruction of our planet. My ordeal consisted in having to experience the destruction. But there was more. I had to climb a steep staircase up to the level of the king and queen. I began the ascent, which was long and difficult. My heart beat violently. I was afraid, but I knew that the fate of humanity was at stake. Then I woke up soaked with sweat. I realized as I awoke that the destruction of the earth was a wedding feast for the king and queen. That is why I had that strange feeling when I saw them.

The first part of the dream reminds us of the Book of Enoch. There it is written that a number of angels sinfully lusted after human women. With them they begat the race of giants, which began to destroy the entire earth. However, the angels also taught humans many new arts and sciences. On account of the protest of the loyal angels, God sees Himself obliged to put a stop to the destruction. Then follows the vision of the "Son of Man." C. G. Jung interpreted this myth in "Answer to Job."[3] It represents a premature invasion of human consciousness by contents of the collective unconscious (hence the new arts). This produces an inflation, an arrogant puffed-up quality, an exaggerated sense of self-importance in people. The vision of the Son of Man points to the actual solution that is being sought by the unconscious.

In our modern dream the solution is the wedding feast of the king and queen. This signifies a union of the psychic opposites. This liberating image can only have its freeing effect if the dreamer takes upon himself the hard work of climbing to the higher level of consciousness that is necessary for the realization of this image. The ascent signifies what Jung called individuation, that is, self-realization. The dreamer has this great task posed to him by his unconscious. In the first half of life, better adjustment to the external world often means the healing of a neurosis. In the case of certain young people and in almost all people over forty, however, there can be no healing if the persons in question do not find something within themselves that they can call the meaning of their life, a solution, or rather, *their* solution to the general problem of the times. For many, a return to their spiritual roots and a renewed understanding and better grasp of the old truths is enough. With others, however, the unconscious seems to be seeking the realization of something that has never been there before, something creatively new—yet something new that does not do away with the old but rather adds something to it, like the new annual ring on a growing tree. These last individuals are those with a creative nature. Such people are never spared the crises and suffering of spiritual birth-giving—the isolation, being misunderstood—but not the thrill of accomplishment either. In the world view of Carl Jung, that which is eternally the same, the old handed down by tradition, and the creatively new do not constitute any kind of absolute antithesis. Indeed the world of archetypes presents basic psychic structures that remain self-identical over millennia, but which at the same time are a driving dynamic element behind every new creation, because they are in movement and reconstellate themselves anew in century-spanning processes of transformation.

Notes

1. Cf. C. G. Jung, *Mysterium Conjunctionis,* cw 14, para. 602.
2. Cf. R. Schärf-Kluger, *Saul und der Geist Gottes. Studien zur Analytischen Psychologie C. G. Jungs* (Saul and the Spirit of God: Studies in the Analytical Psychology of C. G. Jung) (Zurich: Rascher, 1955), vol. 2, pp. 215ff.
3. C. G. Jung, cw 11, pp. 355ff.

ANTICHRIST OR MERLIN?

A Problem Inherited from the Middle Ages

▪▪
▪▪

As C. G. JUNG HAS ATTEMPTED to demonstrate in his book *Aion*,[1] history is not only brought about by economic, geographically conditioned, and military power struggles, but also by spiritual and psychological changes that have their origin in processes of the collective unconscious. In relatively long periods of time (anywhere from one to three thousand years), certain archetypal collective images tend to emerge and recede again, probably in response to spiritual needs of humankind, but also to some *creative* evolutionary process. Insofar as this process shows a certain psychologically logical continuity, prophetic predictions have been made by intuitive "seers" as to the coming dominants in the future aeons. One great system of such predictions is astrology—which is in fact not mirroring "influences of the stars" (for this is probably only a projection) but transformations of archetypal constellations in the collective unconscious. Jung has shown how powerfully astrological speculation was linked with the rise of Christianity. Christ himself was not only symbolized as the slaughtered Lamb (the end of the age of Aries) but from the very beginning was associated with the Fish—thus initiating the age of Pisces.

The age of the Fishes was characterized by an extremely dualistic polarization between light and dark, good and evil. Around the year 1000 (and this was closely linked with astrological speculation) people expected the coming of the Antichrist, personifying the second Fish of Pisces, which—in the astrological image— swims in the opposite direction from the first one. Viewed psychologically this would mean an *enantiodromia* (turning over into the opposite), a complete reversal of collectively dominant values.

The figure of Antichrist coalesced from different sources: Jewish traditions of the coming of a pseudo-Messiah, New Testament sources, mainly the Apocalypse, Persian, and gnostic influences.[2] According to some legends the birth and life of the Antichrist were imagined to be a negative replica *(mimema)* of that of Christ. Satan too decided to become incarnate in the human realm and chose a virgin in Babylon as his vessel for this birth.[3] Thus the Antichrist was either Satan himself or he already became possessed by Satan in the womb. Later he was educated by black magicians in Corozaim.

As a pseudo-prophet or political leader (or both) he will assemble around him a great multitude of Christ's enemies (deceiving them by "phantasms"), and at the end of time he will venture into a great battle. The *civitas Diaboli* (seen as the whore of Babylon) will stand up against the *civitas Dei*. Finally, the Antichrist will be overthrown and destroyed. The Antichrist is a Son of Satan *non per naturam sed per imitationem.*[4] He personifies lawlessness, arrogance, and idolatry. His life is a *mysterium iniquitatis.*

According to apocryphal and sibylline sources, Antichrist has power over nature, over the sun and moon, plants, water, and thunderstorms. He can cure illnesses, revive the dead, and even simulated his own resurrection after death.[5] His country is in the north or he comes from the sea (like the beast or old dragon of the Apocalypse with whom he is identified), and he will erect a counterchurch and regulate all economies. Whoever does not carry his sign will be able to neither buy nor sell. Adso of Moutier describes him as a nature spirit capable of changing shape *(naturas in diversis figuris mutare).*[6] He looks "wild" and monstrous and has horns. He wins people over to his side by terror, gifts, and (false) miracles. Either Christ himself or the archangels Michael and Gabriel will kill him in the end. In later sources he is sometimes understood as an instrument of God's providence. The number 666 of the Apocalypse is an attempt to define by means of gematria his names in different forms: Antemos, Apnoume, Teitan, Diclux, Genshrikos, Armillus (Romulus), etc.[7]

Such an absolute opposition of good and evil, as Jung points out, characterizes the Christian era. This opposition probably has the important function of heightening man's moral consciousness and sharpening his moral conscience, but it can also lead to an insoluble conflict which brings life to a complete standstill. In practical psychotherapy, moreover, we can rarely state what is absolutely good or evil, since these concepts are to a great extent relative: "In view of the fallibility of all human judgment we cannot believe that we will always judge rightly. We might so easily be the victims of a misjudgment. The ethical problem is affected by this principle only to the extent that we have become somewhat uncertain about moral evaluations."[8] Jung stresses that the validity of good and evil per se continues to exist but that in many situations we have to make an ethical decision against conventional rules so that such a decision becomes *a subjective creative act.* Jung differentiates between morality, which means obeying a code of collective rules, and ethics, which means following one's innermost conscience, or the voice of God in one's own heart. These two can collide (to which every dissident in Russia, for instance, could testify). What Jung calls the "fallibility of human judgment" is best shown by the fact that the Antichrist has been projected again and again onto rulers or groups: Nero, Henry IV, some popes, or the Jews, the Huns, heretics, and so forth. Antichrist, in fact, became a label for what or whom the various ecclesiastical writers disliked.

The harshness of this Christian moral dualism calls for a *tertium quod non datur,* for a symbolic solution through which life can continue to flow. One of the first such mysterious reconciling symbols is found in the emergence of the figure of Merlin in medieval literature.[9] The story of Merlin's birth recapitulates exactly that of the Antichrist. While Geoffrey of Monmouth's *Vita Merlini* does not tell of his birth, Robert de Boron's "Merlin" describes how the Devil and his host in hell decide to nullify Christ's work of Redemption through a pseudo-prophet. One devil who possesses the capacity to assume different forms takes on the task. An innocent girl is selected to be the mother. One night when, against her confessor's advice, she forgets to keep a light burning, the devil sneaks into her room and as an incubus impregnates her. The girl then turns to her confessor who makes the sign of the cross over her and sprinkles her with holy water. He imposes on her a vow of lifelong chastity, which she keeps. Thus the devil's spell is broken. Because of her pregnancy the girl, Merlin's mother, is imprisoned and eighteen months later is condemned to death. The baby Merlin appears in court and proves that the judge himself does not know who his own father is either. Thus Merlin's mother is acquitted. Merlin inherits from his mother the gift of prophecy and from the devil the knowledge of the past. Before leaving his mother he dictates the story of Joseph of Arimathea and the Holy Grail: "And because I am dark and always will be, let the book also be dark and mysterious in those places where I will not show myself."

Obviously Merlin is meant by the devil to become the Antichrist, but the positive Christian influences of his mother and the priest prevent this. He develops instead a strangely ambiguous third nature: he is usually good but sometimes also a trickster and a rather shadowy figure. He is nearly immortal, for it is said he will not die before the end of this world. In Jungian terms he represents the natural whole man, good and evil, mortal and immortal—a symbol of the human psychic totality which Jung terms the Self.

Merlin, like the Antichrist, has a special relationship to nature and possesses the gift of changing shape. Moreover, he personifies the archetype of the druid, the shaman and medicine man. Near Merlin's abode, for example, springs a well of water that cures madness. In addition, he is an astrologer, poet, and prophet in one. In him pagan traits unmistakably predominate; they bring back from the depths of the unconscious a relation to nature that the Christian teaching had too harshly suppressed.

Among the later episodes of Merlin's life, I will comment on only a few. Merlin leaves his home because Vortigern, the illegitimate king of Britain, wants to build an impregnable tower, but the walls keep collapsing without reason. Astrologers advise the king to mix the blood of a fatherless boy with the mortar, so it is decided to sacrifice Merlin. When Merlin is brought before the king, he reveals that there is a large quantity of water under the foundation of the tower, and beneath this water two dragons—one white, one red—shake the walls with their continual fighting.[10] As I have elsewhere shown,[11] the fighting red and white dragons are an *alchemical* motif. They represent in the symbolism of alchemy the opposites of male and female which after fighting and death become the partners of the alchemical conjunctio or Hierosgamos—the union of opposites. Merlin thus points to a conflict in the depth of the psyche, covered by water, that is, unconsciousness.

Later in his life, Merlin withdraws from human society into the forest. There he lives the life of a wild animal until emissaries of his sister Ganieda come to soothe him with song and lyre. But at the sight of men he breaks loose and disappears again into the forest. He gives consent to his wife Gwendolena to marry another man, but on the wedding day he appears riding on a stag, pulls off the stag's antlers, and using them as a weapon kills the bridegroom. He flees back to the forest but falls into a river and is saved only by his sister's servants. She tries to keep him with her, but he loses all joy in life, and so she agrees to his return to the forest and helps him to build a tower with seventy windows and doors for his astronomical observations. In winter he lives in the tower provided with food by his sister. In summer he roams about wild. In return for her care he teaches his sister prophecy. During this period Merlin becomes a "wild man of the woods." He maintains a special relationship to the stag, a trait he shares with the Celtic god Kerunnus and with the Irish Suibne.[12]

For the remainder of his lifetime Merlin never mixes directly in worldly matters, but he acts in the background as the godfather and secret counselor of King Arthur, whom he inspires to create the Round Table. He knows all about the Grail,[13] and he appears sometimes to the knights as their counselor. As I have shown elsewhere, he is the very essence of the secret of the Grail.[14]

The image of the circle, then, is associated with Merlin, for not only is he responsible for the creation of the mandala of the Round Table (a symbol of wholeness), but he also built in the sea a rotating island made of a metal wall and held fast by a magnet.[15] Even the last phase of his life is significant in this context, for he finally disappears in a circular stone or miraculous magical bed or house of glass—the revolving four-horned glass island of Celtic myths. This place of retirement is called Esplumeor, a *hapax legomenon.* Helen Adolf interprets it as a cage or "nest" in which the falcons molt, and draws attention to cabalistic traditions according to which the Messiah withdraws during the last judgment into a bird's nest in the Garden of Eden. His soul dwells there "like a swallow in its nest." From his Esplumeor Merlin continues to prophesy "whatever the Lord inspires me," and he will not die until the end of the world.

Merlin shows a close similarity to the prophet Elijah, who is described in Jewish folklore especially as a trickster, a man who can change his appearance, a man who does not die but living awaits the end of the world. Like Merlin, he too is hirsute.[16] According to legend, Merlin dictates his book on the Grail to a cleric, Helyes, who is probably Elijah [Elias], thus drawing the two figures together.[17] In some respects Merlin also resembles John the Baptist. Even stranger than his resemblance to Elijah and John, however, are Merlin's parallels to the figure of Mercurius of the alchemists, who stands behind the transformation of the old king into the new king or Philosopher's Stone.[18] The alchemists sometimes compare him to Christ, sometimes to the Antichrist.[19] Thus he represents the original total man, "the spirit of Truth which is hidden from the World." Ethically he is *duplex* (double) for "he runs around the earth and enjoys equally the company of the good and the wicked."[20]

Jung sums up his commentary on the alchemical Mercurius in the following way: "He is both material and spiritual, the Devil and redeeming psychopomp, an evasive trickster and God's reflection in physical nature. He is also a reflection of the mystical experience of the artifex. . . ."[21] As such Mercurius represents on the one hand the Self and, because of the limitless number of his names, he is also the collective unconscious. But what does all this antiquarian lore mean for us today?

The tearing apart of the psychic opposites in Christian teaching has totally separated spirit and matter, good and evil. The split goes right through our own psyche. In the dreams and creative phantasies of modern individuals we can observe how the unconscious attempts to heal this extreme split by producing *reconciling symbols of totality.* These symbols have either the forms of some mandala, or are representations of the Self in the forms of a wise old man or savior figure that closely resembles Merlin-Mercurius-Elijah. This savior, primarily by his ambiguous nature, softens the conflict between an absolute good and evil, by promoting the *creative act of individual ethical decision* mentioned above.[22] Sometime after the year 1000, when the symbolic figure of the Antichrist began to haunt the minds of people more and more, medieval poets produced from the depths of their creative unconscious the healing figure of Merlin, an intuition that reaches beyond the antithesis of Christ and Antichrist.[23]

The figure of Merlin did not, however, effectively survive the age of chivalry. Except in the writings of a few poets, he became a nearly forgotten literary figure.[24] He thus actually hid himself back in the unconscious, as he himself predicted that he would do. One noticeable exception is Goethe, who sometimes in conversations identified himself with Merlin.[25] Jung, who himself felt he had unknowingly lived traits of Merlin's life by following the voice of his inner Self,[26] sees in Goethe's figure of Mephistopheles in *Faust* more of the symbolic figure of Mercurius (Merlin) than of the "orthodox" Christian Devil. Mephistopheles, Jung points out, is not at all wholly evil but a trickster of indisputable wisdom, and Faust was not up to his seductive ambiguity. The way the angels get rid of Mephistopheles at the end of *Faust,* Jung felt, was rather a cheap trick. Therefore Faust appears in the Beyond as an immature boy (which he had remained) who needed further instruction and help of the "Eternal Feminine."[27]

There is one cluster of motifs around Merlin that deserves some attention in this connection: his ambiguous relationship to the feminine principle. In some versions he has nothing to do with the reign of Venus (his parallel in Wolfram's *Parzival,* Clinschor, is a eunuch!), and in later time he even becomes a model in misogynous literature. But in Geoffrey of Monmouth's *Vita* and in Robert de Boron's description he is, on the contrary, married, and in the latter even has a daughter who helps Perceval with her advice. In this way he is also more complete than Christ or the Antichrist, neither of whom is married. In the legend of the Antichrist it is sometimes said that an evil woman will dominate at the end of time, and Bousset, in fact, has shown that the Antichrist himself represents in a way the old feminine dragon, Tiamat, the enemy of Yahweh.

Merlin, however, cannot keep up his marriage; his longing to live as an anchorite in the forest is stronger.[28] In old age Merlin finally lives in a group consisting of four people, one woman and two other men: his sister Ganieda, who gives up a love affair to be with him, the bard Taliesin, and the madman who had been cured by his spring and whom Merlin orders to make up his lost years of insanity in the service of God.[29] His relationship to the feminine is now characterized as the famous alchemical brother-sister incest. Finally Merlin disappears from the world, according to some versions, in the embrace of the fairy Morgana (Vivien and Muirgen, etc.). Under a hawthorn bush she entices him to reveal to her all his magical tricks, and with them she in turn bewitches him so that he cannot, nor does he even desire to, escape from her eternal embrace.[30] This disappearance of Merlin has been differently interpreted. Heinrich Zimmer, for example, praises it as a voluntary sacrifice of worldly power: "Insofar as Merlin knowingly surrenders himself to Vivien's bewitchment, to enchantment through the arts of enticement, knowing what he is handing over to her bit by bit . . . he raises himself to the calm, untroubled heights of an Indian god, who withdraws unconcerned from the world into the stillness of the Self."[31] On the other hand, some feel Merlin's bewitchment to be a catastrophe, representing a victory of evil feminine forces.

The hawthorn, a member of the rose family, is a revealing symbol in this context. In ancient Greece it served as a decoration of the bride on her nuptial day; the altars of Hymen, the god of marriage, were lit by torches made of its wood.[32] In the cemetery of the Abbey of Glastonbury was a famous hawthorn tree, which came from a staff that Joseph of Arimathea planted at Christmas; it has been covered with flowers every Christmas night since. The crown of thorns of Christ was said to be made of hawthorn, and thus the hawthorn is called a *salutaris herba*. In almost all European countries the hawthorn served to banish or exorcise witches, sorcery, and all evil spirits.[33] This salutary aspect of the hawthorn seems to suggest that Morgana's spell is not to be understood negatively. Instead, it means that *love has overcome magic*. (The latter always contains an element of power, which is contrary to love.) Merlin's eternal conjunctio with Morgana is thus an image of the Hierosgamos, the supreme union of opposites.

The negative element comes only in the fact that the couple disappears into the beyond, that is, into the unconscious. They are *entombés* or *enserrés* in their nuptial bed of stone forever, and only a few knights sometimes hear the famous *cry of Merlin* which calls them to some great adventure. Jung writes: "This cry that no one could understand implies that he (Merlin) lives in unredeemed form. His story is not yet finished, and he still walks around. It might be said that the secret of Merlin was carried on in alchemy, primarily in the figure of Mercurius. Then Merlin was taken up again in my psychology of the unconscious and— remains uncomprehended to this day! That is because most people find it quite beyond them to live on close terms with the unconscious."[34]

Merlin, then, in Jungian psychology, is a figure that unites all opposites. The creative fantasy of medieval poets saw intuitively (in the life of Merlin) a pattern according to which our Western cultural consciousness tends to evolve. Collective consciousness, however, limps far behind in its comprehension of this pattern. An important psychological event in the process of "catching up" occurred when Pope Pius XII made the official Declaration of the Assumption of Mary.[35] Mary, as the text runs, thus "enters the nuptial chamber" *(thalamos)* in Heaven. "The dogmatization of the Assumptio Mariae points," as Jung stresses, "to the *hierosgamos* in the pleroma; and this in turn implies, the future of the divine child, who, in accordance with the divine trend toward incarnation, will choose as his birthplace the empirical man. The metaphysical process is known to the psychology of the unconscious as the individuation process. . . ."[36] As Jung goes on to explain, "The central symbols of this process describe the Self, which is man's totality, consisting on the one hand of that which is conscious to him, and on the other hand of the contents of the unconscious. The Self is the *teleios anthropos,* the whole man, whose symbols are the divine child and its synonyms."[37] "Although he (the savior arising from the divine marriage) is already born in the pleroma,[38] his birth in time can only be accomplished when it is perceived, recognized, and declared by man."[39] It seems to me that now we have to choose if we will do the works of the Antichrist or continue on the path of Merlin and listen to his cry, which calls us to the new adventure, the quest for individuation.

Notes

1. cw 9/ii.

2. Cf. W. Bousset, *Der Antichrist* (Göttingen, 1895) and *Die Apokalypse Johannis* (Göttingen, 1906 [reprint 1966]), and H. D. Rauh, *Das Bild des Antichrist im Mittelalter* (Münster, 1979).

3. This is only one version: others assert his purely human descent or that he was generated "nefasto incesto." (See Rauh, *Bild des Antichrist,* p. 155). The Antichrist is then either Satan himself or his instrument (organon).

4. Haimo of Auxerre, *Patrol lat.,* vol. 117, col. 779.

5. Rauh, *Bild des Antichrist,* pp. 67f.

6. Adso, Abbot of Montier-en-Der, *Libellus de ortu et tempore Antichrist,* v. 950. Cf. Rauh, *Bild des Antichrist,* p. 153, and E. Sackur, *Sibyllinische Texte* (Halle, 1898), p. 108. He sometimes appears as a child, a youth, or an old man.

7. Rauh, *Bild des Antichrist,* p. 219. Another interesting idea can be found in Honorius of Autun, who says that the (plant) Mandragora is a girl from the north without head. She symbolizes the followers of the Antichrist after his death, a mob without head. Then Christ gives this woman a new golden head—a symbol of her return to faith. (Cf. Rauh, ibid., pp. 262f.)

8. C. G. Jung, *Memories, Dreams, Reflections* (New York: Vintage Books, 1963), p. 329.

9. Cf. Paul Zumthor, *Merlin le prophète* (Lausanne, 1943); also A. O. H. Jarman, *The Legend of Merlin* (Cardiff, 1960), and Emma Jung and Marie-Louise von Franz, *The Grail Legend* (London, 1971), pp. 347ff. and further literature cited there.

10. The red dragon signifies Vortigern, the white one the two brothers Pendragon and Uther, who will defeat Vortigern. After this happens, and once Pendragon is also dead, the other brother calls himself Uther Pendragon and becomes king. He is, of course, the father of King Arthur.

11. Emma Jung and Marie-Louise von Franz, *The Grail Legend,* pp. 375f.

12. Huth-Merlin I, pp. 158f.: quoted in Zumthor, *Merlin le prophète,* p. 208. The stag in medieval times is a well-known symbol of Christ because he owns the secret of self-renewal, and also of the Antichrist because of his Superbia. This one animal symbol, therefore, combines the traits of both extremes. In Alchemy it is Mercurius who is often called *cervus fugitivus;* in this form he represents the spirit of the *prima materia,* which is so difficult to obtain.

13. Cf. Helen Adolf, "The Esplumeor Merlin," *Speculum* XXI (1946), pp. 173 and 176, and "New Light on Oriental Sources of Wolfram's Parzival," *Publication of the Modern Language Assoc. of America,* vol. 42 (1947). Cf. also *Visio Pacis* (Pennsylvania State University, 1960), passim.

14. *The Grail Legend,* pp. 361ff.

15. In later times, the erection of Stonehenge is frequently attributed to him.

16. Jung has shown that Elijah, in contrast to Christ's one-sided perfection, symbolizes the complete man, a total incarnation of Yahweh, of his light *and* dark side. In his obscurity he represents the *deus absconditus,* the Ancient of Days. In the legend he is called the metatron or "little Yahveh." See Père Bruno, "Elie le prophète," *Etudes Carmélitaines,* Desclée de Brouwer 156, vol. II, pp. 15ff.

17. Cf. Zumthor, *Merlin le prophète,* p. 198. Elijah is closely related to the Antichrist because at the Last Judgment he will appear as a witness together with Enoch.

18. C. G. Jung, "Alchemical Studies," cw 13, paras. 239–303.

19. Ibid., paras. 103, 105, and 111. The alchemists themselves realized the closeness of Merlin and Mercurois; in the Rosarium philosophorum a philosopher Merculinus (!) is quoted, and there also exists an alchemical *Allegoria Merlini,* an old text that describes the transformation for the "King."

20. Ibid., para. 267.

21. Ibid., para. 284.

22. See above, pp. 3f.

23. For this, see C. G. Jung, "Answer to Job," in cw 11, paras. 746–49.

24. For this, see P. Zumthor, passim. For the German literature see J. Vielhauer, *Das Leben des Zauberers Merlin* (a translation of Geoffrey of Monmouth's *Vita Merlini*) (Amsterdam, 1978).

25. Ibid., pp. 90f.

26. M. L. von Franz, *C. G. Jung: His Myth in Our Time* (New York, 1976), p. 279.

27. Another variation is the strange figure of Gil Martin in James Hogg's *Confessions of a Justified Sinner.* He seems to be just the Devil or Antichrist, but when the hero has done all the evil deeds he suggests, he shows him his disappointment. Probably, as Barbara Hannah shows, Gil Martin is ultimately more a Merlinlike personification of the Self than a personification of absolute Evil.

28. As earlier pointed out, he leaves his wife and even agrees that she may marry again but on her wedding day murders the rival. This

outburst seems not to be consistent with his usual wisdom, and indeed he then nearly drowns in a river. In this episode he becomes the stupid trickster, lacking in animal instinct. But "these defects," as Jung points out, "mark his specially human nature," with its capacity for further development.

29. Geoffrey, *Vita,* verses 1237ff.

30. In the *Vita Merlini,* Morgana is the sister of Arthur and one of the nine fairies of Avallon. She is also called Dame du lac.

31. "Merlin" in *Corona,* IX 2 (Munich-Berlin, 1939), pp. 150–52.

32. E. and J. Lehner, *Folklore and Symbolism of Flowers, Plants, and Trees* (Tudor, N.Y., 1960), p. 59.

33. Cf. *Handwörterbuch des Deutschen Aberglaubens,* ed. Hoffmann-Krayer (Berlin, 1918–1941), under "Weissdorn."

34. *Memories, Dreams, Reflections,* p. 228.

35. *Apostolic Constitution: Munificentissimus Deus* . . .

36. "Answer to Job," in cw 11, para. 755.

37. Ibid., paras. 746–49.

38. The collective unconscious, my note.

39. Ibid., para. 748.

THE TRANSFORMED
BERSERKER

The Union of Psychic Opposites

■■

IN TIMES OF UPHEAVAL and social changes, people call for a leader who shows the way to either an inner change of attitude or an outer change of social reorganization. These two goals are opposed.

The central problem of the relationship between individual transformation and social responsibility arises out of a psychic opposition. For as C. G. Jung explained, "There are always two standpoints and there always will be: namely, the standpoint of the social leader, who, insofar as he is an idealist, sees the general welfare in the more or less total suppression of the individual; and the spiritual leader, who looks for improvement only in the individual." The two types constitute "a necessary pair of opposites . . . , which keeps the world in a state of balance.[1] Examples of social leaders with or without a sense of responsibility for their people are found in plenty in the mass media. I will therefore attempt here to give a detailed presentation of an example of the other kind of leader. I have chosen for this our only Swiss saint, the spiritual leader Brother Niklaus von Flüe. He was a profoundly introverted, solitary hermit, who worked only on his own self-perfection; nonetheless, through this he became the political savior of Switzerland.[2]

Niklaus von Flüe was born on March 21, 1417, in the "Flüeli," the hill country above the town of Sachseln in the canton of Unterwalden. He was the son of a respected local farmer, Heinrich von Flüe, and his wife, Emma Ruberta. In the fifteenth century, the Catholic Church was in a state of decay, corruption, and inner discord—a circumstance that brought many believers to reorient themselves toward an inner approach to religion. The political situation in Switzerland was also a difficult one at the time, because the original cantons, as a result of the pernicious custom of young men leaving their homes to join foreign armies (so-called *Reislaufen*), had been completely drained and were in a state of collapse. Though Saint Niklaus was not himself involved in such fortune-seeking activities, we nonetheless find his name in the lists of several groups that went on marauding expeditions.

Though he evidently even rose to the rank of captain, he is said always to have attempted to prevent unnecessary massacres and senseless destruction. Around the year 1447, when he was thirty years old, he married Dorothea Wyss, who in the course of time bore ten children. From 1459 to 1462 he held the office of judge and was a member of the governing council of Unterwalden. As a judge he was often a witness to injustice and graft. This provoked a profound sense of outrage in him as well as an aversion to all worldly transactions. He once had a vision during a court session of fire blazing from the mouth of an unjust judge.

When he was forty-five years old, he began to suffer from a profound depression, which was accompanied by a feeling of annoyance with his family and by a longing to devote himself to his inner religious vocation. His friend Heiny am Grund, the local priest in Kriens, recommended a practice of regular prayer, but this proved of little help to him. Finally, when he was fifty years old, Klaus (as he was called) succeeded in persuading his wife to allow him to leave home, and he set forth into the unknown world as a mendicant monk.

However, a number of incidents, including a horrifying vision that came upon him as he neared the Swiss border, caused him to return home. With the help of friends and relatives he built a hermit's cell about two hundred and fifty yards from his house in a deep, shadowy ravine. There he spent the rest of his life. He took no food apart from the sacred host. He had many visionary experiences and gradually acquired such renown as a religious healer and adviser that there were often as many as six hundred people to be found waiting in the neighborhood of his cell for an opportunity to speak to him.

At the age of sixty-four, Klaus became involved in a famous political event at the Congress of Stans, the "Stans Accord" of December 22, 1487. A conflict between the original cantons, which were more democratic and rural, and the new cantons, which stood more under aristocratic rule, had reached a critical point. A civil war seemed imminent. In this situation, the priest from Kriens, Heiny am Grund, ran all through the night to reach the hermitage in Sachseln and ask Niklaus to address the hostile parties. Klaus did not leave his cell but sent the message that the parties should come to an understanding. He simply admonished them to keep the peace, to accept the two new urban cantons but without expanding their territory too much, and to settle the conflict by means of a treaty. Klaus's authority was so great that both parties humbly obeyed, though not without a certain amount of grumbling, and put an end to their dispute. If the matter had come to an armed conflict, then probably Austria and France would have intervened militarily, and Switzerland would have disappeared from the map forever. All this is by no means legend, but undisputed historical fact.

The message that Klaus sent contained nothing particularly out of the ordinary. In a certain way, it was simply an expression of good, sound common sense and could have been formulated by any wise old peasant in just the same way. What brought about the extraordinary results was the awe that everyone felt toward Klaus. Later he was frequently called upon for his counsel in political matters by noblemen and diplomats; and in this way achieved in actual fact what Confucius had sought in China but was unable to accomplish owing to unfavorable circumstances—he was able to exercise political influence as a sage.

This leads us now to a deeper question: what really lay behind the extraordinary effect that Niklaus von Flüe had on those around him? In my view, we can learn more about this question by examining a significant vision the saint had, which was as follows:

It seemed to Brother Klaus that a man who looked like a pilgrim was coming toward him. He held a staff in his hands, had on a hat with the brim turned back in the manner of a wayfarer, and wore a cloak. Klaus knew within himself that this man came from the east or from far away. Although the pilgrim did not say so, Klaus knew he came from "where the sun rises in summertime." He stood in front of Klaus singing the word "Hallelujah!" When he began to sing, his voice echoed, and everything between heaven and earth seemed to support his voice. And Klaus heard "three perfect words that stood out from the rest, coming out of one origin," which then closed up again like something on a spring. When Klaus heard these three perfect words, none of which touched either of the others, they nonetheless struck him as being a single word. When the pilgrim had finished his song, he asked Klaus for alms. Brother Klaus suddenly had a penny in his hand and dropped it into the pilgrim's hat. "And the man [Brother Klaus?] had never realized that it was a thing so worthy of veneration to receive a gift in one's hat."

Klaus asked where the wayfarer came from and who he was, and the traveler said only, "I come from there," and was unwilling to say anything further. Klaus stood in front of him and looked at him. Then the pilgrim transformed. He now no longer wore a hat and cloak, but rather a blue-gray vest. He was a fine, handsome-looking man, and Klaus looked at him with joy and longing. The brownish color of his face gave him a noble look, his eyes were black like a magnet, and his limbs of extraordinary beauty. Although he was clothed, Klaus could see his limbs. As Klaus was looking at him so raptly, the wayfarer also looked back at him. In this moment, great miracles occurred: Mount Pilatus collapsed to the ground and was completely flat; the earth opened up; Klaus thought he could see the sins of the whole world. A huge throng of people appeared to him, and behind them appeared the truth, but all the people had turned their backs on it. In their hearts, Klaus saw a great sickness, a tumor as big as two fists. This sickness was egotism, by which people were so seduced that they were unable to bear the sight of the man (of truth), "no more than people can stand fire." In great confusion, fear, and shame, they ran hither and thither, and finally fled; "but the truth remained there."

Then the countenance of the wayfarer transformed "like a veronica," and Klaus had a great longing to see more of him. He saw him again as before, but his clothing had changed, and he stood before him in a bearskin with coat and pants. The fur was spangled with golden color, but Klaus saw clearly that it was a bearskin. The bearskin was very becoming to the pilgrim, and Klaus recognized his extraordinary beauty. As he stood before the wayfarer, so noble in the bearskin, Klaus saw that the figure wished to bid him farewell. Klaus asked him, "Where do you want to go?" and he replied, "I want to go up country" and would say no more. As he departed, Klaus stared after him and saw that the bearskin shone on him as when someone moves a brightly polished sword back and forth and the reflection of it is seen on the walls. And Klaus thought that this was something whose meaning would remain hidden from him. When the wayfarer had gone maybe four steps, he turned around, took off his hat, and bowed to Klaus. Then Klaus realized that the wayfarer bore him such love that he was quite stricken and had to confess that he was not deserving of this great love. Then he saw that this love was in the wayfarer. And he saw that his spirit, his face, his eyes, his whole body was full of this elevated love (Minne), like a vessel that is filled to the brim with honey. Then he could no longer see the wayfarer, but he was so fulfilled that he no longer desired anything from him. It seemed to him that the wayfarer had revealed to him "everything that was between heaven and earth."

Many hours were necessary for the interpretation of this great vision. Here I can only go into a few of its essential aspects. This pilgrim is clearly an image for what Jung called the Self (as opposed to the ego). That is, it is Klaus's eternal inner spiritual core, something like the "inner Christ" that is described in the writings of the mystics. But although the pilgrim sings the biblical "Hallelujah" (God be praised), his clothes characterize him more as Wotan, the Germanic god of war, of truth, of ecstasy, and of shamanic wisdom. In accordance with a number of myths, Wotan traveled through the world, taking lodging with human beings, dressed in a gray-blue cloak and a broad-brimmed hat. With his flaming eyes, he looked like a nobleman. Other myths recount that he could continuously change his form. For this reason, he was also called Svipall, "the changeable," or Grimmir, "the masked one," and Tveggi, "the twofold." In Klaus's vision he comes from the direction of the sunrise, that symbolic location from which arise new enlightenments and revelations of the collective unconscious. This frame of reference is also reflected in expressions like "an idea dawned on me."

In the further course of the vision, the wayfarer appears behind the backs of people as truth personified. Wotan also had the epithet Sannr, "true." He is supposed to have had second sight, and according to some sagas, he could open up all the mountains and see and "take what was inside" (Snorri Sturluson). In Christianity, the Holy Ghost is the spirit of truth, but here it curiously fused with the ancient Germanic god of love (Minne) and spiritual devotion. This pilgrim gives Klaus the feeling that he knows everything between heaven and earth, that is, he confers on Klaus what Jung called the "absolute knowledge" of the unconscious, which characterizes many experiences of the Self.

Yet he also confers on Klaus something more, that is, the feeling of boundless love, described as a brimming vessel, overflowing with honey. The honey motif recalls a verse in the *Brhadaranyaka Upanishad,* which says: "This Self is honey for all beings. For this Self all beings are honey. And that which in this Self is that *atman*—that is, that *purusha* that arises out of light energy, out of the deathless—is that very primordial Atman, Deathlessness, Brahman. It is the universe. And verily is the Self the lord of all beings, the king of all beings. And just as all the spokes are held in the axle and the rim of a wheel, so all beings and all these selves (of the earth, of the waters, etc.) are held in the Self.[3] In India, *madhu* (honey) symbolizes the contact of all beings in the universe with the Self, the anthropos *(purusha);* that means, as Max Müller has explained, an objective, complete, and mutual interdependence or connectedness of all things—which is what Jung called "objective knowledge" as opposed to subjective love, which is full of projections and ego-oriented wishes.

The most striking and most unorthodox motif in this vision of Brother Klaus, however, is that of the bearskin worn by the pilgrim. This detail once again points to Wotan, who among his other epithets, as the god of the berserkers is also called Hrammi, "bear paw." In the Old Testament, the bear represents the dark side of Yahweh, and among the northern shamans, the bear is the most common of the "helping spirits" or allies. In most of the countries of northern Europe the bear was formerly regarded as so sacred that it was spoken of only as "father," "sacred man," "sacred woman," "wise father," "goldfoot," and so on.

For the ancient Germans, wearing a bearskin meant one was a *beriserkr,* a berserker. The ability to become a berserker was a parapsychological gift that was hereditary in certain Germanic warrior families. It manifested as a divine ecstasy, a kind of sacred wrath. It was said of such men that they fell in a swoon to the ground as though they were dead, and at this point their soul left their body in the form of a bear. Then it went raging into battle, slaying all foes, sometimes, however, also its own people by accident. The basic state of mind in this "going berserk" was called *grimr,* which amounts to something like "fury" or "rage." Going berserk was also called *hamfong,* that is, changing one's skin or form as well as one's shadow or protecting spirit. In sum it can be said that the bear aspect of the holy pilgrim in Klaus's vision represents the dangerous and uncanny animal shadow of the Self.

In a letter, Jung writes about this vision: "The mana-charged, or numinous, person has theriomorphic properties and thus reaches beyond the ordinary man not only in an upward direction but also downwards." In the vision of the berserker, Jung tells us, the inner Christ appears in two forms: "first as pilgrim, who like the mystic is making a peregrinatio animae; and second, as a bear, whose fur has a golden luster." This last is an allusion to the "new sun" (sol novus) in alchemy, a new knowledge.[4] Jung continues: "The meaning of the vision could be this. Brother Klaus recognizes himself in his spiritual pilgrimhood and in his instinctive (bearlike, i.e., hermitlike) subhumanness as Christ. . . . The brutal coldness of feeling that the saint requires to separate himself from woman and child, and friendship is found in the subhuman animal kingdom. Thus the saint casts an animal shadow. . . . He who is capable of bearing the highest and the lowest together is hallowed, holy, whole. The vision is telling him that the spiritual pilgrim and the berserker are both Christ, and this paves the way in him for forgiveness of the greatest sin, which is sainthood." Later in his life Niklaus had a vision of God's wrath that horrified him, "for this wrath applied to he who had betrayed his dearest ones and ordinary people for the sake of God."

The Christ-berserker in Brother Klaus's vision thus unites irreconcilable opposites, that is, subhuman savagery and Christian spirituality, the frenzy of war and Christian agape, the love of humanity. Only because Klaus could make room for this figure within himself was he capable of reconciling these opposites in the outer world, of convincing his compatriots to adopt a peaceful solution rather than letting themselves be carried away into a civil war.

In order to understand how this is possible, we must come to grips with certain basic notions of depth psychology. Let us take a look at the situation as it is represented in the accompanying diagram. The points A, A, A located on the outermost edge of the diagram represent the human ego consciousness. Below that lies a psychic stratum B, B, B, which represents the sphere of the so-called personal unconscious, that is, the psychic stratum discovered by Freud that contains forgotten and repressed memories, desires, and instinctive impulses. Below that is the stratum C, C, C, which is a kind of group unconscious that comes to

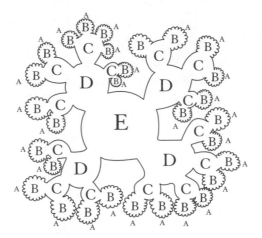

DIAGRAM OF THE STRUCTURE OF THE UNCONSCIOUS.

A = ego consciousness; B = personal unconscious; C = group unconscious;
D = unconscious of large-scale national unities;
E = universal archetypal structures

the fore in family or group therapy. This contains the customary reactions and complexes common to whole groups, clans, tribes, and so on. Still further down, we find the stratum D, D, D, which embodies the unconscious of large-scale national unities. In the mythologies of the Australian aborigines and the Indians of South America, we can see, for example, that they constitute a large "family" of religious motifs that are relatively similar to one another, which, however, they do not share with the whole of humanity. An example is the motif of capturing a demonic solar figure and taking away its strength. We find this motif in the Far East, but not in the West. Finally, the circle in the middle of the diagram, E, represents the sum of those universal psychic archetypal structures that we have in common with all of humanity, as, for example, the psychic notion of mana, of heroes, of cosmic divine persons, of mother earth, of the helpful animal, or the figure of the trickster, which we find in all mythologies and all religious systems.

When someone is working on his own unconscious, as soon as

he reaches C, he makes contact—at first invisibly—with the group; and when he goes yet deeper, he makes contact with the great national unities (stratum D) or sometimes even the whole of humanity (stratum E). This individual then changes not only himself but also has an imperceptible influence on the unconscious psyche of many other people. That is why Confucius (Kung Tzu) said: "The superior man abides in his room. If his words are well spoken, he meets with assent at a distance of more than a thousand miles.[5]

The collective unconscious is actually like an atmosphere that contains and affects all of us. One of the images of greatest significance in our common Center E is the image of a divine human being or a collective hero, which we find in nearly all cultural communities (Christ, Osiris, Avalokiteshvara). In comparative religious terms we might call this figure the anthropos to distinguish it from various gods, spirits, and demons, which are more symbolic of particular autonomous impulses in the collective psyche. In contrast to these, the anthropos represents the core aspect of the collective unconscious, which stands specifically for the quality of humanness, including human cultural consciousness.

In the development of religious cultural communities, there is clearly a fundamental law at work that brings the periodic disintegration and collapse, then the renewal and recombination, of their constituent elements. In principle, all individual instinctive drives—as for example, the sexual impulse, the aggressive drive for power, or the survival instinct—have both a psychological and a symbolic (that is, psychic or spiritual) side. On the archaic level, these two sides function in very close collaboration. The ritual and bodily activities are one with what they represent. However, in the course of historical development, these two aspects tend to separate. When this happens, the ritual and religious teachings develop into something that is no more than a rigid intellectual formalism, against which the physical instincts then rise in revolt. This conflict situation is necessary for the development of a higher consciousness, but the conflict can also go too far and become destructive. Then a reconciliation of the opposites is needed. Such a situation calls for the recollection (anamnesis) of the primordial human person, the anthropos as the archetype of the total human being, who stands at the core of all the great religions. In the notion of such a homo maximus, the higher and the lower aspects of creation are once again reunited.[6]

In the Christ-berserker of Klaus's vision, just such an anthropos figure, which completes the official incomplete image of Christ, spontaneously arises. But this individual vision in which Christ appears as a berserker overflowing with Eros is no isolated image arising in an extraordinary individual. Rather it reaches far into the past and is rooted in an enduring hidden historical context. As Jung has shown, there is within the whole Western Christian culture, with its two-thousand-year-old tradition, an unofficial development of the Christ image. In his work *Aion*,[7] Jung refers to the fact that in the Revelation of Saint John the Divine (chapters 5 and 6), there appears a lamb with seven horns and seven eyes, a monstrous beast that does not at all resemble the sacrificial lamb associated by tradition with Christ. It is praised as a "bellicose lamb, a conqueror" (Rev. 17:14; see also Jung, loc. cit.) and as "a lion of the tribe of Judah" (Rev. 5:5). Thus it would seem that at the end of time a certain shadow aspect of Christ, a shadow aspect that Christ had earlier cast off, will reappear and once again be integrated into his image. When we compare the Church's image of Christ with the God image of the Old Testament, the traditional Christ figure does not seem to fully embody this God image. Yahweh is on the one hand full of boundless goodness; on the other, however, He shows himself boundlessly cruel in His wrath and vengefulness. By contrast, Christ embodies only the first aspect. It is presumably for this reason that he himself foretold that at the end of the Christian era a countervailing process would bring forth the Antichrist. The demonic ram of the Apocalypse, however, is not a form of the Antichrist, but rather a reincarnated, transfigured, or completed symbol of Christ, in which certain dark and vengeful aspects are integrated rather than splintered off.

Perhaps this is a partial return to the Jewish conception of a warlike Messiah, which arose from an anti-Roman resentment. The Christian answer to the knowledge of the good-and-evil double nature of God was, to begin with, one sided: God is exclusively good, and Christ, his incarnation as a human being, is likewise only good. From the year A.D. 1000 on, this symbolic religious solution began to be doubted. The problem of evil forced itself increasingly into the foreground. With regard to this problem, there were two possibilities. The first was the accepted notion that an Antichrist movement would arise and destroy on a gigantic scale all the cultural and moral achievements brought about by Christ. The second possible development was also produced by the unconscious: the idea of completing Christ into a figure that would be both good and evil—a real union of the opposites.

In his work, "Answer to Job,"[8] Jung put forward the hypothesis that the Apocalypse should be regarded as an expression of this second development. In Revelation 12, there appears "a woman clothed with the sun and the moon under her feet; and upon her head a crown of twelve stars." While in the throes of labor she is harassed by a dragon. After she has borne a boy, the child is "caught up unto God," and the woman flees into the desert (Rev. 12:5f.). This seems to be a vision of a kind of rebirth of the Christ figure that is an adumbration of the future of the collective unconscious, an anticipation of a more complete symbol of the self that is no longer split into good and evil halves.

This notion of a more complete Christ figure also did not fail to stir many medieval alchemists. Their "philosopher's stone," which they compared to Christ, was not exclusively good; it was a union of the moral opposites. And beyond that, it also unified mind and matter as well as the human and animal. It was not only a savior of souls like Christ, but also a redeemer of the total nature of the macrocosmos.

If we look at how the history of our Western Christian civilization has unfolded externally, we can see that this union of the opposites has not taken place, or at least not yet. On the contrary,

Europe is split into a so-called Christian western half and an anti-Christian eastern half. Large parts of the rest of the world have taken sides with one of these or the other. The explicit anti-Christian spiritual development in Europe began with the Renaissance, that is, in the time in which Brother Klaus lived. Thus it is all the more striking that it was precisely at this time that the unconscious in Klaus independently and spontaneously produced a Christ figure, which like the philosopher's stone of the alchemists, unified the opposites. The dark side—which looks back to the pagan Germanic tradition—is a berserker. When we consider what was wrought by this Wotan-like berserker in World War II, we realize what gruesome destructivity is brought about when this berserker is no longer unified with its opposite and is left to function autonomously. Jung referred to World War II as a "Wotanic experiment" and expressed the fear that we are now in the process of preparing ourselves for a new Wotanic experiment, but this time a worldwide one (letter of September 9, 1960). Such a catastrophe is only possible when the berserker shadow—that is, aggression—remains autonomous and is not integrated into the inner wholeness of man.

By completely withdrawing into his hermitage in the Ranft during his desperate depression, Brother Klaus forced this shadow to remain entirely within him, where it fused with the inner Christ. But we know from experience that we are unable to integrate such divine powers of aggression into our ordinary ego. All that hopeful, well-meaning prattle we hear about integrating one's own aggression is nonsense. Only through effort and suffering can we lend support to the integration of these powers into the Self. In other words, we can only integrate our personal shadow, not the collective shadow of the Self, the dark side of the Godhead.

Yet if we suffer the problem of the opposites to the utmost and accept it into ourselves, we can sometimes become a place in which the divine opposites can spontaneously come together. This is quite clearly what happened to Brother Klaus. His vision showed him that the divine opposites had become one within the

Self and that this unified figure now overflowed with honey. This is a love that flows from the individual human being who has become whole.

We find interesting parallels to this process in the writings of the alchemists. Many of them describe the philosopher's stone in a way that strongly recalls Brother Klaus's vision of the cosmic berserker overflowing with honey. They praise it as a living thing that streams forth "rose-colored blood" or "rose color" and has a healing effect on its environment. This is certainly one of the most curious images that is to be found in the alchemical writings. The disciple of Paracelsus, Gerard Dorn, for example, said about the philosopher's stone: (The philosophers) "called their stone animate because, at the final operations, (it) sweats out drop by drop . . . a dark red liquid like blood. . . . And for this reason they have prophesied that in the last days a most pure man [*putus* = genuine, not falsified], through whom the world will be freed, will come to earth and will sweat bloody drops of a rosy or red hue, whereby the world will be redeemed from its Fall. In like manner, too, the blood of their stone will free the leprous metals and also men from their diseases. . . . For in the blood of this stone is hidden its soul."[9]

Another alchemist, Henricus Khunrath, says of the same blood, that it is the blood of the "lion lured forth from the Saturnine mountain."[10] Here, in the place of the bear in Brother Klaus's vision, we have a lion from the "Saturnine mountain," who, like the bear, is also a wild animal who comes out of the depths of darkness and depression, but brings with it the healing blood of love. Khunrath goes on to speak of the "Rosy-Coloured Blood . . . that flows forth . . . from the side of the innate Son of the Great World when opened by the power of the Art." Thus this blood comes from a "Healer of all imperfect bodies and men."[11] In contrast to the Biblical Christ, he is not only a savior for human beings, but also—like the lapis, the Christ of alchemy—the redeemer of the whole of nature.

Jung writes: "It seems as though the rose-colored blood of the alchemical redeemer was derived from a rose mysticism that penetrated into alchemy, and that, in the form of the red tincture, it expressed the healing or whole-making effect of a certain kind of Eros." This Eros emanates from the homo totus, the cosmic man whom Dorn had described as *putissimus* ("unalloyed"). "This 'most pure' or 'most true' man must be no other than what he is; . . . he must be entirely man, a man who knows and possesses everything human and is not adulterated by any influence or admixture from without." According to Dorn, he will not appear on earth until "in the last days." Jung continues: "He cannot be Christ, for Christ by his blood has already redeemed the world from the consequences of the Fall. . . . [Rather what we have here] is the alchemical *servator cosmi* (preserver of the cosmos), representing the still unconscious idea of the whole and complete man, who shall bring about what the sacrificial death of Christ has obviously left unfinished, namely the deliverance of the world from evil. . . . [His blood is] a psychic substance, the manifestation of a certain kind of Eros which unifies the individual as well as the multitude in the sign of the rose and makes them whole."[12]

In the sixteenth century, the Rosicrucian movement made its appearance. Its motto, *per crucem ad rosam,* had been anticipated by the alchemists. "Such movements, as also the emergence of the idea of Christian charity . . . ," Jung tells us, "are always indicative of a corresponding social defect which they serve to compensate. In the perspective of history, we can see clearly enough what this defect was in the ancient world; and in the Middle Ages as well, with its cruel and unreliable laws and feudal conditions, human rights and human dignity were in a sorry plight."[13] We may add here that this held true also for social conditions in the time of Brother Klaus. Therefore it seems that this berserker who is overflowing with honey, that is, with love, appears in his vision, because Klaus, as we know, was extremely troubled over the social injustice and cruelty taking place around him.

But what kind of love could this be? Jung emphasizes that love by itself is useless if it is not accompanied by a certain understanding. "And for the proper use of understanding a wider consciousness is needed, and a higher standpoint to enlarge one's horizon. . . . Certainly love is needed for that, but a love combined with insight and understanding. Their function is to illuminate the regions that are still dark and to add them to consciousness [through discrimination]. . . . The blinder love is, the more it is instinctual, and the more it is attended by destructive consequences, for it is a dynamism that needs form and direction."[14] We can see this in the case of mothers who fairly suffocate their children out of pure love; or on the collective level, we see it in foreign aid through which, with all love, we brutally force our own ideas and technologies on underdeveloped countries. For so-called love, humanity has had to bear countless crimes and great upheavals, and the more sentimental love is, the more brutal is its shadow, following behind it. By contrast, in the symbol of the berserker—Christ, this brutal shadow (which appears in the form of a bear) is integrated into the human figure and therefore no longer continues to function autonomously behind its back.

The whole problem is ethical in nature. It is the problem of the differentiation of our emotions. Western civilization has for some time been developing its extraverted thinking and sensation one-sidedly in its technology and its introverted thinking and sensation one-sidedly in its theoretical research. Intuition has not been entirely suppressed, because it has been used for the discovery of new creative ideas. Feeling, however, and the whole world of Eros, love, is in a truly pitiable state. I even believe that at this point in time, everything depends on whether or not we are capable of developing our feeling and our social Eros.

Psychologically, it is impossible to say what Eros actually is, for it is an archetypal force that goes far beyond our power to comprehend it intellectually. From the empirical standpoint, it appears that what lies at its roots is a participation mystique, which Jung called an "archaic identity." This is an unconscious agreement of collective ideas and emotional values. Upon such an archaic identity is based the common presumption that what is good for me is also good for others, and that therefore I have the right to decide the situations of others—for fundamentally speaking, other people are like myself. This is a primordial, fundamental social and instinctive bond that unifies all human beings and that can even include animals, plants, and other elements of the external world. Even Christian brotherly love and Buddhist compassion are ultimately based on this deeply rooted instinctive factor. The symbolic image of the anthropos or divine man includes this aspect, since it is often described in myths as being the basic stuff out of which the entire cosmos is created. This is the case with the Purusha in India, P'an ku in Chinese mythology, the giant Ymir in the Germanic creation story, Gayomart in Persia, or Osiris-Re in Egypt. The Judeo-Christian figures of the first and second Adams (the second Adam being Christ) includes this aspect as well. According to certain midrashim, for example, Adam was at first a cosmic giant in which all the souls of humanity were united "like strands in a wick." Christ has the same function in relation to the Christian community, since Christians are all brothers and sisters in Christ.

The phenomenon of the archaic identity does not account fully enough for the great differences there are between people. In archaic circumstances, such differences manifest in tribal feuds among the various groups within a people and occasionally even in chaotic social conditions in which everyone is at war with everyone else, as has been the case in every interregnum period.

However, the presence of inevitable personal tensions and hostilities also forces us to realize that other people are sometimes different and do not always behave according to our expectations. This leads to a phenomenon Jung called the taking back of projections. In this process, we awaken to the insight that certain presumptions and judgments of ours about other people do not apply to them but rather to ourselves. However, insights of this nature remain quite rare, and it seems that we are only in the initial stages of this global realization. Especially in cases where great differences exist, as for example, between man and woman, or between quite foreign ethnic groups and ourselves, the discernment and realization of projections is of capital importance.

Only when projections are taken back does relationship—as opposed to archaic identity—become possible. This, however, presupposes psychological insight. We have diplomats in foreign countries who really should supply us with psychological information. How badly this functions in actual fact, however, is unfortunately all too well known. In all pluralistically and democratically organized societies, an attempt is made somehow to regulate the cooperation of the various groups and individuals within it without forcing upon them total adherence to the rules of the archaic collective identity. In contrast to this kind of archaic identity, relationship makes room for the idea of a certain distance. On this point, Jung writes: "Decreases in distance are part of the most important and most difficult chapter of the individuation process. The danger is always that the distance will be taken away on one side only, the unfailing result of which is a kind of violation followed by resentment. Every relationship has its optimal distance, which of course has to be found out through empirical means."[15]

We are in all probability eons away from being able to actualize such a free mutual connection between all human beings. A deeper respect for the real differentness of other people or other national groups is just as necessary as the intimacy of a feeling of identity. But even this is not yet the final stage of the development that is possible. It is obvious that on the surface (that is, on the outer edge of our diagram) this sense of differentness would cause excessive fragmentation or isolation of the conscious individual egos. For this reason, there is yet a fourth stage, which Jung referred to as the destined personal connection of certain people through the Self. This is a kind of return to the first stage, but on a higher, more conscious level. It is a relationship with the Self in the other person, with his or her wholeness, with the unity of opposites within him or her. Only love, not intellect, can apprehend another person in this way. This form of love, Jung writes, "is not transference and not friendship in the usual sense, nor sympathy either. It is more primitive, more primordial, and more spiritual than anything we are capable of describing. The upper story is no longer you or I, it is the many of which you yourself are a part, and everyone is part of it whose heart you touch. There differentness does not prevail, but rather immediate presence. It is an eternal mystery; how could I ever explain it?"[16]

It could perhaps be described as a timeless connection in eternity, which appears as a mystery in this world, in our space-time, yet is that which makes possible any true and profound encounter between two people. This mystery also comes into play when we have the feeling with someone we are meeting for the first time that we have already always "known" him—and it turns out to be true, not a mistake, as is sometimes the case with normal archaic identity. This kind of relationship can occur between members of the same sex, for example, in the "eternal" relationship between masters and their disciples, but it occurs more often in love relationships between men and women, who represent the greatest opposites existing between human beings. According to Jung, it is this last problem of relationship that is at the root of all of modern humanity's problems. Either we must become capable of overcoming these opposites within ourselves, or we shall end up contributing to the outbreak of war in the external world. Personal love is the only existing counterbalance to the fragmentation—indeed even atomization—of modern society. In personal love the image of the anthropos can be resurrected, and with it "the truth" that is behind people's backs, as Klaus saw in his vision.

Brother Klaus was not weak and sentimental in the least. In his counseling, he unhesitatingly uncovered the lies and hidden sins of his clients; but he always did it with a humorous wink of the eye and with kindly warmth. Since these are the earmarks of a good therapist, Jung said Brother Klaus should be the patron saint of psychotherapy. In a certain way, it was personified truth as it arose in his vision of the bearskin-clad pilgrim that was at work in him. His love and warmth was always directed toward the person in front of him, for relationships with individual people are always unique—between one unique person and another. Only within such relationships can our psyche awaken to life and manifest the suprapersonal self. In this way, as the figure of the

Christ-berserker shows, a certain inner split within the Self develops into a unity.

I am convinced that Brother Klaus, without the berserker figure in the background, would not have been capable of bringing a peaceful end to the Congress of Stans. The berserker was a visible representation of the invisible authority that emanated from him, exercising an influence that made it possible for the hostile parties to put their conflict aside. In this way, Klaus had a greater political effect than any ruler or diplomat. He is a wonderful example of the way in which individuation and collective responsibility can come together. Of course Brother Klaus is a unique example, which we cannot simply imitate. In the inner development of every person, the opposition between individual transformation and social responsibility takes on different forms and shadings. In the first hexagram of the *I Ching,* "The Creative," one of the lines is connected with this problem. The line for nine in the fourth place reads: "Wavering flight over the depths. No blame." In the commentary to this line we find: "A place of transition has been reached, and free choice can enter in. A twofold possibility is presented to the great man: he can soar to the heights and play an important part in the world, or he can withdraw into solitude and develop himself. He can go the way of the hero or that of the holy sage who seeks seclusion. There is no general law to say which of the two is the right way. Each one in this situation must make a free choice according to the inner law of his being. If the individual acts consistently and is true to himself, he will find the way that is appropriate for him. This is right for him and without blame."[17]

Compared to such holy sages as Lao Tzu or Chuang Tzu, Brother Klaus as a solitary hermit is a humbler figure. In the first part of his life he took part in all the ordinary activities of life; only when an inner vocation came to him did he abandon the world. To begin with, then, he gave himself with burning fervor to the "imitatio Christi" and practiced Christian brotherly love. But then the berserker came upon him, a deep, introverted, wild longing to follow his own inner truth. And the greatest miracle of all was perhaps that the people around him did not interpret this as madness. A few theologians tried to criticize him for leaving his family, but the general public, and particularly the people of Unterwalden took his side, seeing in his withdrawal into seclusion a divine vocation and not an indication of asocial behavior and lack of responsibility. Presumably this may be laid at the feet of the Eros—honey aspect of the berserker pilgrim, which the people must have felt in him.

To return to our diagram: the central area of the collective unconscious is depicted in most religions as an anthropos figure, the symbol of the God-man or the cosmic man. Thus, paradoxically, the berserker embodies the greater personality of the Self in Brother Klaus and at the same time the self of the whole community. It is precisely in this respect that this figure is still a living archetype today. In World War II, a Swiss regiment had a collective vision of Brother Klaus, standing on the Swiss-German border with his arms outspread to protect the Swiss people from invasion by Hitler. The greater archetypal core in the figure of Brother Klaus is still alive in this way in Switzerland today.

Modern zoologists and countless psychologists these days are writing about the problem of aggression and the possibility of integrating it, abreacting it, or suppressing it. Brother Klaus's vision shows us how it is really possible to integrate and transform it. It is then no longer what we usually call aggression, but rather a clearly defined delimitation and solidification of the individual who is capable of steadfastly remaining "himself," without yielding to a group or falling prey to mass suggestion. In the many situations of collective panic that a nation can fall into, everything often depends on whether or not a few individuals are capable of keeping a clear head and not getting swept away by the prevailing delusive emotions. According to Jung, this is the only way war can be avoided.

But this goal remains a remote and distant one for humanity, and until we reach it nations and groups will inevitably continue to fight each other. Yet one thing is sure for me: we have reached a point in history at which the differentiation of Eros is a matter of the greatest urgency. For because the world has become a smaller place today, we are driven inexorably to realize that we are all in the same boat.

Notes

1. C. G. Jung, *Briefe* (Letters), vol. 1 (Olten, Switzerland: Walter Verlag, 1973), letter of Oct. 19, 1934, p. 226.

2. See M.-L. von Franz, *Die Visionen des Niklaus von Flüe* (The Visions of Niklaus von Flüe) (Einsiedeln, Switzerland: Daimon Verlag, 1980), and the literature referred to there.

3. *Brhadanyaka Upanishad* 2.54 (Oxford: Clarendon Press: 1900), p. 116. German cited from von Franz, *Die Visionen des Niklaus von Flüe,* p. 87.

4. C. G. Jung, op. cit., letter to Professor Blanke of May 2, 1945, p. 449f.

5. *The I Ching or Book of Changes,* Richard Wilhelm translation, trans. by C. F. Baynes (Princeton, N.J.: Princeton University Press, Bollingen Series XIX, 1990), pp. 237–38 (commentary to hexagram 61, "Inner Truth," nine in the second place).

6. C. G. Jung, *Mysterium Coniunctionis,* cw 14 (Princeton, N.J.: Princeton University Press, Bollingen Foundation, 1989), para. 605, p. 420.

7. C. G. Jung, *Aion,* cw 9, para. 167, pp. 105–106.

8. Cf. C. G. Jung, "Answer to Job," in cw 11, but especially *Aion,* op. cit. paras. 163ff, pp. 103ff.

9. C. G. Jung, Alchemical Studies, cw 13, para. 381, p. 290.

10. Ibid., para. 383, p. 292.

11. Ibid., para. 384, p. 293.

12. Ibid., para. 390, pp. 295, 296.

13. Ibid., para. 391, p. 296.

14. Ibid.

15. C. G. Jung, *Briefe* (Letters), vol. 1 (Olten, Switzerland: Walter Verlag, 1973), letter of Sept. 20, 1928, p. 79.

16. Op. cit., letter of April 18, 1941, p. 373.

17. *I Ching,* op. cit., chapter 1.

THE UNKNOWN VISITOR IN
FAIRY TALES AND DREAMS

■■
■■

IN THE *METAMORPHOSES* (VIII, 620f.), the poet Ovid tells how once again the gods got the impression that human beings were neglecting them. Thus Jupiter and Mercury decided to come down to earth, disguised as poor wayfarers, to test human beings. And wherever they knocked and begged for shelter, they were haughtily turned away.

Finally they arrived at a miserable hut belonging to an old married couple, Philemon ("having a loving disposition") and Baucis ("the tender one"), who was a servant of the Great Mother. (The name Baucis is related to that of Baubo, the servant of Demeter who, after the kidnapping of Persephone, first made her mistress laugh again by baring her own bottom. A number of inscriptions would lead one to conclude that Baubo is an aspect of the great goddess herself.) The two old people welcomed the wayfarers into their hut and prepared a meal for them, slaughtering their only gander in the wayfarers' honor. On the following day the gods revealed themselves to the old people in their full glory and rewarded them by granting them a wish. The two asked to be allowed to remain together until death and even afterward. Thereupon their hut was transformed into a magnificent temple, in which from then on Philemon and Baucis lived as priest and priestess. When they had reached the ends of their lives, they died at the same time and were changed into two trees, which stood so close together that their branches entwined in eternal embrace. The scoundrels who had refused the gods shelter were drowned in a great flood and repaid in this way for their godlessness.

This tale of Ovid's was extremely timely: as happens periodically in the course of history, all religious life in his time had become calcified into purely external state ceremonies and had thus lost its psychic influence on humanity. In the Roman ruling class, power prevailed rather than interpersonal Eros, form rather than inner experience. Jupiter was no longer a living archetypal figure of order in the human psyche, but rather the guarantor of power to the Roman Empire. As for Mercury, it was primarily his mercantile side that had developed, his deceitful and thievish character. He was no longer the purveyor of hidden messages from the beyond and also no longer the god of love and fertility who had once come from Mount Cyllene. Patriarchal order overshadowed the maternal domain of outer and inner nature. Although the poets of that period compensatorily sang the praises of return to the bucolic life, this remained a sentimental, aesthetic game hovering above the abyss of melancholy that smouldered in the depths of the psyche. This motif of a god or gods who come to men in a disguised form is an archetypal theme that crops up in many areas of culture, but as it seems to me, always as a compensation for a similar need. That is to say, it crops up at a time *when personal encounter with and individual relationship to the divine has become a necessity,* outside the institutionalized forms and views of religious life.

Meeting with the gods is always a surprise. They appear as unknown, inconspicuous, disguised visitors. In the world of Islam, it is not Allah himself but Khidr who takes on this role. He is the Metatron, the first angel of God, who similarly to Jupiter and Mercury, comes down to earth and visits human beings. Once in East Africa, the leader of Jung's safari to Mount Elgon recounted: "Sometimes in the evening when it is getting dark, you hear a knocking on the door and a poor man is standing there outside asking for shelter for the night. He says, 'Salaam,' and you reply, 'Salaam.' Suddenly you know it—it is Khidr! Then you must receive him very well, for he will always bring you luck." He further recounted to Jung that once this had happened to him when he had had no work and was out of money. The next day after the beggar disappeared, the man got a job with a safari, which saved him from his predicament.[1]

This episode proves that the unknown divine visitor still lives on today in the Islamic world. He compensates for the overly great, abstract remoteness of Allah in the official religion. Besides Khidr in North Africa, the prophet Elijah also sometimes appears in the same role. He too visits people as an inconspicuous wayfarer. He protects those who still have a genuine religious attitude toward life, and plays all kinds of tricks on others who have no respect for God. Leo the Great calls him an "earthly angel and a heavenly human."[2] Once, for example, he went disguised as a beggar to a rich man, who refused to give him shelter. Then he continued on to the poor brother of this man, who received him with special honor. On account of this, as he was leaving, Elijah said to the poor brother: "May God reward you for this. The first thing that you do now will continue as if by itself until you yourself say, 'Enough!'" Thereupon the poor man counted his money until he had received so much of it that he finally said, "Enough!" His rich brother heard about this and wanted to get the same blessing. He ran after the beggar and received him into his household with a great deal of pomp. As he was leaving, Elijah said the same words to him that he had spoken to his poor brother. However, before beginning to count their money, the rich man's wife suggested they should first relieve themselves so that they would not later be interrupted by any call of nature. Anyone can imagine what happened then!

Another time the pious Rabbi Meyer Baal ha-Ness had been proscribed by the Emperor Nero. Some people recognized him in the street, and a crowd began to chase him with the intention of handing him over to the emperor. At that point Elijah changed himself into a well-known prostitute of the city, hurried after the rabbi, threw her arms around him, and covered him with kisses.

Then the people said, "That can't be Rabbi Meyer. He never had anything to do with women like that." That is the way Elijah saved the rabbi.

Elijah was particularly given to appearing to Jews as a black man or an Arab. He was also especially fond of appearing to people in dreams. At the celebration of a circumcision, orthodox Jews still keep an empty chair in readiness for Elijah, the unknown visitor.

Elijah is a figure parallel to Khidr to such an extent that the latter is often known as Khidr-Elijah and is venerated in the same place. He is also called "the eternal youth," and he is thought to like dwelling in water, for example, in the Tigris. In Baghdad, the people used to bring the sick to this river so that Khidr-Elijah could bless and heal them. When they were healed, people tossed burning candles into the water as an expression of thanks. Jung wrote of Elijah that he was a living or constellated archetype that is always activated when a state of deficiency that requires compensation develops in the collective consciousness. Elijah is a *theos-anthropos* who is more human than Christ, because he was begotten with original sin; and who is more universal than Christ, because he also incorporates pre-Yahweh gods like Baal, El-Elioun, Mithra, Khidr, and Mercury. The *deus absconditus* of alchemy has the same compensatory function.[3]

In the Ukraine today, people still say, "Guest in the house— God in the house"; and in my opinion the ubiquitous belief in the sacredness and inviolability of the right of the guest to hospitality belongs to the same archetypal motif as the god who comes down to humanity as an unknown visitor. We cannot, however, go into this further here.

It is no coincidence that *two* divine figures knock on the door of Philemon and Baucis, and that Elijah and Khidr also appear as a pair. Duality as a motif always points to the fact that although an unconscious content is actually *single,* as a content of the unconscious it possesses paradoxical qualities. When it begins to appear on the threshold of consciousness, it manifests itself in opposites. For example, Jupiter is the supreme god of the human and cosmic *order;* Mercury, by contrast, is a trickster who creates unexpected "coincidences." In Khidr-Elijah, still more than in Jupiter-Mercury, this trickster nature is especially prominent as a compensation for the lawfulness of Yahweh and Allah.[4] As we shall see, this duality or dual nature of the unknown visitor is very widespread. It points to a strange either-or in this figure—good or evil, divine and human.

We find this motif not only in cultures closely related to our own; it also appears in Chinese folklore and literature. There the motif is that of one or two unknown, often spurned, Taoist mendicant monks, who appear in this role as earthly personifications of the divine. In a Chinese short novel entitled *Nocha,*[5] for example, the daughter of the king of heaven, the wife of General Li Jing, dreamed that a wandering Taoist penetrated into her chamber and called out, "Quick, receive the divine son!" and placed a shining pearl on her body. After three and a half years she bore a ball of flesh with a wonderful fragrance, which began to roll around her room like a wheel. Her father leapt forward and cut the ball in half with his sword, and a gleaming red boy sprang out of the ball. Three days later the Taoist appeared suddenly at a meal and announced, "I am the Great One. This boy is the bright pearl of the primordial beginning, lent to you as a son. However, the boy is wild and unruly and will kill many people. For that reason, I will take him as my student, to tame his wild nature." Then he vanished. The boy indeed proved to be very unruly and killed several people—finally even a pair of dragon kings who dwelled in a nearby lake (as is well known, in China dragons are powers of goodness). In the aftermath, the dragons threatened to avenge themselves on Nocha's parents. To prevent this, Nocha killed himself to expiate the wrongdoing. He became a bodiless spirit and was venerated at a temple from which he went out to perform great miracles of healing. Later the Great One gave him a new body made from lotus blossoms, and after many other adventures he was raised to the rank of a divinity.

In the famous seventeenth-century Chinese novel *The Dream*

of the Red Chamber,[6] two Taoist mendicant monks appear repeatedly in the course of the story as filthy, crippled beggars. They always turn up at decisive crossroads in the action and make predictions about the future in which they attempt to guide and enlighten the hero of the story through obscure and cryptic verses. But this is in vain. The hero does not grasp at all what is meant, what is taking place in the unconscious. Only later in the "Hall of Frightful Awakening" does he finally realize what the thread of meaning in the dark, chaotic movement of his life has been. The two mendicant monks are, like Khidr-Elijah, messengers from the beyond, knowing beings who announce the "will of Heaven."

In Indian tales, too, deities often appear to men in the guise of a yogi or fakir, only to reveal themselves later in their true form.[7]

Since the theme we are dealing with here is such a universal one, it is no wonder that we also find it in the Christian world. In European folktales, either God the Father himself or Jesus with his apostles appear as numinous unknown visitors or beggars. For example, a Russian fairy tale called "Marko, the Rich Man" recounts the following. Once there was a rich man named Marko who had only one daughter and no son. In a dream he once heard a voice, which said, "Make ready, rich Marko, for at such and such a time the Lord God himself along with Saint Nicholas will visit you as your guests." Marko prepared a magnificent welcome. Thereupon, two dirty old beggars appeared and asked for shelter for the night. Angrily, Marko directed them to the kitchen. During the night, a maid overheard a voice at the window, saying, "Has the Lord God lain down to rest?" The beggars replied, "Yes, what do you want?"

"Lord, in such and such a town a woman has borne a son. What good fortune, Lord, would you like to bless him with?"

"With the fortune of Marko the rich man. The boy will grow up and come to possess all his wealth."

At midnight, the two beggars disappeared. Too late Marko realized that they were the Lord God and St. Nicholas! Marko now tried to destroy the newborn boy by laying numerous impossible tasks upon him, for example, conquering "the pagan dragon." The boy was able to accomplish all of them. Then, deceived by an exchange of letters, Marko betrothed the boy to his daughter. He himself died through some mistake, and the boy inherited his entire fortune. He took good care of it and lived long and peacefully, proliferating happiness and joy and warding off suffering.[8]

Here, in contrast to the story of Philemon and Baucis, the two unknown visitors do not reinforce the traditional behavior of their old host, but as in "Nocha" they bless the birth of a new hero and help him to acquire Marko's wealth. And here too they punish improper behavior toward the unknown guests. We can conclude from this that it is neither the new nor the old that the two divine wayfarers support, but rather they always protect *genuine humanity* and destroy those who are unable to recognize them in their hidden, unprepossessing form.

In the Estonian tale "How the Rich Man Threshed," we encounter again the trickster nature of the visitors. When Jesus was still on earth, he came one night with his disciples to a rich farmer and asked him for lodging for the night. The farmer did not provide for them but said that he had no room. Then Jesus went to the nearby hut of a poor farmer, who offered him shelter for the night on the condition that on the following morning Jesus would help with the threshing. As they were beginning work, to the horror of his host, Jesus set the entire pile of wheat on fire. Then, holding a stick, he circumambulated the fire, saying: "Gently, gently, Laurits [the patron saint of fire], don't go into the latticework!" When the fire went out, two piles could be seen: the neatly separated chaff and the wheat. The rich man thought that this was a good idea and promptly set his wheat pile on fire too. His whole house went up in flames. Jesus was passing the night in the vicinity with his followers. One of the apostles went to the window and saw the light of the fire. He said, "It looks bad out there." But Jesus turned in the other direction and said, "That doesn't mean a thing; that's just the rich man doing his threshing."[9]

In the Bible, Jesus does not appear as a trickster. The above story shows that the simple folk missed this archetypal trait, which is part of every savior figure. That is why the features of the alchemical Mercurius are attributed here, in highly unorthodox fashion, to Jesus. Here, like Mercurius, Jesus has a double nature—he is good to the good and evil to the evil. He divides the chaff from the wheat with supernatural means—with fire. This recalls the saying from the Apocrypha: "He who is near me is near the fire, and he who is far from me is far from the Kingdom." Jesus does not punish the rich farmer himself. The rich farmer destroys his property through his own stupidity. This motif appears quite frequently. In another tale from Estonia, it is told how an unknown beggar granted three wishes to a poor widow who had given him hospitality. Thus she received a large quantity of rich linen. Her rich neighbor demanded the same thing from the beggar, but by inadvertently pronouncing a curse, he cursed himself. In this tale, it is not explicitly stated that the beggar is God, but the fact that he is able to grant the fulfillment of any wish clearly demonstrates his superhuman nature.

A story from Livonia recounts another strange incident of this nature. There was once a poor old man who lived in solitude in his hut. Three unknown visitors came to him, and he received them kindly. Because of this, as they were departing, they granted him a wish. He requested that the apples of his only apple tree should remain in place, for they always disappeared in an uncanny manner, and he could never pick any of them. The next day he saw the tree full of apples, but also full of little boys and a man. They had all been caught fast in a spell in the midst of trying to steal the apples. Good-naturedly the old man set them free. One day Death came to fetch the old man, and the old man requested that before being taken, he be allowed to pluck a few apples. Since he was setting about this in a very roundabout manner, Death himself climbed into the tree to fetch the apples. And he too was caught fast! The old man set him free under the condition that he be allowed to live another few years. Death ran off as fast as he could. "And because of that, to this very day, Death is reluctant to carry off old people."

The three visitors were none other than the Holy Trinity who fulfilled the old man's wish. The apple tree (despite its apparently mundane appearance) recalls the Tree of Knowledge in Paradise. Adam's children seem still to be highly disposed to steal its fruit! By catching the thieves, the old man raises this side of human nature into consciousness—without punishing or suppressing it. He does no more than bring it to light, and thus he is able to keep the apples—divine knowledge—and "be as gods, knowing good and evil" (Genesis 3:5). It is this very divine knowledge that helps him prolong his life and keep Death—the dark side of God—at bay for a little while longer.

Death remaining spellbound in an apple tree seems to be a frequent result of the visit of unknown divine wayfarers. In the Grimm's fairy tale "Hans the Gambler," we are told that once there was a man who was such a passionate gambler that people called him nothing else but Hans the Gambler. At a certain time he was once more on the brink of ruin from all his gambling, when the Lord God and Saint Peter paid him a visit. He received them hospitably and as a result was afterward granted three wishes as a reward. Hans wished for cards and dice that would always win, and for the third thing, he wished that whoever tried to pick fruit from his apple tree would remain spellbound there. God fulfilled his wishes, and He and Peter went away. Then Hans began his gambling afresh, worse than before, and won nearly the whole world with his cards and dice. Thereupon God sent Death to kill him. But Hans sent him up the apple tree on a pretext, and there he got stuck fast. For seven years no one on earth died. So God and Peter descended to earth again to free Death. As soon as he was loose, the first one he killed was Hans. But now Peter didn't want to let Hans's soul into heaven, and the people in purgatory were also not well disposed toward gambling. So Hans went to hell and began to gamble with old Lucifer. He won away all Lucifer's servants, the underdevils, and with these he now began to storm heaven. Peter was so frightened that he let him in. But then in heaven, too, he began his wild gambling, until God and Peter finally caught hold of him and threw him back down to earth. And there "his soul was smashed, and the splinters went into all the no-good gamblers that are living to this day."

Gambling is one of the greatest of human passions. The fascination with it, in my view, comes from the fact that what one ultimately comes in contact with here is one's own unconscious, the secret of synchronicity, and thus with the creative activity of God or divine destiny. This is surely the reason too that it is God and Peter who visit Hans. Now, Hans does not behave in such a disrespectful and heartless manner as the previously mentioned bad hosts, but still he also behaves improperly. He is seduced himself by the powers of the trickster, which are the proper province only of God or divine beings; thus he becomes inflated. True, he is able to keep death at bay for a time, like the old man in the Estonian fairy tale, but in the end (like the double-natured Mercurius himself), he is unable to find a dwelling place either in heaven or in hell and is broken into a thousand pieces and scattered.

This recalls the well-known motif of the Gnostic Anthropos, the cosmic man of light, who is divided up in a similar manner among all human souls. But the Grimm's tale describes a negative version of the same archetypal motif, for in contrast to the Gnostic myth, the dismemberment is not followed by a regathering and redemption of what has been broken up. Here the story ends with the dissolution caused by Hans the Gambler's inflation and lack of religious respect for the gifts of his divine visitor.

Many other such tales could be mentioned—sometimes the divine visitors restore the youth of an old man or even bring back the dead—however, these examples suffice to shed light on the typical basic motif. The motif involves a compensatory humanization of the divine image and of the addition of trickster attributes in cases where the divine image lacks them. The trickster or "divine scoundrel" is, after all, as Jung showed, an archetypal personification of the collective shadow.[10]

The extent to which this also contributes to be a living inner experience in later times and even today can be seen in two visions of the Swiss Saint Niklaus of Flüe.[11] He had these visions during his period of fasting and living with the forest brothers in the hermitage of Flüeli near Sachsen. In one vision he saw three unknown noblemen coming to his hermitage. The first of them said to the hermit, "Niklaus, will you yield yourself to our power, body and soul?" He replied, "I will yield myself to no one other than the almighty God, whose servant I long with body and soul to be." Hearing this reply, they turned aside and broke into happy laughter. Then the first of them spoke further: "If you have promised yourself only to the eternal servitude of God, then I promise you with certainty that when you have reached your seventieth year, merciful God, having mercy on your strivings, will release you from all hardships. Therefore, I exhort you in the meantime to unwavering perseverance, and in the eternal life I will give you the bear's claw and the banner of the victorious host; however, this cross, which is to remind you of us, I leave behind for you to wear." Then they went away.

On the one hand, these three noblemen obviously represent the holy Trinity; however, the promised gifts, the bear claw and the banner of the victorious host, allude rather to Wotan, who often wandered the earth visiting human beings as part of a threesome, accompanied by Hönir and Lodur or by Saxnot (Tyr) and Donar. He was also called Björn (Bear) or even Hrammi (Bear's Claw). This same deity (but here only as *one* man) appeared to Niklaus again in a later vision: From the east, where the sun rises, a pilgrim came to him, dressed in a blue coat, with a black hat and a walking stick, and sang "Hallelujah." And as he sang, "the voice echoed back to him, and the earthly realm and everything that was between heaven and earth, held (i.e., supported) his voice as the small organ the large. And from out of the origin he heard three perfect words that stood out . . . and when he had heard these, he was unable to speak a single word." At this point the pilgrim asked Niklaus for a gift. And then suddenly he had a penny in his hand, which he put into the pilgrim's hat. When

Niklaus asked him where he came from, he said only, "I come from there," and would say no more. As Niklaus beheld him, abruptly he changed. His head was now uncovered, his coat was bluish green, and he was of great beauty. After many other miracles, the pilgrim took on another form, and he stood before him and was clad in a bearskin with a jacket and trousers. The bearskin was sprinkled with golden color and "was particularly becoming to him." The bearskin clad one then disappeared after taking four steps and once more removing his hat and bowing to Niklaus by way of farewell. Niklaus felt love for him rising within himself, and he saw in his mind that his whole body "was as full of loving humility as a vessel filled with honey to the point where there is room for not a single drop more." It also seemed to him "as though he had made known to him everything that was in heaven and earth."

The continuously changing god has features of Wotan, who was called Svipall, "the changing one," or Tveggi, "the twofold one," or Grimmir, "the masked one."[12] He is the divine berserker, the bearskin-clad one, who in this form could conquer all his enemies. Thus in this vision, in a process I have explained elsewhere, the Christian image of God is enriched by traits of the pre-Christian god Wotan. This does not mean a regression to pagan religion, but rather progress in the direction of a more complete integration of the Christian message, an increase in the nearness of God and man and an integration of the dark side of God, the *deus absconditus.* Jung writes in a letter about the berserker motif in the vision of Brother Klaus: "The mana-charged, or numinous, person has theriomorphic properties and thus reaches beyond the ordinary man not only in an upward direction but also downwards. . . . As we can see, the figure of Christ appears here in two forms: first as pilgrim, who like the mystic is making a *peregrinatio animae,* and second, as a bear, whose pelt has a golden lustre. . . . Brother Klaus recognizes himself in his pilgrimhood and in his instinctive (bearlike, i.e., hermitlike) subhumanness as Christ. . . . The brutal coldness of feeling that the saint requires to separate himself from woman and child and friendship is found in the subhuman animal kingdom. Thus the saint casts an animal shadow. . . . He who is capable of bearing the highest and the lowest together is hallowed, holy, whole." Later in a horrific vision Niklaus saw the wrathful countenance of God, "for this wrath applied to him, who has betrayed his nearest and dearest and the ordinary man for God's sake."[13]

The German mystic Jakob Böhme (1575–1624) is also supposed to have had an experience that recalls the motif of the unknown, divine visitor.[14] When he was still quite young, a completely unenlightened apprentice in a shoemaker's workshop, one day he was alone in the shop when a poorly clothed but distinguished-looking man entered the shop (in reality, not in a vision!) and asked for a pair of shoes. At first he did not dare sell him a pair of shoes in the master's absence, but the man persisted in his desire and got the shoes. Then he took a couple of steps out the door, suddenly turned around, and called out in a loud, serious voice, "Jakob!" (It would have been impossible for him to know Böhme's name!) Böhme went to him. Then this man, with his serious but kindly air, took Jakob by the hand, looked him hard in the eyes, and said, "Jakob, you are little, but you will get big and be an entirely different person and man, at whom the world will wonder. For this reason, be pious, fear God and honor His word; especially, take pleasure in reading the Holy Scriptures, in which you will find consolation and instruction, for you will have to suffer greatly from privation, poverty, and persecution. But be consoled and remain constant, for you are beloved of God and He will show you His grace!"

Then he squeezed Jakob's hand and departed. The author of this account tells us that Böhme studied "in the school of the spirit of God, today rejected out of great blindness and ill will, from which also the holy patriarchs, kings, prophets, apostles, and men of God received their knowledge, which they made known in similes and figures of speech." He goes on to say it might well also have been the case that something like a hidden flame and fuel was added to this fire of love from the outside through the magical-astrological influence of the astral spirits. (It is at this point that he recounts the occurrence given above.) We would be more inclined to say that this strange external encounter coincided synchronistically with the inwardly constellated archetypal motifs of the divine visitor and the divine call.

The motif of the unknown divine visitor also appears again and again in the dreams of modern people. We shall only mention a few here, just to show how vigorously this archetypal motif is constellated in the present period. The first dream comes from a three-and-a-half-year-old girl and was dreamed shortly after the end of the First World War:

> I was on a walk with my father and mother and my sister. Suddenly off down the road an old and a young man appeared, who were hurrying toward us. My father, horrified, shouted: "Those are the gods! They're coming to test us!" Then he explained to me that each person possesses an enameled plaque with his name and birth and death dates. If the plaque is intact, the gods can't do anything to him, but if the plaque is damaged, the person in question falls into the hands of the gods. We ran home. My father went and got the plaques and gave each of us our own. When I looked at my plaque, the enamel was damaged as though by a blow. Horrified, I showed it to the others, but they backed away from me as if I had the plague. At this moment, a round, brilliant light appeared in the corner of the ceiling. I left my body and went into the light. From there I looked at myself standing there sadly with my plaque. That gave me courage. I went back into my body and thought, "Okay, fine, so I'll just go meet the gods." I walked to the door, and as I stretched out my hand, I saw the door handle being pushed down from the outside. Then I woke up with a scream.

As Jung once explained, this plaque recalls those plaques or inscriptions that, according to the Gnostic teaching, each soul who enters earthly life receives from the archons (astral powers). The Gnostics taught that Jesus freed the souls from these "debtor's chits" by fastening the debtor's note to the Cross. In this way he released the souls from the determining influence of the stars.

The fracture lines in the plaque in the dream described above indicate a breakup of ego fixation; however, this makes possible enlightenment by the Self. Through this, the child is enabled to meet the gods *consciously*. All the same, it is terrifying to fall into the hands of the living God. That is why the child is frightened.

Another dream is that of a roughly forty-five-year-old graphic artist who died nine years later, but at the time of the dream had no idea that his death was imminent. He dreamed as follows:

> I was sightseeing at a Catholic church [he was a Protestant, but made frequent visits to old churches for aesthetic reasons]. The service was just in progress, so I took a seat inobtrusively in one of the rear pews. A nondescript vagrant of middle age came in behind me and sat down next to me. I caught a furtive sideward glimpse of him and, deeply moved, suddenly realized, "Why, it's Christ!" I wanted to jump up and call out to everyone present, but the stranger pulled me down by my coattail and, with a smile, put his finger on his mouth, indicating I should remain silent. Then it was clear to me that the congregation would have reacted in a shocked and incredulous manner if I had said anything. So, shaken, I sat down again quietly, and we gazed at each other smilingly, with mutual understanding.

Obviously, here Christ wants to meet only the dreamer, and this encounter must remain exclusively his personal secret, *his* encounter with the Self. The congregation, the collective, cannot so much as see the stranger and would not believe that he was Christ even if they were told. So far has the conscious collective idea of the Self (Christ) distanced itself from any psychic reality!

The dream of an approximately forty-five-year-old woman was as follows:

> I entered my house toward evening. The entry hall was empty, without furniture; there was only the bare floor. On it, lying on a pile of straw, was a shabbily clothed man who looked like a tramp. I knew it was Christ. He shone with the whitest dazzling light, for his body was made out of glowing-hot metal! Smiling, he said

to me, "You could do me a favor. Take a bowl full of water and pour it over me to damp down my radiance." I carried out his wish, and the water steamed from him with a hiss. Now his body was made of dark metal, but very limber and alive. He said with a smile, "Thank you."

The appearance of Christ in this dream is out of the ordinary. He is more the Mercurius-Christ of the alchemists, of whom they say he is "lighter than air and glows like the hottest metal." This alchemical figure is not only the savior of humanity but of the whole cosmic material world, of which he himself is a part. It recalls the Christ made of greenish gold whom Jung saw in a vision[15] and of whom he wrote that he represented an analogy to the *aurum non vulgi* and to the *benedicta viriditas* of the alchemists. "The green gold is the living quality which the alchemists saw not only in man but also in inorganic nature. It is an expression of the life-spirit, the *anima mundi* or *filius macrocosmi,* the Anthropos who animates the whole cosmos. This spirit has poured himself out into everything, even into organic matter; he is present in metal and stone."

Jung carved this inscription over the door of the first tower he built in Bollingen: "Philemonis sacrum—Fausti poenitentia." It was, after all, the urge to power that caused Faust to kill Philemon and Baucis in order to win more land from the sea. This murder motif anticipates not only Germany's later destructive eruption, but it also symbolizes the attitude of all of us toward inner and outer nature, which we are always trying to exploit. In order to do that we are continually murdering in ourselves that humble human nature that honors the secret of the psyche, that is, its opening to the divine. It seems to me to be one of the greatest contributions of Jung and his work that it taught us to keep our door open for the "unknown" visitor." He also tried to teach us an approach through which we can avoid the wrath of this visitor, which every frivolous, haughty, or greedy host in the folktales brought down on himself. For it depends only on ourselves whether this coming of the gods becomes a blessed visit or a fell disaster.

Notes

1. C. G. Jung, *Memories, Dreams, Reflections.*

2. Père Bruno de Jesus-Marie, *Elie le prophète: Études Carmélitaines* (Elijah the Prophet: Carmelite Studies) (Descée de Brower, 1956), vol. 2, pp. 13ff.

3. Cf. Jung, *Memories, Dreams, Reflections.*

4. C. G. Jung and K. Kerényi, "On the Psychology of the Trickster Figure," in C. G. Jung, *The Archetypes and the Collective Unconscious,* cw 9/i, pp. 255ff.

5. "Chinesische Märchen" (Chinese Fairy Tales), in *Die Märchen der Weltliteratur* (Fairy Tales of World Literature) (Jena, Köln, Düsseldorf: Diederichs), no. 18, pp. 21ff.

6. *Der Traum der roten Kammer* (The Dream of the Red Chamber) (Leipzig: Insel Verlag, no date).

7. H. Zimmer, *Indische Sphären* (Realms of India) (Munich: Oldenburg, 1935).

8. "Russische Märchen" (Russian Fairy Tales), in *Die Märchen der Weltliteratur,* pp. 183ff.

9. "Finnische und Estnische Volksmärchen" (Finnish and Estonian Folk Tales), in *Die Märchen der Weltliteratur,* p. 190. The next story comes from the same book, p. 286.

10. C. G. Jung and K. Kerényi, "Psychology of the Trickster Figure."

11. Marie-Louise von Franz, *Die Visionen des Niklaus von Flüe.*

12. M. Ninck, *Wodan und germanischer Schicksalsglaube* (Wotan and the Germanic Belief in Fate) (reprint, Darmstadt: 1967).

13. C. G. Jung, Letter of 2 May 1945 to Fritz Blanke, in *Letters,* vol. 1, p. 365.

14. A. V. von Franckenberg, in Kayser, *Schriften Jakob Böhmes* (Leipzig: Insel, 1920).

15. Jung, *Memories, Dreams, Reflections,* pp. 210f.

THE PROBLEM OF EVIL
IN FAIRY TALES

■■

MOST FAIRY TALES hinge on the struggle between good and evil. As Max Lüthi said in his excellent work on the subject,[1] fairy-tale style is characterized first and foremost by a simple, unshaded opposition between black and white, good and evil. *Within* the hero himself we find no psychological conflicts; he is not partly this and partly that—each quality is personified in the simplest form: courage is opposed to cowardice, envy to innocence, kindness to malice, renunciation and self-sacrifice to unrestrained lust or greed. Evil is almost always punished, usually by destruction, though sometimes it is only driven away—the good triumphs or is saved by supernatural aid. The hero attains his goal by courage, guile, humor, or luck; the heroine by perseverance amid suffering, fidelity, guile, or luck. Often the evil principle condemns or does away with itself at the end of the story, or it may unconsciously choose its own punishment.[2]

Lüthi observes that fairy tales are poor in "concrete detail and reality; they reflect little depth of experience, little of the complexity of human relations, little shading, but in compensation for this poverty of content, they are clear and incisive in form."[3] "Fairy tales," he writes, "perceive and describe *a world which grows up in opposition to an uncertain, confusing, unclear, and menacing reality* . . . fairy tales *crystallize forms,* they give us firm lines and *rigid unchanging figures.* . . . Behind the growing and fading forms of perishable reality stand the pure forms, immobile and yet effective."[4]

From the standpoint of Jungian psychology, we may say that fairy tales do not recount consciously experienced human events, but that these "pure forms" make visible *fundamental archetypal structures of the collective unconscious.* This accounts for the non-human or, as Lüthi puts it, abstract character of the figures; they are archetypal images behind which the secret of the unconscious psyche is hidden.

By the collective unconscious we mean that part of man's unconscious psyche which, regardless of all the differences between individuals, remains the same in all men and women, just as certain aspects of the anatomical structure of *Homo sapiens* are the same in all individuals precisely because they are human. Since fairy tales throughout the world disclose certain common themes and structures, we may assume that they spring from this most universal substrate of the human psyche. They might be termed the dreams of humankind,[5] sprung from the deepest layers of the unconscious, and for this reason it is not at all surprising that the ethical problems of our *cultural* consciousness, which we know and discuss in other contexts, have no part in them. What we might, on the other hand, find in fairy tales is the guidelines of an *ethos* of the unconscious, that is, of *nature itself.*

Lüthi writes aptly that fairy tales are concerned not with the "justice" but with the "rightness" of actions. With their abstract approach they aim to "reflect not reality but the essence underlying it."[6] Translated into our psychological idiom, this means: Fairy tales represent *natural events in the unconscious psyche.* And here the question becomes acute: Is ethics an achievement of conscious man and his culture—or is there already an ethic in the unconscious and preconscious psychic structure of man as such?[7] It is not difficult to give a general answer: Most fairy tales do indeed contain a kind of natural morality which is elucidated in the course of the action—an ethic of "appropriate" behavior which leads to a happy end, in contrast to inappropriate behavior, which leads to disaster. Accordingly, André Jolles[8] speaks of a *naïve moralité* in fairy tales, in accordance with which "everything that happens is in keeping with what we expect and demand of a just course of events."[9] They contain an ethical judgment that "is concerned not with action but with process." Thus fairy tales present a contrast to the world as we actually experience it.

But what are the "right" modes of conduct glorified in fairy tales, and can we really regard them as ethical? Let us first consider the problem of guile and honesty: Innumerable are the tales in which a peasant or shepherd outwits the Devil[10] by making an agreement with him that everything above ground in his field belongs to the Devil while everything below ground belongs to himself—and proceeding to sow turnips. When the outwitted Devil reverses the pact for the coming year, the peasant sows wheat and again cheats the Devil, who finally goes off in a rage. It is generally known that the Schöllenen Bridge in the St. Gotthard Pass came into being as a result of such a trick.[11] The moral would seem to be that we should combat evil with guile. And yet, what of the tale about the bearskin?[12] Here a young soldier faithfully keeps his pact with the Devil and makes no attempt to get around it. For seven years he goes without washing and wears his bearskin; the Devil rewards him amply for his "fair play," and he too makes no attempt to circumvent the agreement.

In the first example unscrupulous trickery in dealing with the Devil triumphs; in the second it is shown that honesty is rewarded, even in dealings with the Evil One. Thus the question of the morality of fairy tales does not appear to be so simple. And what about courage? On first thought we might suppose this to be one quality that is never lacking in the fairy-tale hero—and yet we find countless stories in which appropriate conduct consists in so-called magical flight. A good illustration of this is provided by a fairy tale of the Siberian Jukagirs.[13]

A girl living alone is pursued by an evil spirit, whose upper lip touches the sky and whose lower lip touches the earth, and who darkens half the sky. While running away from him, she throws her comb behind her; it turns into a dense forest, which delays the spirit for a time. Then in the same way she sacrifices a red kerchief which becomes an enormous fire; but the evil spirit puts out the fire with river water. Then the girl turns herself successively into a silver fox, a wolverine, and a wolf in order to be able to run faster. Finally she reaches a tent, at the entrance to which she sinks down exhausted. Then suddenly a handsome young man appears before her—the evil spirit metamorphosed—and asks for her hand in marriage. Often in this type of story the evil pursuer is not transformed, but he desists from his pursuit or destroys himself.

All over the world we find stories of this type, showing that it can be a heroic achievement to run away from the power of evil, to avoid being "possessed" by it in the literal sense—and it is known to us from practical psychology how great an achievement it can be to withdraw inwardly from a destructive complex such as that which is at work in paranoia, for example, or from an affect or destructive idea. The suggestive power of the unconscious complexes is so enormous that ego consciousness can only escape it with the utmost exertion.

Thus countless fairy tales do not relate the central character's deeds of courage but his or her successful flight. But it is not, as one might suppose, the hopelessness of the situation that makes flight seem preferable to action. In the Russian tale "The Virgin Tsar,"[14] for instance, Ivan, the hero, comes to a pillar on which is written: "He who takes the right-hand way will eat his fill, but his horse will go hungry; he who takes the left-hand way—his horse will eat his fill, but he himself will go hungry; he who takes the middle way will suffer death." Ivan's two brothers go right and left and get lost; that is, they succumb to anti-spiritual instinct or anti-instinctual spirituality. The one who rides to the right finds a copper snake (= congealed life) and ends up in his father's prison (= tradition). The one who rides to the left is caught in a trap-bed by a whore. But when Ivan comes to the same pillar, he cries out tearfully: "It brings the brave lad no honor or fame to ride to the place where he must suffer death." And so he chooses the way of death—that is, *the way of unresolved conflict and of the middle,* and on the way he performs the greatest deeds, *but does not perish.* Thus even in a situation of utter hopelessness, flight does not always seem advisable.

Like most other heroes, Ivan attains his goal through courage and strength.[15] But sometimes the combination of courage and guile is recommended, as in "The Cunning Little Tailor,"[16] who is cocky and quick-witted rather than heroic. Or else the hero's courage borders on unsuspecting simplicity, as in tales of the Tom Thumb or Stupid Hans variety.[17] Indeed innumerable fairy tales seem to recommend innocent naïveté, which goes hand in hand with luck.[18] But in Grimm's story "The Youth Who Went Forth to Learn What Fear Was,"[19] the opposite is the case—the hero has to overcome his naïve courage. He finally learns to do so when the queen's chambermaid, whom he has won as his bride, pours a pail of cold water full of gudgeons over his back. In another version, he learns when someone twists his head, enabling him to see his rear end. Ultimately, it is the unfathomable depths of a man's unconscious, a man's own shadow, which, quite justifiably, arouses genuine dread.

We encounter the same paradox in fairy tales when we try to determine whether asceticism or light-minded enjoyment of life is more likely to bring success. In Grimm's tale "The Golden Bird," only the youngest, who is serious-minded and reserved, and stops at the shabby inn, attains his goal; his brothers, who squander their money feasting at the merry inn, fail to accomplish their task, and turn into scoundrels who are executed at the end. But in the Carinthian tale "The Black Princess,"[20] all the watchers over the dead are torn to pieces by a diabolical black princess, who rises at night out of her coffin in the church. Thereupon the soldier, Rudolf, is ordered to keep watch over her coffin. A lazy, light-headed young fellow who spent most of his time in taverns, Rudolf "was more often in the guardhouse than on duty." But God himself comes to his help, appearing to him in the form of an aged zither player and giving him advice that enables him to save the black princess from her diabolical possession, and Rudolf becomes a king. We find numerous variants of this frivolous hero, such as "Brother Lustig";[21] they are often the favorites of God or of other helpful powers.

It would sometimes seem as though a slight dig at conventional morality were intended; a childless queen who prays to a crucifix on the right side of the bridge remains childless; but after praying to Lucifer on the left side of the bridge she gives birth to the above-mentioned black princess, who, once redeemed, becomes the best and most beautiful of virgins. We can only conclude that it was more rewarding for the queen to pray to the Devil than to the crucifix. In a Low German fairy tale, "The Black Princesses," we even read how holy water and prayer *impede* the deliverance of the black princesses. And numerous farces in which Saint Peter, Jesus, and God himself appear, seem to burlesque man's conscious conceptions of them, or, one might say, to compensate for their sublimity by reducing them to the level of the all-too-human. And what of "Snow White and Rose Red,"[22] in which the innocent maidens are misled by their kindness into helping a malignant dwarf who calls for help when his beard gets wedged in a tree trunk or caught on a fishing pole. But in so doing they only endanger themselves and the future suitor, the bear who is in need of deliverance, until finally the bear puts an end to the nonsense and kills the evil dwarf with a stroke of his paw. Here the girls' helpfulness is condemned as self-destructive foolishness. And yet the very same naïve kindness is recommended in the story of "Little Man Sponnelang,"[23] in which an orphan girl, lost in the woods, meets a dirty little old man and at his request prepares a bath and bed for him and so delivers him. He makes her a present of his beard, which she spins into pure gold. This orphan girl treats the little man exactly as Snow White and Rose Red treated the dwarf, but in *her* case innocent kindness is rewarded.

Another contradiction appears in the fact that some heroes and heroines perform their tasks by their own resources, whereas others attain their goals thanks to the intervention of helpful animals or divine-demonic powers. Thus it looks more and more as if we should have to content ourselves with purely paradoxical conclusions: the helpful factor may be courage, flight, naïveté, guile, kindness, hardness, pious gravity, or frivolity. And psychologists may find it particularly interesting to note that fairy tales show an equally contradictory attitude toward the problem of achieving consciousness. The story of "Rumpelstiltskin"[24] tells how the heroine will have to surrender her child to a demon (who had previously helped her) unless she can discover his name. A servant overhears the diabolical dwarf as he is singing:

Today I bake, tomorrow I brew my beer;
The next day I'll bring the Queen's child here.
Ah, lucky it is that no one can ever know
My name is Rumpelstiltskin. Ho ho ho!

When the queen utters the dwarf's name, he is so angry that he "stamped his right foot into the ground so deep that he sank in up to his waist. Then in his fury he seized his left leg in both hands and tore himself apart." Here—and seldom is this expressed so clearly in a fairy tale—we see how a destructive unconscious content is rendered harmless by being brought to consciousness. To the primitive mind, as we know, to find out the name of a thing is to apprehend its nature—just as in life any number of destructive complexes of the unconscious are cured by being raised to consciousness. This optimistic view is the basis of much of the modern psychotherapy which concerns itself with dreams in order to eliminate the unconscious negative effects of complexes by raising them to consciousness.

But even this insight is rejected in certain other fairy tales. In the Russian tale "The Beautiful Vasilissa,"[25] a young girl is driven from her home by her wicked stepmother and her stepsisters and comes to the house of Baba Yaga, the forest witch. Here she is put to work like Cinderella, separating grains of wheat and poppy seed. Every time her task is completed, three pairs of hands appear and take the sorted grains away. The witch permits the girl to ask four questions. She asks about the three horsemen she has seen in the witch's house and learns that they are the night, the day, and the sun. But she does not ask about the three pairs of hands. The witch asks why, but she persists in not asking this question, and that is her salvation. For the witch mutters:

"You did well to ask what you saw outside and not what you saw inside. I don't like people to wash dirty linen in public." She gives the girl a skull to take home with her, and her enemies are burned by its glowing eyes; later, with the magical help of a doll inherited from her mother, she wins the king's son as her husband.

On closer scrutiny this Baba Yaga is a great nature goddess. In this story she is described as she flies through the air: "She sits huddled in a mortar, she rows with a pestle, she wipes away the tracks with a broom." Of the three horsemen who serve her she says: "This is *my* (!) day, the bright one; this is *my* sun, the red one; this is *my* night, the dark one." If she possesses day, night, and sun, she must be a cosmic nature goddess. Her house is decorated with skulls and bones like the halls of Hel, the Germanic goddess of death. In another tale she is called "Baba Yaga with the thigh bone" and lives in a rotating hut with chickens' feet and roosters' heads. With her gigantic nose she pokes the ashes in the stove, while at the same time, with her eyes, she guards her geese in the fields. She can turn herself into an apple orchard with a well in it: anyone who drinks of the water or enters the orchard is "torn into pieces the size of poppy seeds." Or she turns into a giant sow which threatens to destroy the hero.[26] But she can also help the hero with food and advice if he knows how to handle her.[27] The hands that snatch away the sorted wheat and poppy seeds probably have to do with the death aspect of the goddess or with the ruthless and often so incomprehensible cruelty of nature. This is a dark secret, which the goddess hides from men. In other words, it is wiser not to investigate the dark aspects of nature too closely, but rather to pass them by as the ancients passed their chthonian gods,[28] trembling and with covered heads bowed in awe. Evil has its divine depths, into which it is irreverent to look. The mentally ill often show an unseemly lack of this respect for the divine powers, especially those of the dark side, and this lack of *"religio"* may be in part responsible for their mental derangement. It springs from a deficiency in the function of feeling, which, in addition, usually prevents them from taking themselves and their lives seriously enough. The tragedy of the student Raskolnikov in Dostoyevsky's *Crime and Punishment* offers an excellent illustration of such a loss (and rediscovery) of feeling. Thus it would seem more normal and appropriate for men to fear the principle of evil.

In Grimm's tale "Frau Trude,"[29] a little girl goes—though her mother had forbidden her—to the house of Frau Trude, the great Mother Goddess and forest witch. There she sees a black man, a green man, and a red man, and like Vasilissa asks the witch who they are. Frau Trude tells her that they are the collier, the huntsman, and the butcher, although they are obviously three manifestations of the Devil! But then the child asks the fatal fourth question, which Vasilissa did not ask: "Oh, Frau Trude, I've had such a fright, I looked through the window and I didn't see you, I saw the Devil with a fiery head." "Oho!" Frau Trude replies, "then you must have seen the witch in her true colors: I have been waiting for you for years, longing for you to shine for me." Whereupon the witch turns the child into a block of wood and throws her into the fire. "And when she was in full flame, Frau Trude sat down beside the blaze, warmed herself and said: 'Now at last it shines bright.'" Apparently the powers of darkness yearn for a human light—a yearning that, as in this case, can have the most tragic consequences. This is what happens to those who become submerged in mental illness: the weakness of their ego, manifested chiefly in frivolity, curiosity, and lack of feeling, makes them an easy prey for the archetypal powers of the unconscious. They do not become conscious, but the evil powers consume their vitality. Accordingly, fear of such archetypal destructive contents in the psyche is not cowardice but a sign of maturity.

Thus an Estonian tale[30] relates how a proud young girl is willing to marry only a man with a golden nose. A man with a golden nose finally turns up and becomes engaged to her. He has a habit of slipping away into churches and forbids her to look after him. She does so nevertheless and finds out that he eats the corpses that are lying in state. She tells the gold-nosed demon what she has discovered, and in his rage he "strangles her with a terrible roar." In contrast to the story of Rumpelstiltskin, the discovery of the demon's secret does not bring happiness. In this case an attempt to bring light into the darkness seems only to activate the darkness—or in psychological terms, a latent psychosis is activated by a mistaken attempt to analyze it. The moral of this type of fairy tale might well be: "Let sleeping dogs lie."

In another tale[31] the same Baba Yaga asks the hero in reference to his quest: "Tell me, my little one, are you riding willingly or against your will?" Here again, the desire for knowledge is negative, couched in a skeptical question, tending to paralyze the hero and reduce him to infantilism (note that she addresses him as "my little one"). The question springs from a mother complex—a factor that has indeed led many a life-shy young man to neurotic "philosophizing" or into a pseudoanalysis offering a great deal of soul-searching and discussion but never raising the essential facts to consciousness and ripening them into actions.

These examples show that the question of ethics in fairy tales—at least if we try to deduce general rules of conduct—leads only to subtle paradoxes. Everything seems to depend on the individual context, each fairy tale seems to be an ethical "just-so story"; that is, a story that can only be understood as a whole and in its own terms.

We have the feeling, to be sure, that a natural ethic is recommended: the creatively "authentic" man seems to be praised in contrast to the "inauthentic" man—but any attempt to formulate a system of conduct for this authentic man would culminate in glaring contradictions. This is strikingly consonant with the findings of Jungian psychology, for C. G. Jung stresses time and again that nearly all psychological rules of conduct might be reversed. We should master our affects, or we should give them free play. In our dealings with another person we should lovingly put up with everything, or we should make our own position perfectly clear, in order that the other may learn through friction to experience him- or herself, and so on. Consequently universal prescriptions are useless in depth psychology, just as it seems absurd to try to derive rules of conduct from fairy tales.

Accordingly it will be more profitable to turn to another question: What do dark figures personify evil in fairy tales? Here we encounter a natural distinction, which is known to us also from the study of comparative religion: there seem to be greater and lesser demons and gods. First of all, certain figures who are compelled by a curse to be wicked or to molest people are not always absolutely evil. They can be delivered from their wickedness as from any other enchantment.[32] In such cases the evil originates with another magical power, which, however, does not always appear directly in the story.[33] The innumerable envious brothers, sisters, courtiers, stepparents, stepbrothers, and stepsisters also seem relatively harmless. Their role is chiefly to set the story in motion or to lend it vividness through a distribution of light and shade. In one type of fairy tale[34] found in many countries, a courtier tells the king that the hero is capable of performing some impossible task, whereupon the king forces the hero to undertake it and orders his head cut off if he fails. But instead of perishing—as the envious courtier intended—the hero performs the task and himself becomes king.[35] The envious person represents the principle that "always wills evil and produces good"—he is a stimulus comparable to ambition, aggression, or the spirit of enterprise. The name *"Ritter Rot"* (Sir Red), which he often bears in European tales, shows that he stems from the emotional level of the psyche. This type of villain is dangerous, but he also has a positive aspect.

There are other, truly wicked figures who seem to personify evil as such, figures such as Frau Trude, certain giants, giantesses, wizards, and demonic magicians. Sometimes they are human figures, as in Grimm's tale "The Juniper Tree," but more often they are magical figures who derive pure pleasure, for which no further motivation is offered, from wickedness. In this respect, it seems to me, a certain distinction can be drawn between tales originating with a more differentiated urban layer of culture and those that remained close to nature. In the latter, as far as I can tell from the available material, evil seems more frequently to take the form of a destructive force of nature, against which resistance is impossible. It is like a landslide, a flood, a flash of lightning—you simply have to run away from it, though you may not succeed.

As one example of this type of story, I shall cite the Chinese tale "The Spirit of Horse Mountain":[36] A rather tipsy peasant, who is riding from market to his village at the foot of Horse Mountain, sees a monster sitting by a brook. "His enormous face was blue, his eyes stood out of his head like a crab's. They glittered and sparkled. His mouth was so big that it stretched to both ears and looked like a bowl of blood. It contained a dense thicket of teeth two or three inches long." The monster gurgles as he drinks from the brook. The peasant tries to circle around him unseen, but a voice cries out behind him: "Neighbor, wait for me." He thinks it is his neighbor's son and stops. The supposed neighbor tells him he has gone to get a coffin for old Li and goes on to ask why the peasant has made a detour. The peasant tells him about the monster he has seen. The neighbor says: "Oof, now I am afraid too, let me ride with you." He mounts behind the peasant and asks what the monster looked like, but the peasant is too frightened to speak. Thereupon the neighbor says: "Turn around and see if I look like the monster." The peasant turns around and sees the monster in person sitting behind him. He is so terrified that he loses consciousness and falls to the ground. His donkey goes home without him, and the villagers, suspecting a mishap, go looking for him. They find him lying beside a cliff and carry him home. "Only at midnight did he regain consciousness and relate what had happened to him."

The story strikes us as rather pointless. There are numerous variants: sometimes the peasant dies, sometimes he outwits the spirit and escapes. The crux of the matter is that there is never a concentrated conflict—evil, as I have said, is portrayed as a natural phenomenon, rather in the style employed by peasants to describe the falling of an avalanche or the appearance of corpses washed up on the shore, namely with a mixture of horror and of gruesome pleasure. The evil of the human soul is treated as an element of nature—on this level, of course, completely projected outward. The story does not tell us why one man may succumb to evil whereas another may escape. At this level, evil is some sort of terrifying object that arouses emotion and leaves behind it a shudder of dread, but does not personally concern the individual.

In Asia and among primitive peoples there are also stories involving a conflict or struggle, but these seem to be more frequent in the monotheistic countries of Europe and the Near East, where a personal accentuation of the ethical problem, a struggle with evil, appears to be more common. In stories of this sort, there is one kind of evil that is especially gruesome, taking the form of utter heartlessness or of grim homicidal frenzy.

In a Norwegian tale,[37] for example, a king has seven sons whom he dearly loves. He sends six of them out into the world to look for brides. The youngest, whom he loves most of all, he keeps at home, asking the brothers to bring him a bride. They find six magnificent princesses for themselves but forget to acquire one for their young brother. On the way home a giant appears at the foot of a steep mountain—in the German parallel he is merely an old man[38]—and turns the six couples to stone. Then the youngest goes forth to look for his brothers. On his way he helps various injured animals—a raven, a salmon, and a wolf—who promise to help him in return. He goes to the house of the wicked giant and finds a princess, who falls in love with him and tells him that the giant is invulnerable, *because his heart is not in his body.* But in bed at night, the princess succeeds in wheedling the giant's secret out of him. He tells her: "Far far away in a sea there is an island, and on the island there is a church, and in the church there is a well, and in the well a duck is swimming, and in the duck there is an egg, and in the egg—that's where my heart is." With the help of the grateful animals the hero manages to find the egg. He squeezes it a little, and the giant falls down groaning at his feet. He orders the giant to set free the six couples he has turned to stone, and the giant complies. Then the prince crushes the egg completely and the giant falls to pieces. Whereupon the seven couples return home. In other tales the heartless giant is replaced by "The Magician Tsar" (see below) or by the Devil himself. In other words, he is an *intrinsically evil nature spirit, who derives pleasure from destruction and murder for their own sake.* It is dreadful to think that there is something of the sort in the unconscious human psyche, but the testimony of myths and fairy tales shows this to be the simple fact.

The figure corresponding to the heartless giant is known in Russia as "Koshchei the Deathless"[39] who has his "death" in the sea, on an island, in an oak tree, in a chest buried in the tree, in a rabbit in the chest, in a duck in the rabbit, in an egg in the duck—that's where his "death" lies. When the hero crushes the egg, the giant dies. A similar demon is the Ukrainian forest king, Och,[40] who teaches a peasant lad magic and as his reward wishes to keep him forever in the underworld. He has the appearance of a wrinkled old man with a green beard. Everything in his "world under the earth" is green, and the water maids, that is, the souls of children who have died without baptism, serve him. In his effort to escape Och, the lad turns himself, thanks to the magic he has learned, into various animals, but each time Och turns himself into a swifter and fiercer animal and catches him. In the end the hero is turned into a garnet ring worn by the Tsar's daughter. Och appears as a merchant and demands the ring, saying he has lost it. The Tsar's daughter throws the ring on the ground, and it crumbles into many grains of wheat; Och turns into a chicken who eats them up, but one grain, hidden under the princess' foot, escapes him. From this one grain the hero rises once again, and this time he has escaped the demon Och for good. Another similar figure is the Russian "The Magician Tsar" who bids each of his daughter's suitors hide from him. He invariably finds them with the help of a book of black magic and beheads them. "He took pleasure in this wicked game," we are told. One suiter, the hero of the tale, finally escapes him in the form of a flint stone.

In the North the same demon is often a troll. In one German tale he is an old man of the mountains, who possesses an altar on which lies a prickly fish. Thus this demon bears some relation to certain aspects of these peoples' pre-Christian gods.[41] He is a personification of a partly evil god or nature spirit, which regularly tries to take possession of a man and to make him the instrument of his own evil designs. In states of cold madness characteristic of certain psychopaths I suspect that such a spirit is at work—the madman is justifiably said to be "possessed by the Devil," wholly assimilated by a dark, divine (i.e., overwhelming) power. And yet this evil principle has a weak point, though it is hard to find: the madman *does* have a heart, or a "death," only—in the language of our fairy tales—it is hidden somewhere, far away.

For the present I shall not go into the symbolic significance of island, church or oak tree, well or chest, rabbit, duck, and egg. First I shall take up another point, namely, the motif of the grateful or gratuitously helpful animal (as for example in the Norwegian tale of the king with seven sons related above in which a raven, salmon, and wolf come to the hero's aid). Though, as I have tried to show, all attempts to deduce a fairy-tale morality end in utter paradox, there is *one exception: Anyone who earns the gratitude of animals, or whom they help for any reason, invariably wins out. This is the only unfailing rule that I have been able to find.* It is psychologically of the utmost importance, because it means that in the conflict between good and evil the decisive factor is our animal instinct, or perhaps better, the animal soul; anyone who has it with him is victorious. Good qualities that are contrary to instinct cannot last, but neither can evil when its one-sided demonism runs counter to instinct.

The hero of an Irish fairy tale,[42] for instance, plays a one-sided game of hide-and-seek with a king who is assisted by a magician. On the advice of his helpful white talking horse, the hero hides in all sorts of places, but the king always finds him with the help of the wicked magician, who has a book that simply tells him where the hero is. The prince's head is at stake. In the end he hides under the tail of his talking horse, and here even the wicked magician is powerless to find him. Thus the horse, with its natural wisdom, is superior to the wicked magician's book-learning.

Animals, says Jung, are more obedient to God than is man; they live out their foreordained lives without doubt and without deviating from their inner patterns. This is no doubt why in so many fairy tales an animal is the symbol of "right" behavior. As a non-canonical saying of Jesus has it: "Ye ask me who will lead you to the kingdom of heaven (τὴν βασιλείαν): the birds of heaven and that which is under the earth and the fishes of the sea—they will lead you to the Kingdom of Heaven, and the Kingdom is within you."[43] In the *I Ching,* the Chinese book of oracles, the "firm lines" that the wild goose follows in its flight are a guiding symbol recommended to the contemplation of the Perfect Man;[44] they denote a spiritual guidance in nature itself, that is, the Tao.

The salutary function of the helpful animal in fairy tales is subject only to one condition: that the hero keep faith with the animal. In Grimm's tale "The Two Brothers," a witch is able to turn one of the heroes to stone because, at her request, he has touched his helpful animals with her magic wand; but the second brother says to her, "I will not beat my animals," and overcomes her without difficulty. The helpful animal of fairy tales often conceals an additional secret, just as our word *instinct* refers to secrets of nature that remain to be explored. Often, at the end of a story, the helpful animal—the fox, for example, in Grimm's tale "The Golden Bird"[45]—asks the hero to cut off its paws and head. When the hero does so with a heavy heart, an enchanted prince rises from the body of the fox. In another version the hero drives his talking horse or his donkey three times around in a circle, and the animal becomes a prince or princess, or else turns out to have been *God himself.*[46] Jung once likened the human psyche to the color scale: At the infrared end it loses itself in the depths of the instincts and somatic processes; at the ultraviolet end it reaches into the realm of the archetypes, that is, of the spirit. In the archetypal image, the *meaning* or latent spiritual aspect of instinct is revealed.[47] Thus when a redeemed prince or god steps forth from a sacrificed animal in a fairy tale, this symbolizes the sudden disclosure of the spiritual meaning that seems to lie behind the "rightness" of animal instinct. And at the same time it means that on the one hand people should follow their unconscious instinctive impulses, but that at a certain point in the curve of their lives they will demand that they sacrifice them.[48] Instinct itself demands to be sacrificed, and in so doing reveals its spiritual aspect. Ego consciousness is led to renounce what is dearest to it, a renunciation demanded by its greater inner being, the Self,[49] which is thus manifested in sacrifice.[50] What first appeared as animal instinct and helped in times of difficulty, proves in its profoundest essence to be something human or even divine. As Meister Eckhart said: "The innermost nature of all grain is wheat and of all metal gold and of all creatures man."[51] This is the mystery of which the Christian dogma of the Incarnation gives an intimation.

An especially illuminating version of the sacrifice of a helpful animal is provided in a Turkestan tale entitled "The Magic Horse."[52] Through her father's fault a beautiful princess falls into the hands of a diabolical man-eating *div* (demon). "When he threw his cap into the air, the sky and the land grew dark for seven days—so great was his power." She is constrained to follow the demon to his domain, but she takes a little magic horse from her father's stable with her, and on his advice also takes a mirror, a comb, salt, and a carnation, which—as in the "magical flight" already described—she later throws behind her when she runs away from the demon. The carnation becomes a thicket of briers, the salt becomes an ocean, the comb a mountain, and the mirror a raging torrent. All these delay the *div* but cannot kill him, and later on he begins once again to harry the heroine, who in the meanwhile has married a king and borne him two sons. Then the helpful little talking horse decides to attack the *div* himself, and the two engage in a long, drawn-out fight under water in which the horse is victorious. When he comes out of the water, he asks the dismayed queen to slaughter him.

Then the queen did everything the horse had asked. She threw the head aside, pointed the legs in four directions, threw away the entrails, and sat down with her children under the ribs. Then from the legs grew golden poplars with emerald leaves, from the entrails villages, fields, and wheat, and from the ribs a golden castle. But from the head sprang a silvery brooklet. In a word, the whole region was transformed into a true paradise.

Here the queen remained, and here the king later found her, whereupon the four of them lived happily ever after in the kingdom that had grown up out of the horse.

In this story we find a late echo of the ancient Indian horse sacrifice, as described at the beginning of the *Brhadaranyaka Upanishad:*

> Verily, dawn is the head of the sacrificial horse, the sun his eye, the wind his breath, universal fire his open mouth. The year is the body of the sacrificial horse, the sky his back, the atmosphere his belly, the earth the underpart of his belly. . . . The rising sun is his forepart, the setting sun his hindpart. . . . Verily, day was created for the horse as the sacrificial dish which stands before him; its place is the world-ocean towards the east. Night was created for the sacrificial horse as the sacrificial dish which stands behind him; its place is the world-ocean towards the west. . . .[53]

As Jung explains,[54] the horse sacrifice signifies a renunciation of the world, a sacrifice of all the energy that pours out into the world, and entrance into a creative state of introversion. This applies also to the horse sacrifice of our fairy tale. The golden castle in the rectangle framed by four golden poplars is a mandala; that is, an archetypal image which in the religions of the East, in those of primitive peoples, and in our own tradition, is an image of the godhead. Thus the four figures—king, queen, and their two sons—enter into a state of shelteredness in God. Mandala structures occur in the dreams and fantasies of modern man's unconscious with the same significance: as Jung has shown, they symbolize the *inner psychic wholeness of the individual.* In this symbol of wholeness psychic cleavages are healed, and accordingly such images usually appear at times of extreme suffering and profound conflict. Their appearance conveys a feeling of order in chaos and has a healing effect. Psychologically such a symbol cannot be distinguished from an image of the godhead.

The Turkestan tale outlined above ("The Magic Horse") shows with particular clarity why the helpful animal has a purely positive value in fairy tales: it embodies something that is at first manifested as the animal instinct in man, but behind which the secret of individuation, that is, the acquisition of inner wholeness, is concealed. Anyone who can enter into the innermost center of his own psyche, his Self, is safe against the assaults of the dark powers. That is why, in *Och,* the hero is saved in the form of a grain of wheat and, in "The Magician Tsar," in the form of a flint. Both are symbols of the incarnate godhead or of what in Jungian psychology is called the Self.[55]

It is highly interesting to note that most of those symbols in which the above-mentioned murderous giant keeps his heart hidden—island, church, well, duck, egg, etc.—are also symbols of wholeness. Unfortunately I cannot demonstrate this fact in the limited space at my disposal, but those who are familiar with the works of Jung will bear this out. Thus *divine wholeness* is the strategic "weak point" of the evil one. That is, where he has his heart or his "death," that is where he can be destroyed. The Chinese *Book of Changes*[56] says: Evil, which lives on negation, is not destructive to the good alone, but inevitably destroys itself as well in the end.[57] No doubt this is so because it represents only a split-off part of the whole, to which, for that very reason, God's wholeness is ultimately superior. In the above-mentioned fairy tale the partial existence of evil is symbolized by the remoteness of the giant's heart. The island indicates the isolation of goodness, on which the giant, in spite of everything, is nevertheless dependent. But one cannot help wondering, why does the hero crush the egg, the symbol of wholeness on which the life of the evil principle depends? One would expect him rather to hatch it out, to develop this germ of goodness in the darkness, not to destroy it. But evi-

dently the secret softness, the good impulse hidden in the darkness, is too weak to grow into true wholeness; it is only a germ
or beginning, *which,* according to the story, *does not deserve to be
sheltered or spared.* In a sense it is precisely the good contained in
evil that makes evil so very dangerous.[58] But often in such cases
it seems impossible to separate the good from the evil, so that the
feeble germ of the good must perish along with the dark forces.
Or, applying the same principle to an individual case: Even if a
murderer possessed by the Devil has a little soft spot in his soul,
sentimental pity is not appropriate, for the soft spot is not large
or deep enough to become a seedbed of goodness, but merely
helps him to deceive people more easily. This is the cruel insight
that this widespread type of fairy tale forces upon us.

It is a difficult problem in life to decide whether we should try
to develop the germ of goodness in evil men by loving acceptance,
or whether we should destroy it unmercifully along with the evil.
Every situation of this kind presents a conflict; the individual is
called upon to play the part of fate. In this respect the fairy tale
offers no help; as is so often the case, it merely formulates a paradox.

There is a Latvian tale[59] that seems especially illuminating in
this connection. A woodcutter measures his mettle with the
Devil. While hunting a marten, he gets lost in the woods and
meets numerous animals who are fighting over the privilege of
singing the dirge of an elk who has just died. He settles the dispute by singing it himself. Thereupon the grateful animals reward him with the power to assume their shape, that of an ant,
fly, cat, lion, greyhound, and so on. Then he attempts to rescue a
princess who has been sacrificed to the Devil. In the form of an
ant he follows the Devil into a mountain, and in the form of a
lion tears him to pieces. But then he is faced with a problem:
How is he going to return to the upper world? The ravished
princess leafs through the dead Devil's book and finds out that if
a certain diamond egg, hidden in a tree, is brought from hell to
the upper world, the crystal castle, where the woodcutter and
princess both are, will also rise up. In the shape of a sparrow, the

woodcutter finds the egg. He turns himself into a cat, takes the egg in his mouth, and has himself kicked into the upper world by the doorkeeper of hell, who detests cats. Then, with the help of the egg, he raises up the crystal palace, princess and all, and lives with her there happily ever after.

What is especially significant for our purposes is the diamond egg, for it is not destroyed along with the Devil, but serves as a magic instrument by which to restore what has been lost in the Devil's kingdom to the human world. Crystal castle and egg are symbols of wholeness, of the Self, and they serve the hero as vehicles by which to escape from the Devil's realm. There are still other stories in which the object needed to renew life is with the Devil in hell and has to be retrieved. In "The Devil with the Three Golden Hairs,"[60] the hero, on pain of death, has to bring the king three golden hairs from the Devil's beard. On the way he is given the additional task of finding the answers to three unsolved problems. The "Alder Mother"[61] turns him into an ant and hides him under her skirts. When the Devil returns home tired after his day's work, he lays his head in the "Great Mother's" lap to have the lice removed, and falls asleep. Then she plucks out the three hairs and also obtains the answers to the three questions. The hero returns home and becomes king.

Here we are reminded of Lucifer and the motif of the light hidden in the darkness. Hairs point to insight, knowledge, thoughts—it is the Devil who possesses the precious illuminating insights without which life becomes congealed, and from whom they can be learned through trickery. The theme of the supreme treasure to be found in hell is even more clearly developed in a Transylvanian tale, which I should like to cite in conclusion. It is called "The Prince and the Princess"[62]:

A king loses one battle after another in a great war and is about to commit suicide in desperation when a man appears to him and says: "I will help you if you promise me 'en noa Sîl' from your house." The king takes these words to mean "a new rope" (ein neues Seil) and thoughtlessly agrees to the bargain. Actually the man is the Devil in person. His meaning is "a new soul" (eine *neue Seele),* to wit, the king's only son who has just been born. Then the man snaps an iron four-pronged scourge in all four directions, a large army gathers, and with its help the king is victorious. But at the end of three times seven years the Devil comes for the now twenty-one-year-old heir to the throne, and leads him away to Hell. There the Prince of Hell threatens to burn the prince if he is not able in one night to drain an enormous pond, transform it into a meadow, mow the grass, and take in the hay. But that night the Devil's daughter unexpectedly brings the prince food, steals her father's iron scourge, and whips up demons who perform the prince's task. Disappointed, the Prince of Hell sets a new task: to clear a mountain forest and in its place plant a vineyard, which must grow ripe grapes overnight. Again the Devil's daughter performs the task. The third task set by Satan is to build a church, complete with dome and cross, out of sand. But this time the Devil's daughter is unsuccessful, because the demons she conjures up are unable to build a church. She then persuades the prince to flee and turns herself into a white horse on which he gallops away. In the morning the Devil sees what has happened and curses his "human-hearted daughter." He sends the hosts of Hell in pursuit of the fugitives, who see them approaching like a black cloud. The Devil's daughter now turns herself into a church; she tells the prince to stand at the altar, singing: "The Lord shelter us"—and to answer no questions. Unable to cross the threshold, the pursuers return to Hell empty-handed. The Prince of Hell then commands them to destroy the church; but meanwhile the couple have fled. The Devil's daughter turns herself into an alder tree and the prince into a little golden bird in its branches. She bids him to sing "I am not afraid" over and over again regardless of what happens. Thus they escape a second time. The third time she turns herself into a rice field, in which he, in the form of a quail, runs back and forth singing "God be with us." The fourth and last time the Prince of Hell himself sets out in pursuit. Then she turns herself into a milk pond and the prince into a duck, and says: *"Swim around in the middle and keep your head hidden.* Whatever happens, don't take your head out of the milk or swim to shore." The Devil stands on the edge of the pond and speaks to the duckling so ingratiatingly that it finally ventures a quick look. It instantly goes blind, and a grief-stricken cry rises from the milk. But from then on the duck withstands all blandishments, whereupon the Devil grows impatient, turns himself into a goose, drinks the milk, duck and all, and waddles contentedly home. But then the milk begins to boil, the goose bursts with a loud report, and the prince and the Devil's daughter stand there in radiant beauty. Whereupon they go home and are married.

Generally in fairy tales the king represents the dominant principle of consciousness or the dominant of the collective order,[63] that is to say, the image of God underlying it. Here, as in many such tales, this image of God is in difficulties, that is, it is unequal to the inner and outward demands of life, and consequently can no longer contain the opposing tendencies of the psyche.[64] Thus the king ought to abdicate and leave the throne to his son, but his son is not yet old enough to rule; he would only succumb to the enemy, that is, the opposing principle. Then, though not fully aware of what he is doing, the king accepts the Devil's help and sells him his son. The Devil's concern is to keep the son and so compromise the future of the dominant principle, in this case no doubt the Christian dominant of consciousness, prevailing in Europe. The Devil owes his superior power to his four-pronged iron scourge; he possesses the symbol of wholeness, against which the principle of consciousness, which has grown one-sided, is powerless. In mythology, the scourge is an attribute of the underworld gods Osiris, Hecate, and the like, who are not always as black as the Prince of Hell; and the latter is not solely destructive, because his daughter—as the story tells us—is "human-hearted." In fairy tales the Evil One often has a benevolent female companion of this kind, though usually not a daughter, but the so-called Alder Mother or Devil's grandmother—a title that does not signify degree of kinship, but denotes the "Great Mother." The Great Mother helps certain heroes against her underworldly husband.[65] This must be interpreted as compensation for the patriarchal principle present in our cultural consciousness, for in those mythologies where the struggle against the primordial mother still figures prominently, it is often a male god who helps the hero: Hermes, for example, who helps Perseus in his fight with the Gorgon, or Shamash, the sun god, who helps Gilgamesh against Ishtar.[66]

In the view of the world characteristic of fairy tales, good and evil are not so diametrically opposed as in our conscious attitude; as in the *T'ai-chi-t'u* of the Taoists, a seed of goodness, in the present case the Devil's daughter, is present in the darkness, just as there is a latent evil disposition within the good (in the reigning king, for example). In contrast to the soft heart of the giant in the above-related tale, the Devil's daughter, the personification of the good in Hell, proves not only to be strong but ultimately more powerful than her father. She is a great enchantress, as she shows by the transformations she effects in the course of her flight with the prince—she might be compared with such figures as Isis, Neith, Selene, Hecate, Artemis, or Kore; or with the magical goddess of late antiquity who is invoked in the papyri as "Three-headed, nocturnal, excrement-eating virgin, Persephone holder of the keys, Kore of the underworld, Gorgon-eyed terrible dark one."[67] Or in another prayer: "Shining by night, holy nocturnal one, thou has created all that is cosmic, wanderer in the mountains, subterranean, eternal dark one!"[68] She is also invoked as the "wily compeller of all things,"[69] or as the "universal mother of nature," "the four-faced one": "Thou art beginning and end, only thou alone rulest over all things, everything has its source in thee, and to thee everything returns in the end."[70] At its culmination the Yang is transformed into a feminine Yin, which saves the future king and, in the form of a white steed of the sun, carries him back to the light. The horse—Pegasus as paranatellon of the era of Aquarius—appears as a positive instinctive force of the unconscious, which saves the Christian principle of consciousness and makes possible its further development.

The tasks that the Devil sets the prince are worthy of our attention. They are all unmistakable culture tasks. What an uncanny insight: in our late aeon the fairy tale declares the domestication of nature to be the work of the Devil. But the mockery of a church established in Hell cannot endure. Darkness cannot complete it. On the strength of this image we are perhaps entitled to hope that the totalitarian organizations of our anti-Christian age will crumble into the sand from which they were built, for how can anything enduring be built by men reduced to the level of worthless particles in a mass? But failure provokes the evil power to erupt in all his destructive fury. The loving couple is driven to "magic flight," the meaning of which is already known to us, and then to another form of flight, the so-called flight of transformation. Four times—the number four points to inner wholeness—the two are transformed; each time the feminine is a protective vessel around the male germ—*vir a femina circumdatus!*[71] (Jeremiah 31:22). The significance of the first transformation is clear: the priest who is at one with his bride, the Church. Because of its cultural aspect, this transformation seems the least effective. The second transformation reaches more deeply into nature: the spirit in the form of a golden soul or sunbird,[72] singing in the branches of the maternal tree. Next comes the quail, singing as it runs back and forth in the rice field, an image of fruitful Mother Earth. The word *Wachtel* ("quail") was formerly thought to derive from the Sanskrit *vartika* (or *vartaka*),[73] meaning the "lively, swift, vigilant one." In recent years doubt has been cast on this derivation, and it has been suggested that the name is an imitation of the bird's cry. This cry has been interpreted in a good many ways: as *"Fürchte Gott, Fürchte Gott"* (fear God, fear God), as "wet my feet," "wet my feet," and so forth. In classical antiquity the moon was thought to keep the quail awake: it wandered about screaming, and from its cry the peasants derived forecasts of the weather or of next year's wheat price. It was sacred to Leto and to Leda, who, according to some legends, was not visited by a swan but a quail at the time of her dealings with Zeus. In other stories she was sacred to Herakles, who, through the smell of a quail, recovered the life that Typhon had taken away from him.[74] These ancient tales are significant, for in them the quail is associated with the feminine principle, with Leto the Mother Goddess, just as in our fairy tale it is the feminine principle that rescues the hero. And in the legend of Herakles the quail helps *the hero murdered by the evil principle* to rise from the dead, just as here the hero escapes murder by taking the form of a quail. He is saved, as it were, by becoming a *being in the service of the feminine principle of nature,* or in psychological terms, by ceasing to manifest masculine authority or judgment and subordinating himself in intuitive trust to his unconscious psyche, which in a man has markedly feminine characteristics.

The rice field is obviously an image of fruitful Mother Earth; in Transylvania rice often replaces the millet elsewhere used in fertility magic. Persons in fear of evil spirits and demons throw rice; the devils run away, because otherwise they would be obliged to count the grains.

In the last transformation the Devil's daughter is turned into a pond full of pure, white, maternal milk, which is often employed in fairy tales as a means of putting devils to flight, because it represents the essence of purity. In antiquity milk was used especially in sacrifices for the dead to appease the anger of the chthonian powers. Milk offerings, in contrast to wine, were regarded as νηφάλια, "sober offerings," and milk was drunk by those who had attained spiritual rebirth in the mystery rites.[75]

The duck into which the Devil's daughter turns the prince is an animal able to move in all three realms and is therefore, in the Indian view, a symbol, par excellence, of the soul. It is also an image of the sun, which in the form of a golden duck swims in a celestial pond.[76] In legends and fairy tales it often appears as the bird of the betrothed maiden or as a form taken by enchanted persons. If we attempt to take all these aspects together, the duck symbolizes a psychic being which on the one hand represents a principle of consciousness (sun), but on the other hand is dominated by the feminine (pond, etc.). In other words, *it is a germinal principle of consciousness, wholly devoted to the service of the unconscious.* In a number of creation myths, the creator requires some earth from the bottom of the sea before he can start creating the universe. He sends out many animals in search of it, but only the duck is able to go deep enough. He brings up some earth in his beak, and from it the creator makes the world. Here again the duck represents a germinal impulse to consciousness, which obediently serves the creative processes of the psyche, tending to bring forth a new and wider field of consciousness. By turning the prince into a duck which has to keep its head under water, the Devil's daughter warns him not to serve the logos. The same idea is expressed in the Devil's daughter's injunction not to raise his head out of the milk. He becomes, as it were, all soul, wholly an expression of his psyche. And perhaps, indeed, it was to this end that nature originally invented the human consciousness, not in order that it might ravage the soul with its principles, judgments, and technology, but in order that it might become an instrument for the expression and fulfillment of the soul. The duck, says the Devil's daughter, should *only swim around in the middle.* In other words, it should remain in the center of the mandala, that is, in the Self, as close as possible to God. *Only this psychic middle is stronger than the principles of opposition.* "God is a circle, whose center is everywhere and whose circumference is nowhere," says an old hermetic maxim, which the Church Fathers, alchemists, and medieval mystics never weary of citing.[77] Like Job, the hero must cling to the seed of divine wholeness in order to avoid destruction by God.[78] This advice is given him by the anima figure. Similarly the hero fleeing from Och, the forest king, is hidden as a grain of wheat beneath the foot of the anima and so saved. There is a parallel Christian conception, namely, the notion that the believer enters into the wound in Christ's side and, there hidden, escapes the Evil One. *"O bone Jesu, exaudi me,"* says the "Anima Christi" prayer, *"intra tua vulnera absconde me, ne permittas me separari a te, ab hoste maligno defende me."* Przywara compares this entering of the believer into the body of Christ with the grain of wheat that falls to the earth to rise again a thousandfold.[79] As Jung has shown in his detailed interpretation of this complex of ideas, this is an entrance into something maternal.[80] Because the consciousness of Western man is distinctly active and masculine, his unconscious side, when manifested, shows feminine traits. The Devil is the male principle that wants to lure him back to his former attitude.[81] The Christian believer enters into the maternal wound of the son of the luminous half of God, while the (compensatory) fairy tale prince enters into the "human-hearted" daughter of the Devil; that is, of the dark half of the godhead.[82] This puts a still stronger accent on the tendency to rely on pure Eros. The image expresses a radical realization of the spiritual attitude initiated in medieval mysticism: Follow *only* your feeling and your soul, without casting so much as a glance outward.

The tale ends with an astonishingly optimistic and promising image: Not only is a man who finds shelter solely and absolutely in the innermost center of his soul and who casts not another look outward, saved; he also encompasses the downfall of the Devil. For the Devil becomes a goose, the bird of witches, in antiquity the bird of the goddess Nemesis and other nature goddesses, and in the form of a goose he drinks up pond and duck. Actually he is following the example of the hero in becoming an aquatic bird—we foresee the hero's victory, for he has imposed his own "choice of weapons" on the adversary. And last but not least, the goose is a goose, that is, a model of stupidity. Like those heroes of myth who cut out the heart of the whale that has swallowed them, thus forcing the whale to vomit them up,[83] so the Devil's daughter defeats her father from within. She becomes the "seething fury" that makes him burst, for those whose unnatural one-sidedness puts them at the mercy of their emotional outbursts are defeated in advance. There is a large group of fairy tales in which the hero and the villain engage in a contest to see who will get angry first;[84] the winner is entitled to kill the loser. They do everything possible to infuriate each other. In the end the villain loses his temper and with it, the game, his possessions, or even his life. The hero marries the villain's daughter. These tales embody a profound psychological truth: Often in life much depends on who "blurts out" an intrigue first. For if one sees such an intrigue in another, outside of oneself, and tries to "unmask" it, one invariably takes on the appearance of a scoundrel in the eyes of the world. Accordingly, it is wiser to look within at one's own shadow; then the other is compelled to "show his colors" and burst with his own malice. The same situation often prevails in political life: one need only think of the many allegedly preventive wars in history.

Milk boiling over is a familiar image for an attack of rage. Those who lose their temper "rise" like the hot milk in the pot, *comme une soupe au lait,* as they put it in French. When the Devil swallows his human-hearted daughter in the form of milk, he has her inside him. The function of feeling becomes dominant, and that is his downfall: *"Festinatio ex parte diaboli est"* ("Haste comes from the Devil") say the alchemists, a truth from which fortunately the Devil himself is not exempt. He falls victim to his own haste. The rescued couple symbolize a new principle of consciousness in which the opposites are united; now masculine and feminine, spirit and nature are in balance and the *coniunctio oppositorum* makes possible a new psychic life.

The image of the duck submerging its head in the middle suggests *a state of absolute introversion, which prevents one from seeing evil "outside."* For, as the fairy tale shows so aptly, to look outward would lead directly to psychic blindness, either because the sight of ugliness leaves behind ugliness in one's own soul, or because this outside ugliness is a projection of the evil within. Only through absolute concentration on the essential within, by immersion in the depths of his own psyche, does the prince succeed in escaping the Devil.

As these examples show, fairy tales take the problem of evil very seriously, and in some, which it has not been possible to cite here, the hero or heroine succumbs tragically to the powers of darkness. Good and evil are represented as primordial principles implicit both in a masculine, spiritual image of God and in a feminine view of nature; and it depends only on small but essential imponderables whether the hero himself, the helpful animal, or some other power, is able to tip the scales in the direction of the good. Here the human virtues are relatively unimportant, the divine-demonic powers of fate have the greater share in the decision.

Sometimes we have the impression that fairy tales merely reflect a conflict between opposing images of God or opposing dominants of the unconscious mind. But usually we can discern an attempt to indicate what stands out so clearly in the story we have just been analyzing: that the essential for man is to grasp the principle of individuation in the center of his own psyche; that is, the inner creative germinal point where the *progressive tendency toward humanity and wholeness,* inherent in both the bright and the dark power of God, strives for fulfillment.

Notes

1. M. Lüthi, *Das europäische Volksmärchen* (The European Folktale) (Berne, 1947), esp. pp. 89 and 103.

2. In my choice of examples I have confined myself in the main to European fairy tales, but the general principles implicit in my remarks apply also to extra-European tales; national distinctions are more apparent in matters of detail than in the overall themes of the stories.

3. Lüthi, *Das europäische Volksmärchen,* p. 89.

4. Ibid., pp. 103 and 115f.

5. Cf. H. von Beit, *Symbolik des Märchens* (The Symbolism of the Fairy Tale) (3 vols., Berne: Francke, 1952, 1956, 1957), vol. 1, Introduction.

6. Lüthi, *Das europäische Volksmärchen,* pp. 107f.

7. As Jung showed in his article "A Psychological View of Conscience," the unconscious can disclose moral tendencies, but these are not always in agreement with our conscious moral code. See cw 10, pp. 437ff.

8. A. Jolles, *Einfache Formen* (Simple Forms) (2nd ed., Darmstadt, 1958).

9. Ibid., p. 240.

10. Cf. "Der Bauer und der Teufel," (The Farmer and the Devil) in *Die Märchen der Weltliteratur,* vol. 2, no. 123 (Jena, 1922). All quota-

tions from fairy-tale collections are translated from this volume, unless otherwise stated. In the following references this edition is quoted as *Grimm*. For an English-language edition see *Grimms' Fairy Tales for Young and Old*, tr. R. Mannheim (Garden City, N.Y.: Anchor Press/Doubleday, 1977). On the theme of the outwitted devil cf. A. Wünsche, *Der Sagenkreis vom geprellten Teufel* (Sagas revolving around the Outwitted Devil) (1905), passim; and J. Bolte and G. Polivka, *Anmerkungen zu den Kinder- und Hausmärchen der Gebrüder Grimm* (Comments on the Brothers' Grimm's Fairy Tales) (5 vols., Leipzig, 1913–1932). In the following references this standard work is quoted under the abbreviation *B-P*.

11. A shepherd arranges for the devil to build it on the understanding that the devil is entitled to the first soul who crosses it; when the bridge is ready, the shepherd sends a billy goat across.

12. *Grimm*, vol. 2, no. 120.

13. *Märchen aus Sibirien* (Fairy Tales from Siberia), no. 18, p. 81.

14. *Russische Volksmärchen* (Russian Folktales), no. 41, pp. 236ff.

15. E.g., "Sturmheld Ivan Kuhsohn," in *Russische Volksmärchen*, no. 22, p. 105.

16. *Grimm*, vol. 1, no. 34.

17. Ibid., nos. 26, 27.

18. Cf. Grimm's fairy tale "Der arme Müllersbursche und das Kätzchen" (The Poor Miller's Boy and the Little Cat), ibid., no. 61, and *B-P* under "Dümmling."

19. *Grimm*, vol. 1, no. 40.

20. *Märchen aus dem Donaulande*, pp. 150ff.

21. *Grimm*, vol. 2, no. 116. Cf. also the story "Der lustige Ferdinand und der Goldhirsch" (Happy Ferdinand and the Golden Stag) in *Deutsche Märchen seit Grimm* (German Fairy Tales Since Grimm), vol. 1, p. 25.

22. *Grimm*, vol. 2, no. 174.

23. "Vun'm Mandl Sponnelang," in *Deutsche Märchen seit Grimm*, vol. 1, p. 404. Cf., C. G. Jung, "Archetypes and the Collective Unconscious" in cw IX/i.

24. *Grimm,* vol. 2, no. 2.

25. Cf. the special edition of A. Löpfe, *Russische Märchen* (Russian Fairy Tales) (Olten, 1941), pp. 5ff.

26. "Sturmheld Ivan Kuhsohn," in *Russische Märchen.*

27. "Die Jungfrau Zar" (Virgin Tzar), ibid., no. 41.

28. I have written about this in greater detail in the chapter "In the Black Woman's Castle," in this volume.

29. *Grimm,* vol. 1, no. 53.

30. "Der Bräutigam mit der goldenen Nase," in *Finnische und estnische Märchen* (Finnish and Estorian Fairy Tales), pp. 179ff.

31. "Die Jungfrau Zar," in *Russische Volksmärchen.*

32. Cf., e.g., "Die verwünschte Prinzessin" (The Enchanted Princess), in *Deutsche Märchen seit Grimm,* vol. 1, p. 237. A princess is compelled by a mountain sprite (or by a troll in a Norwegian parallel in *Nordische Volksmärchen* [Nordic Folktales], vol. 2) by whom she is "possessed," to send her suitors to their death by asking insoluble riddles. On this type of fairy tale, cf. G. Hentze, "Turandot," in *Antaios (1959), vol. 1, no. 1.*

33. Thus, e.g., in Grimm's tale "The Golden Bird" we never find out who has turned the prince into a fox.

34. I am referring to the figure of the envious courtier or companion of the Ritter-Rot type. Cf. *B-P,* vol. 33, pp. 18 and 424.

35. Cf. Grimm's tale "The Two Wanderers," in *Grimm,* vol. 2, no. 92, and "Ferenand getrü und Ferenand ungetrü" (Ferdinand Faithful and Ferdinand Unfaithful), in *Grimm,* vol. 1, no. 46. *See* also the parallels to these tales mentioned in *B-P.*

36. *Chinesische Märchen* (Chinese Fairy Tales), ed. R. Wilhelm, no. 48, pp. 134ff.

37. "Von dem Riesen, der sein Herz nicht bei sich hatte" (The Giant Who Didn't Have His Heart with Him) in *Nordische Volksmärchen,* vol. 2, no. 23, pp. 119ff.

38. *Deutsche Märchen seit Grimm,* vol. 1, p. 15, "Vom Mann ohne Herz" (The Man without a Heart).

39. *Russische Märchen,* no. 29, p. 160.

40. Ibid., no. 6, p. 29. In regard to Och and all these dark nature spirits, cf. C. G. Jung, "The Phenomenology of the Spirit," in cw 9/i, pp. 222ff.

41. On the old man of the mountains as a Wotan figure, see M. Ninck, *Wodan und germanischer Schicksalsglaube,* pp. 133ff.

42. "Der Vogel mit dem lieblichen Gesang" (The Bird That Sang So Lovely), in *Irische Märchen* (Irish Fairy Tales), no. 28.

43. M. R. James, *The Apocryphal New Testament* (Oxford Press, 1924, 1945), p. 26, "The Oxyrhynchus-Sayings of Jesus." A somewhat different translation is provided in *Das Evangelium nach Thomas* (The Gospel According to Thomas), eds. Quispel and Puech (1959).

44. Cf. *I Ching, or Book of Changes* (Princeton: Princeton University Press, 1967), no. 53, "Gradual Progress."

45. "The Golden Bird," in *Grimm,* vol. 1, no. 7.

46. "Ferenand getrü und Ferenand ungetrü." For parallels see *B-P,* vol. 3, pp. 18ff., esp. 22.

47. Cf. C. G. Jung, "On the Nature of the Psyche," in cw 8, pp. 159–234.

48. Cf. C. G. Jung, *Symbols of Transformation,* cw 5, esp. chap. 5.

49. On the Self, see below.

50. Cf. Jung's remarks about *Die Symbole der Wandlung,* p. 287 (see *Symbols of Transformation,* cw 5).

51. Meister Eckhart, *Schriften,* ed. H. Büttner (Jena, 1934), p. 37: "Von der Erfüllung: Predigt über Lukas I:26."

52. *Märchen aus Turkestan* (Fairy Tales from Turkestan), no. 9, pp. 236ff.

53. Hume (tr.), *The Thirteen Principal Upanishads,* pp. 73f. Quoted in modified form C. G. Jung, *Symbols of Transformation,* p. 280.

54. C. G. Jung, *Die Symbole der Wandlung,* pp. 420f. (see *Symbols of Transformation*).

55. On the flint as symbol of the Self, see C. G. Jung, "The Visions of Zosimos," in *Alchemical Studies,* cw 13, pp. 203, 214, and on the grain of wheat, "The Symbol of the Tree," ibid., p. 361. Also C. G.

Jung, *Die Symbole der Wandlung,* pp. 598ff., 610ff. (see *Symbols of Transformation*).

56. *I Ching,* no. 23, "Splitting Apart," "Nine at the Top."

57. Cf. also no. 36, "Six at the Top."

58. Cf. C. G. Jung, *Essays on Contemporary Events,* in cw 10.

59. *Lettische Märchen* (Lettish Fairy Tales), no. 3.

60. *Grimm,* vol. 2, no. 83.

61. I.e., the Devil's grandmother.

62. *Deutsche Märchen seit Grimm,* vol. 1, pp. 155ff.

63. Examples in C. G. Jung, *Mysterium Coniunctionis,* cw 14.

64. Ibid.

65. Cf. Grimm's fairy tale "Der Teufel mit den drei goldenen Haaren" (The Devil with the Three Golden Hairs), in *Grimm,* vol. 2, no. 83.

66. Cf. Thot's action against the raging Hathor in Egypt.

67. Cf. K. Preisendanz, *Papyri Graecae magicae* (Leipzig, 1928), p. 119 (Prayer to Hecate).

68. Ibid., p. 149 (Prayer to Selene).

69. Ibid., p. 157.

70. Ibid., p. 163 (Prayer to Selene).

71. Cf. C. G. Jung, *Psychology and Religion,* cw 11 (1958).

72. Cf. C. G. Jung, *Von den Wurzeln des Bewuβtseins* (Zurich: Rascher, 1954), chap. 12.

73. Cf. A. de Gubernatis, *Die Thiere in der indogermanischen Mythologie* (Animals in Indo-Germanic Mythology) (Leipzig, 1874), p. 550.

74. Ibid., p. 548.

75. Cf. K. Weiss, "Die Milch im Kultus der Griechen und Römer" (Milk in the Cult of the Greeks and Romans), in *Religionsgeschichtliche Versuche und Vorarbeiten* (Giessen, 1914).

76. Cf. A. De Gubernatis, *Die Thiere in der indogermanischen Mythologie,* pp. 574ff.

77. Cf. C. G. Jung, *Mysterium Coniunctionis,* cw 14, p. 47, para. 41.

78. Cf. C. G. Jung, "Answer to Job," in cw 11.

79. E. Przywara, S. J., *Deus semper maior: Theologie der Exerzitien* (Freiburg i. Br., 1938), vol. 1.

80. Cf. Jung, *ETH Lectures, 1939–1941,* pp. 64ff. (privately printed).

81. Ibid., p. 69.

82. Concerning the father god who tries to possess his own daughter, cf. Jung's remarks on Wotan and Brünhilde in *Symbols of Transformation.* Brünhilde's betrayal of Wotan, i.e., her love for Sigmund, forms an exact parallel to the tale of the prince and the Devil's daughter.

83. Cf. L. Frobenius, *Das Zeitalter des Sonnengottes* (The Age of the Sun God) (Berlin, 1904), and Jung, *Die Symbole der Wandlung,* p. 545 (see *Symbols of Transformation*).

84. E.g., "Hwekk," in *Isländische Märchen* (Icelandic Fairy Tales), no. 60, and "Böse werden" (Becoming Angry) in *Deutsche Märchen seit Grimm,* vol. 1, p. 394.

THE BREMEN TOWN MUSICIANS FROM THE POINT OF VIEW OF DEPTH PSYCHOLOGY

■■

TELLING FAIRY TALES is an activity probably as old as humanity itself. Fairy tales are among the most primeval of human expressions. Yet they still illustrate the true inner spiritual life of all of us. As Laurens van der Post reports of the Bushmen of the Kalahari, who remain still at the most archaic stage of culture, their stories—all of them animal stories—are their greatest spiritual treasure. A Bushman would rather share his goods, food, and all his possessions with a stranger than the secret of his tales. They are, as van der Post says, "his greatest container of primordial mind, filled to the brim with things without which his life would have no meaning; without stories no life-giving connection would exist with the beginning of things, and there would also be no future." Indeed life itself is a fairy tale for the Bushman. Xhabbo, a Bushman whom the white men held captive far from his people, said to his white master, who wanted to hear his stories from him, "Master, you know that I am sitting here waiting for the moon to come back for me so that I can return to my homeland, so that I can hear the stories of my people again, . . .

110

so that I might sit and listen to the stories, wherever they may come from, stories that come from far away. . . . Here I can't hear any stories. . . . Therefore, I have to wait for the moon to come back. Then I will say to you, master, now the time has come when I should be sitting among my people, who in passing away meet those who are like them. They listen to the stories. I have to sit for a little and cool off in order to ease the tiredness, waiting for the stories that I want to hear. . . . As I sit and wait for them to flow into my ears. Even if there are mountains in the way and the way is long, yes truly, they would still flow to me. Listening, I will return on my tracks, so that I can feel in my ears the story that is the wind." These stories are truly the Bushman's *religio,* which connects him with the origin of the universe and the flowing on of life. And they are nearly all animal stories!

At this cultural level of so-called hunters and gatherers, nearly all the stories are about animals. Among the Bushmen, for example, we encounter the praying mantis as the embodiment of the supreme deity, the hyena as the principle of darkness. The praying mantis is the creator spirit in the joy of creation. Near her lives Dxui, a suffering god, who is water, flower, and bird. Mantis is the bringer of the word and of fire. Porcupine is her daughter, the bringer of light, and so on.[1]

But such animal deities behave mentally and psychically just like people. They are like animal-people gods, and as Jung has shown, we can recognize through these figures that our mental and emotional inner processes were originally fully subordinated to our instinctive animal modes of behavior. These figures are like the mental "inner view" of our animal instincts, which Jung referred to as archetypes. In the process of cultural development more human-shaped deities gradually developed from these animal-people gods (in ancient Egypt the greatest gods still kept the heads of animals), and this reflects a development of consciousness in the course of which we have gradually become conscious of the specifically human quality of our behavior. The old tales about the animal-people gods, however, never died out, but rather continued to survive as animal fables alongside the later hero tales. In that case, later on these stories were often no longer completely understood. In order to justify perpetuating them, they often had moralistic endings tacked onto them, as we know from Aesop's fables or those of La Fontaine. Either that, or the animal stories were given a somewhat farcical touch, which also shows that they were no longer quite emotionally understood and therefore no longer taken seriously. For this reason we have to descend quite far down into ourselves, into the world of little children and of the most primitive peoples in order to be able to understand such animal stories again. But when we do, it emerges that they are often much more profound than the ordinary fairy tales that deal with kings and peasants—that they reflect the very most primal of our unconscious psyche.

Carl Jung was the first to recognize that mythical tales derive from a still living function of our unconscious psyche. They again and again give visible form to the ultimate myth-building structures of the psyche, which he called archetypes.[2] While such images can be shown to appear directly in the dreams of modern people, the stories are made up of traditional formulations that are for the most part incalculably old. They are primal "revelations" of the preconscious psyche, spontaneous utterances concerning unconscious psychic events, and as such, of vital importance. They not only represent, but also *are* the life of primitive peoples. They do not refer to something external and also never to something that is already conscious or has been conscious, but to something essential in the unconscious. For this reason, any interpretation must remain an "as if"; the final nucleus of meaning itself can only be pointed to but not described. Although our intellect continually tries to explain it away in a rationalistic fashion, we never can really get away from it except at the expense of a neurosis. Thus for each new stage of consciousness we must find an interpretation that corresponds to that stage, even if we know that it cannot be definitive. Only in this way do we stay in connection with our psychic past, and there that which heals us reveals itself again and again, even if often in an unsightly, bizarre form. But this we shall see in our story, which is familiar to everybody:

A donkey which had faithfully served his master, a miller, is to be killed by the master, who wants to spare himself the cost of maintaining the animal in its old age. So the donkey flees with the plan of eking out an existence as a town musician in Bremen. On the way he is joined by an old hunting dog and a cat and a cock, who are all in the same plight. During the journey they must pass the night in a dark forest, where they find a brightly lit house belonging to some thieves. They stand one on top of another, begin to make music, and then crash in through a window, causing the thieves to flee in fright. The animals eat and drink and lie down to rest, the donkey on the dung heap, the dog by the door, the cat on the hearth, and the cock on the balcony. Then one of the thieves, sent back by the others, sneaks into the house and holds his match up to the cat's eyes, thinking that they are glowing coals. The cat leaps at his face with her claws. He runs to the door, where the dog bites him. At the dung heap he gets a kick from the donkey, and the cock crows after him, "Cock-a-doodle-doo!" He rushes back to the others and tells them that a cruel witch scratched his face, a man at the door stabbed him with a knife, a black monster in the yard hit him with a club, and on the roof, "there sat the judge and shouted: 'Bring the rascal here!' Then I made my getaway." So the thieves never dared go back to the house. But the four Bremen town musicians were so content there that they never wanted to leave. And the last person who told us about it still has his mouth warm.

There are countless parallel versions of this fairy tale to be found throughout Europe,[3] including among many primitive peoples. The oldest records we have of it go back as far as the twelfth century,[4] when a tale was being told about how a doe, with seven animal companions who were going to be slaughtered at home for a wedding feast, made a pilgrimage to Rome. The thieves in our version are replaced by a wolf called Isengrimm. Georg Bolte and Johannes Polivka tell us that in the oldest versions the enemies of the animals are all wolves or a wolf, and not human thieves.[5] Apart from that, the tales all run more or less the same way: At the beginning of the story, a certain number of domestic animals fall into mortal peril. This is either because, as in our main version of "The Bremen Town Musicians," ungrateful humans want to deny them upkeep in their old age, or they mean to kill them for their own purposes (a wedding feast or a festive meal). This motif is initially derived from the fact that humans have always felt a natural guilt toward the animals they have used or eaten. At the most primitive stage, expiatory rites were carried out to propitiate the spirits of slain animals.[6]

The relationship between men and animals were regulated by religion. If we understand this not only in concrete terms (although this too is entirely valid) but also symbolically, it means that every necessary killing of animals in the external world and also every suppression of our own animal instincts within us for the sake of cultural development has not just been carried out of willfulness and violence, but has taken place in the context of certain spiritual archetypal principles of order.

In effect, the way a human being deals with animals is the same way he also deals with his own instincts, and thus also with the oldest gods, that is, the oldest psychic representation of our instincts, the animal gods. For in nature drives and instincts are never without restraint and restriction, but rather always coupled with a symbolic image. In other words, the drive never appropriates its object blindly, but always in conjunction with a certain psychic image or interpretation. Thus our instinct world, which initially strikes the cultivated rational person as extraordinarily simple, reveals itself on the primitive level as a very complex interplay of psychological facts with taboos, rituals, class systems, and tribal teachings. In these, symbolic interpretations are expressed that impose a priori, that is, preconsciously, a restrictive form on the drive and thus places it at the service of higher purposes.

The primordial connection of image and instinct also explains the bond between instinct and religion in the widest sense. "Religion" on the most primitive level signifies the psychic regulatory system that relates to the dynamism of the drive. On a higher level, to be sure, this primordial bond is often lost, and then religion easily becomes a poison counteracting the drive, and in this way the original relationship of mutual compensation degenerates into the well-known conflict between mind and instinct. But such a split is by no means just an accident and a senseless catastrophe; rather it contributes toward the broadening and further differentiation of human consciousness. In other words, if the conflict reaches a certain unbearable intensity, the unconscious instigates a new reconciliation between instinct and mind by producing symbols that reconcile the opposites. Initially of course people degenerate and fall into conflict with their true nature. They forget their origins, and their consciousness behaves in an autocratic manner that is antagonistic to the instincts.

As we can see, this is also the case at the beginning of our fairy tale. People are egotistic and wish to deprive their poor animals of their hard-earned old-age upkeep. But this brings about the activation of destructive forces in the unconscious, which are embodied in the thieves. The thieves represent murderous lawlessness and greed. Often also the enemy of the animals is a greedy innkeeper, a witch, or simply an evil person. Behind these, however, in the older versions, is always to be found the wolf Isengrimm and his cohorts. Isengrimm, as Martin Ninck has shown,[7] is an animal manifestation of Wotan in his dark aspect as the lord of war and the battlefield. He is seen as a gruesome strangler, the pale gray messenger of death, and a rapacious thief. The word *vagr* means at the same time wolf, thief, outcast, and criminal. Two wolves, Geri and Freki, accompany Odin. The two expressions mean greed and belligerence; and two other wolves, Sköll the Barker and Hati the Hater, harry the sun at the time of the end of the world. But the wolf Fenrir, who brings the end, is a brother of death, Hel, the son of Angbroda, the bringer of misery. Later Isengrimm was the name of an iron specter of horror, a revenant and companion of Wotan to the savage hunter. He is an embodiment of cold, raging anger. In a Russian parallel, he is a one-legged, one-eyed demon, and in a parallel from the Grimm brothers, the evil one is called Mr. Korbes, who gives the fairy tale its title. This name means the same thing as Knecht Ruprecht or the bogeyman—a severe, harsh man who frightens children[8] and who also embodies an aspect of the ancient dark father of the gods that survived into Christian times. Thus the enemy of the animals is ultimately an aspect of the *deus absconditus* and indeed his darkest and most menacing side. He symbolizes the whole hopeless fearsomeness of nature and the darkest pathological and dreadful abysses of the human psyche; in sum, the power of the evil that ponders the annihilation of the world and humanity. Thus ultimately our story concerns nothing less than how to deal with the principle of evil and the problems that it sets us—one of humanity's profound eternal questions!

In certain versions, however, the antagonist of the animals is not directly characterized as evil. Sometimes it is just an old woman or a foolish, apparently harmless girl who is seemingly gratuitously tormented by the animals.[9] From this we can only conclude that an apparently harmless ignorance concerning the exploitation of animals, that is, our deepest religious instincts, can be just as wicked as the personifications of war, murder, and destruction mentioned above; it is the great unconsciousness *(agnoia),* which the Gnostics also saw as the truly worst primordial evil of human existence. C. G. Jung once said that if our world were to be destroyed by an atomic war or a failure to cope with the overpopulation problem, it would happen more as a result of the stupidity than the evil of humanity. Any psychotherapist working in depth psychology could tell us to what a great degree, with regard to their own psychic problems, people's unconsciousness, repression, and unwillingness to see are capable of turning the people themselves and the world around them into destructive monsters. That is why the English saying "he meant well" might be just about the worst thing that can be said about a person. Repression and ignorance of the most profound demands of one's own deep psyche and unawareness of the divine powers at work within it is the worst of faults and one that is seemingly just as severely punished as actual evil.[10]

But who are the heroes of our story? In the musicians of Bremen version, it is the four animals: the donkey, the dog, the cat, and the cock. A group of eight animals is found in the oldest recorded version. Some of the later versions have different numbers of victorious animals, something I would like to go into later on. But the group of four or eight seems to be the oldest and most frequent case.[11]

In order to understand this quaternity motif, we must have some background. Throughout his entire opus, Jung always took care to demonstrate that human beings have not only their conscious ego, with which they ordinarily identify as the center of their psyche, but that the psyche as a whole is governed by another center, which Jung called the Self. This "something," which by its nature at all times transcends and encompasses our consciousness, is scarcely directly knowable for us, but it definitely manifests itself repeatedly in the unconscious psyche in the form of symbols. The most frequent image is the mandala, the circle divided in four parts, or the square with further subdivisions in multiples of four: 8, 16, 32, and so forth. In almost all the religions of the world, a form of this sort is regarded as a divine image. From a psychological point of view it is an archetypal symbol that expresses the psyche as a whole. In other words, it gives visible form to the wholeness of the ground of the psyche; or in mythic terms, it is the appearance of the deity become visible in man.[12]

Experiences of this inner center of the psyche exercise a helpful or destructive influence on people. "He cannot," Jung says, "grasp, comprehend, dominate them; nor can he free himself or escape from them, and therefore feels them as overpowering. Recognizing that they do not spring from his conscious personality, he calls them mana, daimon, or God."[13] Modern psychology calls this the unconscious wholeness of the human psyche, whose center, the Self, strikes us experientially as something alien, overpowering. In this symbol, the opposites of the world and of the human essence are unified[14] in such a way that they are no longer at war but mutually complement each other and give a meaningful shape to life. This also holds for the great opposition of good and evil. This conflict, which we encounter in the image of nature and its creator, can only be reconciled in the unity and wholeness of the Self. This raises the life of the individual to a level where it serves as the place in which the opposites can become one and the blind *deus absconditus* of nature can become conscious. Jung says,

> If the Creator were conscious of Himself, He would not need conscious creatures; nor is it probable that the extremely indirect methods of creation, which squander millions of years upon the development of countless species and creatures, are the outcome of purposeful intention. Natural history tells us of a haphazard and casual transformation of species over hundreds of millions of years of devouring and being devoured. The biological and political history of man is an elaborate repetition of the same thing. But the history of the mind offers a different picture. Here the miracle of reflecting consciousness intervenes—the second cosmogony. The importance of consciousness is so great that one cannot help suspecting the element of *meaning* to be concealed somewhere within all the monstrous, apparently senseless biological turmoil, and that the road to its manifestation was ultimately found on the level of warm-blooded vertebrates possessed of a differentiated brain—found as if by chance, unintended and unforeseen, and yet somehow sensed, felt and groped for out of some dark urge.[15]

The fact that the animals in our tale number four points to this "dark urge" toward the development of consciousness in nature; for our consciousness functions as a general principle in rhythms of four. This is based on the four functions of thinking, intuition, sensation, and feeling. Yet the animals do not represent these conscious functions themselves, but rather their preformed bases in the human psyche. More simply put, they represent that which pushes us to become conscious of our wholeness and the Self. They embody a priori structural forms of the instinctive foundations of our consciousness, and especially the foundation of our ego consciousness.

In Christian art the four Evangelists are depicted as three animals—an ox, an eagle, a lion—and a man, who form the foundation supporting the Christ symbol enthroned in their midst. In ancient Egypt, the four sons of Horus—a baboon, a falcon, a jackal, and a man—were the gods that brought about the resurrection of the supreme deity Osiris. That here one of the figures is human betokens that at least a quarter of the highly significant animal quaternity has grown up into human consciousness. By contrast, in our group all four gods are animals, that is, they are still situated in the unconscious. However, we now understand why particularly this quaternity of animals appears as something like an answer to the constellation of evil, of the destructive side of God. Only these powers of the depths themselves, and not the errant ego of man, can cure the problem that has been activated, that is, only they can make the ruined divine image whole and healthy again. With the four animals and their struggle with the wolf and other evil powers, it is as though God were opposing God in the essential depths of the human psyche—the healing factor that strives toward greater consciousness confronting the abyss of self-destruction. Because these four animals are destined to heal the opposition between good and evil, they participate in the nature of both positions; in their behavior they are simultaneously good and evil. In a group of related fairy tales, they are even referred to as "a pack of no-goods" as in the Grimm's fairy tale of this name. In the Siebenbürgen version of this tale,[16] two lice and two mice (four animals!) are yoked to a wagon in which a bear, a wolf, a fox, and a crab (four animals!), and an egg, a sewing needle, a stickpin, and a millstone (four objects!) are driving to the funeral of a chicken. When a rude innkeeper turns the company away, the wolf and the fox break into the innkeeper's stables, the crab takes its place in the water barrel, the egg in the embers, the needle in the easy chair, the stickpin in the handkerchief, and the millstone over the front door, which in the end strikes dead the fleeing innkeeper, who has been tormented by the others. To top everything off, the cock, the mate of the dead chicken, shouts over him, "Serves him right!" This "pack of no-goods" in spite of its misdeeds has the complete sympathy of the listener on its side, since it was only villainous toward the arch-villain himself. We are reminded in this respect of the nature spirit Mercurius as venerated by the alchemists, of whom they said that he was "good toward the good and evil toward the evil."[17] One might suspect that this pack of animals also fre-quently runs up a bill without paying, as doubtless our Bremen town musicians do as well. They do this out of a natural right they possess in the face of the miserliness of greedy humans.

But let us look at our four animals one by one. The leader of the company and the originator of the idea of becoming a town musician in Bremen is the donkey. In Greco-Roman antiquity, this animal belonged to the entourage of the god Dionysus (he is the mount of old Silenus), and in the famous novel *The Golden Ass* by Apuleius, he is used as the symbol of sexual lust and Dio-nysian uninhibitedness. He also was connected with the phallic fertility god Priapus. In ancient Egypt the donkey was an animal connected with the god Seth, who murdered Osiris and who rep-resented the epitome of murderous brutality and emotionality. Astrologically he was considered to be connected with Saturn, whose turgid melancholy and depths of suffering he shared. Be-cause Saturn was often considered in late antiquity to be the god of the Jews (and frequently for that reason of the early Christians also), the donkey also became a symbol of the Old Testament Father God.[18] He embodied something like the hidden, dark as-pect of God. In the Old Testament story of Balaam, as is well known, the ass, Balaam's mount, suddenly begins to talk and to declare the will of God. Thus he became a proclaimer of Yah-weh's will. In addition, the ox and the donkey are often interpre-ted in the pictures of the birth of Christ as the gods of the Old and New Testaments. Because Christ rode into Jerusalem on a donkey and her foal (Matthew 21:2–7, John 12:15), in the Middle Ages the donkey acquired a high symbolic significance. After all he is the bearer of the "new God." Saint Ambrose says the fol-lowing:[19]

It was not because of outer appearances that it pleased the Lord of the World to have himself borne on the back of a female ass, but rather to bestraddle our inmost heart within the protectedness of mystery. He desires to establish himself as a mystical rider among the secret forces of the soul, as though in the body to guide the steps of the soul through divine influence, to curb the unruly flesh and thus to rule the tamed passions of the nations. Happy are those who have accepted such a rider in their inmost being.

In the Middle Ages, as the Christian mass acquired an ever more elevated and esthetically perfected form, there arose among the people a compensatory need to serve God also with their more primitive side. This led to the so-called Feast of Asses or Feast of the Interment of Hallelujah, at Easter time. At that time a child pope was elected, a little boy who walked around sprinkling holy water. The priest and congregation got drunk on the wine of the mass, played ball in church, and sang:[20]

Orientis partibus
Adventavit Asinus
pulcher et fortissimus

From the furthest Eastern clime
Came the Ass in olden time
Comely, sturdy for the road,
Fit to bear a heavy load.

Then came a French refrain:

Hez, Sire, Asnes car chantez
belle bouche car rechigner
vous aurez du foin assez
et de l'avoine a planter

Sing then loudly, master Ass,
Let the tempting tidbit pass:
You shall have no lack of hay
And of oats find good supply.

121

The last of nine verses goes:

Amen dicas Asine
[hic genuflectabur]
iam satur de gramine
Amen, amen itera
Aspernare vetera [?]

Say Amen, Amen, good ass.
[here a genuflection is made]
Now you've had your fill of grass;
Ancient paths are left behind [?]:
Sing Amen with gladsome mind.

Each hallelujah was now replaced by braying "hee-haw" like a donkey. Because of the excesses that occurred at many such feasts, they were eventually prohibited by the Curia. In my view, however, it is a pity that these feasts no longer take place, because this leads to an unhealthy repression of the more primitive religious nature within us. In this regard Jung said, "One cannot understand modern man without knowing about his longing for Nietzsche's Dionysus experience as a counterbalance to the all too rational and Apollonian quality of our technical age."

The medieval Feast of Asses was an attempt to counteract this development toward a one-sided Apollonianism in Christianity. It was precisely this that the donkey as Christ's mount was an ideal symbol for,[21] since it does not symbolize an enemy of Christ but rather a supportive instinctive basis for the Christ symbol that is its master. Indeed the profane, the ecstatic, the animal-instinctive, and the world of emotions are all elements that belonged to the original religious sphere of humanity and cannot be sublimated away without a certain "loss of soul." For what reason the Dionysian religious longing of modern people is leading them today into a more widespread use of narcotics I hardly need to discuss here. The medieval Feast of Asses was a meaningful inclusion of this aspect in Christian worship. We now can also understand our donkey's inclination toward the musical calling. Music has ever associated with Dionysius and the world of emotional expression and religious passion.[22]

In the Grimm's fairy tale "The Donkey," the hero is an enchanted prince, and this donkey is also described as a gifted lute player, who through his playing wins a royal bride. This fairy tale is derived from a poem of the fourteenth century called "Asinarius." In medieval woodcuts and miniatures, one often sees depictions of a donkey playing the lyre. A music-playing donkey is one of the many "impossible things." That is why we have sayings in German like: "The donkey will play the lute" or "What is the donkey doing with the bagpipes?" or "The donkey who cannot play the lute must carry the sack to the mill." In Czechoslovakia there is the saying "He understands as much about that as a donkey does about a harp or a hen about beer." In Poland, we find, "It is futile to force a donkey to play the lute." So what happens in our fairy tale is a real miracle!

The next animal to join the donkey is an old dog, whom his master no longer wants to feed. So we have a dog who has gone to the dogs. This animal also is a symbol of rich and subtle symbolic meaning. Probably the dog was the first wild animal ever to join man as a friend and companion.[23] Thus for us he has always been a symbol of emotional loyalty and devotion.[24] From time immemorial the dog has done us great service with his keen nose; for that reason he also embodies the intuitive element, the "flair" of the intuitive capability of the unconscious, which often seems far superior to our consciousness. Like the donkey, he has a double aspect of good and evil in mythology. On the one hand, he is seen as godless and immoral; hence the word "dog" as an insult. But then again he is seen as the "hunter of souls," who drives errant sheep back to the divine Shepherd. (One might also think of Francis Thompson's "Hound of Heaven"!)

In very many religions, the dog appears as the guide to the land of the dead, and in Egypt it was the jackal-headed god Anubis who brought about the resurrection of his father Osiris.

Therefore, the entire mummification ritual was placed under the protection of this god. Because of the dog's relationship to the beyond, there are also in many places folktales about ghost hounds, dark wraithlike figures like the "hound of the Baskervilles." They always either harry to his death some individual who has committed evil, or else protect the offspring of one who has died. Good ghost hounds often bring a cure, and in ancient Greece the dog was also one of the most frequently manifested forms of the god of healing, Asclepius. In many regions today, people still believe that a dog's lick can cure. *Langue de chien sert de médecin* (A dog's tongue serves as medicine), say the French.

On the other side, the black poodle in *Faust* embodies the devil, and the dog is also regarded as a witch's creature. These are survivals of the hellhound Cerberus. The hell of the Germanic peoples was also guarded by the dog Garm, just as for many other peoples of the earth the entrance to the beyond is protected by dogs. In Christian times, a dog accompanied St. Rochus on his pilgrimage, and thus this saint remains today the patron of dogs. According to other versions, this role belongs to St. Hubert, who cured rabies. In old icons, even St. Christopher sometimes has a dog's head.

The next animal to join our concert band is a cat, concerning whom the donkey makes the remark that she is especially expert at serenades. With the female cat, the world of feminine deities enters the circle of the musicians. According to the ancient Germanic peoples, cats drew the chariot of the goddess Freyja.[25] In Egypt, the cat goddess Bast or Bastet was highly venerated. A holiday of joyful abandon, sexual license, and musical festivities for the people was dedicated to her. She was in part identical with Isis, as well as with the gentle manifestation of the lion goddesses Sekhmet and Tefnut.[26] In Egypt a tomcat helps the sun god Re in the underworld against the sinister serpent Apep.[27] The eyes of the cat were often likened to the moon.[28] Thus later in Greece, the Egyptian Bastet was equated with the goddess of the moon and the hunt, Artemis. The female cat was considered extraordinarily hard to kill; "she goes on and on," as an old Egyptian inscription says. We also say she has seven or nine lives. In other mythological contexts, the female cat is considered a seer.[29] The Egyptian name Mau means both "female cat" and "to see." Her body is used in many magical preparations to heal the eyes. Thus the goddess of truth was also called Bastet. She also had all kinds of healing effects against snake venom and other poisons, as well as against blindness. She was the great huntress who could even slay the devil's mouse. Because of her avid addiction to grooming, she also was considered a symbol of purity. She was capable of discovering and driving away anything evil, which is why, in China, cat talismans were made for the protection of houses.

In her dark form, she was an animal of the devil, of witches, and of black magic. Especially black cats play this role, as is well known. And not least, she was also a musician; Isis' sistrum was associated with her. In Christian times in Aix-en-Provence on the festival of Corpus Christi, a cat was ceremonially burned as an analogy for Christ. It was thought that at the time Christ was born, a cat gave birth in the same stall. Thus the female cat became parallel to Christ himself, something like his animal shadow.[30]

The last to join our group is a cock. He too is a being of the highest significance. In the Germanic world, he was principally an instigator of battle. The cock in the world tree is called Vissöfnir, "he who harries from the tree." He corresponds to the dwarf "Awakener of the People" and is at once a giver of warning, a spy, and a harbinger of light. Thus Hamlet says, "I have heard / The cock that is the trumpet of the morn, / Doth with his lofty and shrill-sounding throat / Awake the god of day; and, at his warning, / Whether in sea or fire, in earth or air, / The extravagant and erring spirit hies / to his confine." He is nonetheless also an animal from the threshold of the underworld, as the brown cock of Hel and as the watchman of heaven and Heimdall. Also in the fairy tale "Mother Holle," he stands on the threshold of the beyond when he welcomes one back into the upper world as a golden girl but calls the other girl dirty. Because he is the harbinger of day and the day brings everything to light, he is also the harbinger of truth and the symbol of inner conscience. Thus Peter became aware of his betrayal of Jesus when the cock crowed three times and began to cry. Thus the cock—who was also associated with the god of the threshold Janus (who gives his name, connected with *ianua* [Latin, "door"] to the month January)— became the animal of Peter, the gatekeeper of heaven. And yes, the cock too was considered an allegorical representation of Christ. Thus, for example, Prudentius sings:

> *Crowing, the cock, day's harbinger,*
> *Loudly proclaims approaching light,*
> *Wakes in our hearts the call of Christ*
> *And spurs us on to real life.*

And a hymn of St. Ambrose praises the cock's crow as "the wanderer's beacon. It wakes the star of day that drives away the darkness. Evildoers abandon their wicked ways, the sailor finds new courage, . . . the sick feel relief, . . . sinners gain faith." In medieval paintings the Jesus child is often portrayed, riding on a white cock, as the God of the "new light." A white cock was considered auspicious. Thus he has found his place on our church towers as a repeller of demons.

In Islamic legend, Muhammad, when he ascends to heaven, sees four angels standing before God's throne: a cock, a man, a lion, and a vulture. The lion prays for the quadrupeds, the vulture for the birds, the man for the children of Adam; but the cock was so huge that his feet reached down to the abyss of the seventh earth. Of it, it is said, "God gave this angel the form of a cock, because without him we would not know the hour of prayer, for he sings God's praises in each of these hours and at the same time he cries out, 'Give thought to God, O, you thoughtless ones!' And the cocks of earth hear him and they too cry out, and when he stops, they are still."[31]

In antiquity the cock was the animal of Athene. The Greek word for cock, *alektryon,* means "shining one" or again "battleworthy one" or "belligerent one." Thus he was considered a symbol of combativeness as well as of sexual virility. The proud bearing of the cock also drew upon him the projection of blatant exaggeration of emotions; hence his appearance in Edmond Rostand's *Chantecler* as a somewhat quixotic knight. In the Chinese oracular text, the *I Ching,* at the end of chapter 61, "Inner Truth," we find: "The cock is dependable. It crows at dawn. But it cannot itself fly to heaven. It just crows. A man may count on mere words to awaken faith. This may succeed now and then, but if persisted in, it will have bad consequences."[32] Here the cock's crow becomes a symbol of emotional pathos. In our story too, he only crows. He does not fight like the three other animals. But with his "Serves you right!" in the fairy tale "A Pack of No-Goods," as in Mother Holle, he proclaims what amounts to "the moral of the story."

If we try to relate the four animals with the basic functions of human consciousness, then the donkey would be the thinker, since he plans the animals' entire rescue. The dog with his keen nose would be intuition; the cat with her realistic approach would be sensation; and the cock would be feeling. The concert, the harmonious unison of these four, expresses wholeness.

That the thought that occurs to the animals is to become street musicians is of course a joke—we have only to think of their particular gifts of voice. But there is something deeper behind this. Music has always been a religious means for man of driving away evil thoughts and evil spirits. Thus Saul's melancholy and the evil spirit that had taken hold of him yield before David's harp playing. As late as in the Middle Ages, music was recommended as a means to cure Tristitia. We find something similar in the *I Ching,* referred to just above (chapter 59): "Religious forces are needed to overcome the egotism that divides men. The common celebration of the great sacrificial feasts . . . was the means employed by the great rulers to unite men. The sacred music and the splendor of the ceremonies aroused a strong tide of emotion that was shared by all hearts in unison, and that awakened a consciousness of the common origin of all creatures. In this way disunity was overcome and rigidity dissolved."[33] (It should be noted that egotism was the sin of humanity that brought the ani-mals in our story into peril of death.) In the chapter "Enthusi-asm" (chapter 16) of the same book, we read: "When, at the beginning of summer, thunder . . . comes rushing forth from the earth again, and the first thunderstorm refreshes nature, a prolonged state of tension is resolved. Joy and relief make them-selves felt. So, too, music has power to ease tension within the heart and to loosen the grip of obscure emotions. The enthusiasm of the heart expresses itself involuntarily in a burst of song, in dance and rhythmic movement of the body. From immemorial times the inspiring effect of the invisible sound that moves all hearts and draws them together, has mystified mankind. . . . Music was looked upon as something serious and holy, designed to purify the feelings of men. It fell to music . . . to construct a bridge to the world of the unseen."[34]

In our own culture too, music was associated both with Apollo and Dionysus, and once upon a time Orpheus brought back the paradisiacal peace between animals and humans. Thus our four musicians stand with the great peace-bringing deities, and this sheds a new light on their healing, whole-making function, even if it comes down to no more than the love-drunk nocturnal me-owing of the cat, the yapping of the dog, the strange and mon-strous braying of the donkey, and the shattering cry of the cock. They are dark but beneficial gods of the psychic depths; they alone can deal with the problem of evil. As can be shown, all the wise saws about fairy tales are reversible except for one: whoever allies himself with helpful animals and remains true to them is always victorious. That is the only rule without exception.[35]

And now let us turn our attention to the actual nocturnal drama. The thieves' projections of their own evil are piled upon their invisible partners, and it is ultimately from their own pro-jected evil that they flee. They fantasize about evil people, and in their panic they fail to recognize the completely harmless domes-tic animals. In many versions the good animals themselves fall into panic. When a raindrop falls on a cabbage leaf or a chair creaks, the cat screams, "The sky is falling,"[36] and they all tear off. "From that time," runs the tale, "they couldn't put up with the cat." So then, it was touch and go as to who was terrorizing whom. However, in the Bremen musician version, it all works out for the best, and it is the villains who are put to flight. That it is only a small thing that decides this is also made clear in variants in which the animals are riding on a wagon made from paper and drawn by lice and mice—as a result of which we are compelled to visualize them as very tiny. Even when certain objects accompany them on their ride, it is for the most part an egg and a needle, with a millstone as the only large object; and it is these little things that put the villain to flight or even harry him to his death.

We can speak literally here of the "malice of the object," of those tricky little accidents behind which, when they strike us, we can usually discover a false neurotic attitude toward reality in ourselves. It is then as though our unconscious complexes had reached out and taken possession of matter in the outside world and persecuted us in the shape of this malice of the object. The collar button rolls under the dresser, the car key creeps into the lining of our pocket, the battery is suddenly dead, and so on. In a bad case, a deadly accident can even come out of this, for example, through a wasp stinging the face of a person driving a car. Jung called this behaving of objects as though they were part of our inner world and had their meaningful place in it "synchronicity phenomena." This is a problem with profound ramifications, which I cannot pursue further here. But such things have always been familiar to the magical frame of mind. In these cases, we say, "But it is surely no coincidence that . . . !" for the very reason that such accidents fit all too meaningfully into the inner psychic life situation of the victim.

Lice essentially symbolize the demonic, autonomous thoughts that inhabit our heads. Mice, on the other hand, symbolize sexual and other "gnawing" fantasies that keep us awake at night; also guilt feelings, obsessive worries, and the like. In many variants our musicians ride in the company of these small but mighty animals, as though on their wagon. In these versions, as in others as well, sometimes there are more than four animals. As a result of this, the nocturnal spectacle becomes a long chain reaction of comical situations. In fact it is for the sake of prolonging this chain reaction that the animals and objects are multiplied in this way. The accent then lies not so much on four or eight as symbols of wholeness as on the endless concatenation of little things by which ultimately the evil principle is conquered. These versions seem, however, to be of later origin and therefore less significant than the original groups of four or eight.

Finally, as concerns the town of Bremen, it must share the honor of being the destination of these animal gods with Amsterdam, Brussels, and Rome. But only the people of Bremen seemed to have grasped how significant this story is, for they chose the four as protectors of their city. In the oldest version of the story, though, Rome was the destination of the animals, where the cock wanted to become pope and the cat wanted to have her tail gilded. That the religious center of medieval Christendom was the destination, points clearly to the deeper religious meaning of the seemingly so harmless little animal tale.

Notes

1. Laurens van der Post, *The Heart of the Hunter* (London, 1961), pp. 169f.

2. Cf. C. G. Jung, K. Kerényi, and P. Radin, "On the Psychology of the Trickster Figure," in cw 9/i, pp. 255–72.

3. Given in G. Bolte and J. Polivka, *Anmerkungen zu den Kinder- und Hausmärchen der Brüder Grimm* (Leipzig, 1913–32), vol. 1, pp. 237ff.

4. Ibid., p. 255.

5. In the Hanover, Sauerland, and Siebenbürgen versions; ibid., p. 23.

6. Cf. K. Sälzle, *Tier und Mensch, Gottheit und Dämon* (Animal and Human, Deity and Demon) (Munich, Basel, Vienna, 1964), pp. 217ff.

7. Cf. Martin Ninck, *Wodan und germanischer Schicksalsglaube* (Wotan and the Germanic Belief in Fate) (Jena, 1933), p. 50.

8. Cf. Bolte and Polivka, *Anmerkungen,* vol. 1, p. 375.

9. Ibid., pp. 257ff.

10. Cf. also C. G. Jung, *Memories, Dreams, Reflections.*

11. Cf. Hans Sachs, *Fabeln und Schwänke* (Fables and Droll Tales), ed. Goetze and Drescher, vol. 5, p. 211, N. 735, cited in Bolte and Polivka, *Anmerkungen,* p. 238. There we have a female cat, an ox, a horse, and a rooster.

12. Cf. C. G. Jung, *Memories, Dreams, Reflections,* p. 337.

13. Ibid., p. 336.

14. Ibid., p. 338.

15. Ibid., p. 339.

16. Bolte and Polivka, *Anmerkungen,* vol. 1, pp. 75ff.

17. Cf. C. G. Jung, *Symbolik des Geistes* (Zurich: Rascher, 1948), p. 118; see also C. G. Jung, cw 13, para. 267, p. 217.

18. As also shown by the so-called Cross of Scorn on Palatine Hill.

19. In Luc., lib. IX: 9–14, cited in D. Forstner, *Die Welt der Symbole* (The World of Symbols) (Tryolia Verlag, 1961), p. 639.

20. Cf. "On the Psychology of the Trickster Figure," in cw 9/i, p. 258. The English translation of the verses is by A. S. B. Glover, ibid., p. 259.

21. Forstner, *Die Welt der Symbole,* p. 371.

22. In medieval times the wild ass was considered a symbol both of the devil and of the religious hermit going his solitary way (ibid., p. 371). Because, unlike his rider, Balaam's ass saw the angel of God who was barring the way, the ass is also considered spiritually clairvoyant.

23. Cf. K. Lorenz, *Wie der Mensch auf den Hund kam* (How People Went to the Dogs), passim.

24. Cf. Forstner, *Die Welt der Symbole,* p. 388.

25. Cf. also the Austrian fairy tale "Die weissen Katzern," in *Märchen aus dem Donaulande* (The White Female Kitten; Fairy Tales from the Danube Valley), in *Die Märchen der Weltliteratur.*

26. Cf. Patricia Dale Green, *Cult of the Cat* (London: Heinemann, 1963), pp. 2ff.

27. Ibid., p. 8.

28. Ibid., p. 13.

29. Ibid., p. 21.

30. Ibid., pp. 29, 34, 44, 48, 51ff.

31. Cf. M. Grünbaum, *Neue Beiträge zur semitischen Sagenkunde* (New Essays on Semitic Mythology) (Leiden, 1893), p. 284.

32. Trans. C. F. Baynes (Princeton: Bollingen Foundation, Princeton University Press, 1967), p. 239.

33. Ibid., pp. 227f.

34. Ibid., pp. 68f.

35. Cf. M.-L. von Franz, "The Problem of Evil in Fairy Tales," in this volume.

36. Bolte and Polivka, *Anmerkungen,* vol. 1, p. 237.

THE COSMIC MAN

As Image of the Goal of the Individuation Process and Human Development

■■
■■

IN THE DEPTH PSYCHOLOGY of C. G. Jung, which is primarily concerned with the destiny of the individual, we look at individual lives of a historical time span so short that they can hardly give us any information about the evolution of humanity as a whole, an evolution concerning which we know that, if it exists at all, it would extend over millennia. Nonetheless, let us consider to begin with what we *can* learn from individuals; for in their case a development indubitably does take place. Carl Jung called this development the individuation process. One aspect of it is an unconscious process, a growing up, a maturation, and a movement toward death. At first sight, this says nothing more than that from an acorn an oak develops, from a calf a cow, from a child an old person; but there is another aspect—and only this is individuation in the strict sense of the word—a process of developing consciousness, which, continually broadening its frame of reference, works toward the conscious realization and active fulfillment of an original fundamental wholeness. This appears already as potential wholeness in early childhood in the form of symbols in dreams and fantasies which manifest again and again in periods of transformation such as puberty, the midlife period, and in times of crisis. In the first part of his work *Psychology and Alchemy*,[1] Jung gave a detailed exposition of such a process based on the dreams of a young man. He particularly elucidated the symbol of the mandala, which repeatedly recurred in the dreams, as an indication of wholeness seeking to actualize itself.[2] What we seem to be dealing with here is a goal-seeking process in the psyche that is to a great extent independent of external conditions.[3] The goal itself is expressed by the unconscious in symbols, which cannot be distinguished from an image of the divine. The most important of these are the mandala, the cosmic divine man, the divine child, the flower, the diamond body or stone *(lapis philosophorum)*, Christ, Buddha, Khidr, Adam Kadmon, and others. Jung says:

> We can hardly escape the feeling that the unconscious process moves spiral-wise round a centre, gradually getting closer, while the characteristics of the centre grow more and more distinct. Or perhaps we could put it the other way round and say that the centre—itself virtually unknowable—acts like a magnet on the disparate materials and processes of the unconscious and gradually captures them as in a crystal lattice. . . . Indeed, it seems as if all the personal entanglements and dramatic changes of fortune that make up the intensity of the life were nothing but hesitations, timid shrinkings, almost like petty complications and meticulous excuses for not facing the finality of this strange and uncanny process of crystallization.[4]

The most important phases of the individuation process are the integration of the shadow, that is, the "dark" side of the personality, which belongs to the wholeness but is denied or overlooked by consciousness; making conscious the opposite-sex components, which Jung called the animus (in a woman) and the anima (in a man); and finally, experiencing the Self and developing a relationship with the Self, the innermost core of the psyche.

Although, as mentioned above, the image of the goal of this process already appears in products of the unconscious in early childhood, what we have here is not a cyclical process in which the end becomes the beginning, but rather a spiral; for the end lies on a higher level of consciousness.[5] Thus along with the cyclical aspect a progressive development takes place, and—at least in the individual—we see nature striving for an irreversible progression toward expanded consciousness. But does this process also play a role in human history? Or does it just repeat again and again in an equivalent and similar fashion in certain outstanding individuals of all times?

We have three questions before us:

1. Is the unquestionable individuation of, say, a Lao-tzu less than that of a modern person?

2. If not, does the number of individuated people gradually increase by comparison with earlier periods?

3. Does the symbol of the Self change in accordance with a linear form of development in which it is possible to discern an evolution of humanity, at least in the sense of a change if not in the sense of a progression?

The first question, in my view, can only be answered in terms of our subjective sense of the matter, and in my opinion, with a no. For by very definition, being individuated is something unique and thus not subject to comparison. Individuation is not commensurate with a schema of progressive increase. On the other hand, the second and third questions, as we shall see, are so closely intertwined that we are obliged to consider them as one.

To this end, I should like to focus as an example on a particular symbol of the Self, that is, of the goal of the individuation process in individuals—the symbol of the "cosmic man."

The Cosmos as the Form of a Divine Primordial Man

According to numerous creation myths of the most various peoples, the universe arose from the scattered parts of a gigantic

135

human figure. For the Germanic peoples, this was the giant Ymir:

> *From Ymir's flesh was the earth created,*
> *From his bones the mountains,*
> *The heavens from the skull of the snow-cold giant,*
> *The sea-surge from his blood.*[6]

In China, it was the primordial figure of the divine man P'an Ku who made the universe. *P'an* means "eggshell" and "fasten"; *Ku* means "undeveloped," "unilluminated," that is, "embryo."[7] When P'an Ku cried, the Yellow River and the Yangtse Kiang were created; when he breathed, the wind blew; when he spoke, the thunder rolled; as he looked around him, lightning arose. When he died, the five holy mountains of China originated from his body: from the head, the T'ai Mountain in the east; from his trunk, the Sung Mountain in the middle; his right arm became Heng in the north; his left, Heng in the south; his feet became the Hua Mountain in the west. From his eyes came the sun and the moon. Later he was reborn in a miraculous manner to a pure virgin, "the holy mother of the first cause," as a sage and bringer of culture.

A similar notion is found in the ancient Indian tradition. There the cosmic ancestor and the first to die is Yama, who later in the Upanishads is called Purusha, which simply means "man" or "person," and represents the individual as well as the cosmic self that dwells in all things.[8] According to the *Rigveda* (X, 19), the four castes arose from the body parts of the "thousand-headed" Purusha;[9] and when he was sacrificed by the gods, the moon arose from his mind; from his eye, the sun; from his mouth, Indra and Agni; from his navel, space; and from his head, heaven. The Purusha was thousand-headed, thousand-eyed, thousand-footed. He held the earth enclosed in his embrace and towered beyond measurable space. He is everything that was and will be. A quarter of him is all beings; three-quarters of him is that which is immortal in heaven. He is hermaphroditic and gave birth from himself to the first female being *(viraj)*.[10] "Verily, he is the inner self of all things."[11]

In ancient Iran, corresponding to Purusha was the cosmic giant Gayomart. The name comes from *gayo,* "eternal life," and *maretan,* "mortal human life." He is the body or seed of light in the good god Ohrmazd, the first priest king, born at the center of the cosmos. He was murdered in the primordial time by the evil principle, Ahriman. At that time the eight metals flowed from his body, and from the gold of his soul essence, which fell on the earth, and his luminous seed sprouted the rhubarb stalk from which the first human couple originated.[12] Water comes from his tears, the plants from his hair, the sacred cow from his right hand, and fire from his mind.

Before we go on to further examples, let us pause at this point to consider this aspect of the motif from a psychological point of view.

The dissolution of the great man into the universe, or his entry into the universe, points to an utterly primordial, *preconscious process of projection,* which results in the arising of a condition indicated to be the original state of humanity by anthropologists and researchers into individual history. This is the state—in the archaic man as well as the child of any period—of absolute *participation mystique* with the surrounding world. Jung called this condition "archaic identity."[13] In it, there is as yet no ego consciousness and no distinction at all between subject and object, I and self. It is an "all one." If anything individual is ever to arise out of this inchoate whole, first it must, in a preconscious projection process, allow all its individual components to emerge from it or it must dissolve into them, so that afterward they can become conscious individually;[14] otherwise they would remain forever part of an undifferentiated amalgam. In other words, it is as though there existed in the unconscious a completely ungraspable inchoate unity which disintegrated prior to the formation of ego consciousness so that through this process the ego and the other complexes of the individual's psychic makeup can emerge individually. This makes it possible for them, much later, gradually to coalesce again into a conscious unity.

The original archaic identity, however, is not just something that must be overcome in the course of development because in its negative aspect it is the basis for all mass suggestion and psychic infection; for it is also the archetypal precondition of a possible social attitude in people as it has found supreme expression, for example, in Christian brotherly love or Buddhist universal compassion.[15] It is also not only the precondition for projection, but also the basis for its more conscious form: in one aspect, the passive act of empathy with others; in the other, the active act of judgment through which one delimits oneself from others.[16] But on this is based every deliberate, conscious relationship with one's fellow human beings that we are capable of. Thus the archetypal symbol of the Great Man or Anthropos embodies the inborn, preconscious potential to relate individually to one's fellows and to humanity in general. On the unconscious level, it brings about group identity or instinctive group solidarity; on a higher level, it makes possible a sophisticated social attitude toward one's fellows. In this sense, the Anthropos is also a symbol of love in the broadest sense of the word, that is, in the sense of a potential for understanding a fellow human being and for encountering him or her positively without identification. Therefore it is not surprising that the Anthropos symbol is often described mythologically as the "Self" of a people or even of humanity as a whole.

The Primordial Man as the "Self" of a People or of Humanity as a Whole

As we have already seen, the four castes arose from the Indian Purusha. In Jewish legend also, Adam is sometimes described as a cosmic giant. He covered the entire surface of the earth, and God gathered red, black, white, and yellow dust from the four corners of the world in order to form him. According to other versions, Adam was composed from eight parts of the world.[17]

Like the Indian Purusha, he too was androgynous, and according to later Kabbalistic tradition (that of Isaac Luria), all the souls of human beings and spirits were contained in him. Adam's soul was "like the wick of a lamp, twisted together from many threads," that is, plaited from the six hundred thousand souls of all beings.[18]

In these versions, the cosmic primordial man appears as a symbol for the Self of a collective.[19] We are dealing here with an archaic notion, which is to be found in many places. As Mircea Eliade has shown, in most primitive mythologies and religions, all earthly things—animal species, implements, and so forth—possess their archetypal image in the beyond,[20] and this holds for man too. That is to say, humanity as a whole has something like a collective primordial image of its being existing in the beyond (that is, psychologically speaking, in the collective unconscious). This "protanthropos" in the beyond is a kind of unconscious "group spirit," from which all individuals have their being. This meaning of the Anthropos as collective soul also explains why the Jewish tradition of the Great Man as the first manifestation of the unknowable God of the Creation—the Adam Kadmon of the Kabbalists—not only incorporates in his body the ten Sefirot, but also why his body is composed, in a certain sense, of the Ten Commandments of the Torah. At the same time, as Gershom Scholem says, he is the true "mystery of faith" or the "inner man" and the symbol of God appearing in man.[21] The "soul of the people" or its Self manifests on this level exclusively in the religious traditions, and the individual is only connected with the inner man and his own Self, which does not yet seem to possess any individual features, only through the body of religious traditions. They alone express the spiritual and eternal aspects of his being. The individual aspect of the Self, by contrast, in general remained unconscious. As Helmuth Jakobsohn showed,[22] for example, the Egyptian of the Old Kingdom lived entirely within the collective norms, with which his consciousness was fully identified. Only after death did his own individuality emerge, in the form of the so-called *ba* bird or as a star.[23] This would mean that at that time the entire process of development of consciousness, which today we call individuation, remained projected onto the after-death state and only existed as a hope for the future, which one could not accede to in the here and now. Living in the religious collective norm, however, is no different from other instinctive patterns of human behavior, which we possess, just as the animal species do, as an inborn way of life. That is why the symbol of the Anthropos in many myths even has marked animal aspects.

The Animal Aspect of the Primordial Man

The Indian Purusha appears, for example, as the sacrificial horse, from which the world is engendered, and the Iranian Gayomart is wrapped in an animal skin. P'an Ku has horns and according to many versions had a dragon's head and a serpent's body;[24] and Adam, according to certain rabbinical traditions, had a tail.

This animal nature of the primordial man, hinted at in many places, certainly points, on the one hand, to our own origin and our kinship with the animal world, but also to the fact that the primordial man symbolizes the world of drives and instincts within us. This area of our psyche is, however, by no means something simple, but is revealed, as Jung states, "on the primitive level as a complicated interplay of physiological facts, taboos, rites, class-systems, and tribal lore, which impose a restrictive form on the instinct from the beginning, preconsciously, and make it serve a higher purpose."[25]

This mental regulatory system for the world of instinctual drives is very much of the actual essence of religion. However, on a higher level it may happen that the unity of the instinctual drive with its mental form disintegrates, and then the religious teachings contaminate the drive instead of regulating it. Thus a split is produced that is usually directed toward a further development of consciousness. Then, initially, man, in his stupidity and ill will, degenerates and falls into a state of conflict with his original nature; indeed he even forgets his origin. As a result of this, then, the archetype of the original whole man, of the Anthropos, is constellated, for in the symbol of the "great man" the higher and lower are once again unified in the Creation.[26] As we shall see, this is now once again a current problem in our culture.

In our consideration of the aspects of the Protanthropos mentioned so far, we plainly see features that identify him as the origin of human development, an origin to which humanity clearly must repeatedly return in order not to lose itself, but we do not recognize anything that might indicate an evolution of humanity. However, the symbol has still other features, which it now behooves us to look into.

The Quaternary Structure of the Protanthropos

As we have seen, the primordial man often has a striking association with the number four. From the Purusha arose the four castes, from P'an Ku the four world-mountains and their midpoint, and Adam was made of dust from the four or eight corners of the world.[27] Adam Kadmon manifested on four levels of being.[28] In late antiquity and in alchemy, there were extensive speculations connected with the four letters in the name Adam, which were also linked with the Tetragrammaton, YHVH.[29] Pico della Mirandola says very eloquently about this Adam:

> In man at his birth, the Father placed all possible capacities for development and the seeds of the many forms of life. What each one develops will . . . bear fruit for himself: if he cultivates the vegetative, he will become a plant; if he cultivates only the animal, then he will become an animal; if he cultivates reason, he will become a celestial being; if he cultivates the spirit, he will become an angel and even God's son. However, if not content with any lot of created beings, he withdraws into the center of unity in himself, then, one with the spirit of God, in the solitary darkness of the Father, . . . he is ahead of them all.[30]

In certain apocryphal and Islamic traditions, Adam appears as part of a matrimonial quaternity as the spouse of Eve, on one hand, and as Adam Secundus, the spouse of Sophia Mary (or the Church), on the other.[31] In the symbol of Christ, the second Adam himself, the quaternity appears again in the form of the tetramorph as well as in the image of the Cross.[32]

According to the Jungian view, a quarternary structure of an unconscious content in principle indicates the possibility of its becoming conscious, being after all the archetypal foundation of the four orienting functions of our consciousness: thinking, feeling, perception, and intuition. From the psychological point of view, the quaternary structure of the primordial man would then mean that the image of the Anthropos *contains the possibility of a progressive development of human consciousness, an inner dynamic,* which drives in the direction of a broadening of consciousness.

This becomes still clearer through another motif, which is found in many Protanthropos myths. This is the motif of a primordial man submerged in darkness or dismembered and of his necessary "regathering" and return to the light.

P'an Ku, after his first death, is reborn as a bringer of culture. The Purusha lives on in each individual human being as an eternal inner person, and, as it is said, "whoever knows him is released from death and all degradation." From Gayomart springs a lineage of great sages and cultural innovators who lead humanity. And not least of all, over the grave of the first Adam stands the cross of Christ, Adam Secundus. And this motif is much more richly elaborated still in Manichaeism,[33] by the Mandaeans,[34] in Gnosticism and its continuations, and in the philosophy of alchemy.

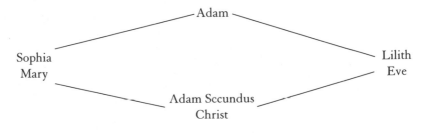

In these traditions a great dramatic myth portrays the primordial man of light, who is identical with the godhead and dwells in a transcendental pleroma. He is conquered by the forces of evil or is won over by the astral powers, the archons, and then falls, sinks, or "flows," ending up broken in a thousand parts, dispersed in matter as sparks of light or as the "crucified world-soul," awaiting his redemption. This work of redemption is carried out either by an emissary of God or a chosen human being and consists of gathering the scattered parts of the great man, reuniting them, and sometimes bringing about their re-ascent to the pleroma. In a certain sense, the lot of the fallen man of light repeats the destiny of the disintegrated primordial giant, but on a higher level. This time it is no longer the utterly primordial preconscious wholeness that is projected into the universe but rather a much more individual and more human aspect of it. Nonetheless, this is still a process of preconscious projection, though it is now one that has moved much closer to consciousness and already contains within it the possibility of the regathering, that is, the withdrawal of the projection, which now falls to the human individual as a task. Here, however, the view of alchemy is distinct from that of official Christian doctrine.

The Christian projection, as Jung made clear, goes as far as the unknown in the human being, whereas the alchemical projection goes as far as the unknown in matter. "In the Christian projection the *descensus spiritus sancti* stops at the *living body* of the Chosen One, who is at once very man and very God, whereas in alchemy the descent goes right down into the darkness of inanimate matter whose nether regions, according to the Neopythagoreans, are ruled by evil." In accordance with this, the goal of the alchemist is not his own salvation through the grace of God, but the *liberation of God from the darkness of matter.* For that reason, the spirit that appears through the transformation is not "the son of man" but the *filius macrocosmi,* the stone.[35]

It is not possible within the framework of this article to give an account of all the impressive individual variants of this drama, which we can present only briefly in its main outlines. What is of importance for us is that here the idea prominently emerges of an evolution that corresponds to the development into consciousness of all humanity. This, however, can also be understood only as an inner psychic process in the individual, for each individual always encounters himself initially as a chaotic miscellany of hereditary components, a particle of a mass and the mass itself, which can reach unity only through becoming conscious. This comes about in part through the efforts of the ego, but at the same time an influence emanates from the unconscious center, from the Self, which makes this work possible.[36] This is reflected mythologically by the fact that frequently the man of light who has fallen into darkness not only regathers himself but also gathers the ones he has called and leads them back to the origin. Understanding this as an archetypal motif, it is clear that this means a growth toward further consciousness on the part of humanity, beginning with an increase in the number of those who devote themselves to their own individuation. For clearly this process can only take place in the present bearer of life, the individual human being.

Nonetheless, this could still also be understood historically as a fragment of a greater cyclical process, if it were not part of a development, discernible over thousands of years, which Jung tried to delineate in *Aion* and "Answer to Job," and that we shall now look at more closely. This process is reflected in a transformation of the symbol of the Self, that is, in the image of the Anthropos.

The oldest historically visible religious systems of our cultural sphere seem to be dominated by a god or gods who, in terms of sheer superhuman power for good and evil, go beyond all human measure. They embody the fearsome mystery of creation as a *coincidentia oppositorum,* of which human beings are completely at the mercy but to which they relate in a devoted and uncritical fashion. In Egypt's Middle Kingdom and also in the Old Testament, a development begins to take shape in which a special human being not only incarnates the Anthropos but also, as such, after death gradually becomes greater than any of the many other gods. Whereas, for example, in ancient Egypt the god-king alone incarnated the sun god (Re) and in his postmortal form, as Osiris-Ba, progressed through many stages of transformation to become the supreme God, in the Middle Kingdom, this process, which illustrates a projected form of individuation, began also to be extended to certain noblemen surrounding the king. Finally in the late period, any person could go through this postmortal transformation into Osiris and thence into the supreme cosmic God. In the late period, this development came to be something that was not only hoped for after death, but in the Isis-Osiris mysteries (as we know of them from *The Golden Ass* of Apuleius) was experienced during life.

In Old Testament Judaism, it was at first only individuals like David or Job who began to suffer from the overpowering amoral problematic of the opposites in their image of God. Likewise in the Old Testament, the myth began to appear of a "man" or "son of man" who possessed a more conscious morality than Yahweh. According to Jung's view, this is the "lawyer" whom Job called upon: ". . . but mine eye poureth out tears unto God. O that one might plead for a man with God." This "lawyer" was none other than the wisdom of God, Sophia, which in the later writings of the Old Testament appeared as a feminine personification of the Anthropos archetype. Through her mediation, a new God-man was created on earth, incarnated in the historical figure of Christ. True, he embodied primarily the good side of God, while the dark side of God, Satan, "fell like a thunderbolt from heaven" and appeared over against Christ as an antagonist. Thus in Christianity the Anthropos was incarnated for the first time in a unique *historical* figure; and at the same time it was affirmed in connection with this process of incarnation that it would also extend to other people through the ongoing influence of the Holy Spirit. Indeed from that point onward Christ was also recognized as an "inner figure" in other individuals. In addition, the archetypal motif whereby the Anthropos embodies the soul of a people also reappeared in Christianity in the view of the Church being the body of Christ.

However, in the second millennium, the Anthropos symbol of Christ underwent a widespread decrease in effectiveness, because it only included the light-related and more conscious side of wholeness, though God apparently sought to become human in his entirety. Since only the light-related aspect of God was incarnated in Christ, already in early Christianity there arose the expectation of an *enantiodromia* in the form of the coming of the Antichrist, which was placed by the astrologers at the end of the Piscine age, that is, the current era. This attack of darkness is portrayed in the Apocalypse in a way that makes it seem almost to be a description of our time. However, after the outbreak of a period of general destruction, the author of Revelation saw a new human figure, a boy borne by a "woman crowned with twelve stars." Jung tells us that this is finally really a symbol of a unitive nature, one that epitomizes the individuation process as a *total* humanization of God in the empirical man.[37] "That higher and 'complete' *(teleios)* man," as Jung says, "is begotten by the 'unknown' father and born from Wisdom, and it is he who, in the figure of the *puer aeternus*—vultu mutabilis albus et ater ('of changeful countenance, both white and black," Horace, *Epistulae,* II, 2)—represents our totality, which transcends consciousness."[38] This figure of a *filius sapientiae,* foreseen by the author of the Apocalypse, was given form in a thousand variants by hermetic philosophy and alchemical speculation in their symbolism projected onto matter. This was their central interest. In begetting Christ, it is as though the higher, spiritual, masculine principle inclined itself to the lower, earthly, feminine principle, and accordingly, by way of compensation, the lower principle accommodated the higher one and produced a son figure, which was not an opposite to Christ, but rather a chthonic counterpart. In this is reflected a healing tendency, which is seeking to resolve the conflict of our present-day world and to heal our one-sided overemphasis on consciousness by restoring the bridge to the nature-related roots of the unconscious and thereby to the experienceable phenomenon of individuation. The dream of a modern graphic artist provides an illustration of how distant the image of the natural, integral Anthropos has become in our time from the officially worshiped figure of Christ.

In the dream, he goes to the Catholic Church. (He himself is a Protestant, but he often visits Catholic churches out of aesthetic interest.) A service is just in progress, so he discreetly takes a seat in one of the rear pews. Then a simply clothed, somewhat vagrant-looking, mysterious and strange man comes in and sits down quietly next to the dreamer. In spite of his unprepossessing quality, he is somehow numinous; and suddenly the dreamer realizes with deep emotion that this is Christ. He turns to him, but the stranger puts his finger on his mouth and smiles. Then the dreamer realizes with what shock and incredulity the praying congregation and the priest would react if he were to tell them that Christ is here.

So he remains quiet and smiles to the "stranger" as a sign of his secret agreement. This dream shows how the Anthropos is constellated today as an image of the Self—as a secret of the *individual:* any contact with a collective context would be harmful to him. Even the name Christ, which is derived from the language of the collective, is almost misleading, because it could lead to collective conscious associations. It is rather the "strange friend" of the individual who shows himself here, only hinting that he is the one who under other circumstances is worshiped as "Christ."

The dream of a forty-five-year-old woman exhibits a similar constellation. She dreamed that in the darkness of evening she entered her vacation house. The hall was dimly lit and entirely empty; only, on the stone floor there was a pile of straw, and on it, a male figure, dressed like a vagrant, of middle age. With deep emotion, she realized that this was "Christ." But his body was not made out of flesh and blood, but of brightly shining, glowing-hot metal. He said, "You could do me a favor and take a bowl of water and pour it over me *to damp down my radiance.*" She did this, the water steamed up with a hiss, and the body became dark metal, without losing its limberness or life. The stranger smiled and said softly, "Thank you."

This figure is a direct analogy to the Mercurius of the alchemists, a spirit emanating from the earth, who both shines brilliantly and glows hot, is heavier than metal and lighter than air.[39] This figure also wants to remain hidden and to damp down its brightness, in other words, remain a secret of the individual, that is, to the extent possible, not visible to the outside.

Today this archetype seems to be constellated in the collective unconscious to such an extent that, because it is not acknowledged, it results in the most bizarre possible possessions and projections. Nazism was already a kind of unconscious, and therefore destructively misguided, attempt at the realization of this content; now the same archetype haunts the background of the apparently rational movement masquerading as an economic theory that we know as Marxism. Not only does this movement also thrive on the eschatological expectation of a kingdom of peace realizable on earth, but the archetypal Anthropos appears in its theory projected on a group, the so-called "revolutionary class." As Robert Tucker demonstrated,[40] Karl Marx was actually seized by a religious myth: he saw human society split between the property owners and the propertyless workers. The former live in a state of self-alienation, but the victory of the latter betokens a reconquest of the Self.[41]

Humanity has lost itself in the production of possessions, and therefore for Marx the revolution is humanity's supreme act of self-realization, through which it can liberate and return to the "natural man" already idealized by Rousseau.[42] In the light of what we have said so far, it is not difficult for us to recognize the myth of the fallen man of light/Anthropos who must be liberated from the hands of *agnosia* (unconsciousness), the archons and evil worldly powers, whose image is projected today on the capitalists, counterrevolutionaries, imperialists, and revisionists. "For Marx," says Tucker, "the world revolution of the Communists is a kind of violent self-change on the part of man, in which man puts an end to his alienation, restores his lost harmony, and realizes himself as a human being."[43] Tucker rightly sees in this the projection of an inner problem onto external society. The goal, according to Marx, is "the complete essential unity of man with nature, the true resurrection of nature, the actualized naturalism of man and the actualized humanism of nature."[44] In Maoism this comes still more clearly to light. Among "Mao's sayings" we find, "The working class is the most far-sighted (i.e., most conscious) and the most selfless; an unlimited creative power inheres in it."[45] In other words, it is the vehicle for the projection of the man of light/Anthropos, and even the division into four is there, since it is said that the revolutionary class that is called upon to save the world consists of *four* elements: the workers, the farmers, the soldiers, and the young intellectuals, which, as is always the case with the fourth element, is the hardest to fit in.[46]

From a psychological point of view, what we have here is a regressive restoration of that primordial state in which the Anthropos once again represents purely a group Self, as was once the case with primitive peoples, and in which this Self is once again seen as fully identical with the collective norms. Because we live in a time of neurotic dissociation, the healing symbol of the Anthropos is being constellated in the unconscious; however, when we do not become individually conscious of it, again and again the kinds of archaic projection of the myth on the outside world are engendered that can have no other result than the struggle for the liberation of the Anthropos from the powers of darkness also being projected on the outside—and this can only lead to war. But even behind this distortion, we can catch a glimpse of the real progress that nature is striving for, that is, an ever broader potentiality for individuation, the coming to consciousness of the human wholeness on the individual level. At first this was the prerogative of individuals, but gradually it became the common property of an entire social stratum; and in Christianity it was extended further and further as the idea of the "inner Christ." But today obviously an extension of the symbol of a complete "inner Anthropos" to all human beings is taking place. As far as I can see, that is the goal toward which the disturbance of the collective unconscious seems to be tending, even though it may perhaps require even greater misfortune and suffering before its content can become conscious for us.

Looking at things on this basis and in a historical framework, it seems to me possible to say, albeit cautiously: first, that humanity has not yet attained the level of its own preconscious archetypal model of existence—we are still at the beginning of our possible development of consciousness; and that somehow a very slow, century-spanning movement of human development seems to be trying to actualize itself from the side of the unconscious. But whether this process represents a real qualitative development or whether, as the Indians believe, it runs down cyclically into itself over hundreds of thousands of years, that is to say, whether it represents a flourishing and dying out and a flourishing once again of the same primordial image, I do not dare say. The most I can say is that by temperament, I believe in the former. This corresponds to the Western, more extraverted outlook, whereas for the people of the East, a static worldview seems to be tolerable. The important thing, however, is not so much this idea in itself as the projection of a *meaning,* either inward or outward. That human existence should have a meaning is of vital importance for us psychically, whether it is to be found outside or inside or a combination of both.[47] As Jung acknowledges, the sole sense of human existence is "to kindle a light in the darkness of mere being,"[48] that is, to create consciousness. This sense is sought by Western man more on the outside, in history; Eastern man, by contrast, discovers it within himself, embodies it himself.

That being the case, in conclusion I would like to add a few more words on the short historical line of development thus far observable in the West. In relatively many myths about the Anthropos who has sunk or scattered into matter, it is only the *female* part of the androgynous primordial figure that has tumbled into the darkness.[49] We have the Gnostic Simon Magus's well-known myth of Sophia, who, imprisoned in the underworld by the astral lords whom she herself created, is left to wander there. For the Ophite sect, she initially belonged, as a female holy spirit, to a celestial trinity of primordial man and son of man; however, she was unable to receive the plenitude of light that these two poured upon her. Then, falling down to the left as "light dew," she became Prunikos-Sophia, who was lost in the waters of the depths. Later, returning to the heights, she was able to save herself. As the fruit of her fall, however, her son, the demonic Jaldabaoth, the author of all evil, remained below. We also find in the system of Valentinus a Sophia who has been abandoned in the lower world of darkness and is seeking the way back upward to the light of the primordial father. From her passion, matter arose, from her return, psychic being; and in a purified state she finally bore pneumatic being. In the Kabbalah, this myth corresponds to the idea of the exile of the Shekhinah.[50] In most Gnostic teachings, the fundamental evil, which stands opposite the Anthropos-Sophia principle, is *agnoia,* unconsciousness, from which salvation can only be brought about through gnosis, that is, inner experiential learning.

Wherever it is only the feminine aspect of the symbol of the Self that has become lost through projection, this points psychologically to the fact that in the collective consciousness the principle of the masculine logos has come to prevail one-sidedly, at the expense of eros, the relationship to feeling. As a result of this, the anima in men as well as the conscious ego of many women is in danger of becoming lost in unconscious emotionality. The spiritual direction in consciousness, Jung says, then loses its connection with reality and degenerates into mere intellectualism. It becomes ruthless, arrogant and tyrannical, and abandons the feminine principle to *agnoia,* unconsciousness.[51] In this way a profound split develops. The world of light will not darken its radiance, and the world of darkness does not want to give up its gratifying emotions.[52] The original wholeness, however, remains a profound desideratum, and for this reason the unconscious brings forth symbols of wholeness in uncommon measure.

This feminine aspect of the Anthropos, too, is seeking today to push its way into the light in unknown and therefore archaic, and in part distorted, collective form. Thus the French poet Éluard, a friend of Picasso's, praises the triumph of Communism, the new world he longs for, as an era of love.

Être unis, c'est le bout du monde
le coeur de l'homme s'agrandit
le bout du monde s'approche. . . .

. . . .

Nous prendrons jour malgré la nuit
Nous oublierons nos ennemis
La victoire est éblouissante
Nous avons pénétré le feu
Il faut qu'il nous soit la santé
Nous nous levons comme les blés
Et nous ensemençons l'amour![53]

But at the same time here again the whole drama is projected into something external—this same Éluard made the following reply to the remark of a friend that one should make one's own life into a masterpiece: "No, it's the life of others that one should make into a masterpiece."[54] What an aberration of the so-called love that he has just praised so highly! Pure violation of the other by force!

And yet the archetypal idea behind this is the notion of an at least emotional accord between peoples and a unification of the whole of humanity, albeit in the regressive primordial form of the "archaic identity" described at the beginning. This can be seen with particular clarity in the Hippie movement, with the rebelling students, with the Red Guard in China, and similar surges of youthful revolt: possessed themselves by the archetype of the *puer aeternus,* the alchemistic Mercurius or apocalyptic *filius sapientiae,*[55] they revere pure emotion, occasionally sketching a culture of feeling through music, flowers, and so on. They do not want to be pinned down to any reasonably formulable goal, and what binds them together is not so much an idea as a powerful emotion in which they feel one with the primordial image of the Anthropos, not without the attendant side effect of inflation with its dangerous consequences. Interestingly, this rift in the human world does not run along the lines of the iron curtain but right across it. This yields a cross in the form of two splits instead of the four-part combination corresponding to wholeness. And as Jung points out,[56] humanity today is approaching the state of either a chaos controlled only with difficulty or a completely amorphous mass. The only way to deal with this is the inner consolidation of the individual, which could protect him from assimilation into the mass. However, if this inner consolidation of the individual is not accomplished *consciously,* it will develop spontaneously in the form of an incredibly asocial hardening of the mass man against his fellows. This is showing itself today in the increasing tendency toward acts of violence, which can be seen on every hand. However, here the psyche, "which lives only from human relationship," is being lost. For as Jung pointed out, the psyche "is never complete in the individual unless related to another individual. The unrelated human being lacks wholeness, for he can achieve wholeness only through the soul, and the soul cannot exist without its other side, which is always found in a 'you.'"[57] For this reason also, individuation does not mean some egotistical isolation, but on the contrary, it creates the precondition for genuine relatedness and a sustainable social attitude. But whether today, now that we are at the end of at least five thousand years of the development of consciousness, we must take a step backward into a primal barbaric state, or whether the Self of humanity will evolve further in the consciousness of the individual, I do not know. The only thing that seems sure is that today this archetype is trying to manifest in many individuals, and that now everything depends on how many of them will be able to understand this occurrence consciously and will undertake efforts for their own individuation, that is, for the liberation of the *homo altus,* the greater inner person.

Notes

1. C. G. Jung, cw 12.
2. Cf. also C. G. Jung, "Concerning Mandala Symbolism," in cw 9/i, pp. 355–85.

3. Jung, *Psychology and Alchemy,* cw 12, para. 4, pp. 4f.

4. Ibid., pp. 217f.

5. Cf. Jung, *Aion,* cw 12, para. 34, pp. 43f.

6. *Die Edda,* trans. von Genzmer (Jena, 1933), p. 86.

7. Cf. H. Maspéro, *Le Taoisme* (Paris, 1950), p. 109; and H. Koestler, *Symbolik des chinesischen Universismus* (Symbolism of Chinese Universalism) (Stuttgart, 1958), p. 40. For further references, see C. G. Jung, *Mysterium Coniunctionis,* cw 14, para. 573, pp. 399f.

8. *Brhadaranyaka-Upanishad* 1.4.3; *Katha-Upanishad* 1.2.25; and *Mundaka-Upanishad* 2.1.

9. Cf. H. Güntert, *Der arische Weltenkönig und Heiland* (The Aryan Cosmic King and Savior) (Halle an der Saale, 1923), p. 320.

10. Cf. further parallels to this motif from Cochin China, Ceylon, Japan, and Egypt (Sarapis), ibid., p. 331.

11. *Mundaka-Upanishad* 2.1.

12. Cf. S. Hartmann, *Gayômart, Étude sur le syncrétisme de l'ancien Iran* (Gayômart, Study on the Syncretism of Ancient Iran) (Uppsala, 1953); and Henry Corbin, "Terre céleste et corps de résurrection" (Celestial Earth and Body of Resurrection), in *Eranos-Jahrbuch* XXII (1953), pp. 150f. See further R. Reitzenstein and H. Schaeder, *Studien zum antiken Synkretismus aus Iran und Griechenland* (Studies in Ancient Syncretism from Iran and Greece) (Darmstadt: reprint, 1965), passim.

13. Jung, *Psychological Types,* cw 6, in the definitions under "Identity."

14. Cf. Jung, *Mysterium Coniunctionis,* cw 14, paras. 593ff., pp. 413ff.

15. Cf. Jung, *Psychological Types,* pp. 441f.

16. Ibid., under "Projection," pp. 457f. In paranoia, the act of judgment predominates in such a one-sided fashion that a cutting off of all relationships results.

17. Cf. A. Wünsche, *Schöpfung und Sündenfall des ersten Menschenpaares* (The Creation and Fall into Sin of the First Human Couple) (Leipzig, 1906), pp. 8f.; and H. Güntert, *Der arische Weltenkönig,* p. 328.

18. A. Wünsche, *Schöpfung und Sündenfall,* p. 13.

19. Cf. Jung, *Mysterium Coniunctionis,* paras. 593ff., pp. 413ff., and further references given there.

20. Curiously, Eliade overlooked the example of Adam.

21. Cf. G. Scholem, *Zur Kabbala und ihrer Symbolik* (The Kabbalah and Its Symbolism) (Zurich, 1960), pp. 172f., 140, 150.

22. H. K. Jakobsohn, "Das Gegensatzproblem im Altaegyptischen Mythos," in *Studien zur Analytischen Psychologie C. G. Jungs* (The Problem of Opposites in Ancient Egyptian Myth) (Zurich, 1955), vol. 2, pp. 171ff.

23. Cf. H. Jakobsohn, "The Dialogue of a World-Weary Man with his Ba," in H. Jacobsohn, M-L. von Franz, and Siegmund-Hurwitz, *Timeless Documents of the Soul* (Evanston, Ill.: Northwestern University Press, 1968).

24. Cf. Jung, *Mysterium Coniunctionis,* para. 573, pp. 399f.

25. Ibid., pp. 417f.

26. Ibid., pp. 418f.

27. A. Wünsche, *Schöpfung und Sündenfall,* pp. 8, 9.

28. E. Müller, *Der Sohar* (Zurich, 1959); and G. Scholem, *Zur Kabbala und ihrer Symbolik,* pp. 54f.: "The number of bones of the Anthropos corresponds to the days of the year and the 'two hundred and forty-eight organs' to the number of commandments in the Torah."

29. Jung, *Psychology and Alchemy,* p. 363; and *Mysterium Coniunctionis,* para. 619, pp. 429f.

30. Opp. Basileae 1601, vol. 1, p. 201, cited in A. Wünsche, *Schöpfung und Sündenfall,* pp. 19f. "Nascenti homini omniferaria semina et omnigenae vitae germina indidit Pater: quae quisque excoluerit, illa adolescent et fructus ferent in illo si vegetalia, planta fiet, si sensualia, obbrutescet, si rationalia, caeleste evadet animal, si intellectualia, angelus erit et Dei filius. Et si nulla creaturarum sorte contentus in unitatis centrum suae se receperit, unus cum Deo spiritus factus, in solitaria Patris caligine, qui est super omnia constitutus, omnibus antestabit. . . ."

31. H. Corbin, *L'imagination créatrice dans le soufisme d'Ibn Arabi* (Creative Imagination in the Sufism of Ibn Arabi) (Paris, 1958), pp. 123f.

32. Jung, *Psychology and Alchemy,* para. 457, pp. 368–70.

33. Cf. G. Quispel, *"Der gnostische Anthropos und die jüdische Tradition"* (The Gnostic Anthropos and the Jewish Tradition), *Eranos Jahrbuch,* vol. 22 (1953), pp. 230ff., 197ff.

34. Cf. E. S. Drower, *The Secret Adam* (Oxford, 1960), passim.

35. Cf. Jung, *Psychology and Alchemy*, para. 413, p. 304, and para. 26, pp. 23f.

36. Cf. in this connection, ibid., para. 34, pp. 28f.

37. Cf. Jung, "Answer to Job," *Psychology and Religion*, cw 11, p. 455.

38. Ibid., p. 457.

39. Cf. "Flying Saucers: A Modern Myth," in *Civilization in Transition*, cw 10, para. 727.

40. R. Tucker, *Karl Max: Die Entwicklung seines Denkens von der Philosophie zum Mythos* (Karl Marx: The Development of His Thought from Philosophy to Myth) (Munich, 1983).

41. Ibid., p. 195.

42. Ibid., p. 196; cf. also K. Marko, *Evolution wider Willen* (Reluctant Revolution) (Vienna, 1968), pp. 27–29, and the other literature referred to there.

43. Tucker, *Karl Marx*, p. 201.

44. Marx/Engels, *Historisch-kritisch Gesamtausgabe* (Critical-Historical Complete Edition), first section, vol. 5, p. 116, cited in Tucker, *Karl Marx*, p. 207.

45. *Worte des Vorsitzenden Mao Tse-Tung* (Sayings of Chairman Mao tse-tung), (Peking, 2nd ed., 1967), pp. 48, 140.

46. Cf. *Peking Rundschau*, no. 34, 27 August 1968, pp. 17f.

47. Jung, *Memories, Dreams, Reflections*, p. 317.

48. Ibid., p. 326.

49. Cf. H. Jonas, *Gnosis und spätantiker Geist* (Gnosis and the Spirit of Late Antiquity) (Göttingen, 2nd ed., 1964), vol. 1, pp. 351ff.

50. Cf. Scholem, *Zur Kabbala und ihrer Symbolik*, p. 144.

51. Jung, *Alchemical Studies*, cw 13, para. 455, pp. 335f.

52. Ibid., para. 456, p. 337.

53. "Les hommes sont faits pour s'entendre, pour se comprendre, pour s'aimer" (People are made to be in harmony with each other, to understand one another, love one another) in *P. Éluard*, eds. L. Parrot and J. Marcenac (Paris, 1964), p. 184. A straightforward translation of the poem is: Being united is the end of the world /

the heart of man gets bigger / the end of the world is coming near.
. . . We'll take the light in spite of night / We'll forget our enemies /
Victory is dazzling / We have gone into the fire / This will have to
be our health / We arise like stalks of grain / And we sow the seed
of love!

54. Ibid., pp. 187f.

55. Cf. Marie-Louise von Franz, "Über religiöse Hintergründe des
Puer-Aeternus Problems" (Religious Background of the Puer Aeternus Problem) in *Der Archetyp* (Basel, New York, 1964), pp. 141ff.

56. Jung, "Psychology of the Transference," in *The Practice of Psychotherapy,* cw 16, para. 443, p. 232.

57. Ibid., para. 454, p. 244.

THE SELF-AFFIRMATION OF
MAN AND WOMAN

A General Problematic Illustrated
by Fairy Tales

■■

A GREAT PART OF THE PROBLEM in the self-affirmation of man and woman is a general human problem, coinciding with that involved in any kind of self-affirmation. Primarily it is a problem of degree: to what extent is it "legitimate" to defend one's own personal life potential against the pressure of other people's power complexes or the pressure of the collective; and at what point does this defense itself start to become tyranny in relation to others? In what follows, I would like to concentrate on the problem of personal self-affirmation in the relationship with the opposite sex, for here specific complications tend to crop up that are deserving of particular attention.

C. G. Jung rightly pointed out that such a powerful attraction as man and woman exercise on each other is only possible where there also exists an equally strong antagonism. For according to the Bible, it was not only that enmity was put between Eve and the serpent, but the curse also extended to the relationship between the sexes. Jung says, "Primal guilt lies between them, a *broken state of enmity,* and this appears unreasonable only to our

rational mind but not to our psychic nature."[1] To reason, especially with its present-day materialistic perspective, the union of
the sexes seems to be *the* sensible instinct. However, a more spiritual point of view would just as strongly require discrimination;
for only where there is detachment and genuine conscious discrimination is a relationship of feeling in a deeper sense possible.
The specific complication I alluded to earlier that makes the relationship of man and woman and the problem of self-affirmation
of one vis-à-vis the other so difficult, consists in a nutshell in this:
both the man and the woman have, not only in their body but
also in their mind, opposite-sex components, of which, however,
they are at first usually not conscious. Because these components
are not consciously developed and cultivated, they have a relatively primitive quality and even a quality of inferiority. It is as
though, for example, women have a petty, stiff, primitive man
they carry around in them, and men an ambivalent, sensual,
somewhat inferiority-afflicted woman. Jung called these components animus (in the woman) and anima (in the man). The situation becomes even more complicated because in general the man
cannot tolerate this second-class masculinity in the woman and
the woman cannot tolerate this dubious femininity in the man,
and they react to them with automatic irritability. As a result,
each time a confrontation develops in connection with the self-
affirmation of one or the other, these two components almost
always become mixed up in the discussion and draw it down to
a lower, irritable level. Through this, unintentional hurting of
feelings comes about, which are afterward often difficult to heal,
and the whole confrontation goes astray and ends up in a dead
end. Thus when a woman feels she needs to assert herself in some
respect vis-à-vis the man, she finds herself face to face with the
problem of a "two-front war"—against the man, on one hand,
and against her own animus, which spoils her plan, on the other.
The same problem also faces the man.

Since this is an age-old, general human problem, it has been
reflected symbolically in myths and fairy tales, and because it is
impossible for me to depict a great number of individual cases in

a fully factual manner, I would like to present two such mythical tales in which everything essential is expressed in a concentrated manner.

The first tale, which relates to the problem as it comes up for a woman, is a Norwegian Cinderella variant with the title "Kari Woodenskirt."[2]

Once upon a time there was a king who had lost his wife and had married, as his second wife, a widow with a daughter. She, however, was evil and hated the king's only and beautiful daughter Kari. The king had to leave the country to go to war, and the girl, in order to escape the persecutions of her stepmother, had to flee to the cattle on the meadow. There she became friends with a blue bull, who spoke to her in human language, promising her consolation and help. From his ear, she could pull a little cloth on which rich dishes of food appeared, from which she nourished herself. Then the stepmother decided to have the bull slaughtered, and Kari made up her mind to escape far way on the blue bull's back. They came to a wood, whose trees all bore copper leaves, and the bull asked Kari not to touch or pick any of them. But unintentionally she did so all the same, and a three-headed troll appeared, and a fight to the death ensued between the troll and the bull, in which the latter, exhausted, barely prevailed.

Now they came to a wood whose trees bore silver leaves, and again the same thing happened, only this time it was a six-headed troll that had to be defeated.

Then they came to a wood with golden trees, and the troll who ruled over it had nine heads. There Kari picked a golden apple, and thus the bull had to overcome this devil also, which he did by the barest margin. Now they came to the border of another kingdom, and the bull said: "In the royal castle you must put on a wooden skirt and live in the pigsty and always say that you are Kari Woodenskirt and you have work there. But now you must cut off my head, pull off my hide, and roll up in it the two leaves and the golden apple and lay it at the foot of the cliff wall here. Against that wall leans a stick. Whenever you want something from me, rap on the wall with it." With a heavy heart Kari carried out these commands and took refuge in the pigsty of the castle, where the cook gave her work. Now one Sunday she brought the prince washing water in his chamber, but since she rattled so in her wooden skirt, he poured the water over her head. Then she went to the cliff wall and rapped on it, and a man came out, and she asked him for a dress to go to church in. He gave her a dress as radiant as the copper forest and also a horse with a saddle. She rode to the church, and everyone admired her beauty, and the prince rode up behind her and asked where she came from. "From Washwater Land," she answered, and then spoke the magical verse:

> *Light before me*
> *Behind me, darkness,*
> *That the prince may not see*
> *Whither I ride.*

Then she disappeared, leaving behind a glove. The next Sunday, all this repeated, only this time the prince threw his handkerchief on her head; and after that she rode to the church in a silver dress. She disappeared, leaving her riding crop behind. The prince fell so much in love with her that he looked for her everywhere.

The third Sunday, again everything happened the same way, only this time the prince tossed his comb on her head, and Kari rode to the church in a golden dress. But when she left the church, her golden shoe was left stuck in the tar, and with this in his hand as a token, the prince now searched everywhere for the beautiful churchgoer. Then everything happened as in the well-known story of Cinderella. The evil stepmother and her daughter came, and the latter chopped off her toes in order to fit in the shoe, but a little bird exposed her deception. Finally Kari, too, appeared to be tested, and the shoe fit her perfectly. Then she threw off her wooden skirt and appeared in her radiant golden gown. Then she and the prince celebrated their marriage.

The initial situation shows us a king who is absent, entangled in war, and at home it is his evil second wife who rules. This corresponds psychologically to a situation of the collective consciousness in which the masculine principle, spirit, is exhausting itself in a conflict situation while the feminine principle of eros, the principle of the culture of heart and feeling, has degenerated and is now only concerned about prestige and power. The masculine and feminine natures are separated and not in a state of relationship. Kari, the daughter, symbolizes a possibility of renewal of the feminine nature, which must find a way to prevail in the face of these difficulties. To begin with, she escapes in a typical feminine fashion—disappears into the realm of Mother Nature, to beasts of the field, that is, the realm of unconscious fantasy. There she meets a blue bull, who provides her with nourishment and help.

The bull, in most religions and myths, is a symbol of the spirit of the earth, a chthonic fertility power of great violence, wild affectivity, and strength. For the woman, he embodies a kind of dark, passionate, realistic, affect-laden conviction, the roots of which are religious in nature—something like an unconscious, nature-related divine image and a still undifferentiated instinctive spirituality. (Blue is the color of the spirit.) From this animus figure, Kari draws her strength and spiritual nourishment, but at the same time it also cuts her off from all contact with her fellow human beings. The bull carries her further away from the perilous source of perverted outlook (the queen), and they go through forests whose trees bear metal leaves. From a mythological point of view, such a thing happens only in paradise; thus one can only conclude that Kari has been transported to the realm of primordial fantasy pre-existing the most ancient times, into the center of the collective unconscious, to a realm of innocence, nature, and nearness to God. But as Eve once tasted of the apple, she too, in a forbidden way, picks leaves from the metal trees and lays a sin on herself that forces her to leave paradise. The germinating ego consciousness of her personality egotistically wants a piece of life *for itself*. Here we have a bit of self-affirmation, this time not vis-à-vis other people, but vis-à-vis the unconscious. It is as though she were saying, "True, when I flee to the realm of fantasy all conflicts are resolved; but I do also want to live myself and have something real in my hands." Three times, her unintentional theft brings about a savage mortal conflict between a troll and the bull. In Nordic mythology, trolls represent the chaotic, unformed primal unconscious, which here turns against the bull, who embodies a higher, goal-directed spirituality. The chaos of untamed affects and emotions breaks loose, but it can be overcome by the strength of the blue bull. The trolls' many heads signify the undirected dissociative force of the emotions. And with this, the paradisiacal state of the dream is over—Kari must go back to the human world, and at this threshold of her own salvation, she has to sacrifice that which is of greatest value to her, the bull. It occurs again and again in many fairy tales that a helpful animal demands to be sacrificed in this way by the hero or heroine. This points to a deep-seated psychological mystery.

The ultimate religious attitude toward life and the most profound urge in human nature, which Jung called the impulse toward individuation, that is, self-realization, is initially simply an unconscious instinct, an irrational "can't-help-it." This profound and wholesome instinct in a human being often saves him or her in the face of all perils. It is a kind of human genuineness or sincerity that cannot be twisted out of shape. But in the long run, that is not enough. A person must by nature also *know* why he is doing something. He must—and this is apparently a destiny imposed on him by nature—become conscious and comprehend *the meaning* of this "dark urge." Therefore he must only sacrifice this instinct in its animal form, and it is the instinct itself that demands its own sacrifice. This is a tragic and frightful moment in the life of every human being. The "dark night of the soul" takes over, and he is now abandoned by everything, even the helpful voices and vital supportive forces within him. But Kari pluckily heeds the bull's demands and performs the ritual killing. She buries *four* parts of the bull, and this indicates the significance of the sacrifice; for in nearly all myths and religions of man, four signifies the making conscious of a content, and through this endeavor to recognize the "bull" in its deeper nature, she discovers that hidden within him was the spirit of a man, who now manifests and from then on remains her invisible helper and advisor.

This masculine spirit is the animus of the woman, mentioned earlier, which now, however, no longer manifests purely as affect, impulse, and vital force, but has become human, can express itself in words and deeds on a human level.

From a practical point of view, this means the following. When a woman gets into a situation in which she has to hold her own or affirm herself and encounters difficulties in doing so, she no longer falls prey to a brutal affective outbreak or to the reverse side of this, the compulsion shyly to completely withdraw and encapsulate herself in her own inner world. Rather she is capable of expressing herself in a reasonable and sensible fashion and of finding her way to her goal.

But in her return to the human world, Kari at first finds herself in an extremely humiliating position. She becomes a Cinderella at the court of a kingdom in which a young, still unmarried prince is the ruler. This prince is a figure representing the renewal of the collective-consciousness principle, a new spiritual and philosophical attitude, which in contrast to the king at the beginning of the tale is not caught up in war. In other words, it offers a new possibility for life which leaves the old conflicts behind. However, the masculine and feminine are not yet harmoniously unified. The two principles are separated from one another—Kari goes crashing about in a wooden dress, and the prince behaves in a coarse and uncourtly fashion.

Kari's wooden skirt symbolizes a "wooden" and unfeminine way of manifesting an awkward and contrary manner that makes her erotically unapproachable. This is a gesture of self-protection by which she is protecting her own inner process of maturation from premature contact.

The prince's uncourtly coarseness can be interpreted in two ways. The prince can be looked at as an animus figure within the woman, and in this case it would mean that when a woman makes an effort to develop the masculine side of herself, she inevitably passes through a temporary phase in which she behaves arrogantly and unskillfully by way of compensation for her otherwise yielding feminine nature. (History shows this, for example, in the behavior of the first feminists before the First World War.) But one can also look at the prince as the woman's outer male partner, and in that case, his behavior clearly shows how willfully the man reacts, and even must react, when the woman relates to him in such a "wooden" and contrary fashion. His manhood reacts with a corresponding affect, and that is probably basically for the best, because he forces Kari to develop herself further.

From the invisible spiritual advisor, the bull-spirit-man, she now receives the beautiful dresses in which she appears in church, that is, very literally, her psychic beauty and higher consciousness begin to shine through, and the prince begins by moments to glimpse her true higher nature behind her contrariness. In true feminine fashion, however, she compels him to find her rather than pushing herself on him. Indeed, judging by the verse she speaks, she remains turned only toward the inner light of her own growth to consciousness, fleeing before the darkness of unconsciousness and the animus affects, until the prince finds her true nature. Through this she reaches her due position of queen, that is, of an individuated, fully developed woman. She gives the prince to understand in a few biting and haughty remarks how discourteously he has behaved, but she takes no revenge, for where real love and a genuine relationship of feeling prevails, no further competitive self-affirmation is necessary. One can reach an understanding in a human and completely ordinary fashion through words or often just little innuendoes. Humor, that single divine quality of humanity, as Schopenhauer once called it, is the bridge of genuinely human and friendly "self-affirmation" between partners.

Now let us turn to the problem of the man who has to affirm himself vis-à-vis a woman. Here the situation is entirely different, for because of his physical superiority and traditional legal situation, at least in our patriarchally shaped religion and culture, the problem ostensibly does not exist at all. If a man is not a Milquetoast but a real man, then he knows instinctively what he has to do to defend himself against a feminine power play. If he does not know, then usually it is because his mother has craftily castrated him through a "good upbringing," that is, taught him that he has to subordinate himself like a good boy to the woman. When it falls to one to help such men, what it comes down to is reminding them of their inborn genuine manhood and giving them some backbone. That means that they will have to become less noble and mannerly and let their darker, animal, shadow side come out. For many very fine and sensitive men this can be quite difficult, but it *must* happen, if they are not to become the disdained patsy of some power-hungry woman or her animus. There is a Greek fairy tale that illustrates this particularly well.

> A hunter went out and caught a fish, but in response to its plea he set it free. It then gave him one of its scales, which he was to rub when he was in trouble. Then he caught an eagle, and again the same thing happened. He spared him and received a feather. Thirdly, he spared a fox and received from it a hair and its promise to help him. Now he came to the court of a beautiful princess, who had until then brought about the destruction of all of her suitors. She set them the task of hiding from her three times. If she could find them, their life was forfeit, but if not, she was to yield to the man. The hunter took up the challenge and hid himself with the help of the fish in the deepest depth of the ocean, but the princess possessed a magic mirror. She looked into it and saw the hunter on the ocean floor. Then he flew with the eagle to the highest height of heaven, but there too the princess's magic mirror found him. Now it was a matter of life and death. The hunter called the fox for help, and the fox dug a subterranean burrow right up to beneath the princess's throne. The hunter, on the fox's advice, crept into it, and as she was trying to see him in her magic mirror, from beneath her he stuck her in the bottom with a needle. She dropped the mirror and yielded to the hunter, who courted her and became the king of the country.[3]

Help comes neither from escape into the depths of the sea, that is, the unconscious, nor escape into the sphere of the intellect (the eagle's flight). Both are forms of escape that many men try: some abscond into the realm of fantasy or into an extramarital relationship that is kept hidden; others escape into the intellect, that is, they bury themselves in newspapers, books, political theorizing— all realms where the evil woman apparently cannot follow. But this is of no help; only the animal of the earth, *the ground of reality,* helps; to wit, the fox, who is famous for his realistic shrewdness. He is an animal of Dionysus and Wotan, also in mythology often a diabolical spirit. With his help, the hunter succeeds in pricking the "weak point," the vulnerable complex of the nasty woman, presumably her power complex, for it is with this—her bottom—that she sits on the throne! Touché, she has to yield, and we may hope that with this the "taming of the shrew" has come to pass.

This fairy tale also clearly illustrates in what way women most frequently illegitimately dominate a man—not by force but through superior cunning. In our fairy tale, this is the magical mirror in which the princess sees everything. In practical terms this means the following: When the man wants to undertake something that does not suit her, the woman does not say that, but at that particular moment, she gets sick. Or when she notices that her man likes other people, men or women, with real feeling, she fears that this might draw him out of her power. Then in advance, long before he has noticed what is going on, she lets slip poison-tipped, slanderous remarks, which nip the relationships in the bud. Since precisely in the area of relationship and feeling, men are often strangely, touchingly, naively unconscious, such a woman often has an easy time of it. She always "sees" how things stand with him inwardly long before he himself knows, and she takes her measures. A man is helpless against this with his naive masculine strength or affects. He has to take the time, with the help of his inner "fox," to find out what game is being played with him.

A Norwegian fairy tale, "The Companion," and a North German variant of it, "The Enchanted Princess," shed more light on this problem.[4]

A peasant lad went out into the world, and the first thing he encountered was an unburied corpse in a village. The deceased had diluted wine or run up debts, and thus no one wanted to bury him. So out of compassion the lad paid for the burial with his last pennies, and shortly thereafter a stranger attached himself to him and promised him his help. This was the spirit of the buried corpse. With the help of the stranger, the lad acquired from three witches a sword, a spool of golden thread, and a hat that made the wearer invisible. Then he and his traveling companion arrived at a royal castle where a princess set her suitors riddles. If the suitor did not guess the riddle, he was executed. The lad took up the challenge. When night came, the princess rode off on a goat "to her darling," but the lad followed her invisibly wearing his magic hat. In one version the "darling" is a troll, in the other, an old white-bearded man who lives inside a mountain, where he keeps an altar on which spiny fish and a fiery wheel appear. The lad eavesdropped while the princess and the evil spirit made up the riddle they intended to pose, and thus twice fulfilled the task. The third time the riddle was to be: "What am I thinking about?" which was to be the head of the mountain spirit. Then the lad chopped off the spirit's head with his magic sword and hid it in a cloth. When the princess asked, "What am I thinking about?" he threw down the head at her feet. Now the lad had won, and after the princess had further cleansed herself from the spell by bathing in milk, their wedding was celebrated.

Here the freed spirit of the dead man, the companion, plays the role of the helpful fox, and we see what he really is. He was a "debtor," that is, he is a shadow aspect of the man that has become conscious. By paying off the "debt" of his dark side, that is, by becoming conscious of his own less positive side, he is now capable of winning his battle with the evil riddle–posing princess. She, however, is not really so evil herself but has rather fallen into the clutches of a troll or sorcerer, who actually is an embodiment of the old Germanic Wotan. Interpreted in terms of the outer woman, she was a very nice woman, but one who was possessed by an evil animus—something like a Kari Woodenskirt in whose case the troll rather than the bull had been victorious. But we must also look at her as an inner figure in the man himself, as a wicked anima figure. In modern psychological language this would amount to something like the following: The anima embodies the capacity for relationship in the man, his feeling, the state or condition of his affects. In the case of our fairy tale, everything would have been just fine in this regard were it not for the fact that the princess had fallen under the influence of the demon. Feeling was unconsciously warped into a lie by the mountain spirit, so that it could not function. But the mountain spirit himself is a raw power of nature.

What this means on a practical level is that a man with such an anima might, for example, imagine that he loves a woman though in reality he is after her bank account; or he might confuse love and sexuality; or he might fail to follow a genuine feeling because it would imperil his position in society. In this way, he is inadvertently serving a primitive god called Mammon, or sex, prestige, or any other dark affective impulse, and imagining that *this* is his genuine feeling. In such a case, what has to be done is literally, as the fairy tale so beautifully shows, to get to the bottom of things, which means getting behind this distorted state of feeling, which makes any genuine love impossible, and disabling the destructive background influence. The freeing of a maiden from a dragon that is depicted so often in fairy tales expresses something similar, except that the dragon embodies the "cold" drivenness of the sexual instinct, whereas the mountain spirit represents "Wotanic" possession.

As long as a man has not freed his anima from such a background influence, the woman often feels that he is only "in love" with her but does not love her—that his feeling is autoerotic and caught up in illusion; and what in our day complicates the problem still further is that *feeling takes time,* and this is something the modern man has very little of. He must fight for it if he is to take his "Mistress Soul" seriously. But only when he succeeds in freeing his inner anima is he really proof against the tricks of malevolent or cold, power-hungry women and capable of finding relationships in which he can have confidence.

But the tales given above point to a still deeper problem, which

I have thus far left aside. The prince in the story of Kari Wooden-skirt discovers Kari on the way to church, and the evil princess of the riddles in "The Companion" secretly serves a mountain spirit, who represents nothing other than an archaic God image. The bull, too, is really an old pagan deity. Here the confrontation of the sexes touches upon the sphere of the problem of religion, for the "interrupted state of enmity" between man and woman goes so deep that the healing of it touches the deepest layers of the psyche.

Jung tried to prove in his life's work that behind the animus and anima in the unconscious of man and woman, a still mightier content dwells hidden, the true "atomic nucleus" of the psyche, which he called the Self to distinguish it from the ordinary every-day ego. The Self is the personality's inmost and most powerfully influential center of meaning, and when it appears in myths and sagas and in people's dreams, it manifests as an image of the divine. Expressed in religious language, it is the "divine spark" residing in the depths of the psyche of every human being. From this center also emanate the ultimate resolves of conscience, when a person seeks to be guided not by conventional morality but really by his "inner conscience"; and it is with this center, too, that the problem of self-affirmation is ultimately connected. For as long as it is only a matter of superficial things—whether to take a little outing together or not, whether the living room should have red or blue drapes—no human ego is injured by generously giving in or making a compromise. Those are not serious problems of self-affirmation. But when matters are in-volved in relation to which one's most authentic "being oneself" is threatened by another person or persons, when, in other words, individuation or self-realization is at stake, then the problem be-comes acute. Out of love, generosity, or desire for peace, a person can give way in many matters without suffering injury to honor or psychic health, but when another person is trying to prevent one from being obedient to one's inner divine voice, that is when the problem of self-affirmation really is posed. It is at this point that, if one does not assert oneself, one can become psychically ill or deformed. And there is the further issue that, even if one has an understanding of psychology, it is very difficult to know in actual practice whether or not one is actually confronted with a challenge to the Self. Women, for example, often confuse the rigid opinion of their own animus with the much softer divine inner voice, which is why the French are wont to remark sardonically, "Ce que femme veut, Dieu veut!" And men have often assured me that their inmost, most authentic feeling was telling them to do thus and so, while I could clearly see the troll smirking behind this "feeling"!

In such situations there are only two things that help to clarify the situation—time and dreams. If one can wait patiently, most of the time the deepest motivations and needs become gradually more visible, and in the place of the impulsive possession by an affect, a kind of calm and sureness come from the inmost core of the psyche and make possible a responsible decision or step. Further help comes from dreams. Through them, if one knows how to interpret them psychologically correctly, one can usually see after a while if a wish for self-affirmation is vitally and genuinely desired in a way that comes from the divine spark and is therefore "necessary," or if it is just the animus and the treacherous riddling princess playing their heartless power games.

According to Jung, here we find ourselves on the brink of a completely new development never before dared; for on a closer look, we see that man and woman have never really been on that level of feeling before, or only in exceptional individual cases. On a primitive level, their relationship is a sexual one and a situation of common interest through which the inherent natural opposites are reconciled. Then comes the phase of the "broken state of enmity," in which either, as in our culture, the masculine principle rules and the woman accommodates it and subordinates herself to it; or as, for example, in South India, where there is a sociological matriarchy and the reverse happens—the man is reshaped in accordance with the woman's wishes. Our task at the present time seems to be to return not to the "enmity" but to its higher stage, that is, polarity, and out of this distinctness to build a real relationship that does not mean the violation of either the man or the woman.

Among today's younger generations, however, another tendency is taking shape, that is, a fairly thoroughgoing setting aside and blurring of the opposites. This is a symptom of the pushing to the surface of the unconscious, which masculinizes the woman through animus possession and feminizes the man through anima possession. This tendency goes in tandem with a general turning of the younger generation toward the unconscious, whether through drugs or through outbreaks of chaotic emotion. It looks as though all the old forms of consciousness have to be melted down before a new order can develop out of them. The great problem that plagues these young people as much as us is lack of knowledge concerning the powers of the unconscious, the animus and anima. It now really seems to be time for us to take this problem of the opposites seriously in hand, so that Kari Woodenskirt can appear in a golden dress and the hunter can learn to solve the riddles of the evil princess, that is, of his moodily destructive anima.

For the relationship between the sexes has more than a biological significance and more than a significance for the harmony of human relationships. Beyond those, it seems to have been chosen by nature to serve the development of consciousness and the realization of the Self; for without a deep psychic relationship and interaction with a member of the opposite sex, one cannot become conscious of one's animus or anima. And as we have seen, these in turn are linking figures, which mediate our relationship to the real inner core of our psyche, the Self. On the level of its deepest background, the problem of self-affirmation is fused with that of individuation or self-realization, that is, the gradual maturation and growth to consciousness of a more complete inner personality or to psychic wholeness.

Notes

1. *Mysterium Coniunctionis,* cw 14, para. 104, p. 89.

2. *Nordische Volksmärchen* (Nordic Folktales), in *Die Märchen der Welt-literatur,* vol. 2 (Jena, 1922), no. 27, p. 146.

3. Cf. "Der Jäger und der Spiegel, der alles sieht" (The Hunter and the Mirror That Sees Everything), in Chr. Hahn, *Griechische und Albanesische Märchen* (Greek and Albanian Fairy Tales), vol. 1 (Munich, Berlin, 1918), p. 301.

4. *Nordische Märchen,* in *Die Märchen der Weltliteratur,* Norway volume, p. 22; and *Deutsche Märchen seit Grimm,* vol. 1, p. 237.

IN THE BLACK WOMAN'S CASTLE

Interpretation of a Fairy Tale

■■
■■

THROUGH THE RESEARCH WORK of C. G. Jung, the discipline concerned with the meaning of myths and fairy tales acquired an empirical, scientific basis for the first time.[1] As a result it became possible to understand mythologems not only in the terms of intellectual history or through poetic interpretations, but scientifically: that is, to understand them in a relatively objective fashion in their functional aspect as vital phenomena of the unconscious psyche. In the framework of the present study, Jung's views and working hypotheses are of course presumed;[2] however, to begin with I would like to present a few general considerations, which have arisen for me in the course of practical interpretive work and which I believe are not unimportant for the psychological interpretation of myths and fairy tales.

One of these considerations concerns the figure of the hero or heroine, that is, in general the main figure in a myth or fairy tale, with whom the hearer or reader of the tale usually tends to identify emotionally. In the dreams of single individuals this figure corresponds to the dream ego. In almost every dream, the dreamer experiences events or images as an ego (active, passive, or just watching); and even when he dreams he is somebody else, he still always feels himself to be an "I." By contrast, though the figure that replaces the dream ego in myths and fairy tales appears as an ego, at the same time it has features that essentially distinguish it from the ego of an individual human being.[3] To single out just one principal element, the main figure of a myth or fairy tale lacks individual uniqueness,[4] which is often evinced through the absence of even a personal name. As Max Lüthi accurately points out,[5] fairy-tale heroes and heroines especially are "pure vehicles of the action," figures of abstract isolation, drawn in the simplest, yet highly colorful and definite, lines.[6] Therefore Lüthi also rightly speaks of the "one-dimensionality" of the fairy tale. What he means by this is that the hero is part of the same transcendent, abstract realm as all the other figures of the tale. Translated into the language of Jungian psychology, this means that the hero himself is also an archetypal image, and therefore, like all the other fairy-tale contents, symbolizes a content of the collective unconscious.

And yet at the same time, along with the features that characterize it as an archetypal image, this main figure has something about it that, in spite of everything, suggests to our feelings that we experience it as an ego and thus identify with it. Therefore we must also see this figure that vehicles the action as the archetypal basis of the individual ego complex. As such it symbolizes that unknown structural aspect of our psychic makeup, inherent and the same in all human beings, that presents a pattern in accordance with which the particular ego of each individual is formed.

However, in its mythical manifestations this archetypal ego complex often possesses traits that suggest that the forms it takes on be understood, not in terms of ego, but rather as symbols of the Self—traits such as divinity, invincibility, magical power, and so forth. Thus we must also see the figure of the mythical hero as a function of the Self, whose special action is to form, further broaden, and maintain the ego and, as it were, to assure its "proper" functioning, that is, assure ego functioning that remains in proper relationship to the wholeness of the psyche. This functional aspect of the Self constitutes the archetypal basis of the ego complex mentioned above. This is precisely why the mythical hero is so often depicted as a renewer of culture, a savior, and a discoverer of the "precious treasure that is difficult to attain"— because he symbolizes a "proper" posture of the ego, that is to say, one that is called for by the psychic totality. Thus for the individual ego, which often deviates from its instinctive basis, he is something like a guiding image.

In this connection, however, a practical difficulty in the interpretation of myths arises—the absence of an Archimedean point outside the myth itself. In interpreting a dream, the dreamer's conscious situation can almost always serve as a reference point for a given dream content.[7] However, with a mythologem, initially such a reference point seems to be lacking. Thus with a fairy tale, which can usually neither be dated nor connected with a specific locale, one finds oneself in a situation similar to that of having to interpret a dream without knowing anything about the dreamer or his or her attitude and situation. One would have to interpret the dream purely on its own ground, without any reference point "outside" the unconscious material. And indeed the mythologem is actually the form taken on by an unknown event, which is played out fully within the collective unconscious itself, purely between archetypal contents.

As an aid to understanding this, one can imagine the archetypes as dynamically charged "nuclei" existing in darkness in a state of latency, which can mutually reinforce, repel, obliterate, or absorb each other. Every mythologem illuminates a fragment of such a process in the collective unconscious; at the same time other aspects, which may also be present, remain latent.

However, it seems to me unavoidable to think in terms of some factor that acts as a trigger, causing this particular psychic process and not another to appear as a sequence of images on the threshold of consciousness. It must be presumed that the roots of the mythologem are, mutatis mutandis, the same as those in dreams observable in individuals,[8] and in that case one must basically think in terms of the following possibilities: (1) The mythologem reflects contents of the collective consciousness, for example, dominant religious views or generally accepted philosophical conceptions and ideas. (2) The myth gives form to contents of the unconscious constellated by the above-mentioned conscious contents. These would be, for example, symbols standing in a compensatory relationship to consciously accepted social and religious symbols, as Jung showed was the case with, among others, alchemical ideas, which compensated for the symbolism of Christianity.[9] (3) In a third category would be contents occasioned by creative unconscious processes. Such a creative function of the collective unconscious can be seen, for example, in such secular processes as Jung demonstrated in *Aion*. He showed in this work that, at the time of the changing of so-called astrological ages,[10] something like a creative moment in the collective unconscious occurs, which is manifested in historical time, inter alia, as synchronicity phenomena. It would be rewarding for a scholar of mythology to attempt an ordering of myths in terms of such "ages." (4) In a fourth category of the roots of myth fall unconscious reactions to physical and psychic environmental conditions, such as those that might come about as a result of migrations of peoples or of invasion and domination by alien cultures.[11]

In my experience, these factors make it possible to date most mythologems accurately within a few centuries and also to connect them with a broadly defined locale. This works best in practice through asking oneself which historically known configuration of consciousness is most aptly compensated for by the meaning of a given tale. This can be further elucidated with the help of the following example.

A further consideration, which has forced itself upon me in the course of many interpretative efforts, can be explained as follows: As an aid to understanding, imagine the archetypes as nuclei or nexus points of a multidimensional network or field where the nexus points represent the archetypes in their relative specificity[12] and where the network or field is comparable to the connections between meanings and their partial overlappings and identities and where all archetypes thus appear as contaminated by all other archetypes and even as in part identical with each other.[13]

The accompanying diagrams only provide a framework intended to suggest a three-dimensional space, but such a model is inadequate insofar as it does not show definite "distances" between the archetypes, because in fact very often in the myths the most distant archetypes[14]—like snake and light, mother and phallus, animal and spirit—unexpectedly show up as identical; or else several archetypes that one usually thinks of as separate suddenly fuse. To get the relationships halfway correct, either we would have to design an unrepresentable n-dimensional model, or we would have to give up on our attempt at a spatiotemporal ordering altogether, since in the unconscious psyche space and time appear as relativized if not eliminated altogether.

Now in every mythologem, the thread of the story follows certain connections between archetypal meanings, which in figure 2 is sketched in with arrow lines. In this way, every individual tale illuminates a quite definite aspect of the collective unconscious, and this is where the meaning and living function of that particular tale lies. This also explains why there are so many relatively similar fairy tales, that is, why from a relatively constant set of building blocks—like the image of the witch, the hero, the helpful animal, etc.—peoples build ever new fairy-tale structures; in the integral just-so-ness of every individual tale there is a special meaning, which is sought out by the collectivity at a particular

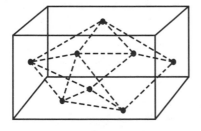 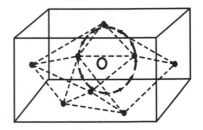

FIGURE 1   FIGURE 2

 ● = archetypes

- - - - = possible connections
of meaning

 ➤ = the course of the story

○ = the one meaning of the story

time and which can be delineated by following the "thread" of that tale in the process of interpretation. The curious thing that emerges in doing this is not only the fact that all the archetypal images in a tale are contaminated—and thus with enough amplification interconnections can be shown to exist between all of them—but also that the "thread," the "how" of the story's movement, itself seems to circumambulate a single meaning or content.[15] Thus, on the one hand, every single archetypal image occurring in a mythologem is a latent representation of the whole, and on the other, the just-so-ness emerging from the sequence of the many images is also a whole.

Accordingly, through amplification of the individual images, on one hand, and the meaning of the entire context grasped as a unity, on the other, one arrives at two complementary results—results that are mutually exclusive logically[16] but which nevertheless represent the best possible description of a "transcendent" reality.[17]

Another practical difficulty we encounter in interpreting mythologems could be called the problem of the right "jumping-in point" for the mythologem. For every mythical story is so much a unity and has such an integral form that, like a drop of water, it exhibits a kind of surface tension, which becomes palpable for the would-be interpreter in the feeling that he or she is helpless in confronting something that is really infinitely simple and of one piece; and that any interpretive grasping at a single image in the context would already destroy this perceived unity. And yet the story is not comprehensible without amplification and interpretive tracing of the thread of the mythologem. Jumping into the process of interpretation is thus always a matter of a decision that causes a psychological backlash in the interpreter, which often even shows up in dreams.[18] What I am calling "jumping in" here corresponds to the notion of the "cut" in modern physics, where "every gain in knowledge of atomic objects through observation must be paid for with an irrevocable loss of other knowledge."[19] The location and choice of the cut is left rather freely to the discretion of the observer. In the interpretation of a mythologem, too, such a "cut" is inevitable and therefore certain potenti-alities for knowledge must also be sacrificed here. This is where the resistance comes from that many people feel against interpre-tive intervention with mythical images. In the location and choice of the "cut" or "jumping-in point" in the interpretation, the na-ture of the observer is always inevitably implicated. Therefore, relatively speaking, the most one can do to approach objectivity in interpretation is to try to make the choice of the jumping-in point as consciously as possible so that one is in a position to take it into account.

In what follows, I shall attempt briefly to interpret a fairy tale that seems to illuminate certain problems related to the feminine principle. It is an Austrian fairy tale called "In the Black Wom-an's Castle."[20]

Once upon a time there was a crofter (*Keuschlegger*)[21] who had seven children. When his eldest daughter was twelve years old, he wanted to find her a place as a maidservant, so he packed up her clothes and set out with her. As they were going along the road, a wagon without any horses drawing it came toward them and stopped in front of them. It was completely black, and a woman who was just as black looked out of it and offered to take on the girl as a maid. She gave the father some money and prom-ised him a further sum if he brought the girl back to the same spot in eight days. "If she's a good girl, things won't go badly for her," she said. After eight days she took the girl off with her to a castle in the forest and showed her to a little room right next to the entrance. The black woman told her that if in that room she thought of anything she wanted, that thing would immediately appear before her. She also gave her the keys to the house, which had a hundred rooms. Each day the child was to sweep and tidy up one of the rooms, all except for the hundredth. "If in three years," the black woman said, "you haven't gone into the forbid-den room, your fortune will be made." At first the "wench" fol-lowed these instructions, but fourteen days before the end of the three years, she could no longer contain her curiosity, and she unlocked the hundredth room. There she saw "the woman inside;

but she was already completely white except for the tips of her toes, which were still black." Quickly the girl slammed the door shut and ran to her room, but the woman was already there, and she asked her if she had been in the hundredth room. In spite of the black woman's horrifying threats, the girl lied steadfastly and said she hadn't been there. Then suddenly she was in the middle of a wild forest, wretchedly dressed and with nothing to eat and nothing to drink. "There she stayed for a while."

Nearby in the royal capital, the young king was dreaming that he should get up, go hunting, and whatever he found, he should love like himself. When the dream had repeated for the third time, he finally obeyed. His hunters found the girl in a cave, the king fell in love with her, brought her home, and soon made her his wife. A year later she gave birth to a wonderfully beautiful little boy. But the third night after that, unexpectedly, the black woman came to her and said, "Now you are queen. You have your child, and now I am asking you, were you in the hundredth room?" "No, no," said the young queen. "I'll take your child away, and you'll go deaf." Still the queen kept up her denial. The black woman disappeared with the child, and the queen went deaf. This happened twice more. Again and yet again the black woman took a child, and the queen also became dumb and blind. For a long time already, the king's mother had been angry; now she persuaded the king that his wife was a witch and child murderer. And after the third disappearance of a child, the king heeded her and condemned his wife to be burned at the stake. She was already at the stake and the fire was about to be lit when all of a sudden a black wagon came driving up, in which sat the black woman, holding the three children. She approached the queen and said, "Now I'm asking you for the last time. You're about to be burned. Were you in there or not?" But this time, too, no was the answer. And hardly had the queen said it when the strange woman turned completely white like snow and said, "All right, go back up to the castle. Everything is again now as it was before. I already know, you were not in there; you only looked inside. If you had once said that you were inside, I would have reduced you to dust and ashes. Now you have completely redeemed me. The castle is yours, and she who has slandered you

181

shall be burned at the stake." So the king's evil old mother was burned as a witch, and the young royal couple with their three princes lived happily ever after.

The resemblances to, and also the deviations from, the widely known Grimm's tale "Mary's Child" are quite evident and will be discussed later.[22] But this parallel was chosen as the main version rather than "Mary's Child," because the latter has obviously been reworked from a Christian point of view, whereas the present variant seems to represent a more intact form of the story.

The Interpretation of the Fairy Tale

While one is still hesitating to face "jumping in" to the interpretation, the question always arises whether this tale reflects more the problem of the unconscious psyche of a man or of a woman. For there are without doubt fairy tales that are more expressions of one side than the other, just as both men and women took part in the shaping and telling of the tales—as they still do today.[23] In general we would be inclined to think—and it often proves empirically to be the case—that stories with a male main character are related to the psychology of men and those with a female main character are related to the psychology of women; but there are also exceptions to this, for sometimes these main figures represent the animus or anima and can therefore better be applied the other way around.[24] In addition, in some fairy tales two children are the vehicles of fate.[25] Thus there is no simple principle that will provide an adequate answer to this question. In the story before us, the fate of the girl could be seen as that of the crofter's anima, but one could also see the girl as a woman, and then one would interpret the crofter as the father-animus figure in the girl. In fact, the question is altogether falsely posed if it takes as its point of departure categories related to individual human personalities. Looking at this story more closely, we see that the girl probably represents neither a woman nor an anima, but is an archetypal Kore figure, that is, a feminine being in whom the archetypal anima of the man[26] as well as the archetypal model of the feminine ego is depicted.[27] In addition, the course of events in which this figure becomes involved can be interpreted in terms of the psychological problems of both sexes. Seen from the point of view of the deeper, collective levels of the unconscious, both patterns are actually interwoven,[28] just as in the outer reality of the simple folk out of whose midst this tale comes, the image of the real woman and the anima, on the one hand, and that of the real man and the animus, on the other, remain, as a result of projection, to a great extent indistinct.[29]

The crofter has seven children. No mother is mentioned; she must be dead. Thus the tale begins with a group of eight figures, among which only the father and the daughter emerge clearly. As Jung has shown, the number eight, like the number four, indicates psychic wholeness. Numbers that are a multiple of four come up with particular frequency in this story. The girl is twelve years old; she has to wait eight days to assume her position definitively; she is not allowed to enter the hundredth room.; the black woman imposes four trials on her (three times taking her children away, and once confronting her with burning at the stake). Thus the rhythm 4, 8, 12, 100 is stressed, and from this we can conclude that here we are dealing with psychic processes connected with individuation.[30]

According to R. Allendy, the number eight has on one hand the meaning of a double quaternity, and on the other it betokens a final equilibrium arrived at through a process of development;[31] psychologically this would mean the Self. But although the number of figures here indicates a psychic totality, an essential aspect is missing from this initial situation, which ordinarily we would expect to find—the image of the mother. It is for that reason that the entire process represented in the story aims at redeeming the "mother imago," that is, lifting her up from her "unilluminated" position into the light and renewing contact with her. At the beginning of the fairy tale, we have an incomplete family; at the end, a relatively complete one. It often happens in fairy tales that at the beginning a symbol of wholeness appears—for example, a group composed of a father with three sons[32]—but this wholeness is lacking an aspect, for example, the feminine element. We can deduce from this that in the collective consciousness an attitude (for example, a religious form) is dominant, which though in principle taking into account the psychic totality, the Self (and nearly every living religion does do this), does not or does not sufficiently acknowledge some particular empirically-psychologically demonstrable aspect of the Self. Thus the archetype of wholeness or totality is inadequately accommodated on the human level and is unable to carry out all of its functions. In the initial situation of the present fairy tale, as already pointed out, the mother image is conspicuously missing; however, we should postpone for the moment drawing cultural-historical conclusions from this.

In a poor farm family with lots of children that is lacking a mother, it is natural for the oldest girl to be charged with the role of filling in as the father's companion and the children's mother. Thus it is by no means an accident that it is the destiny of the girl in this story to have to come to terms with a primal image of the feminine so as to be able to discover her own nature. If we look at this as a personal situation, we can say that such a girl could very easily develop a father complex, and this fits with parallel versions in which the girl is brought to a crisis through the father's erotic advances.[33] If, however, one remembers that this "wench" is not a human individual, we must formulate the situation in more exact terms as follows: The girl represents a Kore, an archetypal component of the collective unconscious, whose tendency is to transform the archetype of the mother and the feminine and to constellate it in an entirely different way. This figure also reflects at the same time an anima need of the unconscious psyche of countless men and the tendency toward individuation in innumerable women. As a feminine being, she is capable of personifying a new form of eros and emotional relatedness in and through which the image of the "black woman"—whatever that may signify—can be redeemed as a psychic function.

The fact that the story stems from a milieu of poor anonymous folk—the "wench" in this version does not even have a name[34]—suggests that the problem of the redemption of the dark mother was not constellated in the first instance on the level of the predominant culture, but rather was constellated in the psyche of natural, simple folk as a psychic need, and that the search for something missing that is implied in it arose from the "inferior," "lower" level in people. Only when the girl becomes queen does the problem develop anything like the potential for becoming conscious on the collective level.

Though in this version the father intentionally indentures his daughter to the black woman for money, in other variants he often sells her unintentionally by promising the demoness in exchange for money whatever is hidden in his house, and it is only revealed afterward that this is the still unborn girl.[35] The father may here symbolically represent a traditional collective disposition;[36] the figure is suitable for portraying a certain quality of inertia that is unwilling to change in the face of crisis, but prefers to sacrifice the future, the child, only to acquire enough energy to continue to persist. Here the father irresponsibly indentures his daughter to an obviously strange, witchlike figure just to be able to keep on going in the same rut. Thus the traditional masculine approach is unfavorable to the female figure. If one looks at the girl as an anima, we would have to think in terms of a habitual neglect of the anima. However, if we see her as a feminine figure of the Self, the father would represent a collective approach to women, which exercises an inhibiting influence on the development of conscious feminine individuality. This can also often be observed in individual cases of father complexes in daughters.

The approach of the black wagon, moving by itself without the help of horses, is the formal beginning of the dramatic entanglement. It moves without a team of animals—without connection to the world of animal instinct—and a folk audience would immediately assume that it is being propelled by the force of magic and witchcraft, which also places the black woman in the coach in the company of black sorceresses and witches. Unknown "super-natural"—in other words, spiritual—forces are at her dis-posal. Also the absence of horses displaces her atmospherically from the realm of a pure *mater naturae,* such as, for example, an Asiatic mother goddess like Cybele, or the Celtic goddess Epona, or the Germanic goddess Freyja, whose chariots are always drawn by animals. The woman of our story has something unnat-ural about her, which is consonant with the motif of her being cursed or in need of redemption. The spiritual component of the black woman emerges more clearly in a Hessian variant of the tale,[37] in which the girl is carried off to a black castle by a beauti-ful black-clad virgin. At the end of the fourth year, the child looks into the forbidden room and sees there "four black virgins engrossed in reading books who seem at that moment to get frightened." This book reading also seems to hint at magic and secret knowledge, which once again removes the figures from the realm of pure nature beings. The quaternity of the black women in this last version, moreover, clearly points to the nature of the black woman as being related to psychic wholeness.[38] The eerie quality of the woman in the coach is further underlined by her color, which places her in the realm of the chthonic gods, in a transcendental realm, and even, from a Christian point of view, in the realm of evil. All the same, this last-mentioned aspect does not seem to me to be a prominent one. Rather the black color is connected with the motif of not wanting to be seen, which is one of the dominant themes in the story. We must also remember that in non-Christian contexts even "good" gods can be black. For example, the Egyptian deities Isis and Osiris are black,[39] and here this color indicates their affinity with the beyond, not with evil. Nonetheless, in our tale the black color is connected with the curse that weighs on the woman, and her unredeemed state and her ambivalence are also expressed by the fact that, on one hand, she wants human help but, on the other, does not want to be seen getting it.

In this connection the question arises why this woman who is capable of sorcery and can effortlessly run her household by mag-ical means would seek a young human child as a maidservant.

To begin with, we are dealing here with a very widespread archetypal motif[40] in which a demonic figure carries off a human being to assist either in housework or in bodily care (washing, combing, lousing).[41] It is as though the dark demonic world itself longed for the ordering function of the human consciousness and could not exist without it. The archetypal powers have need of the human element, for as long as they are not lived on the human level—and, what is more, are not consciously acknowledged—they seem to lack a dimension of reality. In the present example, it is not so much the light of knowledge, of human consciousness, that is sought after, but rather the opus, the effort of cleaning and sweeping. As a result, this work has a double meaning. In the foreground and to all appearances, the girl only has to clean the castle; in the background and on a hidden level, in the "forbidden chamber" the black woman herself is also cleansed through this process and brought from blackness to whiteness.[42] The parallel is obvious with the alchemical opus, in which the materia prima is brought from the nigredo to the albedo through human work[43] (with the work of washing often particularly emphasized).[44] In this phase of the individuation process what is of primary importance is the work on the shadow and bringing to consciousness projections and other unconscious material of an ambiguous nature.[45] The curious thing in the present tale is that the black woman only demands that her castle be cleaned and keeps passionately secret the redemption of her own blackness that is accomplished simultaneously. This is of a piece with the fact that the place she provides for the girl is a little room right by the entrance to her forest castle; in other words she does not admit the girl unreservedly into her realm. At the same time this little room imposes a quite narrow framework on the child, so that she is not overwhelmed by the greater figure of the black woman. Thus a boundary is established, and it is on this "limit line" that the whole further drama is constellated. Seen in terms of personal psychological processes, the likely interpretation of this is that by this means the human ego is set apart from the divine-demonic figure in such a way as to ward off an inflation or an explosion.

We could also see this little room as fulfilling the function of a cloister during an initiation, according to the custom of many cults.[46] To the extent that the girl actually represents an archetypal ego, such an interpretation would not be off the mark; but the motif has still deeper ramifications.

If we take both female figures to be archetypes, then we could say that in the unconscious itself, the differentiation of a dark aspect of the Self from a more human side of the Self is being prepared. This would be a process going on entirely within the core of the psyche itself, which would only become visible in the collective consciousness much later. This process could be compared, *mutatis mutandis,* with the differentiation of the God image in Christianity, in which also, with the incarnation, an aspect of the ambivalent father deity was differentiated into a more human and more kindly image of the Self (Christ) and a destructive aspect (Satan). During this process the archetype of the Kore is, as it were, more clearly circumscribed (in the form of the little room), and at the same time its effective influence is so intensified (the girl is given the power of wish fulfillment) that it begins to become visible in the reality of the outside world (presumably as synchronicity phenomena). On closer examination, we may well conclude that this last interpretation is the right one. Nonetheless, the above parallels from the personal-human sphere provide us with an image in whose forms is reflected a basic process of this same nature on the level of the life of a human individual.

Behind the black woman's gesture of closing the girl in, there lies the intention, as we have already said, of keeping her from penetrating into her realm, and at the same time it is an attempt to do to the girl what has been done to her, namely, to close her in and put her under a spell. In this way the unredeemed condition of the black woman is extended in part to the girl. The one archetype infects the other, which is expressed in the fact that now the girl in her little room can do magic just like the witch herself, since all the wishes she makes in this room come true. On the human level, this means that the girl acquires the *imaginatio vera,* in and through which the psychically real becomes real altogether, but which demands by way of compensation an objectification and thus a delimitation of her individuality.[47] This is the so-called active imagination, which can indeed, when misused for the goals of ego, become black magic, but which applied consciously can bring the possibility of self-knowledge and a coming to consciousness par excellence.[48]

The transference of the ability to create reality by imagination from the black woman to the girl signifies that an archetype that is especially energetically charged, and therefore highly constellated, is particularly bent on making itself visible in the human realm through synchronicity phenomena; that is, on manifesting not only on an inner psychic level but also as coincidences in the configuration of outer conditions. This particular intensity in the way things appear is what is transferred to the girl in the castle, and indeed in a specific "little room." Could it be that this is ultimately related to the intrusion of an archetype into the time-space continuum and the "shrinking" of the archetype that is conditioned by this? From the mythological point of view, the castle is a symbol of the mother-anima or of the feminine Self and is especially connected with the psyche's way of relating to this central content, for it is a form created by the human hand.[49] But we shall examine this aspect in greater detail later on.

The bewitched atmosphere of the castle once again removes its owner from the framework of a nature goddess, who would be more likely to dwell in the forest itself, in water, or in heaven. By contrast to that, the castle points to the past cultural framework of this figure when it was closer to consciousness and had not yet, as now, sunk back into the unconscious. The fact that the cultural framework of the figure is that of the past perhaps points to magic, which is an inheritance from pre-Christian culture, an inheritance that was preserved into the Middle Ages as a form of knowledge but then came more and more to be ignored—in other words, the forest again grew over the castle and hid it.

Not only can the girl now perform magic, but in the course of the story more and more of the black woman's attributes and conditions are transferred to her—suffering, being misunderstood, being isolated—until at the end she even inherits the castle and replaces the black woman in it. The archetypal ego, "properly" fulfilling its function, is more and more assimilated to the Self and finally becomes a new image of the Self. Or: the Self transforms ever more within itself, finally taking on a new form.[50]

Interpreting now in terms of the psychology of a man, we could compare the painful development of the girl with the suffering of the Gnostic figure of Sophia,[51] which sinks into darkness and *agnoia,*[52] because the masculine consciousness identifies too strongly with the world of light of the spirit and neglects the emotional side, the anima.[53] Because of this, the anima regressively fuses with the mother imago and must be liberated from it, which in the present tale occurs through the action of the young king.

But this does not yet explain why the black woman places the task of cleaning her castle in the girl's hands, but hides her personal involvement in this as a numinous and horrible secret. As we mentioned above, when mythologically amplified, the castle is a symbol of the feminine self and thus also an analogy for the black woman herself.[54] Also, in alchemy the *castrum* as well as the *vas* is considered as an image of the anima or mother; and the Virgin Mary is often praised as a tower or palace.[55] The castle is the feminine symbol that contains the black woman and also the one that is inherited at the end by the girl from the disappearing redeemed figure. If the girl had just done the cleaning and had never known what she was doing to the black woman in the process, then she could have been compared to an alchemist who distilled his chemical substance and never had any inkling that his own psychic *mysterium* was mirrored in this. Such a person remains stuck in projection by definitively projecting her unconscious into what the Christian view sees as "dead" matter—just as in the present case the castle made of stone represents something inanimate. As a man-made construction, it would also be possible to regard the castle as a form for conceiving the numinous. In that case the cleansing of the castle would mean cleansing one's own religious views from elements of the shadow, but not yet an immediate experience of the numinous itself, which would go beyond that. Only when the girl opens the door of the forbidden chamber and commits the sacrilege of seeking an immediate experience does she transgress into the realm of the deity, as Adam did when he ate from the tree of knowledge.[56]

In fairy tales there is no such thing as a forbidden chamber that is never opened,[57] and such a chamber always contains a *tremendum numinosum*.[58] In the pre-Christian religions this factor was still contained within the religious framework, in that in most cults there was an adytum that could not be entered by lay people except after certain initiations. It was there that the essential religious mystery unfolded.

Related to the framework of the individual, the forbidden chamber—for example, in dreams[59]—represents the "shell" of a complex that is fully splintered off and is therefore utterly incompatible with the prevailing set of conscious ideas. It is a content that provokes panic as well as fascination. But in this fairy tale the image reflects how one archetype is encapsulated vis-à-vis the sphere of the rest of the archetypes. At this point, now, relationship to something outside the narrative becomes indispensable, for such a phenomenon cannot be explained without reference to a particular set of the collective conscious ideas. To wit, presumably the forbidden chamber contains, as in the dream of an individual, an archetypal content that is incompatible with the prevailing consciousness and therefore cannot function as an "organ of the soul." As a result, it becomes energetically charged and thus is repelled by the other psychic contents and becomes isolated in a special position. Here it is the image of the dark mother that has clearly been repressed into such an encapsulated, and at the same time, highly charged special position in the unconscious. After all, even according to the fairy tale itself, there is a curse on the woman, and this curse must have been laid on her at some time by someone; that is, a previous drama is hinted at which led to the current situation. And there is indeed something like a fatal history for each individual archetype, a history that is connected with the human development of consciousness. Now this tale depicts an isolated and unredeemed state of the dark mother imago which obviously cannot function within the living wholeness of the psyche.

The incompatibility of what the girl saw in the room is clearly confirmed by her immediate repulsion; and after she has refused to admit her deed, she is thrown into the darkness and misery of the forest,[60] and even further into a state of total disorientation and loneliness. It looks as though this were the punishment for her lie, but we find out at the end that admission of her deed would have had much worse consequences still, for in that case, the black woman would have "reduced her to dust and ashes." So whatever the girl had done, she would have been contaminated by the tormented state of the black woman, and her lying even turned out to be the relatively "right" and good way out. We might well ask what would have happened if the girl had not opened the hundredth room.[61] Supposedly then she would have received a good wage and could thus have returned to her village eligible for marriage. But then she would have missed her essential destiny of becoming the queen of the country—that is to say, in the realm of the collective consciousness, no transformation would have taken place.

The raging and senseless fury of the black woman about the girl's deed is difficult to understand at first, and since we are dealing here with a central motif, this requires some amplification. In the present version the girl does not really see anything frightening; she only feels her mistress's need for redemption. But the variants reveal another aspect here. There the girl sees a cage with three snakes in it, a green goose or a green toad, a woman who is half fish, and by way of frightening visions, a witch, a nodding skeleton, or the mistress Mary the Cursed who is in the thirteenth room swinging on a blazing swing.[62] In other words, the girl catches a glimpse of an animal-subhuman or a horrifying aspect of her mistress, a side of which hitherto she knew nothing. Particularly informative concerning the rage of the woman is a version published by August Ey, "The Green Maiden,"[63] in which the girl sees this green maiden, who is half fish, half human, in the following setting: she is surrounded by twelve dwarves who are petrified up to their knees and are squatting on little steps.[64] This "maiden" later presses the heroine with the words, "How could you look upon me in my distress?" It is clearly the subhuman and suffering aspect, her helpless and evil side, that this figure wants to hide, and yet it is precisely this same side that makes her dependent on human help. The ambivalent posture of the black woman toward the heroine reminds us of the attitude of Yahweh toward Job, of how Yahweh, in conflict with himself and suffering from his own shadow, Satan, plays a cruel game with the man in order to convert himself by reflection, and finally even being incarnated, in a human being through this process.[65] Like Job, this girl has demands placed upon her and is persecuted at the same time by a clearly superior figure, and it is her knowledge of the helplessness and the suffering of this figure that places her in danger.[66]

The girl is driven off into the woods, where she dwells without food or drink—in the depths of the unconscious in its aspect of nature, pure and without connection with human forms of life.[67] Like an animal, she lives in a cave—a mother symbol stemming from an even deeper, more archaic level of the unconscious,[68] something like the lowest depths of the psyche, where the suffering is so great that, for that reason, suffering can no longer reach one.[69]

Just at this moment, in a distant and unexpected place, the situation is beginning to turn—through the dream of the young king. In the "royal capital," where he lives, a situation prevails that is in many ways compensatory to the one portrayed in the family of the heroine. Whereas in the latter, a father and his daughter predominated and the mother was missing, in the king's court, there are a royal mother and her son, but no father. The old king seems to have disappeared or to be dead. In general "the old king," who is a typical fairy-tale figure, represents the dominant element within the prevailing collective outlook and is thus for the most part originally a symbol of the Self, which, however, in the course of time has become a mere concept, the conventional central notion of the religious and social order.[70] In this late stage, therefore, the aged king often represents an outdated and rigid dominant system that is urgently in need of renewal. When the king dies, then usually a chaotic and dark interregnum begins,[71] which lasts until a new religious symbol has won acceptance. And often the old king stands in the way of such a renewal.[72] In the royal capital in our tale, behind the scenes the old queen[73] obviously continues to a great extent to be in charge; and in our tale it is not the old king who stands in the young king's way, but the old queen who does not want to let the young woman come into her own. The witchlike old queen signifies an emotional tradition, and also perhaps the habit of a material order that is no longer animated by the spirit, with the result that more and more false emotional values and inauthentic forms of human relationship prevail.[74] The new spiritual dominant, the prince, is isolated in this atmosphere, and his unconscious therefore advises him to bring forth a new form of eros—that is, an anima—from the depths of the forest, who is destined to him as his proper companion. Frequently in fairy tales we find the motif of a simple lad who becomes king against the resistance of the old ruler,[75] and such reversals of fortune have to do with processes of transformation in the spiritual orientation of the collective consciousness, which probably ultimately derive from transformations and internal life processes in the interior of the Self.[76] However, in the fairy tale under consideration, this aspect of the problem does not seem to be acute, that is, the young king has already begun to rule, and this assures a proper continuation of the spiritual order. By contrast, however, in the realm of the feminine, that is, of the anima and the feminine mode of life—and thus of course in the area of eros and relationships of feeling—a critical transformation is brewing. This announces itself first in the realm of consciousness in the form of dreams, which force the young king to find and marry the girl, that is, to open himself to an unexpected emotional experience. His hunters find the girl, and with the brevity and simplicity so characteristic of fairy tales, he rescues her and without further ado brings her home with him as his wife.

The girl gets out of her critical situation so suddenly and effortlessly that we involuntarily fear ex post facto difficulties. Considering matters from the girl's side, we must see this elevation
to queenhood as somehow connected with, if not a direct consequence of, her having looked into the forbidden chamber—as
though it was precisely through this that she brought her extraordinary destiny on herself. Through this she was raised out of the
anonymity of the ordinary collective life into the center,[77] and on
top of it became a symbolic individual, whom all look up to as a
guiding image. From amplifications we know that she always
was this already, but the fairy tale portrays the turning point in
which this content became visible.

Seen from the point of view of the psychology of a woman,
the young king would represent a collective animus figure, and
becoming connected with him would mean that through her isolation in the forest cave,[78] the girl had achieved a spiritual connection with the collective consciousness. While—from the point of
view of the realm of the archetypes—the psychic content reflected
in the girl sinks into darkness, conversely, looked at from the
point of view of the sphere of human consciousness, it arises out
of the unconscious collective psyche onto the surface, where unexpectedly it suddenly becomes visible. "Immortal: mortal; mortal:
immortal; for the life of the former is the death of the latter, and
the life of the latter is the death of the former," says Heraclitus.[79]
Here he is certainly alluding to the fact that the archetypes (im-
mortals) must be diminished if they are to be realized within the
human realm, and conversely, that a human being is burst apart
if he or she is assimilated by an archetype.[80] The expulsion of the
girl from the castle in the forest and her elevation to queenhood
is therefore, from a psychological point of view, a completely co-
herent sequence of events.[81]

A further possibility in the present tale is that seeing the black
woman had such unfortunate consequences because it was the
girl alone who saw the dark figure of the Self while still without
a connection to the king, that is, while she was still in a state
without the potentiality for a spiritual understanding that would

have helped her to relate to the experience with clarity. Perhaps it was for this reason that destiny led her first on the sidetrip to the union with the king before the second phase of her confrontation with the black woman was constellated.

At the court the young queen bears a boy. She becomes a mother herself, and at this moment the problem of the "dark mother" reappears. The symbol of the boy, seen in the framework of female psychology, indicates a potentiality for conscious, creative enterprise, which here comes to life but is at once seemingly destroyed again by an evil stroke of fate.[82] The fact that there are three births indicates a dynamic element.[83] Various details have already shown that there is something like a hidden spiritual element connected with the black woman. This is hinted at by the "spirit-driven" coach, the book reading of the young black women (in the variant), and in the self-fulfilling wishful thinking that is possible in the black woman's castle.[84] But this spiritual element, so long as it is part of the black woman's realm, seems very ambiguous, in dubious proximity to black magic and witchcraft. At last in the realm of consciousness (the king's court), it is transformed through a new birth into a creative spirituality.[85] But precisely at this moment the problem of the black woman is constellated afresh at the ultimate level of intensity, and through her persistent lying the queen not only loses her child three times, but is also struck deaf, dumb, and blind and falls under suspicion of infanticide. She is, as it were, identified from the outside as the black woman, the horrific mother, and she loses every possibility for human expression and contact. It is as though it were now she who was in the forbidden chamber. Interpreted on the personal level, this corresponds to a state of severe depression, if not of psychological dissociation.[86] And although the queen in this critical situation gives birth to a child twice more, that is, although her positive feminine being is preserved, this cannot emerge into the light, for the "shadow" of the black woman covers her completely. We should try to keep in mind what an almost supernatural and heroic sacrifice the queen's persistence in her lie means, for in so persisting she consciously sacrifices one of the most profound female instincts, maternal feeling for her child. The individuation process leads here to a sacrifice and thus to a making conscious to the ultimate degree of merely blind instinctive motherliness,[87] and it is precisely this sacrifice that "redeems" the archetype of the dark mother through this process of making conscious, in other words, that brings it back, in the figure of the new queen, to its meaningful psychic function.[88]

During this last trial, the young queen's mother-in-law, the king's mother, suddenly appears as a negative figure and a helper of the black woman in her tormenting role, so that in effect during the day and out in the open the girl is plagued by the old queen, and at night and in secret, by the black woman. By itself this episode of the queen's being falsely accused of infanticide is a well-known old motif[89] that stems from medieval times, and it is found as an element in the plot of many other fairy tales, though in a different relationship to the overall meaning.[90] The duality, however, of the slanderer is relatively rare. A Russian parallel to the present fairy tale, reworked from a Christian perspective, varies the motif in the following manner: The heroine in this case is named Maryushka and is the godchild of the Holy Mother and God-bearer Mary. In the forbidden room, the girl sees her godmother carrying and swaddling the Christ child and placing him on a throne. Later when Maryushka has become the queen, the Holy Virgin admonishes her to confess her transgression of her command, and she punishes the girl's lying by each time ripping a hand or a foot off her child, sticking it in the mother's mouth, and disappearing with the child. This causes her husband to repudiate her. When she finally admits the truth, she gets back her children and, finally, her husband too.[91] This parallel illuminates the secret identity of the nocturnally appearing feminine figure and of the female slanderer who during the day portrays the queen as an infanticide.[92] When the black woman is redeemed in the tale we have chosen as the main version, the old queen is burned as a witch. She represents a purely "destructive" (time-bound) shadow aspect of the black woman herself.

Now the peripeteia of the tale reaches its climax: the young queen must be bound at the stake as a witch. The symbol of being burned represents the emotional suffering of the conflict reaching its most acute point, but even in this moment of the girl's greatest torment, she still denies her deed. Thereupon, completely unexpectedly and as though by a miracle, the reversal occurs through which everything turns to good. Only the old queen—an evidently untransformable aspect of evil—is burned, whereas the black woman becomes entirely white. She is redeemed and disappears into the unknown. She gives her former castle to the girl, who on this account now commands two domains at once—at court she is the queen and in the forest she is the mistress of the castle. In other words, the girl becomes a symbol in which the realm of collective consciousness and the depths of the collective unconscious are vitally connected.[93]

But all this happens in the version before us because the girl denies her deed to the end—a strange motif, worthy of closer examination. In the numerous Christianity-tinged versions, like "Mary's Child" and the Russian version mentioned above, as well as others, the motif has been turned around, that is, the denial brings the suffering, and an eventual confession brings the redemption. Evidently, the motif of redemption resulting from consistent denial was found repugnant, against the grain of Christian ethical sensibility. In our version, too, the motif is somewhat deflected in that the black woman seems to be making a hair-splitting distinction between whether the girl only looked in or had actually been inside the room. But the variants enumerated in Bolte-Polivka[94] in which unadulterated denials leads to redemption are so numerous that we are compelled to take them seriously as a valid version of the story. This deed can hardly be considered merely a childishly cowardly or wily lie, for the conscious sacrifice of the children is completely out of proportion to this. Therefore there must be a secret hinted at in this behavior that is not so easy to understand. As we consider this initially, here too, a certain parallel destiny between this girl and the biblical figure of Job strikes us; for as Job is confronted with the inner divine opposites (Yahweh-Satan) and through his insight into

Yahveh's suffering arrives at a critical point, so here the queen is plagued by the black woman and her shadow, the old queen, but is still not supposed to know anything of the goddess's ambivalence. Thus the girl's silence can be compared to the wise gesture of Job when he said, "Behold, I am of small account; what shall I answer thee? I lay my hand on my mouth. I have spoken once, and I will not answer; twice, but I will proceed no further" (Job 40:4–5).[95] It seems to me that this girl also shows something of the wisdom and self-discipline of Job.[96] Clearly, however, there is the difference from Job that, whereas he rightly felt completely innocent, the heroine of the fairy tale actually did commit a transgression, though it seems in no way commensurate with the threatened punishment.[97] However, the words of the green maiden, "Child, how could you look upon me in my distress?" reveal that in the wrath of the dark mother, her rage about being caught in her shadow aspect by far outweighs her irritation over the transgression of her command.

In my opinion, a parallel to this strange motif of denial is the so-called negative confession of sins of the ancient Egyptians. At the judgment of the dead in the beyond, the deceased enumerates a long list of sins with the assurance that he has *not* committed those. Despite this, it must be presumed that he knows of some that he did commit. As H. Jakobsohn has explained,[98] for an Egyptian of those ancient times, confession of his sins would have seemed blasphemous, since he would thus be ascribing to himself the individual potentiality or power to stand up to the gods on his own. Thus the negative confession of sins is to be understood as a gesture of humility and awe.

Still more archaic but it seems to me along the same lines of religious behavior is the gesture of "not doing the same thing" of the dairy farmers of Uri, Switzerland, whom E. Renner described in his book *Goldener Ring über Uri* (Golden Ring over Uri).[99] Whenever anything extraordinary, that is, "numinous" happens, for example, when the "it" makes the cows disappear, or the mountain milking hut suddenly seems to have melted away by magic, then the most important thing for the dairyman is "not to do the same thing," through which he avoids, as it were, getting emotionally entangled with the demonic; as a result "it" will let go of him.[100]

Although in these examples we have expressions from entirely different stages of culture, of which the last-mentioned gesture of "not doing the same thing" represents the most archaic and the wise silence of Job the most differentiated form, nevertheless it seems to me that we can recognize in these examples a common primal form of religious behavior, which is characterized by the following common elements: safeguarding of the human boundary with the numinous, in which a certain humility is expressed; a self-disciplined protection of oneself from one's own emotion (panic) and from the emotion of the deity by preventing getting affectively entangled with it; and an awe-conditioned letting the divine be as it is.

It is possible that the denial of the girl in our present tale represents a return to such a primal religious gesture; and it seems to me no accident that this forgotten form of behavior crops up in a fairy tale that illuminates problems of the development of feminine psychic nature. For in this gesture there is not only a safeguarding of the boundary with the divine, but beyond that a certain feeling of emotional relatedness to the divine, which could be characterized as a tactful, protective letting-it-be-as-it-is.[101] "For the spirit searches all things, yea, the deep things of God" (I Corinthians 2:10) is a confession of the masculine logos; but it is far more the nature of the feminine to cover up the dark abysses of the deity with the mantle of love. (These are not two opposed approaches but rather complementary ones.) Thus the silence of the heroine could represent a differentiated form of eros in which there is acceptance of an antinomy within the divine principle.[102]

Also in the most ancient Chinese wisdom book, the *I Ching,* the feminine principle, *kun,* is characterized by an ability to bear things without judging them ethically, and by taciturnity and discretion.[103] One of the oracular pronouncements even says, "bound-up sack, no blame, no praise," which is interpreted in the commentary as meaning "strict reserve." Whereas it befits the masculine principle *(ch'ien)* to structure things and make things manifest, in a rhythm of opening and closing, it is the latter that seems to correspond to the feminine principle. By behaving in this manner, the girl in our fairy tale shows herself a match for the dark mother.

The masculine-active animus of a woman continually tries to seduce her into "taking over" even this aspect of her nature and destiny, and thus hinders her inner development. The girl, however, is a guiding example for a certain kind of right behavior. Erich Neumann speaks of a dimming of ego activity. The black woman represents a very dark root of feminine life, a wishful dreaming from which intrigues and a secret influence over others are born.[104] This dark feminine power here should not be dragged into the light by ethical judgment, for in this darkness the germ of individuation also lies hidden.

It is unmistakable that in this motif of denial is to be found the compensation for a certain Christian ethical ideal of truthfulness, and this is also shown by the fact that the Christianity-tinged versions of the story have done away with this motif.[105] At this point, our interpretation comes to the problem, touched upon in the introduction, of the cultural-historical place of the present mythologem.

General Psychological Conclusions

It has become palpable at various points in our interpretation that this fairy tale about the "black woman" could compensate for a collective attitude of consciousness connected with Christianity.[106] Let us now briefly go over its most important features. In the lower strata of the people the lack of a mother image makes itself felt,[107] and unfavorably against the feminine in this situation stands a masculine, habitual attitude. In the upper layers of society, behind the scenes, an image of woman gone negative is dominant. In the collective unconscious itself at the same time there is a dark mother imago, encapsulated and cut off from all its vital functions. The castle hidden in the forest indicates, for the dating of the fairy tale, a period following the Middle Ages, for although magic and witchcraft were condemned during the Middle Ages, they were not forgotten. Here, however, a content is reflected of which nothing whatever is known any longer. The past "curse" under which the black woman labors could well refer to the medieval witch hunts. Thus we are justified in dating the tale between 1500 and 1800 and placing it in Christian Europe. Since it deals with the reign of a still young king, we might narrow the time down more precisely to the beginning of the era of rationalism, which represents a masculine spiritual heritage of the Middle Ages, in the beginning period of which the forgetting of the dark mother takes place. The beginning of rationalism was not consciously anti-Christian in orientation,[108] and as a result there was no crisis in the succession of the king's lineage, but there was a transformation in the realm of the feminine, both of the anima and the real woman.[109] There, the archetypal background was forgotten, and at the same time a crisis began to take shape that was only later to reach the threshold of consciousness.

In the action of the tale, not only is this problem of a past time reflected, but at the same time a development is anticipated, which we are only beginning to realize consciously today. We are speaking of a transformation in the attitude toward the feminine, which first became visible in the field of the collective consciousness in phenomena like women's emancipation, in other words, not until around 1900.[110]

Therefore it seems of essential significance that this tale was diffused in Christianity-tinged variants and is even more well known in those forms than in the one presently under consideration, and that in them the "black woman" is for the most part equated with the Virgin Mary. This must express a perception on the part of the people, who sensed that this black or green woman really represented a mother goddess, whom one could of course only identify with the Mother of God. Conversely, however, the particular popularity of "black madonnas" seems to suggest a longing for a more earthy, darker form of this mother imago.

The name given to the figure in a Russian variant seems to be particularly revealing in this respect. There she is called "Maria the Cursed," and in the forbidden thirteenth room she is swinging on a swing. This swinging surely points to a movement of opposites within the figure itself,[111] which can only be interrupted through an intervention on the part of human consciousness. This fairy-tale figure, the black woman, is in fact an archetypal figure that could be characterized as the shadow of the Virgin Mary, analogous to Satan as the shadow of Yahweh. However, in the case of God and Satan, an irreconcilable rift opened up, whereas this dark woman seems much less unequivocally cut off from the light. She embodies a somewhat darker aspect of the anima image in men and the Self in women, which in the dogmatic figure of Mary is inadequately represented and therefore is driven down into the unconscious. Here the witchlike features of the figure are particularly revealing. In this connection, Jung, in *Psychological Types,* pointed out that the belief in witches was psychologically of a piece with the increasing prominence of the cult of Mary.[112] Through the anima image of the man being assimilated to the general symbol of Mary (whereas before that in courtly love it was represented by a lady the man chose himself), it lost its *individual* expression and the potential for further individual differentiation. "Since the psychic relation to woman was expressed in the collective worship of Mary, the image of the woman lost a value to which human beings had a natural right." As a result, this individual value sank into the unconscious and there animated infantile-archaic dominants. The relative devaluation of the real woman was compensated for by demonic features—woman appeared as a persecutor and witch. "The consequence of increasing Mariolatry was the witch hunt. . . ." What Jung elucidates here particularly in relation to the anima problem can also be applied to the development of a woman, which is to say that women's individual potential for development was also inhibited by this cultural-historical situation.[113] However, these potentialities for feminine individuation are archetypally personified in the present tale, and the tale shows how this germ of individuation must prevail in the face, simultaneously, of a false image of woman in the collective consciousness (the old queen) and an archaic mother and female image in the collective unconscious (the black woman) in order to attain its own potential.

But what does "the shadow of the Virgin Mary" mean here? To begin with, hidden within this figure are certain (particularly animal) aspects of pre-Christian nature and earth goddesses,[114] which are still preserved in "Mother Holle," "The Devil's Grandmother," and other similar fairy-tale figures. This nature-mother aspect is indicated by the black (earthy) and green (vegetation) variations in the color of the demons and their animal forms of appearance, such as goose,[115] lizard, and serpent. A further aspect is represented by the form of the "nodding skeleton," which moves the figure into the vicinity of death. The feminine principle is equated to such a great extent with the notion of life— because woman is a child-bearing, life-giving being—that the death-related aspect of the "great mother"[116] was forgotten, which was venerated as "the black woman" in the pagan religions, for example, in the Greek Hecate and Persephone,[117] in the Germanic Hel, or in the Latin personification of death (*mors* is feminine). Also the aspect, described by Karl Kerényi, of the wrathful and mournful mother goddess—who was venerated in Phigalia, for example, as black Demeter and Demeter Erinys—is a parallel to the figure we are now considering.[118] The hiddenness and the wrath against those who "reveal" the goddess is also an archetypal motif, for the goddess Neith, who as Plutarch says, "many held to be Isis,"[119] proclaims of herself, "I am everything that was and that will be, and still no mortal has ever lifted my robe." This Neith is a goddess of the underworld, who is depicted with a green face and green hands (!). Later she fused, as mentioned above, with black (!) Isis.

Finally, in this "shadow of Mary" also lies the element of the medieval witch as a specific form of evil, who expresses herself, inter alia, in uninhibited lust, jealousy, intrigue, sucking other people dry, and general egocentrism. A part of this witch aspect is destroyed at the end of the fairy tale in the person of the old queen, because at least *this* form of her human influence is conditioned by time and can therefore be eliminated. The eternal dark root of witchhood, however, though it has ostensibly disappeared—it ceases to be depicted in the tale—cannot in itself be susceptible to elimination. Those dark forces that would have made it possible for the black woman to reduce the girl "to dust and ashes" are, in other words, no longer mentioned, just as the question is also left open about where the redeemed woman who turned white vanished to. Thus in this fairy tale only a part of the path to the solution of the problem it deals with is archetypally sketched out, but not a complete lysis,[120] and this is perhaps expressed in the number five, the number of figures remaining at the end of the story, and in the vagueness about where they live.

The figures remaining at the end are: the young king and queen and their three boys. The number five, according to R. Allendy, points to the *natura naturata,*[121] that is, there are the four elements and qualities which represent an abstract equilibrium, and the fifth element is the field of their action, the substrate, and is therefore connected with the natural, individual corporeal beings of the time-space continuum. Therefore the number five is also correlated with the physical outlines of the human body.[122] From the negative point of view, five is associated with the *illusion* of material reality.[123] It is the number of the mother goddess Juno and of Hecate (!), whose countenance was adorned with a five-petaled rose. Also, along with four, it was the number of Mercury.[124]

Thus the number five belongs to the sphere of the chthonic mother and her son, but it also has, as *quinta essentia,* the meaning of the one that binds the four to unity. Therefore perhaps we should imagine the group remaining at the end of the tale, not as in figure 3, but as in figure 4. Here the girl represents something like the central reference point of a masculine quaternio. But even when the situation is illuminated in this way, we are left with the salient fact that the world of masculine consciousness still has very youthful features, whether we interpret this as a still

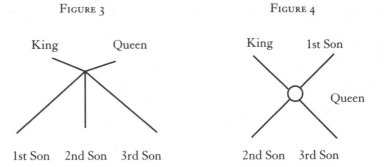

FIGURE 3

King   Queen

1st Son   2nd Son   3rd Son

FIGURE 4

King   1st Son

Queen

2nd Son   3rd Son

immature attitude of the collective consciousness or—as related to a woman—we see it as a still undeveloped form of the animus.

The queen's three sons constitute a triad of relatively vaguely drawn boys. If the fairy tale had a more ancient, non-Christian outlook, this triad could be connected with the Celto-Roman, Germanic, and Slavic triads of deities.[125] As Jung explains in his "A Psychological Approach to the Dogma of the Trinity,"[126] the number three has to do with a process of development in time, and at the same time the three is "the One that has become knowable."[127] Thus the threefold birth in this fairy tale could well be interpreted as the birth of a divine child, but with the additional nuance that this new divine child manifests itself three times, that is, by taking form within the earthly time flow. This makes these boys close to the *Mercurius triunus,* whom Jung interpreted as a *correspondentia* or *analogia Christi* in physical nature.[128] In "The Green Maiden," the three boys are the sons of the king and of the golden stag, which latter clearly suggests Mercurius. When in "Mary's Child" the heroine sees the Holy Trinity in the forbidden chamber, the finger with which she touches their splendor is turned into gold. Could we perhaps draw the conclusion that in the destiny of the godchild something is repeated here that was prefigured in the destiny of her godmother, the *domina creaturae* and mother of the Trinity? Also the three little sons of Mary's Child, while they are dwelling with Mary in the beyond, play with the globe of the world! It is as though the three boys represented an earthly reflection of the "metaphysical" trinity. This can also be connected with a charm for the protection of their flocks spoken by the dairymen of Uri in the springtime, in which the Trinity also takes the form of three boys:[129] "The dear cattle walk, over many days and through the year, over many ditches. I hope and trust that there they meet the three boys. The first is God the Father, the second God the Son, and the third is God the Holy Spirit, who watch over my cattle for me. . . ."[130]

Drawing the Trinity symbol in and down into such an earthly, human form compensates for a perception of the Godhead in which it is set too far "out there," too far away in some metaphysical realm, in such a way that human relations to it are in danger of getting lost. By contrast, in the motif of the three boys an interiorization of the contents of Christian belief may be anticipated, similar in some respects to that hinted at in the works of the Romantics and to that made possible by Jung's psychological understanding of the religious symbol. But this development in which the Christian God image becomes real and understandable within the inner psyche could represent only the first step, on the basis of which the problems of darkness, evil, and the fourth element can first be posed in a real way. However, it is just this last problem that our fairy tale does not go so far as to resolve, for we do not learn where the woman goes, nor do we find out anything about the one who cursed her. This incompleteness of the tale's lysis is connected with the fact that what we are dealing with here is a representation of a collective pattern, whereas any resolution going beyond that would only be possible in the individuation process of an individual human being. Nonetheless, such a tale can serve as a path-blazing symbol, which can shed some light for individuals on their quests.

Notes

1. On the position of psychology within the sciences, see C. G. Jung, "Analytical Psychology and Education," in *The Development of Personality,* cw 17, paras. 163–64, pp. 88f.

2. Cf. particularly C. G. Jung and K. Kerényi, "The Psychology of the Child Archetype" and "The Psychological Aspects of the Kore," in cw 9/i, pp. 151–206; and the practical examples of Jung's fairy-tale interpretation in "The Phenomenology of the Spirit in Fairytales," ibid., pp. 207–54; as well as the rest of Jung's works, passim.

3. This does not hold true for the local saga. Max Lüthi, in his outstanding study *Das europäische Volksmärchen* (The European Folk Tale) (Berne, 1947), showed that the hero of the local saga appears as a real person in our sense of the word, who encounters events from another transcendent dimension; by contrast the hero of the fairy tale is not a person in this sense, but rather is himself part of the transcendent realm. I refer the reader for details to Lüthi's presentation. The hero of the myth is not considered by Lüthi, but he seems to me to occupy a middle ground. He is less human than the vehicle of the action in the local saga, but is less abstract and somewhat more individual than the fairy-tale hero.

4. Individual uniqueness is part of the ego; cf. C. G. Jung, *Aion,* cw 9/ii, para. 10, p. 6.

5. Ibid., p. 21; the fairy-tale hero lacks, as Lüthi says, the "depth quality" and the actual human world of feelings.

6. Cf. ibid., pp. 29, 37–39, 48, passim.

7. Because of the compensatory function of the unconscious; see C. G. Jung, cw 8, para. 545.

8. On this see C. G. Jung, ibid., and Jung, *Seminar über Kinderträume* (Olten: Walter, 1987), pp. 18ff. There the following roots of dreams are mentioned: (1) conscious contents; and (2) constellated contents of the unconscious. The latter are in turn subdivided into: (3) constellations occasioned by conscious contents; and (4) constellations occasioned by unconscious productive processes. Certain dreams seem to have no direct relationship to consciousness, but rather represent, inter alia, reactions to psychic or physical environmental conditions, or are derived from purely creative processes in the unconscious. Cf. "A Seminar with C. G. Jung: Comments on a Child's Dream," trans. E. H. Henley, in *Spring* (Zurich: Analytical Psychology Club of New York, 1974), pp. 200–23.

9. *Psychology and Alchemy,* cw 12, Introduction.

10. Taurus, Aries, Pisces; cf. C. G. Jung, *Aion,* cw 9/ii, passim.

11. For instance, it is possible to observe changes in the rites and myths of the American Indians that can be understood as unconscious reactions to the invasion of the whites. Similarly, we can discern in Greek mythology the reaction to the pre-Greek Mediterranean culture; or in Jewish myth, the reaction to the Exile; and here we are not merely talking about influences that can be understood in cultural-historical terms, but about unconscious, psychic reactions that have taken on symbolic expression.

12. Although each archetype represents an unknown, nevertheless we can speak empirically of the archetype of the Divine Child or of the Wise Old Man or the Great Mother; that is, we can character-ize individual structural elements of the unconscious in a relative manner as functionally definite units.

13. The analogy with the particle and wave nature of light is obvious.

14. "Most distant" is meant here in the sense of "on the average rarely connected, but on the contrary more usually contrasted."

15. See Figure 4, page 206.

16. In the following tale, for example, two separate mother figures appear, of which at the end one is revealed as positive, and the other is burned as a witch. The movement of the story contrasts the two, but amplification of the figures shows their hidden iden-tity. Thus the figures are both identical and not identical. In other words, the movement of the tale specifically isolates certain aspects of an archetype, which comparative consideration (amplification) brings together. This contradiction is explained by the fact that the movement of the story represents an individual case, whereas amplification proceeds statistically, that is, by relating many paral-lel examples.

17. Concerning the significance of the idea of complementarity in psy-chology, see C. G. Jung, *The Structure and Dynamics of the Psyche,* cw 8, para. 545; and C. A. Meier, "Moderne Physik—Moderne Psychologie," in *Die kulturelle Bedeutung der Komplexen Psycholo-gie* (The Cultural Significance of Complex Psychology) (1935), pp. 349ff; and W. Pauli, "Die philosophische Bedeutung der Idee der

Komplementarität" (The Philosophical Significance of the Idea of Complementarity), in *Experientia*, vol. 6 (2) (Basel), pp. 72ff.

18. Cf. C. G. Jung, cw 8.

19. Cf. W. Pauli, "Die philosophische Bedeutung der Komplementarität." The same state of affairs, which Jung describes for psychology in general in *The Structure and Dynamics of the Psyche* (paras. 440ff.) holds particularly true for the description of the archetype. Jung even goes so far as to assert that it is not even certain that the archetype can be described as psychic in nature.

20. From *Märchen aus dem Donaulande* (Fairy Tales from the Valley of the Danube), in the collection F. van der Leyen and P. Zaunert (eds.), *Die Märchen der Weltliteratur* (Fairy Tales of World Literature) (Jena: Diederichs Verlag, 1926), pp. 92ff. The story comes from Styria. I have retold it in a shortened form.

21. A *Keuschler* or *Keuschlegger* is a small farmer who possesses a *Keusche* (hut) and a couple of goats or a cow at the most.

22. For an immensely comprehensive collection of parallels to "Mary's Child" and thus also to this fairy tale, see J. Bolte and G. Polivka, *Anmerkungen zu den Kinder- und Hausmärchen der Brüder Grimm* (Commentary on the Brothers Grimm's Fairy Tales), 5 vols. (1913ff.), vol. 1, pp. 13ff. Hereinafter this work is abbreviated as *B-P*.

23. Cf. the remarks of Pater Pramberger in his introduction to *Märchen aus dem Donaulande*.

24. For example, in fairy tales of the Amor-and-Psyche type.

25. For example, in "Hansel and Gretel," "Little Brother and Little Sister," and so on.

26. The anima has both an archetypal and a personal aspect; in this case of course only the former is in question.

27. Or an aspect of the Self of a woman.

28. Note that C. G. Jung also interprets the Demeter-Kore myth in this twofold fashion in "The Psychological Aspects of the Kore," in cw 9/i, paras. 310ff., pp. 183ff.

29. Cf. C. G. Jung, "The Psychology of the Transference," in *The Practice of Psychotherapy*, cw 16, para. 433, p. 225, according to which in a state of primitivity and total absence of self-knowledge,

the relationship to a woman consists essentially of no more than an anima projection, the same also being true for the image of the man.

30. Cf. C. G. Jung, *Aion,* cw 9/ii, paras. 351ff., pp. 223ff., where, concerning symbols of totality, we find: "The most important of these are geometrical structures containing elements of the circle and quaternity; namely, circular and spherical forms on the one hand, which can be represented purely geometrically or as objects; and, on the other hand, quadratic figures divided into four or in the form of a cross. They can also be four objects or persons related to one another in meaning or by the way they are arranged. Eight, as a multiple of four, has the same significance. A special variant of the quaternity motif is the dilemma of 3 + 1. Twelve (3 × 4) seems to belong here as a solution of the dilemma and as a symbol of wholeness (zodiac, year). Three can be regarded as a relative totality. . . . Psychologically, however, three—if the context indicates that it refers to the Self—should be understood as a defective quaternity or as a stepping-stone toward a quaternity. Empirically, a triad has a trinity over against it as its complement. The complement of the quaternity is unity." Concerning the number 100, see Jung, "The Psychology of the Transference," in cw 16, paras. 525ff., pp. 306ff.

31. *Le symbolisme des nombres* (Paris, 1948), pp. 230, 241.

32. Cf., for example, the Grimm's tale "The Golden Bird" and the numerous parallels to it given in *B-P.*

33. Cf. *B-P,* vol. 1, p. 19. The story then begins to closely resemble the Grimm's tale "Thousandfurs" ("Allerleirauh").

34. In the version influenced by Christianity, she usually bears the name of her godmother, the Virgin Mary, who replaces the black woman. Thus she is called Maria, Mariechen, Maryushka, and so on.

35. Cf. *B-P,* vol. 1, p. 13 and the parallel versions of the Grimm's tale, "The King of the Golden Mountain." Selling children to demons is a widespread archetypal motif. Cf. also *B-P,* vol. 1, p. 21; vol. 2, pp. 318, 320, 516, 526; vol. 3, pp. 97, 107, 465; vol. 1, pp. 98, 302, 490.

36. For a similar interpretation of the father figure, see C. G. Jung, *The Archetypes and the Collective Unconscious,* cw 9/i, para. 396, pp.

214f. There Jung makes this interpretation with regard to the image of the father god, but it seems to me that the same interpretation is also applicable to mythological father figures.

37. Cited from *B-P,* vol. 1, p. 13. This Hessian version, like "Mary's Child," came from Gretchen Wild in Kassel in 1807, and is one of the fairy tales included by the Grimm brothers (1812).

38. This motif, in connection with others, was a key point in my decision to interpret this fairy tale as pertaining more to a woman's psychology, for in this way the black woman or the quaternity of the black woman could be interpreted as an aspect of the Self. Nonetheless, the anima can of course also appear in a quaternity and with symbolic attributes of the Self as a result of contamination. The anima would then in some way represent the (feminine) quaternity principle vis-à-vis a presumably trinity-oriented masculine collective consciousness.

39. Cf. Plutarch, *Über Isis und Osiris* (On Isis and Osiris), text and commentary by T. Hopfner (Prague, 1940), vol. 1, p. 25. Osiris is called "the black one," and a pyramid text addresses him as follows: "Thou art black and great is thy name, Great Black Fortress." His sister-consort Isis is sometimes actually called "the black woman" or "the black-red woman."

40. See also the Grimm's fairy tales "Mother Holle," "The Miller's Drudge and the Cat," and "The Water Nixie"; or the Austrian fairy tale, "The Wild Man."

41. Cf. *B-P,* vol. 1, p. 207.

42. This is suggested by the fact that after the nearly fulfilled three years of cleaning, the woman has become white down to her toes; thus the full three years of cleaning would mean the whitening of the "black woman."

43. Cf. C. G. Jung, *Psychology and Alchemy,* cw 12, passim.

44. Cf., for example, the statement of Maria Prophetissa: "Wash and wash, until the blackness of the Stimmi (antimony?) yields, and that is what they symbolically mean by the albedo." M. Berthelot, *Collection des anciens alchimistes grecs* (Collection of Ancient Greek Alchemists) (Paris, 1887/88), vol. 1, p. 99.

45. Cf. C. G. Jung, "The Psychology of the Transference," in cw 16, para. 471, pp. 262f.

46. This could be compared, for example, to the notion of *katoché* in antiquity, the meaning of which oscillates back and forth between "cloister" and "possession." Cf. Marie-Louise von Franz, *Die Passion der Perpetua* (Zurich: Daimon, 1982), pp. 71f.

47. In alchemy this corresponds to the symbol of the retort or the vessel; cf. C. G. Jung, *Psychology and Alchemy,* cw 12, paras. 408ff., pp. 299ff.

48. Here I must presuppose an understanding of the notion of active imagination. See Jung's commentary on Richard Wilhelm's *Secret of the Golden Flower,* in cw 13, paras. 20ff., pp. 16ff.

49. The castle itself somehow seems to be a kind of dream castle or wish castle, a creature of the imagination. We may think of such expressions as "promising someone a castle in Spain," or "building castles in the air." In the human sphere, such "castles" are often built inwardly by neglected children in order to protect their inner psychic space.

50. On such processes of transformation within the Self, see C. G. Jung, *Aion,* cw 9/ii, para. 381, pp. 242f.

51. The girl could also be compared to the figure of psyche in Apuleius's *Amor and Psyche*. Cf. E. Neumann, *Amor and Psyche,* passim.

52. Unconsciousness.

53. On the meaning of this myth, see C. G. Jung, "The Philosophical Tree," in cw 13, paras. 488f., p. 333.

54. C. G. Jung, *Psychological Types,* cw 6, paras. 427ff., pp. 252ff.; paras. 439ff., pp. 261ff.

55. Cf. ibid. and *Psychology and Alchemy,* cw 12, paras. 338ff., pp. 236ff.; and on city, tower, and wall as mother symbols, C. G. Jung, *Symbols of Transformation,* cw 6, pp. 207ff.; and *Alchemical Studies,* cw 13, para. 433, pp. 324f.

56. It might be felt as a contradiction that sometimes in paraphrasing I characterize the girl as a human being (like Adam) and then again as an archetypal being. But the comparison with Adam is particularly illuminating, because this figure also is sometimes experienced as an ordinary mortal and sometimes as Anthropos. We are dealing precisely with an archetypal image, one of whose essential qualities is that of being human, as opposed to other archetypal figures in which the nonhuman aspect predominates.

57. Cf. *B-P,* vol. 1, pp. 21, 399, 410; vol. 3, pp. 97, 108; vol. 4, p. 239.

58. This can be something horrifying, as in "Bluebeard"; or an unredeemed animus or anima figure; or an animal helper as in the Icelandic fairy tale "Prince Ring and the Dog Snati-Snati"; or something divine, as in "Mary's Child," where it is the Trinity.

59. Cf., for example, the dream of a woman in L. Hoesli, "Jugendträume als Künder eines aussergewöhnlichen Schicksals" (Dreams of Youth as Harbingers of an Extraordinary Destiny), in *Archiv für Neurologie und Psychiatrie,* vol. 72 (1/2), p. 3953, and the parallels educed there.

60. On the meaning of the forest, see Jung, *Alchemical Studies,* cw 13, paras. 241ff., pp. 194ff.

61. One hundred, as mentioned above, is, like ten, a number of completeness; the almost completed three years are four years in the Hessian variant; this reflects the dilemma between three and four.

62. See *B-P,* vol. 1, pp. 13–15; further variants not particularly pertinent here were: twelve cursed old men, twelve cursed men, a cursed man in a gray mantle—in other words, animus figures; as well as Christian motifs, such as Mary washing the feet of the Christ child, the Holy Trinity, and so forth.

63. *Harzmärchen oder Sagen und Märchen aus dem Oberharz* (Fairy Tales from the Harz Region or Sagas and Fairy Tales from the Upper Harz Region) (Stade, 1862), pp. 176ff.

64. The green maiden is married to a golden stag, and she does not shut the girl up in a little chamber but places her on a golden throne.

65. For lack of space, I am compelled here to presume knowledge of Jung's remarks in "Answer to Job," in *Psychology and Religion,* cw 11, pp. 355–470.

66. That the girl, also like Job, becomes withdrawn and silent, see below.

67. How such a content of the collective unconscious can be pushed into the unconscious is incomprehensible. It would be more accurate for us to speak of qualitatively different spheres within the unconscious itself. The forest, for example, represents a purely natural aspect. Cf. C. G. Jung, cw 13, paras. 241ff., pp. 194ff.

68. On the cave as a mother symbol, see C. G. Jung, *Symbols of Trans-formation,* cw 5, para. 182, pp. 12f.; para. 313, pp. 213f.

69. This could be compared to the life of Thousandfurs (Allerleirauh) in the tree, covered with animal hides, up to the time when the king finds her.

70. On this meaning of the king figure, cf. C. G. Jung *Mysterium Coni-unctionis,* cw 14, the chapter "Rex and Regina."

71. Cf., for example, the custom in old African cultures that during the three-day interregnum anyone may kill anyone else. L. Frobe-nius, *Erythräa, Länder und Zeiten des heiligen Königmordes* (Eritrea: Lands and Times of the Sacred Regicide) (Berlin, Zurich, 1931), passim.

72. Cf. the end of the Grimm's fairy tale "Faithful Ferdinand and Faithless Ferdinand."

73. Every spiritual culture and social order is accompanied also by specific forms of eros and feminine life and by a specific attitude toward the anima. These latter values are represented by the queen.

74. This could represent, for example, a false mundanity of the eros principle, prestige orientation, or sentimentality.

75. Cf. the Grimm's fairy tale "The Devil with the Three Golden Hairs."

76. Cf. C. G. Jung, *Aion,* cw 9/ii, paras. 374ff., pp. 236f.

77. Cf. the fairy tale from the Harz region cited above, "The Green Maiden," in which the girl is enthroned by the green demoness!

78. Which could represent a king of rebirth or incubation.

79. Cited from H. Diels, *Fragmente der Vorsokratiker* (Fragments of the Pre-Socratics), W. Kranz (Berlin, 1951), vol. 1, p. 164, fragment 62.

80. This could also be compared to the *kenosis* idea in Christian theol-ogy, according to which Christ, as a figure that has existed forever in the beyond (Logos), must "empty" itself in order to become human. Cf. Jung, *Mysterium Coniunctionis,* cw 14, p. 170.

81. There are variants of the fairy tale (see above footnote) according to which not a woman but rather an unredeemed male figure ap-pears, a spiritual content which in our version only resonates in the magic or the women's book reading. This animus figure in

need of redemption would be identical with the groom in our tale. These variants reflect a much less deep-seated animus problematic, which is why I give them less attention here. In "The Green Maiden," it is two figures: the green maiden and her consort, a golden stag, who is identical with the man who later becomes the girl's husband.

82. In the following remarks I must presume familiarity with the problematic of the animus and therefore refer the reader to the fundamental essay of Emma Jung, "Essay on the Problem of the Animus," in *Animus and Anima* (Analytical Psychology Club of New York, 1957).

Emma Jung speaks in detail about this unconscious spirituality, that is, animus activity in the woman, ibid., pp. 319f.: "Where the man grapples with problems, the woman amuses herself with solving puzzles, where he attains knowledge, the woman is content with belief or superstition or makes exceptions. . . . So-called wishful thinking also corresponds to a certain level of spiritual development. This exists as a fairy-tale motif, often characterizing a past time when this functioned, 'at a time when wishing still used to work.' . . . Grimm points out . . . the connection between wishing and thinking: . . . 'Wishing is the measuring, outpouring, giving, creative force; the constructive, imagining, thinking force; thus also imagination, idea, image, form.' And elsewhere: significantly, in Sanskrit wish is *manoratha,* 'the wheel of the mind'; wishing turns the wheel of thoughts." Cf. further on the connection between wishful thinking and synchronicity phenomena (magic), C. G. Jung and W. Pauli, *Naturerklärung und Psyche* (Natural Explanation and Psyche) (Zurich, 1952); and C. G. Jung, "Synchronicity: An Acausal Connecting Principle," in cw 8, para. 956.

On the boy as a symbol for a woman's own developing masculine component, cf. Emma Jung, "Essay on the Problem of the Animus," p. 29.

83. Cf. C. G. Jung, *Seminare über Kinderträume,* pp. 220f. See also "A Seminar with C. G. Jung."

84. We might also think of the dwarves in the parallel, "The Green Maiden," who are an indication of the creative activity of the unconscious.

85. In "The Green Maiden," the father of the three boys is the king, but he also appears at the same time as the golden stag, cursed, at the side of the green maiden. He is an animus figure that recalls the "spirit Mercurius" as *cervus fugitivus* (fleeing stag). Cf. C. G. Jung, *Alchemical Studies,* cw 13, para. 259, p. 211.

86. Professor B. Klopfer once pointed out to me in an oral communication that this archetypal constellation might well be behind postpartum psychoses, the course of which is different from and less dangerous than that of ordinary psychoses. It would be worthwhile to look into this more closely.

87. On the sacrifice as a process of making conscious, cf. C. G. Jung, *Psychology and Religion,* cw 11, paras. 381ff., pp. 252ff.

88. On this assimilation of the archetype, not through living out its instinctive aspect, but rather by making conscious its "spiritual" pole, cf. C. G. Jung, *The Structure and Dynamics of the Psyche,* cw 8, paras. 415f. See also Jung's essay "The Psychological Aspect of the Mother Archetype," in cw 9/i, p. 98.

89. Cf. *B-P,* vol. 1, p. 20.

90. For example, in the Grimm's Tale "Thousandfurs" (Allerleirauh). See also in this connection the parallels in *B-P,* vol. 2, pp. 45ff; also the Turkestani fairy tale "The Magic Steed," where the nocturnal kidnapper is a *div,* that is, an animus figure.

91. From *Russische Märchen,* same collection, no. 51. That the incredible brutality of the Virgin Mary was not regarded as repellent is astounding!

92. In "The Green Maiden," the motif is structured as in "Maryushka."

93. On this as precisely the living function of a genuine symbol, see C. G. Jung, *Psychological Types,* cw 6, para. 824, p. 478.

94. *B-P,* vol. 1, pp. 13ff. In "The Green Maiden," too, it is the denial that is the heroic deed. There the "maiden" says, "Because you were so discreet and did not let even a horrible death at the stake loosen your tongue, you and I and your husband, the golden stag, are saved."

95. Cf. Jung's remarks on this in "Answer to Job," in cw 11, paras. 564ff., pp. 367ff.

96. Ibid., paras. 583ff., pp. 376ff.

97. This motif reminds us more of the Paradise story, where also a childish curiosity on the part of humanity was punished with tragic disproportion.

98. See Helmut Jakobsohn, "Conversation of a World-Weary Man with his Ba," in *Timeless Documents of the Soul* (Evanston, Ill.: Northwestern University Press).

99. Zurich, 1941, p. 152f. This is a magical gesture that is even more archaic than the sacrifice or the Saturnalia customs, something, however, that seems connected with the more ancient roots of these; cf. Renner, *Goldener Ring über Uri* (Zurich, 1941), p. 154.

100. He protects himself from the bad consequences of panic, and he also protects the "it" from getting involved in a prestige struggle with a human being.

101. This is by no means to be confused with sticking one's head in the sand and repressive unwillingness to see what is there, for after all, the denial was preceded in the fairy tale by an act of knowledge (opening the chamber). Rather it is as though the girl, who now knows the nature of the black woman, wanted to spare her the pain of feeling seen through in the midst of her suffering with her own shadow.

102. Note also that Jung stresses that loyalty and constancy (as emotional values) are of crucial importance in Job's behavior.

103. Edited by R. Wilhelm (Jena, 1923), vol. 1, chap. 2.

104. Cf. B. Hannah, "The Problem of Women's Plots," in *The Evil Vineyard* (Gould Pastoral Psychology Lectures, no. 51, 1948); and E. Neumann, *Zur Psychologie des Weiblichen* (The Psychology of the Feminine) (Zurich, 1953), pp. 107–109 *(Amor and Psyche)*.

105. When I speak of Christianity in this sense, I am referring less to its dogmatic and theological tenets than to the collective Christian popular outlook.

106. The time-related quality of the myth becomes clear most easily through considering for a moment the difference between this mother-daughter narrative and that found in the Demeter-Baubo-Kore myth. Unfortunately the scope of the present work prevents me from further pursuing this difference.

107. Cf. Jung's remarks in "Answer to Job," in cw 11, paras. 748ff, pp. 461ff., to the effect that the dogma *Assumptio Mariae* was to a great extent required by a need within the people.

108. Consider, for example, that scholars such as Johannes Kepler and Isaac Newton had a definitely Christian worldview.

109. Cf. Jung's remarks in "Answer to Job," (in cw 11), and in *Die Frau in Europa* (Woman in Europe) (Zurich, 1929); and E. Neumann, *Amor and Psyche,* passim.

110. Cf. A. Jaffé, *Religiöser Wahn und schwarze Magie* (Religious Delusion and Black Magic) (Einsiedeln: Daimon, 1986).

111. Such things can be observed, for example, in the unconscious material of schizophrenics, where the personality apparently continuously builds itself up and falls apart again. In antiquity, swinging played a role in the cult of the dead and in the Dionysius cult, and seems to have served as expiation in cases of suicide, as a means of driving out demons, and as a fertility charm. Swinging back and forth is also used as a means of receiving inspiration. Cf. J. Frazer, *The Golden Bough,* vol. 4, (3rd edition, 1914); also *The Dying God,* pp. 281ff.

112. cw 6, paras. 239ff., pp. 235ff.

113. As a patriarchal religion, Christianity gave inadequate consideration to women, which easily produces in women either a mimicking of the masculine (animus possession) or an unconscious falling back upon a primitive mother imago. Cf. in this connection E. Jung, "Ein Beitrag zum Problem des Animus," passim.

114. Cf. in this regard A. Dieterich, *Mutter Erde* (Mother Earth) (Berlin, 2nd ed., 1913).

115. The goose is associated, for example, with Nemesis, Aphrodite, and in the Germanic tradition, with *witches.*

116. On this, see C. G. Jung, *Symbols of Transformation,* cw 5, p. 271, para. 415; pp. 369ff., para. 577.

117. On the latter, cf. C. G. Jung and K. Kerényi, *Einführung in das Wesen der Mythologie* (Introduction to the Nature of Mythology) (Zurich, 1951), pp. 182ff.

118. Ibid., pp. 178ff., 182ff.

119. Theodor Hopfner (ed.), *Griechisch-aegyptischer Offenbarungszauber* (Leipzig: H. Haessel Verlag, 1921), p. 83.

120. In my experience, almost no fairy tale represents a complete lysis. Unfortunately in the scope of this study it is not possible for me to document this; however, I would still like to mention it.

121. R. Allendy, *Le Symbolisme des nombres* (Paris, 1948), p. 113.

122. Ibid., pp. 113–15.

123. Ibid., p. 132.

124. Ibid., pp. 143f.

125. Cf. *inter alia* P. Sarasin, *Helios und Keraunos* (Innsbruck, 1924), pp. 172ff.; and D. Nielsen, *Der dreieinige Gott* (The Triune God) (Berlin, London, 1922), passim; and W. Kirfel, *Die dreiköpfige Gottheit* (The Three-headed Deity) (Bonn, 1948), passim.

126. In cw 11, para. 180, pp. 118f.

127. Cf. the remarks in ibid., para. 119, pp. 69f.

128. See "The Spirit Mercurius," in cw 13, p. 241.

129. Cf. E. Renner, *Goldener Ring über Uri,* pp. 216, 217.

130. The fact that in this dairyman's charm the Trinity appears as three shepherd boys clearly corresponds to a need to experience them in a more human form.

THE DISCOVERY OF MEANING IN THE INDIVIDUATION PROCESS

■■
■■

C. G. JUNG ONCE DIVIDED the main events in a psychological treatment into four stages: confession, elucidation, education, and transformation. The first stage, confession, represents a historical continuation of the confession practices in the ancient mystery cults and in the Catholic Church. The purpose of it is to relieve the individual of painful, repressed secrets or affects that isolate him from his fellow human beings. "It is," says Jung, "as though man had an inalienable right to behold all that is dark, imperfect, stupid, and guilty in his fellow men."[1] And, "It seems to be a sin in the eyes of nature to hide our inferiority—just as much as to live entirely on our inferior side. There would appear to be a sort of conscience in mankind that severely punishes everyone who does not somehow and at some time, at whatever cost to his virtuous pride, cease to defend and assert himself, and instead confess himself fallible and human. Until he can do this, an impenetrable wall shuts him off from the vital feeling that he is a man among men."[2]

The second stage is elucidation of the origin of certain disturbances and fixations, which are mostly based on wishful childhood fantasies. This is the area in which Sigmund Freud made so many helpful discoveries. Elucidation makes use of interpretation of dreams in order to gain access to the hidden material.

The next problem facing us, now in the third stage, is educating the patient as a social human being, a necessity Alfred Adler first highlighted and that today plays a central role particularly in group therapy and self-development groups.

The fourth stage, transformation, responds to a further need, which is not included in the previous stages, or is included only implicitly. This has to do with the notion that social adjustment and so-called normality is not the ultimate goal for all people. It is that for the unsuccessful, but for those who can perform adequately without difficulty, it spells deadly boredom. Although we are herd animals and are therefore only happy when we can function as social beings, there nevertheless persists along with this a longing for one's own uniqueness and for a "meaning" in one's own life that goes deeper than mere social adjustment.

The inner development process, which leads to the realization of this fourth stage, Jung called the individuation process. It involves the development of what is known as a mature personality, "a well-rounded psychic whole that is capable of resistance and abounding in energy,"[3] which is capable of choosing its own path and self-reliantly remains true to its own inner law.[4] Especially in times of collective neurosis, the existence of such mature people is of crucial importance. Also in this stage, according to Jung, only dreams can point the way, for this development follows a purely inner bent or is determined by destiny.[5] Dreams that are an index of the individuation process have, as we shall see, a strange religious or mythological character, for after all it is really religions that have served humanity in the discovery of inner meaning from time immemorial. Today, however, there are all too many people for whom the existing religions are no longer capable of providing any meaning and who are also not satisfied by the purely extraverted worldview of contemporary science or by the intellectual word games of modern philosophers. It is at moments like these that many people are called by an inner voice and find themselves compelled to set forth on an inner quest.

Instead of presenting a general set of ideas concerning the Jungian notion of individuation, I prefer to base my further explanations on a practical example, the dreams of a thirty-eight-year-old doctor who was not undergoing any treatment based on depth psychology. This has the advantage of letting us observe the process as an uninfluenced development taking place naturally, outside the context of psychological treatment. In the context of treatment, of course, the process is more concentrated, and through the greater understanding of consciousness, many false directions, such as we shall also see here, can be avoided.

This doctor came from somewhere far to the north and was a successful general practitioner with a normal "happy" marriage and two grown children. He had in every respect attained the third stage of normality and satisfactory social functioning. He had been raised a Protestant but hardly ever went to church anymore and subscribed to a sensible, "Christian," humanitarian idealism without all that much depth to it. He came to Zurich supposedly to study at the Jung Institute; however, on the only occasion that I saw him during that time, I discovered that he had fled from a conflict back home. He had fallen in love with a married patient and, in order to escape the entanglements that could be expected, had decided to study in Zurich. Discussion, however, showed that this was practically not possible, especially for financial reasons, and so I advised him to return home to his "inner hell" and remain there. He returned home and became an assistant at a psychiatric clinic so as to be able to switch over into psychiatry. Somehow he felt that he should devote himself more to people's psychic problems. He also began to read Jung's writings. From then on, spontaneously, he kept sending me his dreams, partly with his own interpretations. His was a very intuitive, almost mediumistic nature, and thus he understood his dreams astonishingly well on his own. Only from time to time did I signal him when he was in danger of erring into a precipitous decision or an inflation. As a result, we are able to catch a glimpse of a nearly uninfluenced period of what Jung called individuation.

The initial situation is already typical, for individuation usually begins in the midlife period and with an unresolvable conflict. In this case, it seemed to him immoral to break up his marriage and that of the woman he was in love with, and it also seemed to him immoral to suppress a genuine feeling of love on account of convention, especially since the woman in question was already on the verge of self-destruction because of his rejection of her love so far. This is the typical kind of no-way-out situation in which the heroes of so many myths and fairy tales find themselves at the beginning of their quests, a plight against which reason, conventional morality, resolves of will, and so on, are helpless. But major conflicts, as Jung points out, can only rarely be "resolved"; one can only outgrow them through inner ripening.

When the doctor returned home, at first he attempted to maintain a conventional distance from the woman he was in love with, although he suffered deeply from the fact that he was unable to come to her aid. Then suddenly his potency in his marriage began to fail. He sent me the following dream:

A ship lay off the shore of my childhood home. I looked it over carefully and found it to be in excellent shape. I knew I had crossed the sea in it several times. I asked myself: Why in the world don't I take a voyage? I thought, because I didn't understand the engine well enough.

The same night his wife dreamed he had slipped and fallen in the water. She helped him out, and he remarked, "I suddenly felt a weakness in my foot and slipped." His own interpretation was as follows:

The ship is a psychic-energy process, which I don't yet know well enough and which therefore could cause complications. The weakness in the foot is the Achilles' heel. The whole thing has to do with Alberta [the woman he was in love with]. I am often in a depressive mood. I worry about Alberta. She still goes on living but has severe depressions over the suffering in the world. I feel something similar—perhaps she is my relationship to humanity?

I have an inescapable feeling that without Alberta I won't get any further. I'm ambitious and could easily continue to dwell on outer things. I can't let her go. I can't get rid of the feeling that both are meaningful: my marriage and my—call it that for all I care—obsession with Alberta. Perhaps it has something to do with Jung's idea of individuation? What I do know is that when I just talk to Alberta on the telephone, my joy in life comes back. But that, too, is clearly no solution! Anyhow, it keeps death from the door. Any help I am able to give other patients, I feel, is something I am really doing for her, but I still can't use that as an excuse, can I? My responsibility toward her person doesn't become less if I work myself to death for others! Surely one cannot betray love with a doctor's compassion. . . .

From these comments it becomes clear what Jung meant by an anima projection. The young man's magical image of woman has devolved upon Alberta, and there is no trick in the world that can pry it loose from her. Only the path of living through one's suffering can bring a development. We also see how he tried in vain to sublimate his love into medical compassion, and yet deep within himself knew that this was a deception.

As we know, what Jung means by anima is the inner image of the feminine that a man carries in himself, of all feminine figures—mother, daughter, sister, beloved, wife. Originally it is derived from the image of the mother, the first woman he meets. The character traits of this figure correspond to the attributes of the feminine side of a man, to the style of his unconscious approach to life. In our case, the anima is suicidal and depressive, because until now he has neglected her, and thus he also has a kind of hidden depression. Whenever a man meets a woman who entirely or to a great extent fits this inner image, he falls prey to a hopeless fascination. Then a feeling of primordial familiarity appears: "Oh, in times gone by you were my sister or my wife!" Every beloved, says Jung,[6] is the vehicle or embodiment of this perilous reflection, the "Mistress Soul," as Carl Spitteler called her. She belongs to the man, and "she is the loyalty which in the interests of life he must sometimes forgo; she is the much needed compensation for the risks, struggles, sacrifices . . . ; she is the solace for all the bitterness of life. And at the same time, she is the great illusionist, the seductress, who draws him into life . . . and not only into its reasonable and useful aspects but also into its frightful paradoxes. . . ." Through integration the anima becomes an eros of consciousness and a function that mediates contents of the collective unconscious to consciousness. For if a man attempts to draw the fantasy images that lie behind his irrational moods and sudden "states" into consciousness, he can in this way gain access to the psychic contents behind them. Therefore, the anima is also the *femme inspiratrice* in his creative activity. Only through a relationship with a real woman can a man realize his anima.[7]

But let us return to the dreamer. For many months he continued to live absorbed exclusively in his work. He felt oppressed, obsessed, a feeling "like before a thunderstorm or an earthquake," a feeling "that something is about to happen." "Perhaps," he said, "Jung's collective unconscious?" Then he had a dream:

A dream man is standing with me, somebody who is kindly, a wise friend. He says, "Are you sure that you really want to help her [Alberta], even though you might have to put your life on the line?" "Yes," I reply. Then we move through space with the speed of the wind and stop somewhere in the middle of Europe. There, suddenly a man is standing next to us. He is, I know, evil, and somehow I also know that he has taken the "light" away from Alberta, and that I can heal her only if I get it back. She herself could not get it back; I have to do it for her or she will remain incurable. The only solution is to dive into the evil man. "You know the danger," says the dream friend. "If you don't go as straight as you can and if you don't pay attention to anything besides your task, you will never be able to find your way back into life." (I understood this literally in the dream, that the following morning my dead body would be found in the bed.) "Yes, it's clear to me," is my answer. Then somehow I dive into the man; it is as though I am climbing into a deep cave. I wander around in the darkness, always looking for the "light," and at last I find it. . . . I take it with me and hurry back. I wake up with the feeling of having come out of the cave.

He did not have much of an idea what he could say about this dream. He thought it might have to do with finding his inferior side, which was part of him, or with finding a light for Alberta, or with something connected with healing ailing humanity. Then he fell prey for a period of time to an acute fear of going mad, and then a feeling came to him that if he were able to empathize with a patient, "the patient would become conscious in himself." Obviously he had dived into the darkness and was in no less danger than the dream predicted.

When we look at this dream more closely from the point of view of Jungian psychology, the evil man into whom the dreamer had to dive must represent what Jung referred to as the shadow. Since the dreamer took a conscious position that was far too idealistic, he had strongly repressed his egoistic, instinctive, "evil," and especially, aggressive side. Into this side of his nature he now had to penetrate knowingly—a major moral task, for the shadow contains obsessive affects and emotions that can overwhelm one at any moment. However, only if the dreamer penetrates into this dark side can he find the healing light for Alberta. The good dream friend will crop up again; he is a personification of what Jung called the Self, the wholeness of the personality. Characteristically, this dream friend guided him to the center of Europe, that is, to the inner center of his psyche. And there, in this center, he must confront his dark side.

In a subsequent dream, red cows and bullocks are running around like mad, but it seems that through this the earth was being turned over, and this made it fertile. The instincts and affects have broken out. In a further dream, then, a "spirit" appeared out of an old coffin in the cellar of a four-cornered castle with four corner towers. This castle is a variant of the motif of the center in the foregoing dream and again a symbol of the Self. In the depths there, something that is dead wants to come to life. The dreamer thought it was something that always made him scatterbrained when he wanted to please his mother. In accordance with that, it seems that it is once again evil, the aggressive masculine element, that is waiting in the coffin for resurrection. After this dream he suddenly became occupied with the question, whenever a clash of any kind came about, of how much evil there was in him and how much in his environment, and how this question could be decided. He came to the conclusion that in relation to the problem one must "find a medium," a midpoint between the two. After this insight, he dreamed he was on a ship that was sailing to the land of freedom, the "homeland." He himself could have flown ahead in a plane to the destination, but only if he left behind everything personal and all his possessions. Thus, he now went on that voyage that had been heralded by the first dream described above, but he had to give up everything in order to reach inner freedom. This freedom is nothing other than being conscious, for wherever we are unconscious, we are unfree. The dreamer understood freedom otherwise, that is, as being liberated from the prudish, conventional inhibitions that he had nurtured until now, and he dared to take the leap of entering a relationship with Alberta, albeit, to begin with, a platonic one.

A gigantic sex wave inundated him with dreams of nightclubs and stripteasers, behind whose smiles, however, as he said, "the longing for 'real love' shone through." At this time he wrote me:

> I'm working a lot, and my career is progressing, but I feel strangely unenthusiastic. It's that my wife doesn't understand my deep inner life; I could deal with it better if she understood it. But that's a general problem, isn't it? My yearning to see Alberta is partly seeing and partly blind, a mixture of love and obsession. My greater part, the part that sends the "inner voice," feels responsible for both, my wife and Alberta, and for everyone else involved—there is this growing sense of responsibility versus my continually erupting egotism. My greater "I" has driven my little "I" into a corner, and this upsets neither my health nor my work. I pull myself together and do my work, but as soon as I have to take part in empty surface life, I feel tired—it's such a horrible waste of time! My ego is impatient and forgets that life proceeds

step by step on a spiral staircase; one can't leap into heaven. And yet I experience heaven in my heart, moments of truth and beauty that give me strength and profound gratitude but also intensify my suffering.

And again:

I am happy, and so is Alberta. After all, I have my inner teacher, and she is coming along with me. So I must simply follow "the light of my heart."

And:

I used to think that the sexual relationship in marriage meant "being one flesh" and that misfortune awaited any who violated their marriage. But now the shattering insight has come to me that I have always been married to Alberta from the beginning of time. We were both somehow aware of this. But if we were to conduct ourselves irresponsibly toward our partners and children, that would then be a violation of our marriage. It has nothing to do with sexuality. Sometimes we feel that sexual relations with our legitimate partners are like a violation of marriage. The world would surely think that divorce is the only decent solution; according to the collective ethos, our love is something profane, even though this same love is praised in the churches and in rituals as something glorious. Naturally we have thought about the"decent" solution of divorce. But our loves lies between two millstones: passion and responsibility, and it must remain there, so the grain can become bread. Who could understand this?

At this time he had the following dream:

I was in a Catholic school and walking over a meadow to church. It was winter. I knew the world was divided into two parts: the "free nations" and the "totalitarian states." As I entered the church, I heard rifle shots. I saw a man like Father X hide behind a column. (X is a good priest but weak in matters of wine and women.) Before him a woman was standing, a spy from the totali-

229

tarian enemy states, and she shot at him until all her ammunition was used up. Then she came out and held up her hands to signify surrender. The priest also threw his rifle aside. Then a man came up from the cellar (he reminds me of an earthbound, simple, but artistically gifted friend who sees me as "hopelessly cerebral"; he is helpful, loves animals, and is practical and completely unconventional). Now all three of us went for the woman. She wanted to attack, but the man from the cellar held her tight, and she yielded and handed him an object as a token of her surrender. He touched it but recoiled as though it were a hot iron and dropped it. I picked it up and felt that it was very significant and not harmful for me. It was a round object made of copper, like a flat ashtray with snakes around the edges in wave patterns. In the dream I thought, "Christ's crown of thorns." In the middle was a red translucent yolk of great beauty. I took it and thought, "If it weren't for this red yolk, I would not know how beautiful copper can be." I went home and showed my wife the object, but she was afraid of it, so I kept it for myself. I knew it was a treasure that could only be kept by someone who had earned it through hardship and effort. I also knew that the yolk meant "blood and tears."

Instead of interpreting this dream, he added a second one to it, which he had had two years earlier and which we will examine later. First I would like to comment on the first dream briefly myself. The Catholic environment means for the dreamer, as emerges from his remarks in his letters, the world of religious symbols that has been lost by Protestants. Here the dreamer still has to learn, hence the school. Then he tells us it is as though the world were divided by the Iron Curtain. This motif appears frequently in the dreams of modern people and symbolizes, on a first level, their own neurotic dividedness. But it also points to the neurotic split that has become visible in our entire culture. Our whole world is dissociated, Jung tells us,[8] like a neurotic person. "The Western man sees himself forced, an account of the aggressive will to power of the East, to undertake extraordinary defence measures, and at the same time, he brags about his virtue and his good intentions. He does not notice, however, that his

own vices, which he has covered up with good international man-
ners, are being systematically taken up and manifested by the
Communist world. . . . His own shadow smirks at Western man
from the other side of the Iron Curtain."

Behind the two separated worlds stand two archetypal powers.
In the West, the cosmic principle is called God or father; in the
East, it is mother, which means matter. "Essentially, we know as
little of the one as of the other."[9] In the dreamer, too, these principles of the Christian spirit and the material, that is to say, bodily
principle of love are face to face with each other. That is why in
his dream the East is represented by a woman. The Christian
spirit, however, is represented by quite a lax priest—lighthearted,
merry Christianity with a little wine and sex. For after all, we are
adults and have read Freud. As in the dream, the enemy from
the material side surrenders; it is she who hands over that round
small copper bowl with snakes, an article of supreme value. This
round object is a mandala, and as Jung endeavored to prove in
nearly every one of his works, a symbol of the Self, the inner,
higher wholeness of the personality. It is made of copper, the
metal of the goddess Venus-Aphrodite. The coiling snakes suggest the healing staff of Aesculapius, according to the dreamer's
own associations. The red yolk is like a piece of primal living
matter, the *prima materia* of the alchemists, the secret of life,
which is spirit and matter at the same time. The object reminds
the dreamer of Christ's crown of thorns. It also has to do with
the "thorn in the flesh" of which Paul spoke, since for Christians,
this Aphrodite symbol is a source of suffering and conflict. This
dream shows very nicely what Jung was always pointing out, that
in the imitation of Christ we are not meant to mimic Christ out-
wardly; rather, being Christian should mean taking one's own
cross, one's own conflict, upon oneself. The saving symbol is a
paradox: it is an article of supreme value, the secret of life, and at
the same time, blood and tears. No one else can hold the "hot
iron" but the dreamer himself, for it is his cross and his life secret,
which he must keep for himself.

After this dream, the dreamer began also to have physical relations with the woman he loved, for he interpreted the yolk as the physical person, "consisting of body cells." After all, as he says himself in the dream, without this yolk he would not know how beautiful copper, the metal of Venus, could be. His male potency was now once again fully restored.

But now let us turn our attention to the dream of two years earlier, which was sent to me along with the one above, as though the one should explain the other:

I was with my teacher, an invisible presence, on the edge of a sphere, which he had called "the ultimate reality," something without time and space, indescribable. Only those who have seen it can understand this experience—an "everything-nothing," an "everywhere-nowhere," an "everybody-nobody," the "not-yet-spoken word." Somehow the teacher helped me to pull two beings or somethings out of this ultimate reality. I didn't see them, but I knew of them. In order to make them visible, the teacher helped me to extract a silver-gray, mistlike material from the space we were floating in, and we coated the two beings, and a third something that separated the two, with that. When I saw them coated, a profound astonishment came over me. "Those are angels!" I shouted. "Yes," he replied, "that is you." I saw the gray curtain that separated the two angels, and the teacher explained, "That is the veil of illusion." It had lots of holes in it. I was deeply moved and called out, "Oh, it's dissolving, it's dissolving," and I felt that thousands of years that had been lived in the half-conscious hope that this could be broken through were now fulfilled. I went to the angel who was "me" and saw a silver string hanging down from him into a little creature that was also "me" in the realm of illusion. Another string hung down into a woman. It was Alberta. The two angels seemed to be identical and sexless, and they could "think together" in a kind of identity. (That has happened to me with Alberta in reality, "down here.") And we thought: "Such a small part of our consciousness lives in these little creatures, and they worry about such trivial things. Poor little creatures! And we saw that their union could only come about properly if the two little creatures kept up their responsibilities to their relatives and didn't follow their egotistic desires. And at the same time it was clear to us that it would be a sin against this "ultimate reality" (sin against the Holy Spirit?) if we didn't continue on with the process of mutual development of consciousness.

He added to that:

I could write an entire book as a commentary to this; however, I don't have the time. But I must confess there is something in me that simply believes in this path. God uses conventional duty as a weapon in order to cause us to live against his own law. I'm still seeking something that Francis of Assisi obviously found, the "living heart," or that "God is love." But my dependence on the world keeps hindering me. And maybe my so-called virtue contains more sin against life and more pride than love?

This dream about angels in the beyond who are secretly identical with the two little creatures on earth, the two "egos" involved in this drama, points to an archetypal situation that Jung described in detail in his "The Psychology of the Transference," and therefore I must here refer the reader to that work.[10] Whenever man and woman face each other in a love situation, there are actually four figures involved: the two "egos" and their two unconscious personality components, which Jung called the anima and the animus. In the alchemical tradition, the latter are symbolized by the sun and the moon or by the king and queen. In our dream they are symbolized by two sexless angels. I have already attempted to describe the anima. Her counterpart in the woman is the animus, a derivative of the father image. It manifests negatively as prejudices, rigid opinions, traditional spiritual patterns, brutality, and other forms of masculine inferiority. It manifests positively as buoyancy, creativity, and steadfastness of character. The fact that here in our dream the two figures are sexless angels could be understood as a compensation, because at this stage sexuality seemed so very important to both partners.

Jung pointed out in his work that the tendency exists for both animus and anima to be projected onto a human partner, or in the framework of the Christian tradition to be projected onto the dogma.[11] In the first case, an immeasurable fascination is engendered, as in the preceding example. In the latter case, Christ represents the inner groom, while Mary or the Church (*ecclesia*) is the inner bride. In this case, then, these figures are unconscious as the individuals' own personality components. These projections onto the dogma have today become to a great extent dysfunctional. This has gone hand in hand with the demise of Christian collective norms. "Our 'civilization,' however, has turned out to be a very doubtful proposition, a distinct falling away from the lofty ideal of Christianity; and, in consequence, the projections have largely fallen away from the divine figures and have necessarily settled in the human sphere . . ." (namely, onto ersatz gods like *Führer* figures and the like); or ". . . the lapsed projections have a disturbing effect on human relationships and wreck at least a quarter of the marriages." Nonetheless, this step backward has an advantage to it, in that it forces us to turn our attention to the human psyche. The present dream expresses in a very refined fashion how one aspect of what is in play is something personal. It is said of the angel that he is the dreamer and yet that this does not mean the ephemeral little ego, which ekes out its existence as one more ego below on earth. Both angels, who on earth belong to the dreamer and Alberta, are actually one. It is an illusion to believe, in accordance with the way it is presented in the dream, that they are two. The unconscious urge symbolized by the union of two angels is ultimately striving for an inner connection of the personality components, a "spiritual" wedding as an inner experience that is not projected. This urge is leading toward the discovery and experience of the Self, the goal of individuation. Only such a unification in the Self, according to Jung, can preserve the modern human being from dissolution in the mass psyche.[12]

But this inner synthesis cannot take place without a conscious and accepted relationship to one's fellow human beings. "That mysterious something in which the inner union takes place is nothing personal, has nothing to do with the ego, is in fact superior to the ego, because as the self, it is the synthesis of the ego and the suprapersonal consciousness." This brings about an inner consolidation of the individual, but not a hardening. "That is the core of the whole transference phenomenon, and it is impossible to argue it away, because relationship to the self is at once relationship to our fellow man, and no one can be related to the latter until he is related to himself." That is why individuation has two principal aspects: on the one hand it is an internal process of integration, and on the other, it is a process of objective relationship. This double aspect has two corresponding dangers. The first is the danger of the patient's using the opportunities for spiritual development arising out of the analysis of the unconscious as a pretext for evading the deeper human responsibilities, and for affecting a certain "spirituality" which cannot stand up to moral criticism [this is what the dreamer was doing at first, at the time that he was remaining aloof from Alberta]; the other is the danger that atavistic tendencies may gain the ascendency and drag the relationship down to a primitive level. Between this Scylla and that Charybdis, there is a narrow passage. . . ."[13]

In the present dream, the "teacher" presents a personification of the self, and he tries to show the dreamer that he must keep up his moral obligations to his family and yet must also not evade his relationship with his beloved. The cosmic elevatedness of the image is trying to point to the higher significance of the way that should be taken and to lift the dreamer above the futility of his all-too-earthbound worries and desires onto a higher level, and to show him the suprapersonal aspect of the whole situation, which is aiming toward the realization of the Self, of the God image within himself. For an angel (*angelos*) is after all a messenger of God.

At this point I would like to end the discussion of this phase of development. The drama on earth continued on for better or for worse. The two lovers remained in their marriages and with their children. Gradually the intensity of the fascination dwindled, but a good, understanding friendship continued to exist. We could say that the dreamer was able to integrate his anima at least partially, and the differentiation of the eros principle came to benefit his therapeutic practice.

However, with this the goal was still far from being achieved and the adventure was still far from ending. Instead a new problem cropped up, which arises from the experience of the Self. This new problem is clearly reflected in a dream the dreamer sent me several years later:

I had made the journey on foot from England to Switzerland with an unknown girl. We were good friends and experienced a great deal of joy and suffering together. In Zurich there was a big institute called "The Institute of Positive Intentions" with different departments for the different "positive intentions." There were several fountains there, green plants, and bright light. I listened to the lectures going on there, and as I was looking around, I came into a room where John C., a well-known theosophist, was lecturing. There I saw a table at which twelve white-haired, dignified old men in red robes were sitting. They looked very wise. There was, however, an additional seat that seemed to be empty. I asked John C., "Are you still preaching about the One who is to come and occupy that chair (the world teacher)?" He blushed and said, "It is difficult in institutions that favor certain conventions to go against them" (meaning against those who know better). I understood that he wanted to save certain values by serving certain conventions that he did not believe in himself. Suddenly I felt a kind of higher consciousness come up in myself. It was like a voice that said, "Positive intentions can blind inner vision so that people only think in terms of positive expectations. Their expectation to see that empty seat occupied leads them to the deception of thinking that it is presently empty. In truth it is and always has been occupied by the 'formless One,' the supreme teacher, who is himself reality. The twelve wise men not only know that He holds the seemingly empty seat, but also that He is in them themselves and in everyone. They know that, whereas the others do not know it." Now I left the institute, because the lectures seemed sterile to me. And I found my girl again . . . and asked her if she wanted to go to Russia with me. . . . I knew I was asking a lot of her and even added, "I cannot promise never to leave you; we have to go together without any conditions." At first she was surprised, but then she understood. . . . Our gazes met and we found it best simply to trust one another without promises. And I soon saw that she wished for nothing better than to go with me in freedom and without assurances and just to live and let the "formless One" guide us.

The dreamer had planned to get further psychological training in England as well as in Zurich. Thus these two places symbolized continuation of the inner path. The institute of "positive intentions" is obviously a projection onto the Jung Institute, but since, in contrast to reality, a theosophist was lecturing there, this represents something in the dreamer himself, for at this time he had developed a sudden interest in theosophy. The table recalls the Round Table of the knights-errant, which was built on the model of the table of the Last Supper, and at which, there also was an empty seat, the *siège perilleux* left vacant by Judas. The earth opens and devours whoever sits in that seat. In the Grail saga, Percival unwittingly sat in that seat and as a result was forced to seek the Grail.[14] Thus the empty seat is a place where numinous things happen, where the course of history turns in the direction of good or evil. People's expectation, presented in the dream as false, that at some time the "teacher of the world" will appear there, corresponds to the Christian expectation of the Second Coming of Christ or the Jewish expectation of the Messiah. In contrast to that, the dream states that the "formless One" has always been there and still is. It is the God image active in the human psyche, which is no longer to be expected in an external development projected onto history, but to which we should submit in the here and now. The dreamer then leaves this circle because he feels the lectures to be sterile, and continues with his travels to Russia, a further journey on his inner path into the beyond, beyond the Iron Curtain, that is, his still dark inner side, or the unconscious. Russia, as the land of materialism, means for him the world of sensation, his inferior consciousness function, where he still had plenty to learn, and also where his shadow, in the form of not-yet integrated ambition, still awaited him as a task.

When the problem of the anima is integrated, Jung said, a further danger appears on the inner way, namely, the identification with the so-called mana personality or the Self, the "great wise man." Whoever falls prey to this danger loses his individuality and again becomes, without noticing it, inwardly collective. That is why in the dream there is an institute with many people and many schools of thought. The inner direction seems to be lost. And this is a trap that the dreamer then fell into head over heels. He began to present himself in his letters more and more as the Great Wise Man who had noble intentions of helping the human race. And regressive collectivization also hit him in a very concrete way. He became a member of an alchemical-hermetic Masonic lodge, which exercised considerable influence in his homeland. At that point, he broke off his correspondence with me, since he "no longer needed spiritual help." Also, he was cut off from me by his "initiation's" rule of silence. During this time, he appeared in Zurich for two days, and we had only a limited contact. His inflation had isolated him entirely from any human conviviality.

In his essay "The Relations between the Ego and the Unconscious,"[15] Jung described this danger on the inner way in detail. It is, he says, "a masculine collective figure who now rises out of the dark background and takes possession of the conscious personality." This "entails a psychic danger of a subtle nature, for by inflating the conscious mind, it can destroy everything that was gained by coming to terms with the anima." One then experiences oneself as capable of proclaiming the nature of the ultimate reality. "In the face of this, our pitiably limited ego, if it has but a spark of self-knowledge, can only draw back and rapidly drop all pretense of power and importance." Coming to terms with the anima "was not a victory of the conscious over the unconscious, but the establishment of a balance of power between the two worlds."[16] What especially seduced our dreamer were his "positive intentions"; he was always wanting to "help suffering humanity," and that also drove him to become a member of a politically active lodge. Fundamentally, he was unable to admit that up to this point he had more passively undergone the process of development than actively achieved it. He had, like Jacob at the ford, wrestled with the angel of God; something outside of him and stronger than he had taken possession of his life. "But anyone who attempts to do both," says Jung, "to adjust to the group and at the same time pursue his individual goal becomes neurotic." Such a "Jacob," Jung continues with a wink of the eye, "would be concealing from himself the fact that the angel was after all the stronger of the two—as he certainly was, for no claims were ever made that the angel, too, came away with a limp."[17]

For me, this phase of the development of my relationship with the dreamer provided an opportunity to sacrifice my own claim to power in the form of "positive intentions." I could only hope that the "formless One" would help. And he did help. After about a year the dreamer began to write me again in an entirely civilized fashion, and he sent me a dream in which, in long dramatic scenes, he was finally able to save himself from the power of a dangerous, malevolent dictator in a red robe. The dreams that followed insisted that he should give creative form to his inner experiences. He considered collecting some folkloric motifs of his homeland and working on them, and then immediately thereafter dreamed that his father had offered him some magnificent jewels he had found in his country. The father here signifies the spiritual tradition offering him the supreme psychic values to be found in those myths.

So now the way forward lay open again. Twelve years had passed since his first dreams, and he was now fifty years old, with his inner way still far from over—if we are to believe the dreams of the dying, the process continues even after death.

I have tried only to give a very brief sketch here, which provides but a glimpse into this process, and have left out many ups and downs—worries about wife and children, personal problems of all kinds—that came between the main moments. For those who are not familiar with such inner processes, it is difficult to decide what in this process is personal and what is of general human significance. Typical, first of all, is the need for coming to terms with one's own dark side, the shadow, as the dreamer here had to look for the "light" in the evil man. Also typical is the need to subordinate oneself to the Self, or as it is called here, "the formless One" (without identifying with it) and to pursue one's path under its guidance. Everything else in this case is more or less personal. This path is not only pursued by socially more elevated individuals but also by those from among the simple folk—always only individuals, however.

That the path of individuation has a religious character is clearly obvious from the dreams that have been presented. This has caused representatives of the various religious denominations to express the concern that the path of individuation might lead to a scattering of the community. "This would indeed be a retrograde step," Jung answered them, "but it cannot be blamed on the 'true man' [the Self]; its cause is rather all those bad human qualities which have always threatened and hindered the work of civilization. (Often, indeed, the sheep and the shepherd are just about equally inept.) The 'true man' has nothing to do with this. Above all he will destroy no valuable cultural form since he himself is the highest form of culture. Neither in the East nor in the West does he play the game of shepherd and sheep, because he has enough to do to be a shepherd to himself."[18]

The way to the "true inner person," or subordination to the "formless One," is, as we can see, dangerous. The development of the personality is an act of daring, and it is tragic that it is precisely the demon of the inner voice who means at once supreme danger and indispensable help.[19] For this reason, no one pursues this path who is not inwardly forced to, but it is important for pastors and doctors to be aware of its existence, for when a person is called by the inner voice and does not follow it, he wastes away in neurosis or is even destroyed. As long as a person still believes in the light of the truth as already revealed, he is at least protected from this difficult path, but when the light of all the truths of preaching and faith has gone out, for many there remains no alternative but to seek the "light" within themselves. Therefore, I would like to conclude with a citation from the *Brhadaranyaka-Upanishad* (4.3:2–7):

2. [Janaka questioned thus 1:1] "O Yajnavalkya, which is the light of the person?" "The light of the sun, O king," said [he], "by the light of this sun, indeed, one sits, walks about, works and comes back." "So it is, indeed, O Yajnavalkya" [said Janaka].

3. [Janaka then questioned thus]: "O Yajnavalkya, which is the light of this person after the sun has set?" "The moon indeed becomes his light, by the light of this moon, indeed, one sits, walks about, does work, and comes back" [replied Yajnavalkya]. "So it is, indeed, O Yajnavalkya" [said Janaka].

4. [Janaka asked again:] "O Yajnavalkya, which is the light of this person, when the sun and the moon have set?" "Fire indeed is his light, by the light of this fire, indeed, one sits, walks about, does work and comes back (replied Yajnavalkya). "So it is, indeed, O Yajnavalkya" (said Janaka).

5. [Janaka now asks:] "O Yajnavalkya, which is the light of this person when the sun and moon have set and fire also is put out?" "Speech indeed is his light; by the light of this speech, indeed, one sits, walks about, does work and comes back. Hence, O king, even when one's hand cannot be distinguished, then wherever speech is uttered one can indeed approach there" [replied Yajnavalkya]. "So it is, indeed, O Yajnavalkya" [said Janaka].

6. [Janaka puts the next question thus:] "O Yajnavalkya, which is the light of this person when the sun and moon have set, fire has gone out, speech has been hushed?" [Yajnavalkya answers thus:] "The Self indeed is his light. By the light of the Self, indeed, one sits, walks about, does work and comes back."

7. [Janaka seeks further explanation thus:] "Which Self [do you mean]?" [Yajnavalkya explains:] "This person consisting of intelligence [residing] among the organs [and which is] the internal light within the heart. . . ."[20]

In the language of our dream, the formless One. The only dangerous reality that we can under no circumstances elude and at the same time, the only thing of value that no power in the world can take away from us, is the reality of our own psyche.

Notes

1. C. G. Jung, cw 16, para. 132, pp. 58f.

2. Ibid.

3. Cf. C. G. Jung, "The Development of Personality," in *The Development of Personality*, cw 17, p. 169.

4. Ibid., p. 173.

5. Cf. C. G. Jung, *Memories, Dreams, Reflections*, p. 120.

6. C. G. Jung, cw 9/ii, paras. 24ff., pp. 12ff.

7. Ibid., para. 42, p. 22.

8. C. G. Jung, *Man and His Symbols* (New York: Doubleday, 1964), p. 85.

9. Ibid., p. 95.

10. In *The Practice of Psychotherapy*, cw 16, pp. 163–202.

11. Ibid., paras. 441, 442, pp. 230f.

12. Ibid., paras. 442ff., pp. 230ff.

13. Ibid., paras. 444ff., p. 233ff.

14. Cf. E. Jung and M.-L. von Franz, *Die Graalslegende in psychologischer Sicht* (The Legend of the Grail from the Point of View of Psychology) (Olten, Switz.: Walter Verlag, 1980), pp. 390ff.

15. In cw 7, pp. 123ff., especially the chapter "The Mana Personality," pp. 227ff.

16. Ibid., paras. 378, 381, pp. 228f.

17. C. G. Jung, *Memories, Dreams, Reflections*, p. 344.

18. C. G. Jung, *Mysterium Coniunctionis*, cw 14, para. 491, pp. 348f.

19. C. G. Jung, *The Development of Personality*, cw 17, para. 319, pp. 184f.

20. Swami Sivanada (trans.), *The Brihadaranyaka-Upanishad* (Tehri-Garhwal, U.P. India: Divine Life Society, 1985), pp. 403ff.

INDIVIDUATION AND SOCIAL
RELATIONSHIP IN JUNGIAN
PSYCHOLOGY

■■

We are living in a time in which the problem of human relationships has become more urgent than ever before. The reasons for this are well known: the development of technology has brought about rationalism and led to the industrialization of our society. Small rural communities with their closely woven network of personal relationships have dissolved or are dissolving. The inhabitants of the great industrial cities live side by side like strangers. All are oppressed by the thought of their own insignificance in the face of the gray meaningless mass of unknown people surrounding them. With the exception of small groups held together by common religious convictions or shared customs, there exist only communities of interest, which are bound together by commercial, sports-related, or political interests and in general any sort of deeper personal bonding is not present.

This critical situation, which affects humanity as a whole, has led to an increased interest in sociology and, by extension, in psychology as well; but this interest is confined to matters of social behavior. The United States has led the way in behavioral research. There the most varied sorts of group experiments have been undertaken, which in the meantime have also caught on in

Europe, but these are primarily applicable in the field of psychiatry. In a certain way this development has led to belated recognition of data in part already brought to light by Alfred Adler. In any case, now aggression and the restraint of it, the "pecking order" and the social role we play (which Jung called the *persona*), stand in the foreground of discussion.

From the Jungian point of view, however, all of this remains on the surface of the problem. We must penetrate deeper into the instinctive level of the human unconscious in order to find out what it is that conditions our social behavior and our capacity for personal relationship.

So far as we know, man has lived from earliest times as a *zoon politikon*, a "social animal," as Aristotle called him, and indeed, in small groups of from fifteen to fifty individuals. Therefore we may well assume that there is some instinctive basis for this social behavior of ours. Now, we can look at people from the outside and statistically represent their average actions and reactions, as behaviorism does. In this way we discover behavioral patterns of human beings, which do not fundamentally differ from those of animals. But we must also look at the inner psychic processes that go on at the same time. When we investigate these processes, it becomes clear that in the course of their instinctive actions, people also have inner experiences that take the form of fantasy images, emotions, and thoughts. As we know, this is the aspect of the structure of the unconscious that Jung called archetypal. The archetypes are inherited dispositions, which cause us to react in a typical way to basic human problems, inner or outer. Presumably, every instinct has its corresponding archetypal inner aspect. Jung called the totality of these inherited structures the collective unconscious. We can take as an example the instinct of aggression, which can appear inwardly in dreams as the god of war, Mars, as Wotan, or as Shiva the Destroyer. As a counterpart to this, the maternal instinct appears in the mother figures of myths and religions; and the instinctive urge toward renewal and change manifests itself in the symbol of the divine child, which we find in all religions and mythologies.

Such archetypal images rise spontaneously to the surface of the unconscious of individuals at times in their lives when a profound basic human problem is constellated. At such a time it is as though we must draw upon the wisdom of our instinctive inheritance in order to find the solution to our problem amid the chaos of outer and inner circumstances.

When we give up the quest for rational and external solutions to our difficulties and begin to look within us to see what is amiss with us there, initially, as Jung showed, we discover all kinds of aberrant, suppressed, and forgotten psychic tendencies and thoughts, which for the most part are incompatible with our conscious view of ourselves. In our dreams these tendencies often take the form of our "best enemies," for they are in fact a kind of enemy within us—though sometimes not so much an enemy as someone we utterly loathe. This aspect of us Jung called the shadow. If we do not see our own shadow, we project it onto other people, who then have a fascinating effect on us. We are compelled to think about them all the time; we get disproportionately stirred up about them and may even start to persecute them. This does not mean that certain people whom we hate are not also in truth intolerable; but even in such cases we could deal with them in a reasonable manner or avoid them—if they were not the projection of our shadow, which never fails to lead us into every possible exaggeration and fascination. Jung called the process of conscious development that we carry out with the help of objective unconscious material the individuation process. This process inevitably compels us, as the first order of business, to consciously perceive our shadow. As a result of this, our personal relationships go through a considerable change. Above all, we are cured once and for all of our grand idealistic delusions about reforming society and our fellow human beings. We become more modest and at the same time less naive in relation to malicious attacks from the outside. The pot can no longer call the kettle black. The blackness of one recognizes the blackness in the other, which is beneficial for both of them. Most of our so-called "bad" qualities are not entirely useless in our lives, for a person is justified in showing his claws when he is unjustly attacked; he has a right to make use of his slyness in order to ward off an intrigue or to be brutal in order to suppress dangerous tendencies within himself. It is all a question of conscious knowledge of the shadow and the reasonable and measured integration of the shadow into our lives. The shadow, at least in our part of the world, is generally the animal-like, primitive personality within us, which is not bad or evil in itself as long as consciousness keeps an eye on it, but which can become really base and perverse if we suppress it.

It does not have to be proven that this phase of individuation—becoming conscious of one's own shadow and taking back the shadow's projections—has a beneficial social effect. This is obvious. Jungian analysis, which can seem from the outside like an individualistic, self-absorbed preoccupation with oneself, is often accused of being socially useless. But it does not take long for it to become obvious that this is not the case. For example, when a teacher integrates her power shadow and adopts the more mature approach of a conscious personality, countless children reap the benefit. Unconscious, neurotic people are hell itself for those around them; thus every improvement in such people helps a lot of others. Innumerable futile and energy-draining quarrels arise because we are not conscious of our shadows and thus project them onto others. All political strife is also based on this state of affairs.

But this knowledge is only the first step on the path of individuation. When a person has more or less integrated his shadow, his unconscious takes on another shape: this manifests as the image of the partner of the opposite sex—for a man, in a female figure called by Jung the anima; and for a woman, in a male figure called the animus. These unconscious components of the personality are not always projected on the partner of the opposite sex. In former times, they were often experienced as deities belonging to the prevailing religion, as, for example, as the image of a goddess, of the medieval Virgin Mary, or of Dionysus or Christ. This is substantiated by many dreams and visions. The projection of anima and animus onto religious figures was in many ways quite useful, because it protected people from over-valuing and deifying the opposite sex, the result of which was that there was more room for straightforward, realistic personal relationships. However, there was a debit side to this, which was that people were only able consciously to perceive the general, collective aspect of this inner factor and failed to see or experience its individual aspects. In the chivalry of the Middle Ages, courtly love was a first attempt to get beyond this problem. The knight chose the lady of his heart and served her like a goddess, but she was a woman with individual characteristics, an embodiment of his anima, not *the* anima. In this way he gained the opportunity to become acquainted with the specific features of his own inner feminine nature. However, this first attempt at an individualization of the anima was soon suppressed by the Church.

Today the religious symbols that could have served as a vehicle for the projections of anima and animus have lost their meaning for many people. Anima and animus have fallen back into the unconscious of men and women, where, as Jung showed, they create complications in people's relationships. To this we can as-cribe the enormous number of shattered marriages we see around us today.

When the anima shows its negative aspects—and this she does especially when the man is not conscious of her—she manifests as irrational states, sentimental or frigid moods, hysterical out-breaks, sexual fantasies remote from reality; and, not least, she leads the man to choose the wrong partner. She can even bring him to a state of possession. Hitler, with his irrational, hysterical attacks, which drove his mind into a feminine mode, is a well-known example of this. In other cases the anima makes men whiny and depressive, childishly jealous like a woman with feel-ings of inferiority, or vain. All this affects others, particularly women, in an extremely irritating fashion.

An unconscious animus makes women contentious, stubborn, and sometimes brutal; or else it makes them constantly talk at tangents to the matter at hand—all things that men do not like in women. Through the influence of anima and animus, both become involved in lies.

In the present-day women's liberation movement, the animus plays a very prominent role. Often the tyrannical boss that women are struggling against is not so much an external man as the tyrannical animus within themselves, which they have projected onto him. Such women even seem to attract the tyrants in their environments or to choose them as partners. They fail to see that this is connected with their inner worship of their own animus, which is suppressing their femininity. The same thing also sometimes holds true for men. They become woman-scorning homosexuals and never see that the cold, inconsiderate, and tyrannical behavior that they criticize in women is seated within themselves.

When men and women get to know more about their own anima or animus, they get along better with the opposite sex and also redeem these figures within themselves. This means that a man can develop positive feminine qualities such as greater sensitivity and capacity for personal relationship as well as creative and artistic abilities—for the anima is also the mediator between his rational consciousness and the deeper levels of the unconscious. Like Beatrice in Dante's life, the anima becomes the guide to the spiritual heights and depths of the soul. In a similar fashion, the woman's animus can give her courage, steadfastness, strength, and intellectual inspiration and creativity.

Thus while the integration of the shadow has the effect of making us able to get along better with members of our own sex, the integration of animus and anima bridges the gap in understanding between the two sexes and prevents many unnecessary and childish tragedies. All who work in the social professions know how much the generation suffers that grew up in unhappy or broken homes.

Through these examples, I have attempted to show that the process of individuation can eliminate many serious disturbances in our social life. Nevertheless I must admit that it is extremely hard work to bring people to the point of seeing their shadow, and it is even more difficult to make them conscious of their animus or anima. People seem to have a great resistance to thinking honestly about themselves. When things in their lives go wrong, they are far more likely to blame external circumstances.

Up to this point, the process of individuation has seemed to consist primarily in withdrawing our illusory projections from other people and giving up our childish prejudices about them. We become more reflective and more reasonable, but also less dependent upon others. However, we have yet to find an instinctive basis for people actively relating with each other. Only when we go a step further into the depths of the unconscious do we encounter the archetypal factor that unites all humanity and constitutes the basis for our social instincts. We are referring to the inner essence that Jung called the Self.

From the moment that a man or woman attempts to begin work with the anima or animus, he or she is led into deep and critical conflicts, for which there seem to be no solutions. When the ego faces its suffering rather than running away from it, the deepest level of the psyche, its, so to speak, atomic nucleus—a center that seems to regulate the total psychic system of the individual—is activated. Jung observed that in the dreams and fantasies of his patients at times of serious crisis, loss of orientation, or major conflict, a symbol frequently appeared that expressed unity and wholeness. This was a rectangular or round form, which he called by the Sanskrit term *mandala*. The appearance of this symbol is accompanied by inner balance and order. It is an image that stands for the unity of the cosmos and the individual as well as for the meaning of all life. As such it plays a central role in Eastern religions. The Indologist Giuseppe Tucci calls it a psychocosmic order. In the West we find the same symbol, but here it represents either the godhead or the structure of the world. In the latter case, the structure of the world is an image of its creator and in the deepest sense also corresponds to the structure of the human psyche. This symbol of wholeness may be generally described in these terms: "God (and the cosmos) is an infinite spiritual sphere (ball) whose periphery is nowhere and whose center is everywhere." In the German philosophy of the late Romantic period, this conception was also seen as a description of the transcendental, creative ego (not the usually everyday ego!).[1] From the empirical point of view, this center seems to be the core that regulates the equilibrium of our psychic system; from this core the healing and ordering function of dreams arises. It is often perceived as the ultimate goal and fulfillment of life and gives rise to a religious experience which resembles the *satori* of Zen Buddhism.

This inmost core of the psyche, the Self, appears in dreams and fantasies, not only in an abstract mathematical form, but also as a person. In the psyche of men, it appears as a divine or semidivine male being—as a wise old man, a leader, or a teacher. In the psyche of women it presents itself as a kind of cosmic mother figure, as a wise earth mother, or as Sophia. In both cases the Self often has hermaphroditic features, because it unites all opposites, even masculine and feminine.

Whenever the Self is constellated in a person's unconscious, it brings with it a unique and creative solution of his or her problem. In this way, it is the cause of a great leap forward in the direction of consciousness and freedom. For this reason, Jung saw in it the central factor in all human development. Coming into contact with the Self is without a doubt the supreme goal of the individuation process. The fact that the Self is the source of all creativity is of great significance not only for the individual but also for the community. Polarization of the creative individual and collective social behavior seems already to have existed on the animal level of development. The zoologist Adolf Portmann has shown that all innovations in collective animal behavior patterns arise from the independent spirit of enterprise of individuals who try out something new at their own risk.

Thus individual creativity seems to be a lot older than the ego consciousness of human beings. For example, a bird belonging to a species that normally migrates to South Africa spends a winter in Europe. If it dies, nothing further happens. However, if it survives, other individuals begin to do the same thing, and in the end this can lead to an entire group changing its habitual pattern. Japanese biologists studying a group of macaque monkeys living on an island observed a single young female who induced the entire group to wash its food in seawater before eating. A so-called abnormal sentient being seems to be doomed to defeat, whereas creative individuals are destined to enrich their community. To this extent, the problem of the individual versus society already existed among our animal forebears, and isolated individuals have always either threatened or enriched their tribe.

When isolated human individuals act in a destructive manner against the community, we see by closer examination of their unconscious that they are governed by an autonomous complex—which is what was known in former times as demonic possession. This condition of being controlled by a complex, or possession, always provokes fear and hate in other people and brings about isolation. The creative individual, by contrast, usually has an intimate connection with the Self. In his work on shamanism, Mircea Eliade compiled an abundance of material that clearly documents this fact. The shamans of the North are, like the medicine men of other primitive peoples, for the most part individuals who have been "called" by the gods or spirits of their tribes. Following a serious psychic crisis, which has isolated them from their communities—sometimes they also seek out this isolation themselves—they learn under the guidance of an older medicine man how to carry out an appropriate dialogue with these powers, which today we call the archetypal contents of the unconscious. They are not possessed by these powers, except during a short voluntary trance state. They do not lose their normal status as human beings, but they acquire knowledge concerning the powers of the beyond (of the unconscious) and are thus able to function as prophets and healers, and in many regions, also as the artists and poets of their tribes.

On this early cultural level, magical animals are often the symbols of the Self. In the North, it is usually the bear who is the embodiment of the Self for the shaman, because he is a great nature deity. The shaman acquires his healing power and creativity from the bear. In Africa, lions and elephants represent the Self, and sometimes also other magical animals who embody the supreme divine power of the psyche and nature. From the fact that the Self appears in animal form in the dreams and visions of medicine men and creative individuals, it is clear that it is first perceived as a purely instinctive unconscious force, greater and more powerful than the ego but entirely unconscious. It embodies the complete wisdom of nature yet does not possess the light of human consciousness.

In nature there is no animal instinct that does not have its particular form in which we can read its purpose and meaning. Moreover, instinctive impulses do not appear without certain restrictions; they have their own temporal sequence, their objective, their special mechanisms and restraints. For human beings, the restrictive forms of the instincts are the religious customs and taboos. When we look at the inner side of these, we see that they express the sense of our instincts as they manifest in symbols and fantasies. Thus it appears that religion was originally a psychological regulatory system, which ordered our instincts and drives. Only when a religious system hardens into a rigid formalism does it become antagonistic to the instincts and negative. Normally, mind and instinct constitute a compensatory pair of opposites, harmoniously complementing or counterbalancing each other. In countless historical examples the tension of opposites between mind and instinct has become negative, which is what has happened in the last two centuries in our own culture as well. In such cases, the unconscious brings forth new religious symbols, which are meant to bridge the gap between the two and restore to humanity the memory of its original nature. Usually it is a symbol of the Self, the psychic wholeness, that reunites the opposites that have fallen away from each other.

While the totem animal expresses a deep unconscious form of this wholeness and social unity and cohesion, we find in its stead on a higher cultural level a new symbol—a great, all-embracing human figure, which Jung called the Anthropos. Like the totem animal, the Anthropos is regarded as an ancestor of humanity, who unites all people. In many myths, he is even the raw material out of which the whole cosmos is formed. He is seen as the vital principle and the meaning of all human existence and is considered the totem of all of humanity, not just of one tribe.

In many creation myths, belonging to the most various of peoples, it is told that the universe was originally formed from the parts of a gigantic human figure. In the Germanic *Edda*, it was the giant Ymir: "From Ymir's flesh the earth arose, the mountains from his bones. . . ." In China, the cosmos was formed from the dwarf P'an Ku, who was at the same time a giant. *P'an* means "eggshell" as well as "make solid," and *Ku* means "underdeveloped," "unilluminated," "embryonic." When P'an Ku cried, the Yellow River was created and the Yang-tse Kiang; when he breathed, the wind arose; when he spoke, thunder sounded; and when he directed his gaze, there was lightning. At the time of his death the four sacred mountains of China were formed from his body, with Mount Sung, as the fifth one, in the middle. From his eyes came the sun and the moon. After a long time, he reincarnated in the womb of a virgin, "the holy mother of the first cause," and became a venerated hero. The meaning of these myths of the Anthropos as the primordial origin of the cosmos corresponds to the fact that our entire perception of reality is preformed by our psyche and our psychic structures.

We find similar notions in the Vedic literature of ancient India. Here the cosmic ancestor of humanity was Yama, who in the later Upanishads became Purusha, which means "man" or "person." He represents the individual Self or the inmost psychic core in each individual; but at the same time he also represents the collective Self, even the cosmic Self, an all-pervasive divine principle.

In the *Rigveda* (10.19), the four castes arose from the body of the thousand-eyed Purusha. Subsequently, as the other gods were sacrificing him, the moon arose from his mind, the sun from his eyes, the air from his navel, and the heavens from his skull. "He is," we are told, "everything that was and everything that will be. . . . Verily he is the inner self of all sentient beings" (*Mundaka-Upanishad*, 2.1.).

In the ancient Persian religion, Gayomart corresponds to this figure. His name comes from *gayo*, "eternal life," and *maretan*, "mortal existence." Gayomart, who was the seed of the good god Ahuramazda, was the first priest king. When he was killed by the evil god Ahriman, the eight metals flowed from his body. From the gold, which was his soul, there sprouted a rhubarb plant, from which arose the first human couple, which produced the human race.

These myths make clear, among other things, the idea that humanity originally had a collective soul: psychically, all people were a unity. This points to an observation that we can still make: wherever we are unconscious, we are not distinct from other people—we act and react, think and feel entirely like the others. Jung used a term of Lévy-Bruhl's to describe this phenomenon, calling it a *participation mystique*, or an archaic identity. When we analyze the dreams of small children, we can often see that they do not dream of their own problems but rather of those of their parents. In family groups or other intimately connected communities, individuals often dream about the problems of the people around them. It seems that in the deeper levels of the unconscious we cannot delimit ourselves from our fellow human beings. Our unconscious psyche fuses, so to speak, with that of the others. The negative side of this phenomenon lies in the fact that to the extent we are unconscious, we are wide open to psychic infection. The complexes of other people can affect us to such a degree that we become possessed by them. They can even trigger a collective possession.

Another aspect of this archaic identity is shown in the fact that we think other people are psychologically exactly the same as we are. That seems to us to give us the right to pass judgment on them and to wish to "straighten them out," to manipulate them, or to impose our point of view on them.

But the archaic identity also has a positive side. It is the basis for all empathy, the archetypal foundation of all our social instincts, even for their supreme expression in the form of Christian agape or Buddhist universal compassion. Any sense of relationship with our fellow human beings is based on the archetype of the Anthropos; in a certain sense he is the Eros personification par excellence.

In Jewish legend, Adam, the first man and the Jewish version of the Anthropos, is often described as a cosmic giant. God gathered red, black, white, and yellow dust from the four ends of the earth in order to form him. According to the Kabbalist Isaac Luria, all the souls of humanity were contained in Adam "as the wick of a lamp is woven from many fibers." In this tradition, too, the primordial man is the Self of an entire nation, of humanity altogether. He is a kind of group spirit, from whom all draw their life. This vision of a collective soul also explains why certain scriptures maintain that the body of Adam Kadmon is composed of all the precepts of the Law. From a psychological point of view, that would mean that the personality of humanity at this stage of historical development expresses itself solely in the religious tradition. The individual becomes aware of his or her individual inner Self, or "eternal person," only through the religious tradition, for only that tradition expresses the spiritual essence of his or her being. As shown by Helmuth Jacobsohn, the Egyptian of the Middle Kingdom period (up to 2200 B.C.) still believed that he met his noncollective, personal soul only after death, in the form of the so-called *ba* soul, a birdlike being that embodied his true inner Self. During his lifetime, however, the Egyptian felt himself to be real only as a member of the community, only insofar as he functioned according to the rules and laws of his religion.

Only after 2000 B.C. did the Egyptian begin to perceive his individuality in a more conscious fashion and begin to try to locate it in this present life. This led to the spread of the Isis-Osiris mysteries, which fused with other mystery cults of the Mediterranean region that had similar meanings. They all presented certain aspects of the process of individuation in a projected symbolic form.

Here we encounter a confusing paradox. The symbol of the Anthropos seemed to the individual to represent his Self, that is, the unique inmost core of his or her individual personality; but at the same time in the myths and religions, he represented the "totem" of humanity—the archetypal factor, which quite actively brings forth all kinds of potentialities for positive personal relationship.[2] Clearly the philosophers of Hinduism were right when they described their Purusha as the inmost Self of each human being and at the same time as a kind of cosmic Self. In this symbol the opposites of the one and the many are reconciled: it is individual and collective at the same time.[3]

In practical terms what this means is that the more we individuate ourselves, that is, the more truly we become ourselves, the better we are able to relate with our fellow human beings and the closer we get to them. As Jung pointed out, we can only attain inner wholeness through the psyche, and the psyche of a human being cannot exist without relationship to other human beings. But one cannot have a genuine relationship with another person until one has, through an inner psychic process of uniting the opposites, become oneself. Jung says:

> If the inner consolidation of the individual is not a conscious achievement, it will occur spontaneously and will then take the well-known form of that incredible hard-heartedness which collective man displays towards his fellow men. . . . His soul, which can live only in and from human relationships, is irretrievably lost . . . for without the conscious acknowledgment and acceptance of our fellowship with those around us there can be no synthesis of personality. . . . Relationship to the self is at once relationship to our fellow man, and no one can be related to the latter until he is related to himself.[4]

This paradoxical state of affairs is expressed through the symbol of the Anthropos, which is the inner center of every one of us and at the same time the totem symbol of the whole of humanity. The Anthropos not only reconciles the opposites of the individual and the multitude, but also the opposites of ordinary people and culturally sophisticated ones. In dreams and fantasies he often appears as a nameless man of the lower classes, especially when the conscious attitude of the ego tends toward social, intellectual, or aesthetic snobbism. Yet he also appears just as often as a regal figure—when an individual feels overwhelmed by a sense of his collective insignificance. The Anthropos is quite simply the human being, in its lowest and highest aspects. Christ, the figure of the Anthropos in our culture, is thus referred to as both "the king of kings" and as "the least among us" or the despised slave.

Modern researchers in group psychology have shown that all groups, after the initial chaos, begin to concentrate around a center. This can be the group leader or an idea, a cause, a theme of discussion, and so forth. The center can thus be—as is frequently the case in sports clubs or political or commercial groups—a simple common goal, or it can be on a higher level, as is the totem in primitive communities or the God-image in the higher cultures. The more archetypal the center is, the more solid and enduring the cohesion of the group is.

It is the world religions that have hitherto kept the largest human groups together. Their center is the symbol of the Anthropos: Buddha, Christ, Muhammad. By living out their inner wholeness to the utmost, these men have drawn the projection of the Self—or of the cosmic man or the divine cosmic spirit—upon themselves. Both Buddha and Christ have therefore been depicted as a mandala or its "in-habitant," the center of a mandala. In our time Marxism, too, began to play a role that is not far from that of a religion. Its mythical Anthropos is not, however, projected on an individual person—perhaps with the exception of Mao Tse-tung (in the Soviet Union the personality cult was forbidden)—but on the totality of a social stratum. This is, as Robert Tucker has shown, the working class, which is lauded as the embodiment of the individual, noble, creative, and unhindered human person, as a giant who will be able to overcome all difficulties, to cite Marx. He has no shadow—rather, it is projected onto the Capitalists and Imperialists.

One can see the same thing, for example, in the Utopian ideas of the Chinese reformer K'ang Yu Wei, who is still being intensively read in Communist China.[5] His entire system is based on the concept of *jen*, which means humanness, social love, and responsibility. However, this is to be actualized exclusively through external social and political measures. Nobody seems to be aware of the simple and obvious fact that without *jen* in the individual, there can also be none in society—that we must first find the source of *jen* within ourselves, that is, in our own Self, before we can establish relationships with our fellow human beings. In other words, the factor of humanness or love is projected onto a group and in this way infinitely fragmented.

This Marxist projection has as a consequence a collective multiplication of the Self, which is thus disintegrated in the individual and in society. When the idea of the community is overstrained, it leads to general fear and mistrust. Even in small collectivities, the inner voice of the Self in the individual is stifled, and in the same measure the ego with its will to power is strengthened. This results in a falling back of the principle of group cohesion onto a level of archaic, animal-like behavior patterns, as we can see today, for example, in various youth groups and their revival of totemic symbols. On a larger scale, the mass delusion of Nazism also exhibited all the symptoms of such a regression: Wotan as the God image, which was embodied in Hitler; the black eagle and the skull totems with their dreadful implications and the concomitant mass psychosis. Even small groups, which are known to be more reasonable than large ones, can suddenly fall into a state of emotional possession, as may be observed from time to time. As a result, in modern sociology the mass tends to be evaluated negatively, whereas groups are seen in positive terms. This seems to me, however, to miss the essential point, since both the mass and the small group can be either reasonable or possessed. A dictatorial group composed of a small powerful clique can act in just as dangerous a fashion as the blind masses. The real distinction is to be found elsewhere: everything depends on how many individuals are conscious and personally related to their inner selves and as a result do not project their shadow onto others. That and only that is capable of preventing an outbreak of mass hysteria and mass delusion.

Thus we must return to the problem of the archetypes and the question of being consciously aware of or possessed by them. I have already described what anima or animus possession in men and women is like. But the archetype of the Self is also capable of triggering a possession, the effect of which is that an individual identifies himself or herself with the inner "great man" or "wise woman" and as a result becomes hopelessly inflated. Every madhouse has a few Jesus Christs, Napoleons, presidents of the United States, and Virgin Marys. When people are outright mad, the danger ends there. However, there are many people who only in secret overestimate themselves through identification with a Self figure. In such cases they just feel a little bit too much in the right, and this is one of the worst things that can happen. They become secretly inhuman as a result of some fanatical conviction or self-righteous attitude. Exactly this lies behind many of the massacres of our time, far more than the emotional outbreaks of single individuals that we are familiar with as the cause of murder and manslaughter. Most of those who set off bombs in public places have some "righteous" conviction in their heads, which in their eyes justifies what they do.

All ideological fanaticism and every overwhelming affect arise from the constellation of an archetype. The archetype of the Self is no exception to this. It too can produce these sorts of effects. Thus we must have great respect for the old Eskimo shamans, who in relating to the world of the spirits were able just to be healers and not let themselves be possessed by its powers. Those who became possessed by the spirits were sick in their eyes. They caused schisms in the community rather than helping it.

Now considering our present-day situation in the Western hemisphere, we can sketch the following general picture. Christ, the Western Anthropos figure, united humanity for a millennium and a half. We were at least theoretically all "brothers and sisters in the Lord." Christ, as the second Adam, was also the primordial man; he was the God-man, and according to the experiences of the mystics, the inmost Self of every individual. However, the fact that Christ is only good—evil is not part of him but is attributed either to man or the devil—meant that he could not reconcile all opposites. What could find no place in his wholeness was projected on the heathens or other people and powers outside of Christendom. This along with the rise and increasing overvaluation of rationalism—a latter-day descendant of scholasticism—weakened the Christ symbol to an ever-increasing degree. Thus a great number of people lost the religious symbol that had formerly held the people of the West together. Many people now seek it in Buddhism, others in Marxism with its regressive totem symbols, and still others simply feel lost and cling to superficial values and ideas while assuming a generally Christian attitude toward their fellows. However, this is such a bloodless approach that in critical situations it immediately collapses and gives place to archaic barbarity.

However, as with all neuroses, whether in the individual or in the collective, the unconscious here too shows its tendency to reconcile the opposites once again and to heal the split. We are not yet able to predict how this will work out on a worldwide scale, yet we can now already see and regard as certain that a new Anthropos figure is forming in the collective unconscious which bears a resemblance to the "round or square man" or the "true man" of the alchemists. This is no anti-Christian figure, but rather, so to speak, a more complete form of Christ, one that really contains the opposites of the individual and the multitude, the masculine and the feminine, mind and matter, and good and evil. This figure appears in every individuation process that goes deep enough. Up till now, it has only cropped up as the inner experience of individual seekers who have given up their external struggles and looked at their own shadows in order to achieve a more profound and more authentic relationship with their fellow human beings. Toward the end of his life, Jung was not particularly optimistic about our future. Too much pointed toward war, mass psychosis, and impending disaster. But one thing seemed sure to him: only if an adequate number of individuals become conscious in the sense we have described can our civilization renew itself and survive. Otherwise, we shall surely fall back into barbarity, a regressive tribal mentality, and endless war, possibly to the point of final extinction.

Since Jungian psychology is not very widespread among the masses, we must ask ourselves how it can be of any use to the world, being that the process of individuation is the only help for this problem and its only solution. To this we may reply that in truth the process of individuation is not only brought about by Jungian analysis, but is in itself a natural process, which can be carried to a fruitful conclusion by every individual who works on himself or herself with honesty and perseverance. Jung's achievement consists primarily in having brought this process into consciousness and in having found out how it is possible to support it. Fundamentally, it matters little what this process is called as long as one experiences it consciously. Based on what I have seen, there also exist strange and unusual paths found by unusual people with the help of the unconscious. The Anthropos brings all of them together. Perhaps the healing powers of the deeper collective unconscious will save us and bring forth a new form of human community. But the divisive forces of those who are possessed by demons—that is, by one-sided unconscious complexes and the distorted ideas and emotions that are part of them—are also very great. There is no point in denying their existence or in fighting against them. The "true human being," as Jung called the Self, will never take part in the game of "shepherd and sheep," because he has enough to do just with himself. He plunges into the deeper levels of the psyche, where in truth he is one with the whole of humanity, beyond the reach of everyday power struggles. From this level comes all creativity. A person can only be creative in connection with the "ordinary man" within himself—and that is why perhaps, out of these depths, we shall be able to renew our culture.

Notes

1. According to Fichte, the ego constitutes its own being and becomes the point of departure for all experiences by also creating the non-ego.

2. C. G. Jung, cw 16, para. 454, pp. 244f.

3. Ibid., para. 474, pp. 265f.

4. Ibid., paras. 444f., pp. 233f.

5. Ta Tiung Shu, *Das Buch von der Grossen Gemeinschaft* (The Book of the Great Community) (Cologne and Dusseldorf, 1974).

NIKE AND THE WATERS
OF THE STYX

■■
■■

THE DESTINIES OF PEOPLES, as Jung once pointed out, are like an untamed current that rushes heedlessly onward, carrying everything along with it. Depending on the viewpoint of the given historian who is describing it, its course is determined by military, demographic, or economic factors, or factors related to the history of ideas or sociology (that is, intellectual-spiritual ones). Here the so-called zeitgeist plays an important role, not only in the movement of history but also in the continuously changing point of view of historical writing. This brought the philosopher Hans Georg Gadamer to speak of "effective history" (*Wirkungsgeschichte*).[1] In themselves, the past cultures that the archaeologists dig up are forever sunk in the rubble and ashes. What we think we know about them is at best made up of spurious approximations, and these continuously change with the transformations of the prevailing zeitgeist. The changes in the zeitgeist, however, are based on creative processes in the collective unconscious. This is the hidden current of events that flows beneath the surface of what can be grasped as history. C. G. Jung tried to show, for the first time in his work *Aion*,[2] how activated—that is, constellated—contents of the collective unconscious are at work behind the historical course of events—and especially how the spontaneous transformation of the symbol of the Self (that is, of the god-man and the God image of every period of history) has played a role in structuring historical events and is still doing so today.[3]

Behind the chaotic white water of the external historical events our newspapers tell us about, there still flows a hidden stream of unconscious archetypal factors, which seemingly accidentally collide with one another, but in reality may well be ruled by an unfathomable destiny, law, or meaning. This is portrayed with incomparable vividness, for example, in the *Iliad*, where on one level men contend with one another through brute force in war, while on another, in the Olympian beyond, the gods, too—that is, the archetypal powers—are caught up in strife. Or in the Indian *Bhagavad Gita*, in which the hero Arjuna suddenly sees behind the visible battlefield the true form of the god Krishna (who is an incarnation of Vishnu), and praises him in the following words:

> *Your gigantic body with many mouths and eyes,*
> *With many arms, many thighs, many feet,*
> *With many bellies, jaws full of teeth—*
> *The world heaves, and seeing it I quake too.*
> *Touching the sky, streaming light, of many colors,*
> *With open mouth, great flaming eyes—*
>
> . . . .
>
> *Just as a river's mighty surge of waters,*
> *Bent upon it, runs to the sea,*
> *So these heroes of the human world*
> *Enter your jaws of flame.*
> *As butterflies toward a blazing fire*
> *Rush headlong to their demise,*
> *So these humans rush to their demise,*
> *Headlong into your craw.*[4]

What is depicted in the *Iliad* as discord among the gods is drawn together here into a superordinate unity, the *one* universal god. But in Greek mythology, too, there is a unity under which the many gods are subsumed, the goddess of the waters of the Styx, the great underworld river hidden under the earth. Her daughter is Nike, the goddess of victory in single combat (Olympia) as well as of military victory, through which the movement of history is often given a new direction.

Nike is one of what Hermann Usener was the first to describe as "gods of the moment," or to put it in Jungian language, gods who embody the quality of a synchronistic moment.[5] The best known of these, depicted as a winged youth, is Kairos himself, an embodiment of the "favorable opportunity," which has to be seized on the spot—in other words, a god of the meaningful coincidence.[6] Since Nike is a feminine figure, she is connected with a fighter's or an army's anima, that is, connected with their irrational inner state of mind. But this is by no means merely what is called in military reports "the morale of the troops" but rather a far more deep-seated, fundamental inner disposition of an army, an unconscious conviction—not arising from any considerations of reason—to the effect that either victory or defeat is imminent. This conviction has a lot to do with the "absolute knowledge" of the collective unconscious, the existence of which Jung was the first to point out. It is as though the unconscious psyche of the warrior already knew in advance whether victory or defeat lay ahead, as if this were already predetermined by a kind of providence—but a predetermination that is not really absolute, because, as is well known, the fortunes of war can also change at the last moment or through the action of a single individual.

Because the outcome of a battle often seemed somehow to be "known," almost all peoples used to consult oracles before a battle or paid attention to certain "signs." The ancient Germanic peoples, for example, used to attend to the whinnying of the sacred horse or to whether the flag flew in the wind or hung slack, the Romans to the signs that the *haruspices* and augurs watched. In ancient China, sometimes the emperor would play chess with his head general; the moves were noted and those of the winner were taken as military tactics, for in them the victory was thought to be prefigured.[7] The chess game was considered an earthly enactment of the "battles" of the stars in heaven, what we call in our language the archetypes. The Celts, too, were familiar with the divinatory chess game before a battle. This was seen as a mixture of predestination and the free will of men. Nike, however, embodies the anima mood of a fighter, closer to consciousness, which is already sure of the positive outcome and also in part brings it about.

Because a victory often is suddenly "just there," Nike was represented for the most part in pictorial art as a winged female figure moving at a fast run, like the Nike of Samothrace.[8] The wing motif links Nike with the Eros gods, the deities of death, Hypnos, and the messengers of the gods, Hermes and Iris. In Athens, Nike was often seen together with Pallas Athena and later was also often equated with her as Athena Nike. In addition, in representations on vases she accompanies the gods Zeus, Apollo, and Dionysus. In the last case, she resembles the maenads, the drunken, ecstatic, wild companions of Dionysus. She not only guided warriors to victory, but also inaugurated the sacrificial rites, that followed every victory. Sometimes Nike was portrayed as the power that decided the victory by itself, sometimes only as the messenger who brought the victory decided upon by Zeus or by the four children of the Styx.

The type in art of the winged Nike later became the model for the figure of the angel who received the Christian martyrs in the beyond and crowned them with the crown of victory.[9] This shows a radical psychic reversal of poles: this victory in the latter case is one that happens purely in the beyond and is paid for on the earthly level with death. This new Christian approach also clears away a bit of primitive mind that exists in all of us, the notion that a victory is a kind of divine judgment that justifies one's own reasons for war. "Since we won, we were right, despite the atrocities we committed." Christianity seeks to liberate us from this opportunistic mentality.

Along with this type of artistic representation of Nike, we also find her as a little statuette in the hand of a deity—very often Pallas Athena, who through her confers victory upon the hero or the army. This is connected with the notion that in the battles of the gods (archetypes), it is always one god who is victorious and confers victory on the army that venerates this archetype the most. A war, from this point of view, is always also a battle between archetypes represented either by stars or gods.

What was depicted by the Greeks as Nike or by the Romans as the goddess Tyche-Fortuna, was also known to the ancient Germans. With them it took the form of an anima figure who accompanies the individual warrior, the so-called *fylgia*, an invisible feminine companion spirit, or "follower," who possesses a supernatural knowledge of impending fate, victory or defeat, death or life, and is capable of making this known.[10] One can perceive one's own *fylgia* while asleep, in a dream, or in trance, usually as a white winged female figure or often also as a weapon-bearing, supernaturally large, winged woman. The *fylgia* is the same as the valkyrie and the swan maiden, a kind of warrior's personal goddess of fate. Normally she follows the warrior invisibly, and only when marvelous, unexpected events are imminent, which go against the expected causal sequence of his life, does she show herself as *forynia*, literally, "precursor," or *bysn*, literally, "model" or "command," in other words, as the harbinger of great events.[11] When she showed herself in this way as the precursor, this usually meant disaster or death. Usually she hovered behind the warrior, moving in the same direction.

It could be said that when the warrior was in harmony with her, moving in the same direction, she was behind him. However, when she became *forynia*, or precursor, then she had separated from him—then his soul was running away from him, or he was running to meet his fate, death. Whereas the Germanic war god, Wotan, kindled the battle rage of an army (his name in Switzerland meant "rage in the army"), the *fylgia* was more an affectless conviction or knowledge of fate. Because this factor, along with Wotan, seemed also to be important, seeresses were highly honored in the Germanic army, for there was a need to connect with this knowledge of the unconscious. The *fylgjur* (plural of *fylgia*) were also called "battle rulers," and one of them, Brynhilde, Siegfried's *fylgia*, has often been compared with Pallas Athena,[12] who we already know as the double of the Greek victory goddess.

Brynhilde was also called Sigdrifa, "Wreaker of Victory." The valkyries of the Germans usually helped the warrior to victory, but also sometimes were ultimately unable to ward off his death. Once this was determined by Fate, then she came to get him in the form of the winged goddess of death and took him away to the realm of the beyond.[13] The Greek Nike was also sometimes depicted with a pomegranate in her hand and thus marked as a goddess of death, which is anyway hinted at by her connection with the Stygian waters of death. She is also sometimes considered a sister of Persephone, the goddess of the realm of the dead, and in this role she is related to the Harpies, birds with women's heads who carry the dead off to the beyond.

Nike also sometimes appears, like the *fylgjur*, in multiple form as the companion of the single individual; here she comes closely to resemble the Erotes of ancient art.[14] The numerous Erotes of the art of antiquity (like the putti of the Renaissance) represented, in contrast to the single god Eros, a kind of indefinite *mood* of love, which has not yet developed to the point of an individual love experience; and the multitude of Nikes might well also embody something similar—a kind of elusive "disposition to victory" of the army, which precedes the actual victory but also helps bring it about.

As Heino Gehrts has pointed out, the mutual affinity of death and victory is particularly palpable in the archaic Roman ritual (probably of Etruscan origin), the so-called *devotio*.[15] Before a battle of the Romans against the Latins, both Roman generals, the consuls Titus Manlius Torquatus and Publius Decius Mus, had the same dream, the content of which was confirmed by the *haruspices* that were then cast: of the two opposing armies, one fell entirely to the gods of death and Mother Earth, but of the other, only the general. Thus whichever leader would voluntarily sacrifice his life could assure the defeat of the enemy. Both consuls had the same opportunity. However, they decided not to make the decision themselves, but instead to leave it to fate: the general of the wing of the army that yielded first was to consecrate himself to death. In the event, however, it was an external process that decided. The sacrificial priests declared that the sacrifice of Publius Decius Mus foretold his death, whereupon he performed the *devotio*. This consisted of the following rite: The consul consecrating himself to death stands on a spear placed on the ground, dons the *toga praetexta*, covers his head, and says: "I dedicate myself, along with the enemy, to the gods of the underworld and to Mother Earth (*diis manibus et terrae matri*)." Then he picks up the spear and charges into the enemy army. He then has such a fearsome effect—because according to the Roman outlook he is already dead—that the terrified enemy recoils before him. No one can touch him, because he is already a corpse. Through the *devotio* he becomes a dead man; then he dies in the battle. Gehrts asserts, I believe correctly, that this is not the act of a Winkelried* in which a single individual throws himself on the enemy in an attempt to breach his line. Rather the idea is that he casts himself into death and as a dead man becomes the leader of the foe, taking them all down with him to the realm of the dead. When, afterward, the second consul wins the victory (not only Publius Decius Mus committed this act but also, later, various other members of the Decius family), then he could celebrate the triumph just as would any other consul.

As we know, a consul celebrating a triumph would drive into the capital on the *currus triumphalis*, wearing royal garb. On this occasion he wore a mask streaked with red lead, the meaning of which remains unsure today. Most likely the interpretation is that through this he represented the dead, for it has been the custom since the most ancient times, as early as the Stone Age, to rub the bodies of the dead with red lead. Many authors have interpreted this that the bodies were colored with red lead in order to give them the color of the living. In any case, it is sure that it was only the dead who were smeared with red lead. So the wearing of a mask painted with red lead by the *triumphator* probably actually

*Winkelried was a soldier in a Swiss army who at the cost of his life turned the tide of a deadlocked battle by charging and breaching the enemy line single-handedly.—Trans.

represented the other dead consul. Then behind him always stood a slave of the state, that is, one drawn from a conquered people, who held the golden *corona triumphalis* over his head and called out to him, *"Respice post te, hominem te esse memento"* ("Look behind you and remember you are human"). Gehrts points out that this marvelous double-edged relationship could also be interpreted the other way around. The shadow behind the fully alive *triumphator* is the dead man, that is, when he looked behind him, he saw himself as a man, as a living man, who was holding the victory crown over the dead man's head and in this way once again shedding the light of life on the dead man. Thus Gehrts advocates the viewpoint that the consul celebrating the triumph actually also represented the consul who had sacrificed his life. The basic idea would be as follows: There are two consuls. One casts himself as a dead man, along with the enemy, into the realm of the dead. When subsequently the other consul celebrates the triumph, he represents the dead consul who has returned from the realm of the dead to celebrate the triumph—that is why he wears a red mask of death. The man standing behind him, the slave, would be his actual ego, that is, the living consul. One could also turn this around and say the slave is his shadow and he is the dead, namely, those who have been conquered.

The spear on which the consul who is consecrating himself to death stands before the sacrifice symbolizes directed psychic energy. Throwing the spear into the ranks of the enemy actually represents the process of projection through which the thrower becomes the psychic leader of the enemy army and drags them all with him into death so that the second consul can achieve the victory.

The Roman custom of having two consuls as supreme regents derives from the saga of the founding of Rome. According to this, Rome was founded by Romulus and Remus, who were twin brothers. At that time, Remus jumped over a wall that Romulus had built in order to mock him, and Romulus killed him. Thus after the abolition of the monarchy in Rome, two consuls were installed, who were in some way meant to represent these brothers. There are Roman texts that explicitly present this analogy (Livy).

Taken from a general psychological point of view, two brothers as rulers symbolize the fact that the prevailing collective consciousness principle rests on a secret opposition. Indeed our consciousness is maintained by an ongoing process of opposition, by an interaction of conscious and unconscious factors. Now at the moment a battle begins, a remarkable dissolution of the prevailing consciousness takes place: one part of it becomes unconscious and is projected onto the enemy, and through this it is possible to drive the latter down into death, into the unconscious. In order to be able to arouse oneself to a resilient and enduring battle rage, one's own shadow is projected on the enemy. One throws (pro-jects) it at the other like a spear and then one can subjugate it.

When the one consul then celebrates his triumph, he is possessed by the shadow of the dead man that had been projected onto the enemy. In the moment of the triumph he is no longer himself, but plays the role of the other. Again and again, one sees in history how the victor is psychically in danger of enacting precisely that which he regarded as the shadow in the other and had externally beaten down. Just as in the case *Graecia capta victorem cepit* (Greece, defeated, conquers the victor), again and again in history the defeated have psychically conquered the victors. This is tantamount to a general law. When one projects the darkness, then at some point it comes back, and the victor is easily dehumanized, while the slave stands behind him with the symbol of the Self, the golden crown, and says, "Take a look behind you, remember that you are a human being!"

This is a deeply meaningful and differentiated ritual. In our context, what is important is that it shows what always happens when a war breaks out: a psychic meeting of opposites which are supposed to function together in culture, or consciousness (embodied by the two consuls), falls apart and takes sides with the two opponents in battle. Then it never comes back together again properly, for when one wins, he takes over the role of the other.

In this way an enantiodromia is always engendered, unless the *triumphator* looking behind him is really able to integrate the idea that he is *also* the conquered slave and the dead man. If he were really able to understand that, then the interaction of opposites could function properly once again.

So much for the strange interwovenness of death and victory, which is expressed in Greek mythology in the relatedness of Nike to the Styx and Persephone. Nike, however, is not the only child of the goddess Styx; she has three brothers: Zelos (Battle Piper), Kratos (Strength), and Bia (Force).[16] This triad, with Nike as the fourth, constantly accompanies the universal ruler Zeus, embodying his power of victory. Whereas in our present-day view it is the will to fight and strength (military potential) and force that decide a military confrontation, Greek mythology adds a fourth factor, an anima element, a *psychic* quality, ennobling the crude triad of aggression through the feminine-psychic. The unconscious psyche also possesses a decisive power in the apparently meaningless and brutal unfolding of historical processes. That the decisive factor is a quaternity is highly significant, for a symbolic quaternity, according to Jung, always points to the psychic totality, the Self, and indeed to its becoming conscious. This would mean that if enough individuals concentrated on the inner center, the Self, then the possibility would arise that nature, through *synchronistic events*, might take the side of their military group. That sounds almost superstitious or absurd, but if we reflect that it probably corresponds to an evolutionary tendency of nature that human beings, in comparison to other higher mammals, have developed a significantly higher level of consciousness, it might then also be inferred that this evolutionary tendency continues its thrust in us and that those human groups and single individuals who are situated along the line of evolution have the best chance of survival in the course of world history.

That these four siblings who, according to the ancient Greek view, play the crucial role in the decisions of world history, are not only a culture-specific set of symbols is shown by the fact that we find a parallel to them in the Old Testament. The ancient

Israelites, in accordance with ancient Canaanite-Semitic custom, possessed a war fetish, a portable sanctuary, which they took with them into battle in order to gain the victory. This was the Ark of the Covenant, a chest fastened to two carrying poles or placed on a wagon, in which four objects were kept: the tablets of Moses (or the seven-branched candelabra), a golden oil jar, a vessel containing manna, and Aaron's staff. On the lid were two winged cherubim, the messengers of God.[17] This Ark was supposed to represent the immediate presence of God in the battle; that is, it was thought that God took part invisibly in the battle, enthroned on the arms of the cherubim. It was said that the Shekhinah of God—that is, his presence in the world—rested on the Ark, and this was considered to be a *feminine* figure. The Shekhinah also signified the interest that God took in humanity. According to historically later notions, this figure was also present in every human act of love, so here too there was a connection with the god Eros! When God was separated from his Shekhinah or had withdrawn with her on high, things went badly for the nation, and it was the task of men to restore this connection.[18] Here one can see a certain parallel to Nike: The Shekhinah mediates the will of God on earth just as Nike brings victory as a messenger of the gods. Nike is winged and the Shekhinah is enthroned on the arms of two winged beings. Particularly striking is the quaternity motif. Nike is one of four siblings who make crucial world decisions; in the Ark of the Covenant there are four sacred objects. These four things all recall events of the past in which God manifested immediately and miraculously in the realm of ordinary reality: the tablets of the Law, through which God made his will known; the oil signifying the living substance of the divine; the manna that rained from heaven when the people were starving in the desert; and the staff of Aaron, which unexpectedly blossomed.[19]

As Jung showed, when the quaternity motif occurs in a dream, it points to an all-embracing consciousness of the individual, to the greatest possible realization of his inner wholeness, which in the background is what his life is aiming at. For the totality of a human life reveals a kind of central pattern or meaning, which ego consciousness, subsisting only in the moment, rarely glimpses as a whole yet still somehow senses. Thus Winston Churchill is said always to have felt that he would one day have something great to do for England, and trusting in that, he ventured into the fray. When in the most critical of circumstances the fate of England was placed in his hands, he knew that this had been the meaning of his life from the beginning. In such moments a kind of certainty breaks through—one simply knows that one has to do this thing or that. This phenomenon is not particularly rare: many people from all levels of society have experienced such moments in their lives. Before the First World War, there was even a medal in the Austrian army that was only awarded to someone who had *acted against orders* and in this way brought about a favorable turn in the battle. If it went wrong, he was shot; but if the outcome was good, he received this order, which, significantly, was instituted by a woman, Maria Theresa. For this individual had not only served the rational organizational apparatus of the army but had also, as though following the goddess Nike, followed his feeling-based knowledge of destiny.

Today we easily permit ourselves to be blinded by rational statistical calculations and fall victim to the idea of big numbers. Nonetheless it is often also possible for a single individual to turn the tide of a collective situation. We can never say in advance with certainty that the statistically computed majority is the only possible winner. Sometimes an entire battle can be lost through a single officer's moment of inattention. In advance we never know into whose hands such a turn of fate will play; only in historical retrospect do we see that sometimes suddenly a certain insignificant Mr. X, without knowing it himself, had the whole situation in his hands. And this is where the unconscious comes into play: just as the functioning of consciousness suddenly lapses in an individual when an unconscious complex is activated, in the same way in a military organization, which pretty well corresponds to a system of consciousness, the unconscious lapse of a single person, or his positive act, can bring about a change of fate of the greatest collective proportions. We can therefore make the statement that the more conscious individuals who live a meaningful life in harmony with their unconscious are present in a people, the greater the chances for Nike to manifest.

Moreover, we know today that a soldier who is alone in his military task and not operating as part of a group is the most liable not to be able to hold his own in battle. However, it is to be expected that the development of modern warfare will take a direction that will result in there being more and more such "lonely" soldiers, and in that case it will be even more crucial for the greatest possible number of individuals to be inwardly firm and thus able to stand fast when they are no longer carried along by collective emotion and the spirit of comradery.

To sum up, Nike can be interpreted as the warrior's anima, that is, a kind of unconscious feeling-related expectation based on still more deep-seated inner factors, namely, the "truth of the Styx." As we know, the feminine side of the unconscious in a man mediates the relationship to the deep-seated meaningful wholeness of his personality. If a man heeds this element of feeling, which is also involved in his relationships with women, rather than rejecting it as "nonsense," he can only cause it to be more favorably disposed toward him. In this way, like Nike herself, he becomes inspired and acquires wings in reaching his goals. And this is not all. He can also establish a connection with the ultimate "fate factor" in the uncanny waters of the Styx, in the realm of the dead. Also at the same time, Nike embodies an irrational temporal factor, a kind of divinely willed "momentum" that can miraculously cross over into the dimension of real events, appearing there as an irrational turn of fate.

The winged youth Kairos was depicted in a relief carrying a pair of scales. This expresses the fact that in certain states where two opposed factors are in equilibrium, it is he who tips the balance. That this can also happen in a battle may easily be inferred, since in any war, as a result of the vital threat that it poses to a people, there is intense activation of the collective unconscious and its archetypes, and this heightens the likelihood that synchronicity phenomena will make an appearance.[20]

This brings us to the figure that stands still deeper behind that of Nike, the goddess of the subterranean waters of the Styx. In antiquity flowing waters were considered masculine, standing waters feminine. Styx, more an underworld pool or marsh lake than a river, was thus a feminine deity. The word *styx* was also used to refer to penetrating cold; it is connected with the shuddering coldness of the corpse and death.[21] *Stygein* means "to hate," "to loathe," probably originally, "to become cold," or "stiffen with hate." So we are also speaking of a "frigid reception" or "frosty atmosphere," where unspoken hatred predominates. The goddess Styx was the eldest of three thousand daughters of the aged sea god Oceanos, the origin of the world, the gods, and the human race. Her consort was the Titan Pallas (*Pallas* means "blooming youth" or "virago," as for example, Pallas Athena). Pallas was the first to come to the aid of Zeus, the god of heaven, against the demonic Titans, who embodied chaos and brutality. As a dark chthonic power, he took the side of the higher spiritual order.

The Styx, the sluggish underground river that rings the underworld is a body of water that is said to dissolve anything: crystal, clay, stone, wood, and all metals, even gold. For this reason, it cannot be contained in any vessel except in a hollow hoof or the horn of a legendary type of unicorn ass living in Scythia. The gods swore by this water, and when one of them perjured his oath, he fell as though dead for a period of a year and had to avoid the society of the other gods for nine years thereafter. Any other being was immediately killed by the water of the Styx. For example, according to legend, Alexander was killed by a drink of Styx water, which he drank from a horse's hoof. According to another version, this drink made him immortal. For when drunk or bathed in on specific days, it also had the property of conferring immortality. The water itself was described as bloodcurdling and ice-cold, and therefore the goddess Styx lived in seclusion in Tartarus, avoided by all the other gods even though she was a particularly old and venerated deity and possessed an ultimate authority over people, nations, and gods.

What does this mean translated into the language of psychology? An individual consists of an ego consciousness and an unconscious psychic sphere, and the same is true for the sum of individuals that make up a people. From the many unconscious psychic parts arises an unconscious group psyche, the source of the phenomena of mass psychology. This collective unconscious is symbolized in myth as well as in the dreams of modern people by the image of the sea, Oceanos, whom we know as the father of Styx. Whereas the sea god simply embodies the life- and death-bringing unconscious psychic basis of life, Styx has more to do with death, but also with a secret principle of justice and truth. (For the Greek god of the sea is also called *nemertes*, "undeceiving.") The Styx contains a kind of unconscious principle of order of ultimate authority, which in all likelihood rests on a certain unconscious spiritual tendency in the collective unconscious. The water of the Styx is obviously such an overwhelming phenomenon of nature that there is no way of dealing with it through conscious human measures. As the motif of dissolution of its vessel shows, it is "ungraspable." But precisely in this element there is a kind of ultimate fateful justice or truth, which stands even above the gods. For the gods embody certain psychic structures and principles of order of only relative power. When these archetypal principles lose their power to influence the collective consciousness, then their energy is lost to the unconscious, which is correspondingly strengthened. This always happens when traditions and religious and social ideals and convictions lose their force within a people, when they become a mere habit and no longer "work." Then disorientation develops in the individual and in the collective—restlessness and a tendency to indulge in destructive mass movements or to sink as a whole into amorphous indifference, into a state of seething accompanied by malaise, out of which there can come either an outburst of fresh creativity or the demise of the nation, that is, death or Nike, decline or a new possibility of life. In this way, even the life of the gods is dependent on contact with the collective psyche, for a god who is no longer functional in the unconscious collective psyche of the human race is as good as dead. For example, a German professor who was very attracted to the Nazi ideology and was thinking of joining the party, had the following dream in 1933: On the other side of a marsh, he saw groups of workers marching, spades on their shoulders, and singing a song. Full of yearning to reach them, he leaped into the swamp, but as, covered with muck, he reached them, he heard more clearly what they were saying: "Our power, it is over! Our power, it is over!" As early as 1933! Already by that time the knowledge of the outcome of the Second World War was present in the collective unconscious.

On the level of myth, the problem consists in the fact that the water of the Styx is ungraspable, because it destroys any vessel. Psychologically, this refers in a literal sense to a problem of "creativity." Chapter 7, "The Army," in the *I Ching*, or *Book of Changes*,[22] illuminates this problem; it contains the image of water under the earth (like the Styx). There we learn that the ancient Chinese, like the Swiss, had an army levied from the general populace. Just as ground water is hidden under the earth, an army was latent in the peasant population, which could be called up at a time of war and used as a potential for war. Delved into a bit deeper, this image would mean that the potential for unconscious tension is present beneath the field of consciousness (the earth), and that this might become dangerous if it cannot be drawn off. If this hexagram is to be interpreted for an individual situation, then, as Jung once indicated, it is related to the *danger of a precreative state*. Many people, for example, artists, are familiar with a state that arises before they write or paint, or in the case of creative scientists, before they discover something new: a state of enormous irritability, or a depressive or even destructive mood. It is derived, as dreams will usually tell us, from a state that is like too much water being gathered under the earth. This is an energy potential out of which, if we are unable to give it creative expression, prepsychotic states may arise. On the collective level, exactly the same holds true, and on that level the psychosis corresponds to the outbreak of war.

The individual lines of hexagram number seven are also revealing. The first line says: "An army must set forth in proper order. If the order is not good, misfortune threatens." We may understand this as saying that in the precreative depression, one should not let oneself go, but maintain conscious discipline and routine. The second line says: "In the midst of the army! Good fortune. No blame. The king bestows a triple decoration." This refers to a leader of an army who commands from the midst of his troops. That would be the ego consciousness in service of the king, that is, the Self. Consciousness actively engages in the conflict instead of letting itself be pushed around. That way the Self, represented by the king, can help the ego. The third line reads: "Perhaps the army carries corpses in the wagon. Misfortune." The commentary speaks of a defeat, because an unauthorized person (a boy) has become involved in the leadership. A failure occurs because infantilism and mass psychology have spread. The fourth line speaks of an orderly retreat. That is clear enough and requires no commentary. The fifth line is more complicated. It reads: "There is game in the field. It furthers one to catch it. No blame. Let the eldest lead the army. The younger transports corpses; then perseverance brings misfortune." The commentary speaks of a wild animal getting into the fields and ravaging them, which means an invasion by the enemy. The eldest who leads the army is an experienced strategist; the younger who transports corpses is an irresponsible leader who simply charges blindly ahead. I will discuss the wild animal's intrusion later, and the rest of this line is clear. The last line speaks of the proper exploitation of a victory and says that one should not let inferior people gain power. For us the important thing is that "water under the earth" means something similar in China to the Styx, that is the danger and mighty potential of a precreative state, which can bring renewal, but also murder, war, and death.

As already mentioned, the waters of the Styx cannot be contained by any vessel, not even crystal, metal, or gold. Its corrosive force dissolves everything. Here we are clearly talking about finding the proper "container" for the urgent creative potential arising from the unconscious. Obviously this would have to be a new religious-symbolic container, for only a symbol is capable of synthesizing the forces of the unconscious and the collective consciousness, that is, of making it possible for the energy of the unconscious to flow into a conscious cultural form. According to what Aelian says, the only thing that can contain the waters of the Styx is a hoof or the horn of a particular type of unicorn Scythian ass.[23] In general, horses and asses represent the animal sphere of instinct in a human being, the unconscious ground of his vital impulses that carries him along. Because they embody this animal aspect, horses and asses are associated with the devil, who is known to have horse's feet, which he inherited from Wotan. But many heroic horses in mythology have also stamped forth springs of healing water from the earth with their feet (as Pegasus did with the Hippocrene spring), which is why hoof prints are considered in many places to be legendary symbols of fruitfulness and prosperity. And in our culture horseshoes are still considered lucky today.

As Richard Broxton Onians explained,[24] hooves and horns are outgrowths of a being's vital essence, in which the vital fluid, as in sperm, is especially concentrated ("hoof" in Latin was also sometimes *cornu*, the word for "horn").

The Aelian text about the waters of the Styx, which could only be drawn in the horn of a unicorn Scythian ass is probably a later reflection of a passage from the Persian *Bundahishn* (chap. 19):

> Regarding the three-legged ass, they say that it stands amid the wide-formed ocean, and its feet are three, eyes six, mouths nine, ears two, and horn one, body white, food spiritual, and it is righteous. And two of its six eyes are in the position of eyes, two on the top of the head, and two in the position of the hump; with the sharpness of those six eyes it overcomes and destroys. Of the nine mouths three are in the head, three in the hump, and three in the inner part of the flanks; and each mouth is about the size of a

cottage, and it is itself as large as Mount Alvand. Each one of the three feet, when it is placed on the ground, is as much as a flock of a thousand sheep comes under when they repose together; and each pastern is so great in its circuit that a thousand men with a thousand horses may pass inside. As for the two ears, it is Mazendaran that they will encompass. The one horn is as it were of gold and hollow, and a thousand branch horns have grown upon it, some befitting a camel, some befitting a horse, some befitting an ox, some befitting an ass, both great and small. With that horn it will vanquish and dissipate all the vile corruption due to the efforts of noxious creatures.

When that ass shall hold its neck in the ocean its ears will terrify, and all the water of the wide-formed ocean will shake with agitation, and the side of Ganavad will tremble. When it utters a cry all the female water-creatures, of the creatures of Ahuramazda, will become pregnant; and all pregnant noxious water-creatures, when they hear that cry, will cast their young. When it stales in the ocean all the earth—it is even on that account when all asses which come into water stale in the water—as it says thus: "If, O three-legged ass! you were not created for the water, all the water in the sea would have perished from the contamination that the poison of the evil spirit has brought into its water, through the death of the creatures of Ahuramazda."[25]

The ass stands in the spot in the ocean where, according to the *Bundahishn*, the tree Gokard often stands, a tree that has a universal healing effect. Both the ass and the tree symbolize, as Jung points out, the vital, procreative, and healing power of the deity. "The power of the deity is revealed not only in the spirit, but also in the wild instinctive urgency of nature both inside and outside human beings." It is a *complexio oppositorum*, demon and alexipharmacon, devil symbol and Christ symbol, at the same time. The horn in particular represents directed energy, thrusting power, and also often aggression. But significantly it is the cut-off horn that becomes the receptacle for the water of the Styx, that is, the psychically overcome aggression of the inner god. For this also we find parallel notions in ancient China. In the seventh hexagram of the *I Ching*, "The Army," of which we have already spoken, the fifth line says, "There is game in the field. It furthers one to catch it." This means a wild animal that has invaded the cultivated fields. The commentary connects it with the enemy and also with a wild lack of discipline in one's own army, which must be overcome. We find the same idea in more detail in hexagram twenty-six of the *I Ching*, which as an image has heaven, the creative, below, and the mountain, keeping still, above. This is a sign that describes how creative force begins to establish itself on the collective level. The fourth line of this hexagram says: "The headboard of a young bull. Great good fortune"; and the fifth line: "The tusk of a gelded boar. Good fortune." The commentary advises that "a good way to restrain wild force is to forestall it." It also says, "where men are concerned, wild force should not be combated directly; instead its roots should be eradicated." So here also what is being talked about is preventing a destructive psychic outburst through a creative grasp of unconscious forces.

Karl Schmid, in his essay "Über Aspekte des Bösen im Schöpferischen" (Evil Aspects of the Creative),[26] pointed out that the fashionable word "creative" is nowadays mostly used in a positive sense, whereas in the past it tended to signify something revolutionary, subversive, and dangerous, and that a development of this dangerous notion of creativity via Romanticism and Nietzsche had led to Nazism. Since that time it has become fashionable for destructive collective movements to write "creativity" on their banners as a pretext or excuse for the wholesale overthrow of order. Schmid postulates that the state, as the preserver of order, should always relate conservatively to the kind of creativity that degenerates into collective movements. He ends his presentation with the following words:

> The unrest of individuals in cultures may perhaps be a stirring of nature. For collective unrest, according to the law creativity is no alibi. The nature of the state demands that it affirm the law, otherwise it loses its meaning and value. The individual languishes

and becomes incapable of performing his tasks if he merely steers blindly according to collective signals of Left and Right, forbidding and allowing. When, however, the collective discredits that act of stabilizing and clarifying that is the epitome of law and no longer permits itself to be guided by it, it is shattered overnight. The individual needs an undisturbed connection with the unconscious in order to remain creative. But what does the collective need? It needs everything that the Enlightenment sought—unceasing heightening of consciousness, ever stronger acknowledgment of justice, law, and consensus. For the collective, exactly that is supportive and good that is diminishing and evil for the individual.[27]

What Schmid is really describing is a double pair of opposites:

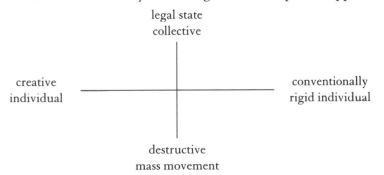

Such a tension between opposites is resolved only through the spontaneous revelation of a new symbol that reconciles the opposites, a new middle term. It is always a case of using the ass's horn—that is, the conquered but not suppressed wildness—to draw from the waters of the Styx that which, in accordance with a mysterious order, is thrusting its way toward the light out of the collective unconscious.

The horn as the vessel has a unique double nature. As a horn it is phallic and masculine—penetrative thrusting power, directed energy. But for use as a vessel it must be turned over, that is, an enantiodromia or reversal is needed. So then as a vessel it is a feminine, receptive principle. Better known than the ass's horn is the so-called unicorn cup, which Jung discussed in detail in *Psy-*

chology and Alchemy.[28] It is an alexipharmacon, that is, all poison that is poured into the cup becomes harmless. It also protects anyone who drinks from it from pain and sickness. Thus the unicorn cup is a "uniting symbol,"[29] and as such it is the "vessel" or the means of harmlessly assimilating suprapersonal contents of the unconscious psyche instead of letting oneself be carried away into wildness and inflation. Only under this condition is the water of the Styx, that is, of the collective unconscious, not dangerous.

The water of the Styx also has another property. This is the power that is sworn by and by which even gods are severely punished if they perjure their oaths. Thus it contains a kind of truth or ultimate justice that stands above even individual gods, which is what the Greeks later called *heimarmene*, "providence" or "doom." The double meaning of doom and providence shows that this principle can be fortunate or unfortunate, and in regard to good and evil, it is often neutral. It is connected, however, with something else: according to Epimedes of Crete, the consort of Styx is not the Titan Pallas, but rather a figure named Peiras. Peiras means (according to Onians) "surrounding band" (boundary) and, derived in a figurative sense from this, "rope end" or "knot." It is said in myths of Oceanos (the ocean surrounding the earth) and his consort Tethys, the parents of Styx, that they are *peirata*, the boundaries of the earth. With Peiras, Styx produced the serpent Echidna, a monster. The relationship of Styx with Peiras probably is connected with her death aspect and with her aspect of historical impermanence, for death is the inevitable factor that is the ultimate boundary of life, the definitive noose around all things. But the word *nike* is also often linked with *peirar* or *peiras*, undoubtedly because a victory represents a result that remains irreversible for a long time. The victor and the defeated are confronted by definite conditions (it is no accident that sports victories are measured by clock and tape!). It is a matter of final limits that nature sets us, which we do not always experience as good or just. Nevertheless, for the ancient Greeks, as well as for the Chinese, it was wisdom to hold oneself within these limits and not to infringe upon them.

Styx contains not only certain limits; as a goddess of oaths she also has something to do with ultimate inner truth, since she punishes any oath-breaking so fearsomely. Even the gods must submit to her truth. This boundary-setting truth, later also called cosmic law, is difficult to grasp in itself; however, it manifests itself, in the destiny of peoples as well as in the destiny of individual human beings, as that which ultimately is just as it is.

Thus what Jung once called the "mysterious flow of events" has to do with the effect of the collective unconscious on the course of world events. The collective unconscious, however, is not something static, but rather over long periods of time certain archetypes more than others are constellated within it, and that, generally speaking, is what we mean by changes in the zeitgeist. And that raises the question of whether behind this process of constellation of archetypes determining the character of a given historical period some lawful principle of order can be detected or whether it is blind chance that reigns. In his work *Aion*, Jung pursues this question and shows that the central symbol in the collective unconscious, the symbol of the Self, seems to come under the influence of an internal process of transformation that gives its mark to a given historical period. Jung outlines this process with the help of Christian, alchemical, and Gnostic symbolism.

But before getting into this, we must look still further afield. In the ancient Greek cosmology, not only is the underworld ringed by the River Styx, but also the disk of the earth is surrounded in similar fashion by the "Oceanos" (which is depicted in the form of Ouroboros). And finally the upper cosmos is ringed by a river in the form of a serpent, who bears on his back the signs of the Zodiac. These three encircling serpents or rings of water—the *peirata gaies*—are fundamentally identical with, that is, they symbolize, three aspects of the same psychic reality; namely, that everywhere—below, above, and on the level of the horizon—where our consciousness comes to an end, the sphere of the unconscious begins. With the sluggish waters of the Styx, however, the quality of inertia and the death aspect of the unconscious come more to the fore; with Oceanos it is more the life-giving and preserving aspects; and with the serpent of the Zodiac, it is a spiritual, temporally conditioned order. This last, as it were, qualitatively colors all the archetypal manifestations of a given historical period. We are presently, as is widely known and much discussed, at the end of the period of the second fish of the Piscine age and are approaching the beginning of the age of Aquarius. Along with this traditional model of the background of the movement of history, in *Aion*[30] Jung outlined a second century-spanning process, a constant internal transformation of the God-man or Self-symbol.

Figure 1 shows a chain of four double pyramids, beginning from the top with the Gnostic symbol of the Anthropos, a cosmic God become human, who comes into prominence at the beginning of the Piscine Age. This symbol broadens to a quaternity in order to be received by consciousness, and peaks in the realization of the God-man of light, Christ. Then the same process repeats in the period of the second fish but this time reversed to the negative—a shadow quaternity, which peaks in the image of the serpent, the symbol of the devil. This is followed by the descent of the same symbol into inanimate nature, which culminates in the alchemical "stone" (*lapis*), and finally, this is followed by the

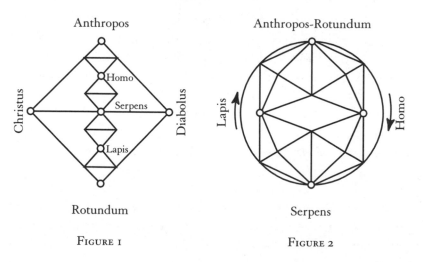

FIGURE I

FIGURE 2

descent into cosmic matter, culminating in the symbol of the rotundum or model of the atom. On the level of the serpent the opposition between good and evil yawns to its widest, whereas elsewhere the symbol of the Self represents more a uniting of the opposites.

Figure 2, with its four double pyramids wound into a spiral, is actually more accurate. This model represents a process of self-renewal of the Self symbol in which (through the linear shift of circle into spiral) at the same time an evolution of consciousness seems to take place. For all this, I must refer the reader to Jung's work *Aion*; however, I mention it here because it represents an attempt to get a fix on the mysterious "truth" or order in the hidden River Styx.

Where are we today within this century-spanning movement? As, among other things, the sporadically appearing rumors of flying saucers show, we are roughly at the level of the serpent on the turn away from the tension of opposites Christus-Diabolus (*serpens*) on the way back to lapis and rotundum. Jung writes in this connection about the serpent.[31]

Most people do not have sufficient range of consciousness to become aware of the opposites inherent in human nature. The tensions they generate remain for the most part unconscious, but can appear in dreams. Traditionally, the snake stands for the vulnerable spot in man: it personifies his shadow, i.e., his weakness and unconsciousness. The greatest danger about unconsciousness is proneness to suggestion. The effect of suggestion is due to the release of an unconscious dynamic, and the more unconscious this is, the more effective it will be. Hence the ever-widening split between conscious and unconscious increases the danger of psychic infection and mass psychosis. With the loss of symbolic ideas the bridge to the unconscious has broken down. Instinct no longer affords protection against unsound ideas and empty slogans. Rationality without tradition and without a basis in instinct is proof against no absurdity.

The *ouroboros*, the serpent who bites his own tail, is according to Jung also a symbol of the demonic human being who devours himself. Napoleon, Hitler, and others are examples of such possession by the collective unconscious.[32]

So we are at a turning point where it is a matter of continuing to exist or not. But if it is true that Nike is part of a quaternity of consciousness, then becoming conscious of the divine image of humanity is a task that has been set us by nature. Thus we might hope that this evolutionary tendency will be able to defeat the powers of destruction.[33]

According to the Greek mythologem, in the quaternity Zelos, Bia, and Kratos predominate by three-quarters; but the fourth, a feminine human figure, constitutes a promise that it is yet possible for humanity and Eros to take the victory. The mythologem of the ass's horn, however, provides a hint about what we can actively do to prevent the outbreak of war: we must cut off the horn of aggression within us—even though it is part of the self— turn its receptive feminine side up and use it to draw up from the collective unconscious that very thing that is thrusting toward the light. In this way we can reduce the perilous pressure of the "water under the earth" from which wars seem to arise. So instead of waiting like a herd of sheep huddling together from fear until some unauthorized figure presses the atomic button, we can actually do something. And the creative element that we must bring up to the surface is, if Jung's schema is correct, comprised of everything that leads, not to a further dissolution into the mass (*serpens*), but to the lapis, a symbol of the free, mature, and responsible individual.

Notes

1. *Truth and Method* (New York: Seabury, 1975).

2. *Aion*, cw 9/ii.

3. J. Hohmann, in *Friede, Wirkungsgeschichte und kollektives Unbewusstes* (Peace, Effective History, and the Collective Unconscious) (Frankfurt: Europäische Hochschulschriften, 1984), has pointed out

that Gadamer's effective history corresponds to the Jungian concept of the collective unconscious.

4. *Bhagavadgita*, tr. L. von Schroeder (Eugen Diederichs Verlag), eleventh song. There are several English-language editions available.

5. H. Usener, *Götternamen* (Names of Gods) (Frankfurt, 1948).

6. For a picture, see M.-L. von Franz, *Zeit: Strömen und Stille* (Time: Flowing and Stillness) (Frankfurt: Insel Verlag, 1981), p. 90.

7. For more detail, cf. M.-L. von Franz, *Number and Time* (Evanston, Ill.: Northwestern University Press, 1968).

8. A Baudrillart, *Les divinités de la victoire d'après les textes et monuments figurés* (Victory Deities on the Basis of Texts and Illustrated Monuments) (Paris, 1874). A Nike excavated in Delphi even had six wings, i.e., two additional pairs on the arms and feet.

9. G. Berefeldt, *A Study on the Winged Angel* (Uppsala, 1968), pp. 60ff.

10. Cf. M. Ninck, *Götter und Jenseitsglauben der Germanen* (The Germanic Tribes' Gods and Belief in a Beyond) (Jena, 1937), p. 30: "The fylgias and the accompanying spirits originated in a different way (from the *mare*). Although they did arise out of the experience of dreams and related ecstatic states, they did not derive their influence from the overwhelming force of some particular effect . . . but rather their power of persuasion flowed from the experience of a remote connection between dreams and events later coming about in fact."

11. Cf. M. Ninck, *Wodan und germanischer Schicksalsglaube* (Wodan and Germanic Beliefs about Fate) (Jena, 1935), p. 199.

12. Ibid., pp. 251–53: "The curious affinity of Athene and the valkyries has already occasionally been pointed out. . . . What we are dealing with here is the double-sided inheritance of a common past. . . . Here the names correspond even down to individuals, for example, Promachos to the valkyries Mild and Gund, Ageleia ("Booty Capturer") to Horya ("Army Woman"), Goj ("Noisemaker") to Hlokk ("Weapon-Clashing Warrior Woman"). Athene is depicted on ancient monuments in a manner resembling a Gaironul ("Spear Charger"). She is Harrier (Laossoos) and at the same time Nike (Victory), as is Sigdrifa ("she who charges to victory"). She . . . alone knows the way into the chamber where the thunderbolt (of Zeus)

lies. . . . Athene, the unfathomable, the well-versed in wisdom, the clairvoyant (*pronoia*), is the destiny that hangs over the hero. . . . As the voice of Nemesis, she intrudes into the life of the individual hero; as a mediator, she stands between him and the parcae; as the radiant Nike, she is the fulfillment of the warrior's existence."

13. Ibid., p. 237.

14. Cf. Berefeldt, *Study on the Winged Angel*, p. 39.

15. *Das Märchen und das Opfer* (Fairy Tales and Sacrifice) (Bonn: Bouvier, 1967), pp. 15, 24ff.

16. Cf. K. Kerényi, *The Gods of the Greeks* (Baltimore; Penguin Books, 1958), p. 30; and M. Ninck, *Die Bedeutung des Wassers in Kult und Leben der Alten* (The Meaning of Water in the Worship and Life of the Ancients) (Darmstadt: Wissenschaftliche Buchgesellschaft, 1960), pp. 37ff. and passim.

17. Cf. H. Gressmann, *Die Lade Jahwehs und das Allerheiligste des salomonischen Tempels* (The Ark of Yahweh and the Holy of Holies in Solomon's Temple) (1920): "When the Ark was taken into battle, Moses said, 'Rise up, Lord, and let thine enemies be scattered; and let them that hate thee flee before thee' (Numbers 10:35). And when, after the victory, they put it down again, he said, 'Return, O, Lord, unto the many thousands of Israel' (Numbers 10:36). In time of peace the Ark was hidden in the inmost Holy of Holies of the tabernacle tent and guarded by a consecrated youth."

18. Cf. G. Scholem, *Von der mystischen Gestalt der Gottheit* (On the Mystical Figure of the Godhead) (Zurich, 1962), pp. 15f; and H. Adolf, *Visio Pacis, Holy City and Grail* (Pennsylvania State University Press, 1960), pp. 63ff. and the literature referred to there (pp. 183ff.).

19. Things similar to the Ark of the Covenant are still to be seen in the present century. Among the Rwala Bedouin who live in a border area of the Syrian desert, a portable *utfa*, arranged as a camel's howdah furnished with a baldachin, represents a kind of magical presence of *mana* and of the destiny of the tribe and is at the same time the seat of the protecting and guiding power of the divine. In a life-or-death battle of the tribe, for which, traditionally, one set out by the light of the morning star, this howdah, mounted on a camel, preceded the warriors just as, according to the earliest recollections of the Old Testament, the Ark of the Covenant was sent

ahead in order to "scatter the enemy." This sanctuary of guidance and war was "loaded" with a love prize, for under the baldachin sat the virginal, naked daughter of a sheik, who served to inflame the warriors and as a promise to the bravest among the youths that, if it was not to a marriage with death that he was rushing, at the end of the battle nothing less beckoned than the Hierosgamos with Ishtar. For it was no one else but the *gadistu ilani*, the holy one, the hierodule of the gods, who was embodied in the virgin daughter of the sheik. Cf. J. Morgenstern, *The Ark, the Ephod and the "Tent of Meeting"* (Cincinnati, 1945), cited by V. Maag in *Kulturgeschichte des Alten Orients* (Cultural History of the Ancient Orient), ed. H. Schmökel (Stuttgart, 1961), p. 586. I am grateful to Dr. René Malamud for bringing this article to my attention.

20. Cf. C. G. Jung, "Synchronicity: An Acausal Connecting Principle," in cw 8, para. 870.

21. Cf. R. B. Onians, *The Origin of European Thought* (Cambridge University Press, 1954), p. 95 and passim.

22. *I Ching or Book of Changes*, trans. Cary F. Baynes (Princeton, N.J.: Princeton University Press, Bollingen Series, 1967).

23. Aelian, *De natura animalium*, X, 40; cited in Onians, *The Origin of European Thought*, p. 246.

24. Ibid., p. 246.

25. C. G. Jung, *Psychology and Alchemy*, cw 12, para. 535, pp. 456ff.

26. In *Das Böse* (Evil) (Zurich: Rascher Verlag, 1965), p. 237.

27. Ibid., p. 257

28. cw 12, paras. 550ff., pp. 466ff.

29. Ibid., para. 553, p. 471.

30. Jung, *Aion*, cw 9/ii, paras. 390f, pp. 247f.

31. Ibid., para. 390, note 79, pp. 247f.

32. See *C. G. Jung im Gespräch—Interviews, Reden, Begegnungen* (Conversations with Jung—Interviews, Talks, Encounters) (Zurich: Daimon, 1986), pp. 176f.

33. C. G. Jung, *Memories, Dreams, Reflections.*

THE INDIVIDUATION
PROCESS

■■

The Structure of the Process of Psychic Maturation

At the beginning of his essay "Man and His Symbols," C. G. Jung presented the concept of the unconscious, with its personal and collective structures and the ways in which it manifests in symbols. Once we have recognized the profound meaning of the symbols of the unconscious, the problem of their interpretation still remains. In this regard Jung showed that a great deal depends on whether or not a dream interpretation rings true for the dreamer, since dreams can only really perform their meaningful function within the framework of conscious reactions.

In Jung's consideration of the unconscious, however, this led to the further question of what meaning a person's dream life might have as a whole, that is: what is the significance of dreams, not just in terms of the immediate regulation of our psychic equilibrium, but for our life as a whole?

In the course of observing the dreams of a great number of people (it has been estimated that he himself worked on at least eighty thousand dreams), Jung discovered that dreams are of significance not only for the life of an individual but that, taken as a totality, they represent parts of an immense "web of destiny," which seems to exhibit a dynamic structure that applies to humanity altogether.

Jung called the development of this existential pattern the process of individuation. Since night after night our dreams produce new scenes and images, many dreamers might tend to overlook this large-scale pattern; but when we interpret our dreams over a long period of time, we see that many themes appear repeatedly, then disappear and reappear again. In fact many people dream frequently about the same figures, landscapes, and situations, and these pass through a gradual process of change. Moreover, this process of change can be considerably accelerated by effective interpretation of the dreams. Thus our dream life actually resembles a woven pattern in which individual threads are visible at one moment, disappear the next, and then unexpectedly appear again.[1] As this process goes on, it gradually becomes clear that a hidden goal-orientation is at work in it, which is bringing about a slow psychic growth. This is a process of self-realization, of becoming oneself. A more comprehensive, more mature personality becomes visible and also tangible to others. Since this process of psychic growth cannot be deliberately "done," but is something given by nature, it is often symbolized by the unconscious through the image of a tree, whose slow growth follows an individual pattern.

The psychic center that organizes this growth seems to be a kind of atomic nucleus of the psyche. We could also say that it is that which invents and orders our dreams. Jung called this center the Self. It represents the wholeness of our psyche, in contrast to the ego, which constitutes only a small part of our living psychic sphere.[2]

From the earliest times, humanity had some inkling of the existence of this psychic core. The Greeks called it the inner *daimon*, the Egyptians called it the *ba* soul, which took the form of a star or bird; the Romans worshiped it as the "genius" of the individual person. Many primitive peoples conceived of it as a protective spirit in the form of an animal or as a helper dwelling in a fetish.

This symbol appears in a particularly authentic form in the conceptions of certain inhabitants of the Labrador peninsula, the so-called Naskapi Indians.[3] These forest hunters lived in small family groups so isolated that they were not able to develop tribal customs or tribal religious views or rites. Thus the Naskapi hunters relied purely on their inner inspirations and dreams. They taught that the human soul was nothing other than an inner companion, which they called "my friend" or *mista'peo*, "great man." This inner companion lived in the heart of the individual and was immortal. Those Naskapi who paid special attention to their dreams and tried to decipher their hidden meanings and test out the truth of them were able to enter into a deeper relationship with the "great man." He favored such people and sent them more and better dreams. In addition to the primary obligation on the part of an individual to follow the indications of his or her dreams, there was a further duty: to immortalize the dreams in works of art. Lies and deception drive off the great man within, whereas generosity, neighborly love, and love shown to animals attract him. In this way, dreams provided the Naskapi with a complete orientation, also in relation to external nature, that is, in relation to the fortunes of the hunt, to the weather, and to other circumstances on which they were dependent.

I mention these primeval, simple folk here because they were not influenced by our civilization and therefore still seemed to possess an unspoiled, natural knowledge of the psychic guide that Jung called the Self.

The Self can be defined as an inner guiding center, which does not coincide with our consciousness and which can only be further explored through dreams, which show that it works toward a lasting expansion and maturation of the personality. To begin with, however, this great center in us is no more than an inborn potentiality. In the course of a lifetime it can be realized to a greater or lesser degree, depending on whether the ego is willing to pay attention to its messages. The Naskapi noted that someone who heeds the promptings of the "great man" receives more numerous and better dreams, and we could also say that in such a person the great man is more clearly realized than in people who neglect him. Accordingly, it seems that the ego was not made by nature to follow its own arbitrary will unrestrictedly, but rather to help the inner wholeness toward realization by lending it the light of consciousness. If, for example, I possess an artistic talent of which I am unaware, it might as well not exist; only when my ego perceives it can it be realized. In the same way, the inborn potentiality for individuation is not the same as the consciously recognized and consciously lived development of psychic wholeness.

We can picture it like this: In every mountain pine the image of this very mountain pine with all its potentialities is present, as it were, in the seed; but each real pine seed falls at a particular time in a particular place, and there are many special circumstances in play, like the nature of the soil, stones, the inclination and wind orientation of the slope, and the time of exposure to the sun. The whole of the nature of the pine reacts to these circumstances, for example, by growing crooked, growing around a stone, inclining toward the sun; and in this way the unique, unrepeatable individual pine tree that is the only real one comes into being, for after all a "pine in itself" is only a possibility or an idea. This growth of the individual, the unique, is what Jung called, in human beings, the individuation process. However, this must be seen from two aspects. Initially, it is an unconsciously flowing process of growth, such as takes place in humans as in every other sentient being, one through which a human being lives out his or her humanness. But in the true sense, this process only becomes a reality when a person becomes conscious of it.[4] We do not know whether the mountain pine tree knows, suffers, is happy, and so forth, when it encounters the various strokes of fate that form it; but a human being can participate consciously in these events and even experience the feeling of being able to play a role in determining details through free decisions of will. This is the process of individuation in the true sense. There is also something else that happens with the human person that is not contained in the simile of the pine tree: *the process of individuation is more than just a collaboration of the core of wholeness and the circumstances of fate.* Experientially, it is as though something divine and creative intervenes in the life of the individual, and indeed in a personal and individual fashion. We have the feeling that something is watching us, something that we do not see—perhaps that "great man" in one's heart, who communicates his intentions to us in dreams.

In any case, this creative aspect can only develop if the ego frees itself from all thoughts of gain and achievement in order to get nearer to this truer and deeper being; it must give itself over, free of all purpose, to this inner need to grow.

Actually, the philosophy of existentialism looks toward such a state, but it gets stuck in mere negation of the illusions of consciousness. The existentialist marches bravely right up to the doors of the unconscious and then does not open them! People who live in less uprooted circumstances than we understand better than we do that all utilitarian thoughts have to be given up in order to give the process of psychic growth room to occur. I once met an old woman who complained that she had not accomplished much in her "external" life; however, she had coped with a difficult marital situation and through this had developed into a mature person. I told her the following story of the Chinese sage Chuang-tse, and she felt consoled by it.

A wandering carpenter named Stone saw during his travels a gigantic old oak tree standing in a field by a shrine to the earth. The carpenter said to his apprentice, who was admiring it: "That is a useless tree; if you tried to make a ship out of it, it would soon rot; if you tried to make tools out of it, they would soon break. . . . From that tree nothing can be made, it can be used for nothing; that is why it was able to reach such a great age." But that night when the carpenter was in bed, the oak tree appeared to him in a dream and spoke: "Do you compare me to your cultivated trees, like the hawthorn, the pear, the orange, the apple, and the others that bear fruit and berries? They can hardly ripen their fruit, people mishandle and abuse them so! Their branches are broken off, their twigs are cut. Thus through their own gifts they imperil their lives and do not live out their full tally of years. . . .

This is the way of things everywhere. For this reason for a long time I have made every effort to be completely useless. Poor mortal! Let us suppose that I could be used for something; would I have reached such a size? And besides, you and I are both creatures. How does one creature come to be in a position to pass judgment on another as though from on high? You mortal and useless man, how can you talk about useless trees?!" The carpenter woke up and thought about the dream, and when his apprentice asked him how this tree among all others had come to serve the shrine to the earth, he answered him: "Hold your tongue! Not another word about it! It grew there on purpose, because otherwise those who did not know it would have abused it. If it were not the tree of the earth shrine, it surely would have run the risk of getting cut down.[5]

The carpenter obviously understood his dream, that is, that the tree, which did no more than realize its God-given destiny, represents the highest principle, before which human goal-oriented thinking has to hold its peace. Translated into psychological language, the tree represents the process of individuation giving teaching to the shortsighted ego.[6] In Chuang-tse's story, beneath the tree that is only itself stands a shrine to the earth. This was a rough stone, on which it was the custom to make offerings to the God who possesses and protects every plot of earth.[7] This earth shrine symbol conveys the meaning that actualization of the individuation process requires devotion to the suprapersonal powers of the unconscious. This means that I ought not to think about what I should do or about what is generally considered the right thing to do, or about what usually tends to happen, but rather I should pay heed to what the inner wholeness, the Self, wants from me now in *this* situation or what it wants to bring about through me.[8] To stay with the image of the tree, it is as though, in the process of its growth, it came against a stone, and instead of feeling irritated or making plans for how to overcome the obstacle, it just tried to feel whether it should now move more to the left or to the right, and as if it then yielded to the slightest yet strongest signal, which is the very urge toward creative uniqueness in which one feels compelled to find out what has never yet been known. The guiding impulses do not come from the ego, but rather from the psychic wholeness, the Self. In this respect, it does not help to imitate other people, for each person has his own unique task to fulfill. It may well be that human problems always remain similar, but they are not the same. All pines resemble one another, otherwise we would not be able to recognize them as such, and yet none is made exactly like any other. As a result of these individual differences, it is difficult to describe the endless possibilities of individuation. For this reason, Jung's views were often accused of not being clear. But here we are talking about things that can only be grasped by feeling, through living experiences, things that are not susceptible to theoretical abstraction.

Here the psychology of the unconscious runs into the same boundary as modern atomic physics has encountered. To the extent that we are dealing with statistically expressible, average facts, we can describe them exactly; however, the individual event can never be grasped in exact terms—we can only describe it as honestly as possible. Just as the physicists cannot say what light is "in itself," but only, on the basis of two experiments, describe it as particles or waves, psychology too runs into similar difficulties. We cannot say what the unconscious and the process of individuation are in themselves, but we can attempt to describe some of their relatively typical manifestations.

The First Encounter with the Unconscious

A person's childhood is usually characterized by a gradual awakening to the world and to his or her own being—in a state of great emotional intensity. The majority of childhood dreams, and often also the first vivid memories, already exhibit in symbolic form a person's most essential determining traits—sometimes, however, these are memories of real events, which, when looked at symbolically, are in effect prophetic.[9] Thus a young woman who, suffering from pathological states of panic, took her life at the age of about twenty-six. As a small child she had dreamed that she was lying on her bed when Jack Frost came into her room and pinched her in the stomach. When she woke up, she saw that she had pinched herself. The odd lack of reaction that characterized the child's meeting with the demon of cold and of life brought to a standstill was not a good sign for her future; and in the end she did cold-bloodedly take her life with her own hand. Her childhood dream had presaged her whole tragic destiny.

Sometimes it is not only a dream, but the inextinguishable memory of a real experience, that elicits early on in symbolic form certain fateful components of the personality. These memories can be regarded like dreams, for they remain in memory only on account of their symbolic significance.

The beginning of school is followed in most cases by a phase of increasing ego growth and adjustment to the world. This is a time that rarely passes without a few painful shocks. With many children, this time is also associated with the growing feeling of being different or peculiar that is often part of young people's loneliness. That which is imperfect and evil in the world and within oneself becomes conscious, and the pressing inner potentialities for development that have not yet had a chance to be actualized lie like a weight on the shoulders of many young people, who have to find their way in life despite this and in the face of the world around them. When the building up of consciousness that is natural during this time is disturbed, the child often withdraws into a kind of protected inner world, which in dreams and symbolic drawings exhibits with particular frequency the kind of circular, rectangular, and nuclear motifs that we will be speaking about later on. Such images are related to the existential center of the psyche referred to above, which organizes the entire development of the personality. Thus there is great likelihood that this image will appear in phases when there is a serious threat. As far as we are able to say today, it is also from this center that the impetus for the development of the conscious ego in humans emanates, the ego apparently being a duplicate or structural counterpart of the original center, the Self.[10]

Already in this early phase of life, many people find themselves compelled to seek intensively for the "meaning of life," for it seems that only finding this will make the chaos both inside and outside them bearable. Others, by contrast, continue during this period to be carried along by the dynamism of their instinctive patterns and thus do not consciously inquire into the meaning of their existence, experiencing as they do specific aspects of it, such as love, nature, sport, work, as having an immediate and satisfying meaning. They are not necessarily more superficial than the first type but are simply carried along frictionlessly by the current of life. The situation is parallel to riding in a windowless railway car: it is only when it stops or starts up suddenly that one notices it is moving at all.

The true process of individuation—the *conscious* relationship with the great inner man or one's own psychic center—usually begins with an injury or some state of suffering, which represents a kind of vocation that is not often recognized as such. Instead ego feels it is being obstructed in the fulfillment of its will or desires; or the obstructing factor is projected onto the outside, and God, the world situation, the boss, or one's spouse are made responsible for whatever does not seem right. Or else things seem to be all right on the outside too, but one is tormented by deadly boredom—nothing has any real meaning any longer. This initial situation is depicted in many myths and fairy tales. It takes the form of the reigning king being old and sick, of the royal couple not having any children, of a monster stealing all the women, children, horses, or treasures of the kingdom, of the devil casting a spell on the king's army or ship and rendering them motionless, of darkness covering the earth, of the rivers running dry, or of flood, drought, or cold afflicting the land. It is as though the approach of the "great inner man" cast a shadow before it, or as if it came in the guise of a hunter and caught the helplessly wriggling ego in its net.[11] At this point in the myths it is always something quite definite that is required to heal the crisis. To be restored to health, the king needs a "white blackbird" or a fish "that has a golden ring in its jaw," or he demands the elixir of life, three golden hairs that grow on the devil's head, or the golden braid of a woman's hair that hangs in a tree, and thereafter, of course, its owner. Thus it is always something quite special and hard to find that could heal the woe, and this is also the case in a crisis in the life of the individual described above: he is seeking something unattainable or something whose nature he does not even know.

At such times, all the advice of so-called good common sense—to be reasonable, to go on vacation, to have relationships with more people or fewer people, to work more or less, to take up a hobby—is all but useless. There is only one thing that always seems to help: to turn toward the impending darkness and try to explore it and its hidden purpose in the most nonjudgmental and naive fashion possible. The purpose within the darkness is usually so strange and unparalleled that the only way to discover in which direction the creative stream of life now wants to flow is with the help of dreams and unconscious fantasies. When one turns to the unconscious in this fashion, without prejudices, it very often spews forth an abundance of helpful images and symbols. But sometimes it initially yields up a whole series of bitter medicines that have to be swallowed, that is, painful insights about oneself that one doesn't want to be true, although one readily imputes them to others. These are things like egotism, intellectual laziness, indulgence in fantasies, lack of precision, cowardice, greed for money—all those little sins about which one thinks at the moment: "Oh, it doesn't really matter, no one will notice anyway," or "After all, everybody else does it too."

Insight into the Shadow

If you feel an almost insuperable irritation arising in you when someone accuses you of certain failings, then you can assume with some certainty that that is exactly where your sore point lies. When others point out your shadow, you become understandably defiant, because "after all, they are no better than I am." However, when your own dream, that is, your own inner judge, accuses you of something, what can you say? Then the ego is caught in the hunter's net. The result is usually a sheepish silence. After that, an arduous process of self-education begins, which is described so aptly in the myth of Hercules. As we know, Hercules had to clean the Augean stables, in which hundreds of cows had left the dung of decades, in a single day. A paralyzing laziness overcomes the ordinary person at the mere thought of such a possibility!

But the shadow does not consist only of what one has failed to do. It manifests just as often in rash and impulsive actions. Before one has had a chance to think, the nasty word has already been spoken, the intrigue is already under way, the wrong decision has already been made. On top of this, the shadow is especially vulnerable to all manner of collective infections.[12] By oneself one can manage more or less all right, but when "the others" do dark and primitive things, then one is afraid of being seen as failing to do one's bit or of being seen as a fool if one did not go along. In this way one falls prey to sudden impulses that really are not part of oneself. It is primarily in dealing with people of the same sex that one stumbles over one's own shadow and that of others, whereas with the opposite sex one sees the same things but for the most part feels a certain tolerance. In dreams and myths the shadow therefore appears as a figure of the same sex. The following dream can serve as an example. It was dreamed by a forty-eight-year-old man, who was very withdrawn and was trying to live by himself. He was all too earnest and disciplined about his work, but on the other hand, as far as his own basic character was concerned, he suppressed his joie de vivre and spontaneity much too heavily.

> I owned and lived in a very large house in the city, so big that I was not yet familiar with every part of it. For this reason, I used to wander through it, and I discovered, especially in the cellar, a number of rooms that I was completely unaware of, as well as exits that led into other cellars (or maybe subterranean streets?).

It made me feel uneasy to find that some of these exits were unlocked and some of them had no lock at all. Laborers were working on a job in the neighborhood, and one of them could have
slipped in completely unnoticed. . . . After going back up to the
ground floor, I crossed a courtyard, where once again I found
exits to the outside and into other houses. I was just about to have
a closer look at them when a man who was laughing loudly
walked toward me across the courtyard and called out that we
were old acquaintances (from primary school?). Then I remem-
bered this too. As he was telling me about his life, I went outside
with him, and we strolled aimlessly through the streets. A strange
chiaroscuro light lay over the scene as we were walking along an
immense ring road. Just as we arrived at a large expanse of grass,
three horses galloped by us, wonderfully powerful wild animals,
who nevertheless looked to be very well cared for. There were no
riders and no one was leading them. (Could they be runaways?
From the army?)

The tangle of unknown passages and unlocked doors in the
cellar recalls the depictions of the underworld of the ancient
Egyptians;[13] it is an image of the unconscious and its unknown
possibilities. It also shows how in the domain of the shadow one
is exposed to alien influences, which can infiltrate secretly. In the
back court—an as yet unknown psychic space of the dreamer's—
his old school friend crops up, obviously an aspect of the dreamer
himself, which he knew as a child and has forgotten in the meantime. Often qualities someone had as a child (such as joie de vivre,
a violent temper, or also naiveté) can disappear in the course of
his development, and it is surely such a lost side of the dreamer
that reappears here and tries to join him—presumably in this
case, it is his extraverted joie de vivre. We also soon learn why he
feels fear toward such a harmless figure: when he is taking a
stroll with his school friend, horses gallop by, perhaps from the
military—which means from the discipline of consciousness.
Since the horses have no riders, it is clear that they are instincts
that have not been mastered by the ego. And yet this old friend,
who brings danger with him, represents the life that is missing in
his consciousness.

Such a problem often arises in the encounter with "the other side." The shadow often contains important elements that consciousness is lacking, but in a form that does not allow them to be incorporated in the conscious sphere without further processing. The many passages and the large house in the dream also show that the dreamer does not yet know the full range of his personality. The shadow in this sample dream is typical for an introvert, that is, for a person who tends to be too withdrawn from external life. In the case of an extravert, a person more attuned to the external world, the shadow would look a lot different.

For example, a young man had the following dream. He was a person who as a result of his lively temperament repeatedly let himself get carried away with external busyness and work in pursuit of success in his career, despite the fact that his dreams kept insisting on his completing some private creative work he had undertaken:

A man is lying on a couch and has covered himself up with the blanket. He is a Frenchman, a desperado who is willing to do anything. An official is conducting me out of an office and down a flight of stairs. There is a plot against me. The Frenchman is supposed to kill me as though by accident. And in fact he is following us to the exit. I am on my guard. A large, imposing man (prominent, rich, influential) collapses against the right wall right next to me. He is feeling ill. I make use of this opportunity to kill the official by stabbing him in the heart with lightning speed. "You feel only a little dampness," something says, as though by way of commentary. Now I am free, for the Frenchman obviously is not going to do anything now that the man who hired him is out of the way. (Probably the official and the large man are the same figure; that is, the latter replaces the former.)

The desperado represents the dreamer's "other side," the introvert in him, who has nothing to lose. That he is lying on a couch covered by a blanket shows that he is looking for passivity, solitude, and introversion. The official and the successful man who are secretly identical symbolize the outer efforts for success mentioned above as well as external obligations. The collapse of the successful man is a reference to the fact that the dreamer had often fallen sick when he had become too dynamically outer-directed. This is seen in the fact that this successful man obviously has no blood, only a little water in his veins, which shows that the external attempts at success no longer contain any genuine life. For this reason, there is no great loss in stabbing him. The desperado is contented in the end, for he is really a positive shadow, who only became negative because he was provoked by the inappropriate conscious attitude of the dreamer.

The dream shows that the shadow can consist of the most diverse elements, for example, unconscious ambition (the bloodless successful man) or introversion (the Frenchman). In connection with the Frenchman, the dreamer had the particular association that the French know what they're doing in matters of love. Thus the two figures in dreams represent two well-known instincts: the will to power and sexuality. The power drive appears here in a double form, as the official and as the successful man. The official embodies more the collective adaptation aspect, whereas the successful man more represents ambition. As soon as the dreamer gets rid of these dangerous inner qualities, the Frenchman becomes benevolent, that is, the dangerous element of the sexual impulses also falls into place.

It is clear that the shadow problem plays a major role in political factionalism. If the dreamer of the last-cited dream had not had an understanding of psychology, he might easily have identified the desperado with "those evil Communists" or the official or the successful man with "those evil Capitalists." Then he would no longer have had to seek the fault within himself! When a person sees his unconscious tendencies in other people, this is called a projection.[14] The malicious political propaganda of all countries, like backstairs gossip among individuals, is swarming with such projections, which obscure all chance of an objective view of other people and obstructs the possibility of genuine human relationship.

Whether the shadow becomes a friend or a foe depends on ourselves. As the dreams of the unknown cellar and the Frenchman show, the shadow is not always an inner enemy. Rather, just like any external person around us, it is a being with whom we must come to terms through—depending on the case—acknowledgment, resistance, or love. It only becomes hostile when it is treated entirely without understanding or is ignored.

Sometimes, though not often, a person feels compelled to act out his worst side and repress his better ego. When this happens the shadow appears in dreams as a positive figure. This can be observed in the dreams of criminals, who dream unusually often about figures of light who do good for humanity and even of savior figures. In such cases, the positive aspect of the personality is repressed. This state of affairs, however, is also found in connection with particular elements in ordinary people. They repress some character trait that is positive in itself because it does not fit in with the image they have of themselves or because it is difficult to reconcile with other inclinations of theirs. A human being comes into the world as an incredible mixture of hereditary factors, and among these are often conflicting traits that are very difficult to make work together.

In the case of a person who acts out his natural affects and emotions too strongly, the shadow can also appear as a cold intellectual. It then embodies venomous judgments and evil thoughts that have been repressed. In brief, the shadow always represents the ego's "other side" and embodies for the most part those character traits one most dislikes in other people.

It would be relatively simple if the shadow could be made conscious by sincere efforts to gain insight into it and then incorporated into our lives. Often, however, attempts at insight are "useless," that is, there is such strong passion and such an intense sense of compulsion connected with the shadow that reason's efforts have no effect. Sometimes what may help is a bitter experience coming from the outside. In other words, a brick has to fall on our heads before we are able to "turn off" the shadow's constant pushing. Either that, or it takes a heroic resolve, which can come about with the help of "the great man."

But we should not take the view that the intense drivenness of the shadow is always to be heroically sacrificed. For it is sometimes the case that the reason the shadow has become too powerful is that behind it, the great man within us, the Self, is pushing in the same direction. In such a case we do not know whether it is the Self or the shadow that is producing the inner pressure. Unfortunately, the unconscious is like a landscape in moonlight: all its contents are vague and melt into each other, and we can never know for sure where anything begins and ends. This is called contamination (interfusion) of the contents of the unconscious.

When Jung called a certain aspect of the unconscious composition of the personality the shadow, he was referring to a part that was only relatively clearly defined; for often everything that the ego does not know about itself is mixed up with the shadow, even very valuable elements. For example, who could have said with categorical certainty that the Frenchman in the dream given above was a ne'er-do-well or a valuable bit of introversion? And the runaway horses of the previous dream—should they be allowed to run away or not? Whenever the dream itself is not clear on this point, it is the ego consciousness that must make the decision.

When the shadow contains elements that are valuable for life, they should be incorporated into life and not combated. Then the ego might perhaps have to give up a bit of its moral high ground and live through something that might seem dark and sinister to it, but is not so in fact. This can be just as heroic a sacrifice as the overcoming of the instincts. The moral problems that can arise in the encounter with the shadow are very well described in the eighteenth chapter of the Koran.[15] In this story, in the desert Moses meets Khidr, "the green one," "the first angel of God," and they travel on together. But Khidr warns Moses he will not be able to witness Khidr's deeds without indignation; and if he proves unable to do so, he must quit Khidr's company. And in-

THE INDIVIDUATION PROCESS

deed Khidr sinks the boat of some poor fishermen, kills a handsome youth without reason before Moses' eyes, and senselessly causes a city wall to fall down. Each time Moses becomes morally outraged, and Khidr has to leave him behind. However, in departing, Khidr explains to him the real state of affairs in each case: the fishermen's boat was saved by his deed from approaching pirates, because the fishermen would be able to salvage it after the pirates had passed; the youth was on his way to murder his parents, and in this way his soul was saved; and through the collapse of the city wall, the buried treasure of two pious young people was revealed. Now Moses understood too late that his moral judgment had been hasty.

Looking at him naively, Khidr seemed to the law-abiding, pious Moses like a lawless, evil, moody shadow. But he was not. He embodied the mysteriously creative ways of God. A similar problem is found in the famous Indian tale "The King and the Corpse," which has been interpreted by Heinrich Zimmer.[16] A mendicant monk, through his gifts, makes a noble king feel obligated to fetch him a corpse by night from an execution ground. In the corpse dwells a demon (Vetāla), who tells the king confusing stories and asks him questions and repeatedly spirits the corpse back to the tree where it had been hanging. Tirelessly, the king struggles against the demon, until in the end the demon reveals to him that the mendicant monk is an arrogant, power-hungry evildoer who intends to murder him and that he, the demon, has rescued him. The monk is a typical shadow of a pious person, that is, the hidden arrogance that develops in a person from doing good deeds; and the demon is only seemingly an antagonist and really is on the side of life. Later he even guides the king to an experience of God.

It is no accident that I have not chosen a dream to illustrate this subtle problem. We are dealing with problems here that often synthesize the experience of an entire lifetime, and these can be gotten at more clearly by using a mythical tale rather than one individual dream.

When dark figures appear in our dreams and demand something of us, we cannot at once be sure whether they are the embodiment of shadow parts of ourselves or of the Self or perhaps of both at the same time. Being able to tell whether this dark other represents a failing that we should overcome or a vital element that we should accept is one of the most difficult problems that we meet on the path of individuation. It feels like a divine act of grace when a dream provides a clear answer to this; but often the dream symbols themselves are so complicated that one gets tangled up trying to interpret them. In such situations there is no choice but to endure the torment of moral uncertainty, to the extent possible to avoid making any definitive decisions and faithfully observe our further dreams. This resembles the situation Cinderella found herself in when the evil stepmother tossed her a heap of good and bad peas and then, though it seemed hopeless, patiently began to sort them. Doves (and in other versions of the fairy tale, the ants) unexpectedly came to her aid. These latter symbolize helpful thoughts arising from a loving attitude and deep unconscious stirrings that can be felt almost only with the body, that are capable of showing the right way.

Somewhere in the deepest part of the psyche, we usually already know what direction things are going in, but very often the buffoon we call the ego sets up such a racket that the inner voice cannot be heard.

When despite all attempts to explore the inner indications we still cannot achieve insight, sometimes there is nothing left but, "in God's name," to come up with the courage to make a responsible decision—of course while still maintaining an inner readiness to change course if at last, after all, the unconscious provides signs that point in another direction. Of course situations do arise, though rarely, in which it is better to resist the will of the unconscious psyche absolutely and bear the negative consequences of this rather than deviate from the ethos of humanity. This is the case, for example, when a person would have to act out a criminal aspect of his makeup in order to realize himself completely. Sometimes it seems as though the Self wants the ego to make a free choice—or perhaps also the Self depends for its realization on human consciousness and its decisions.

Jung was able to show in his works that in the human psyche, often two "moral" powers are at work: the collective moral code (the Freudian superego) and an individual "ethical" voice of conscience that speaks to us directly. The latter comes from the Self, the Great Inner Man, and is often experienced as a divine bidding. For us, however, the great difficulty is to feel which of these two authorities is applicable in a given situation, since this is not always immediately clear, and our own wishes often cloud our vision. Thus we see that ethical conflict is a proper part of the process of individuation, one that cannot be dealt with successfully without our accepting the feeling side of us.

When such difficult moral problems arise, no one is in a position to judge others. We all have to solve our own problems and find out ourselves what is right for us. Thus an ancient Zen master said that we should do as the cowherd does, "who stands watch with his stick, so that his ox will not graze his neighbor's field."[17] It is clear for all to see that the insights of depth psychology relativize officially prevailing moral rules and compel us to make many subtle, individual judgments in *all* areas of law, education, and moral theology. The discovery of the unconscious is perhaps the most revolutionary thing that has happened in recent centuries, but it is so new and so radically different that great numbers of people prefer to behave as though nothing has happened. It takes inner uprightness and courage to enter into relationship with this newly discovered force and to take it seriously, thereby running the risk of a revaluation of existing values.

The Anima as the Woman within the Man

The "ultimate" questions referred to above do not always come up in the encounter with the shadow. Much more often behind him or her another inner figure emerges as a personification of the unconscious. This takes the form of a woman in a man, and in a woman, that of a man. Often it is they who are at work behind the shadow, throwing up new problems. C. G. Jung called them anima and animus. The anima embodies all feminine psychic qualities in a man—moods, feelings, intuitions, receptivity to the irrational, his personal capacity for love, his sense of nature, and most important of all, his *relationship to the unconscious*.[18]

It is no accident that in ancient times many peoples used priestesses (think, for example, of the Greek Sibyls) to enter into relationship with the will of the gods.

The way the anima initially manifests in an individual man usually bears the stamp of his mother's character. If he experienced her in a negative way, then his anima often takes the form of depressive moods, irritability, perpetual malcontent, and excessive sensitivity. If the man is able to overcome these, precisely these things can strengthen his manliness. Such a negative mother anima will endlessly whisper within a man: "I'm a nothing," "It doesn't make sense anyhow," "It's different for other people," "Nothing gives me any pleasure," and so on. Continual fear of disease, impotence, or accidents are her work, and she constellates a general sense of gloom. Troubled moods like these can intensify to the point of temptations to suicide; thus the anima can become a demoness of death. She appears in this role in Cocteau's film *Orpheus*.

The French call such an anima figure a *femme fatale*. The sirens of the Greeks and the Lorelei of the Germans embody these dangerous aspects of the anima—in a word, destructive illusions. The following Siberian tale gives a particularly apt portrayal of such a destructive anima:

A solitary hunter once had the experience of seeing a beautiful woman appear on the opposite bank of a river. She waved to him and sang, "Come, come. I've missed you, missed you. Now I want to put my arms around you, put my arms around you. Come, come, my nest is nearby, my nest. Come, come, lonely hunter, right now in the stillness of twilight." As he threw off his clothes and began swimming across to her, she suddenly flew away in the form of an owl, laughing mockingly. Swimming back, he drowned in the ice-cold river.

Here the anima symbolizes an unreal dream of love and happiness, of motherly love and security (the nest), an illusion that holds a man back from life. The hunter freezes to death because of his pursuit of an erotic fantasy.[19]

The man with a positive mother complex relates to life like a little boy going into a pastry shop with his mother. His approach is: "I'd like this one, give me one of those," and so on, all without any effort of his own. Life should give him everything like a warm loving mother, and when this does not occur, he cries out in pain or defiance. When this kind of neglect of the feeling aspect and the inner life takes place, feeling demands attention to itself, but on a relatively low level, which then certain women know how to exploit to their benefit.

When the neglected anima produces this sort of compulsive state, we call it anima possession. This brings about an ill-adjusted effeminization of the man, who then either takes on a feminine role and becomes a homosexual or else is drawn into relationships with hard, masculine women.

Another type of common negative-anima manifestation is characterized by "femininely" venomous remarks that sting like a wasp and always contain a bit of a lie. Because of this we find throughout the world mythological tales of so-called poisonous maidens, as this figure is called in the East, who contain poison or weapons in their bodies, with which they kill their lovers on their wedding nights.[20] In this form, the anima embodies an aspect of cold unscrupulousness in the man, which can lead him to sudden arbitrary actions. When a man falls under the spell of such an anima, he can irresponsibly abandon his family or do other cruel things in which the sense of inferiority of his eros becomes evident. In the Middle Ages, this was explained as the work of witches, and for this reason many myths and fairy tales deal with the theme of a man who must free himself from a witchlike "false bride" in order to find his "true bride," that is, his genuine capacity for love. In Heinrich von Kleist's *Käthchen von Heilbronn* (Katie of Heilbronn), this motif was also introduced into literature.

If, on the other hand, a man's first experience of his mother was positive, this influences the nature of his anima in another way. The anima can then make him effeminate, a prey to women, and make him incapable of dealing with the hardships of life. Such an anima often makes a man react sentimentally, like an old maid or the princess in the fairy tale who could feel a pea through thirty mattresses. A particularly refined form of this kind of anima figure appears in fairy tales as a princess who gives her suitors riddles to solve or orders them to hide from her. If they are unable to fulfill the task she sets them, they must die. This type of anima embroils a man in intellectual games.[21] One can observe the trick of this type of anima in all those neurotic, pseudo-intellectual conversations which keep a man from contact with reality. In such cases, he thinks so much about life that he himself is no longer able to live, since all his spontaneity and all genuine feeling have been lost.

This form of the anima is represented by the Greek sphinx, who poses a riddle to the hero Oedipus. When he answers it seemingly correctly, the sphinx pretends to commit suicide. This makes Oedipus think he has defeated her, and he walks straight into the very trap of mother-anima entanglement he wanted to avoid. This Greek saga still serves as a valid warning for us today, for it was in the Greece of those times that the development of the European scientific intellect began. The saga shows us that if we think we can solve the problem of the unconscious psyche and of eros with this kind of intellect alone, we are falling prey to a disastrous illusion.

The anima manifests with particular frequency as erotic fantasy, with the result that many men are compulsively driven to ogle women's beautiful curves or to dwell on them in films, magazines, or striptease shows, or else alone in daydreams. This primitively aesthetic and purely nature-related aspect of the anima usually only becomes compulsive when a man remains in-fantile in the domain of eros.[22]

All these aspects of the anima have the same tendency as the shadow—to project themselves on an external person, so that they appear to the man as the properties of a real woman. It is also this process of projection that causes a man suddenly to fall head over heels in love and to feel at the first meeting, "That's her!" as though he had always known this woman to the core. He then often becomes so helplessly enthralled with her that it seems to an outsider like pure madness. Especially women with a certain vague "elfish" quality attract such anima projections onto themselves, because as a consequence of their vagueness, men can impute all possible qualities to them.

Such sudden passionate attractions brought about by the anima upset many marriages and frequently create the well-known tri-angle situation with all its afflictions. A tolerable solution can be found in such situations only if the anima is recognized as an inner power. It even seems to correspond to a hidden intention of the unconscious to bring about such chaotic situations in order to ripen the personality of the man and to force him to integrate more of his inner unconscious personality.[23]

But enough of the negative side of the anima—after all, it has just as many positive aspects as negative ones. The anima makes a man able to find "the right woman," and beyond that, to distin-guish in the half-light of the unconscious, where his understand-ing does not fully penetrate, the contents that are of value to him from those that are not. But even of more practical importance for his life, *this attunement to the right contents opens up the way into his own depths*. It is as though an inner radio receiver were tuned to a particular wavelength on which he received none of the nonsense described above, but only the voice of the great man. With this, the anima attains the status of a guide to the inner world. She appears in this role, for example, in the initiation of shamans, as described by Mircea Eliade. This is the function of Beatrice in Dante's *Paradiso* and also that of Isis as she revealed herself in a dream to Apuleius, the author of *The Golden Ass*, in order to initiate him into a higher spiritual way of life.

The following dream of a forty-five-year-old psychotherapist may serve to illuminate this anima's role as inner guide. As this man was going to sleep the evening before having the dream, he was feeling sorry for himself for being so alone in life, without the support of an organization or a "church." He envied all those who were secure in the bosom of such an organization. Then he dreamed the following:

> I am in a large old, double-aisled church, crowded with people. With my wife and my mother, I am sitting at the back of the nave in makeshift seats.
>
> *I am to celebrate the mass as a priest,* and I have a thick missal in my hands—really more of a hymnal or an anthology of poetry. Since I am not familiar with the book, I have lost my place. This is very upsetting, because I am about to have to begin. On top of that, my mother and my wife are having a completely trivial conversation. Now the organ has already stopped, and everything is waiting for me. I resolutely stand up and ask a nun kneeling behind me kindly to give me her missal and show me where we are in the mass. She does this very willingly. *Now she precedes me to the altar like an acolyte,* which is *back and to the left,* as if we were approaching it from a side aisle. *The missal is now a kind of pictorial frieze,* like a thin, yard-long, foot-wide board, on which text and ancient pictures are arranged next to each other in columns. First it is the nun's turn to do a part of the liturgy before me, and I still haven't found my place. She did tell me, "Number 15," but the numbers are blurred and I can't find it. I resolutely turn to face the congregation. Although by now I have actually found panel number 15—it's the next-to-last on the board—I still do not know if I am going to be able to decipher and read the text. In any case, I was going to try, but then I woke up.

This dream represents a reaction to the thoughts of the evening before and says to the dreamer in symbolic form: "You yourself have to be the priest in your own inner 'church,' in the church of your psyche. The many people present—all component parts of his psyche—demand that he act as a priest and celebrate the mass, but here the actual mass cannot be what is meant, for the missal is very different from a real one. The image of the mass is rather to be understood as a symbol, a symbol for a holy service in which the divine principle is present so that human beings can communicate with it.

This type of solution is naturally not generally valid but, rather, is an answer on the part of the unconscious to this individual dreamer. It is a typical answer to the religious problem of a Protestant, for a believing member of the Catholic Church experiences his anima in the image of the Church itself and its symbolic images, which for him contain the images of the unconscious.

Our dreamer lacked these ecclesiastical symbols and therefore had to travel a purely inner path. The dream provided further hints for him; it told him, "Your mother bond and your extravertedness (represented by his extraverted wife) are distracting you and keeping you through their meaningless gossip from celebrating the inner mass of your psyche. You should follow the nun, who is the introverted anima; as the servant of the mass and a priestess, she can guide you. She has a strange missal made up of sixteen (four times four) ancient pictures. Your mass consists in the contemplation of the psychic images that the religious anima will show you."

If the dreamer could overcome his uncertainty, produced by his mother complex, he would find his life's task in religious service to the inner images of his psyche.

In this dream the anima functions as a mediator between the ego and the Self. The number of four times four pictures indicates that the inner mass is a service to wholeness. As Jung has shown, the inner core of the psyche (the Self) is usually symbolized by fourfold structures.

Nonetheless, the number four is also bound up with the anima, because, as Jung showed, there are four stages of realization of the anima.[24] The first stage has its clearest mytholical symbol in the figure of Eve, who is an image of purely biological relationship. The second stage is illustrated, for instance, by *Faust*'s Helena. She symbolizes a romantic and aesthetic form of eros, mixed with sexual elements. The third stage is exemplified by the Virgin Mary, a symbol of spiritualized eros. The fourth stage frequently appears in the form of love personified as Sapientia (Wisdom), since Wisdom, as a lesser partner of the supreme principle, reaches even further than love. Another image for this last stage is the Shulamite in the Song of Songs. She embodies a stage of development only seldom reached by modern humanity. The Mona Lisa comes the closest to her.

But what is the practical significance of the anima role of guide to the inner world? Her positive function develops at the point at which a man takes his feelings, moods, and unconscious expectations seriously and captures them in some sort of a form, for example, by writing them down, by painting, sculpting, or expressing them in music or dance. If he then ponders them with patience, more and more contents will rise out of the depths. This pondering must, however, be both intellectual and moral, that is, it must take place in the presence of feeling, and the fantasies must be related to as completely real, without sly secret thoughts to the effect that "after all, this is only a fantasy I'm dealing with." If one practices this sort of devotion toward the unconscious over a long period of time, the process of individuation becomes the only reality altogether, and it then unfolds in all its aspects.

The role of the anima as guide to the inner world is also depicted in many literary works: in Francesco Colonna's *Hypnerotomachia*,[25] Rider Haggard's *She*, in the "eternal feminine" in Goethe's *Faust*. A medieval text has this figure saying of herself:

> I am the flower of the field and the lily of the valley; I am the mother of fair love, of knowledge and of sacred hope. . . . I am very beautiful and without taint. . . . I am the mediator among the elements, who reconciles one with the others; what is warm, I cool; what is dry, I make moist; what is hard, I soften—and the

reverse. . . . I am the law in the priest and the word in the prophet and the counsel in the sage. I can kill and bring to life, and there is no one who can deliver (anything) out of my hand."[26]

At the time this text was composed, religion, poetry, and psychic culture were going through a major upswing, and the world of fantasy was receiving more recognition than hitherto. This was the time of chivalry and courtly love, in which the man of the time attempted to develop his feminine aspect both in relation to a real woman and in his inner world.

The lady to whom the knight consecrated his service was a personification of the anima for him. The female bearer of the Holy Grail in Wolfram von Eschenbach's Grail epic has a highly significant name: Conduiramour, which means "she who guides in matters of love." It was she who taught the hero how to differentiate his feeling and his behavior in a relationship with a woman.[27]

Later, however, this individual effort on the part of men to develop a relationship with the anima was abandoned, and instead the spiritual aspect of this figure was identified with the Virgin Mary. But since only the anima's positive side was embodied in Mary, her negative aspects fell forfeit to the belief in witchcraft, which began to flourish at that time.

In China, the figure parallel to the Virgin Mary is Kwan Yin or a figure of the folk culture known as the moon fairy, who confers on her favorites the gift of music and immortality. In India, the same archetype is represented by Shakti, Parvati, Rati, and many other goddesses. Among the Muslims, she is mainly represented by Fatima, the daughter of Muhammad. When the anima is venerated in this way as an official religious figure, there is the disadvantage that she loses her individual aspects. On the other hand, when she is experienced only on a personal level, there is the danger that she will remain entirely projected onto external love relationships.

On this level, only the painful but ultimately simple resolve to take one's own fantasies and emotional moods seriously can prevent stagnation in a man's inner development. For only in this way can he discover what this image of a woman means as an inner reality. Then the anima becomes once again what she was originally: the inner woman who conveys the vitally important messages of the Self to the ego.

The Animus, a Woman's Inner Man

The embodiment of the unconscious of a woman as a figure of the opposite sex, the animus, also has positive and negative features. The animus, however, does not express itself so often in women as an erotic fantasy or mood, but rather as "sacred" convictions.[28] When these latter are expressed loudly and energetically in a masculine style, this masculine side of a woman is easily recognizable. However, it can also manifest in a woman who appears very feminine externally as a quiet but relentless power that is hard as iron. Suddenly one comes up against something in her that is cold, stubborn, and completely inaccessible.

The favorite themes that the animus of the woman dredges up within her sound like this: "I am seeking nothing but love, but 'he' doesn't love me." Or, "There are only two possibilities in this situation," both of which of course are unpleasant (the negative animus never believes in exceptions). One can seldom contradict the animus, for it (he) is always right; the only problem is that his opinion is not based on the actual situation. For the most part he gives utterance to seemingly reasonable views, which, however, are slightly at a tangent to what is under discussion.

Just as the mother influence is formative with a man's anima, the father has a determining influence on the animus of a daughter. The father imbues his daughter's mind with the specific coloring conferred by those indisputable views mentioned above, which in reality are so often missing in the daughter. For this reason the animus is also sometimes represented as a demon of death. A gypsy tale, for example, tells of a woman living alone who takes in an unknown handsome wanderer and lives with him in spite of the fact that a fearful dream has warned her that he is the king of the dead. Again and again she presses him to say who he is. At first he refuses to tell her, because he knows that she will then die, but she persists in her demand. Then suddenly he tells her he is death. The young woman is so frightened that she dies. Looked at from the point of view of mythology, the unknown wanderer here is clearly a pagan father and god figure, who manifests as the leader of the dead (like Hades, who carried off Persephone). He embodies a form of the animus that lures a woman away from all human relationships and especially holds her back from love with a real man.[29] A dreamy web of thoughts, remote from life and full of wishes and judgments about how things "ought to be," prevents all contact with life.

The animus appears in many myths, not only as death, but also as a bandit and murderer, for example, as the knight Bluebeard, who murdered all his wives. The animus then embodies those half-conscious, cold, unscrupulous thoughts that many women permit themselves in the "quiet hours," especially when they are neglecting matters that are obligations from the feeling point of view—thoughts about the division of the family inheritance, manipulative plans in which they go so far as to wish other people's death. "If one of us dies, I'm moving to the Riviera," a wife, for example, says to her husband as they take in the beautiful Mediterranean landscape.

Through her destructive secret judgments even a mother can, in hidden ways, drive her children to the point of illness or death or hinder their marriage, all without this hidden evil ever coming to the surface of her consciousness. A naive old woman once showed me the deathbed photograph of her drowned son and said, "It's better this way than that I should have lost him to another woman!"

Also a strange paralysis of feeling together with a profound lack of self-confidence is frequently the effect on a woman's own inner world of an unacknowledged animus judgment. In such situations, the animus whispers to the woman in the depths:

"You're a hopeless case; why try? It's all to no avail anyhow. Your life cannot, and never will, be any different."

When these figures of the unconscious penetrate our consciousness, unhappily we think we ourselves are having these thoughts or feelings, and the ego is often so identified with them that it is unable to deal with them objectively. We become truly "possessed" by these figures, and only later, after such a state of mind has fallen away, do we discover to our horror that we have said or done things that in reality we did not feel or want at all.

Like the anima, the animus, too, consists not only of negative properties. It too has an extraordinarily positive and valuable side, in which it, like the anima, can form a bridge to the experience of the Self and perform a creative function. The following dream of a forty-five-year-old woman shows this clearly:

> Over the balcony into the room climb two figures shrouded in gray hooded cloaks. Their intention is to torture my sister and myself. My sister hides under the bed, but they get her out with a broom and torment her. Then it's my turn. The leader of the two shoves me against the wall. But suddenly the other one lays out and draws a picture on the wall. Then I say as I see it, "Oh, but how well drawn that is!" Then the two of them let me pacify them, and they become quite friendly.

The tormenting aspect of the two figures was well known to the dreamer, for she repeatedly suffered from serious panic attacks in which she could not help imagining that people she loved were in danger of death or had died. The duality of the figures, however, shows that these intruders represent something that has two possible ways of working, that these animus figures might bring about something besides tormenting thoughts. The dreamer's sister, who tried to escape from them, is tortured—in reality she died relatively early from cancer. She was artistically talented but did not try to make anything of her gift. In the dream, it is now revealed that the intruders are artists in disguise; and when, as a result of their actions, the dreamer acknowledges her own talent, they drop their intention of torturing her. This shows the meaning of the dream. Behind the panic attacks are, on one hand, a serious danger of death, but on the other, a creative potentiality. The dreamer was extraordinarily gifted at drawing and painting but always doubted the meaningfulness of this activity. The dream lets her know in no uncertain terms that this gift should and must be developed. If she did that, the destructive animus could turn into a creative force.[30]

The animus frequently appears, as it does in this dream, as a group of men, or as some other collective image. Thus also the pronouncements of the animus-possessed woman usually begin with "one should" or "everyone knows" or "it is always the case . . . ," etc.

Many myths and fairy tales tell of a prince, who has been turned into an animal or a monster by sorcery, being saved by a woman. This is a symbolic representation of the development of the animus toward consciousness. Often the heroine may ask no questions of her mysterious lover, or she is only allowed to meet him in darkness. She is to save him through her blind faith and love, but this never works. She always breaks her promise and is only able to find her beloved again after a long quest.

As the anima does with men, the animus also creates states of possession in women. In myths and fairy tales this condition is often represented by the devil or an "old man of the mountain," that is, a troll or ogre, holding the heroine prisoner and forcing her to kill all men who approach her or to deliver them into the hands of the demon; or else the father shuts up the heroine in a tower or a grave or sets her on a glass mountain, so that no one can get near her. In such cases, the heroine can often do nothing but wait patiently for a savior to deliver her from her plight. Through her suffering, the animus (for both the demon and the savior are two aspects of the same inner power) can be gradually transformed into a positive inner force.

In real life, too, it takes a long time for a woman to bring the animus into consciousness, and it costs her a great deal of suffering. But if she succeeds in freeing herself from his possession, he changes into an "inner companion" of the highest value, who confers on her positive masculine qualities such as initiative, courage, objectivity, and intellectual clarity. Like the anima in a man, the animus also commonly exhibits four stages of development.

In the first stage he manifests as a symbol of physical force, for example, a sports hero. In the next stage, in addition he possesses initiative and focused ability to act. In the third stage, he becomes "the word" and is therefore frequently projected onto noteworthy intellectuals, like doctors, ministers, and professors. On the fourth level, he embodies the mind and becomes a mediator of creative and religious inner experiences, through which life acquires an individual meaning. At this stage he confers on a woman a spiritual and intellectual solidity that counterbalances her essentially soft nature. He can then act as a liaison connecting her with the spiritual life of the time. When this occurs, women are often more open to new, creative ideas than men. That is why in the past women were often used as mediums able to make knowledge of the future available to the world of the spirit. The creative courage in the truth conferred by the animus gives a woman the daring to enunciate new ideas that can inspire men to new enterprises. Often in history women have recognized the value of new creative ideas earlier than men, who are more emotionally conservative. The nature of woman is more closely related to the irrational, and this makes a woman better able to open to new inspirations from the unconscious. The very fact that women normally participate less in public life than men do makes it possible for their animus to act as a "hidden prince" in the darkness of private life and bring about beneficial results.

The "inner man" in the psyche of a woman, when projected, can lead to difficulties similar to those the anima creates. And then the situation is complicated even further by the fact that animus and anima act as mutual irritants—with the result that every confrontation between them degenerates onto a lower emotional level, as is shown by the stereotyped imagery of love quarrels.

As mentioned, the woman's animus can lead to courage, a

spirit of enterprise, truthfulness, and in its highest form, to spiritual depth and intensity; but this only happens if beforehand she musters the objectivity to call her own "sacred" convictions into question and to accept the guiding messages of her dreams, even when they contradict her convictions. Then the Self as an inner psychic experience of the divine can get through to her and confer meaning on her life.

The Self

When a person has inwardly struggled with his anima or with her animus for a sufficiently long time and has reached the point where he or she is no longer identified with it in an unconscious fashion, the unconscious once again takes on a new symbolic form in relating with the ego. It then appears in the form of the psychic core, that is, the Self. In the dreams of a woman, the Self, when it personifies itself, manifests as a superior female figure, for example, as a priestess, a sorceress, an earth mother, or a nature or love goddess. In the dreams of a man, it takes the form of someone who confers initiations (an Indian guru), a wise old man, a nature spirit, a hero, and so forth. An Austrian fairy tale recounts the following:

> A king posts a soldier to keep watch on the coffin of a cursed black princess who has been bewitched. It is known that every night she comes to life and tears the guard to pieces. In despair, not wanting to die, the soldier runs away into the forest. There he meets an "old zither player who was, however, the Lord God himself," and this old musician advises him how to hide in different places in the church and what to do so that the black princess cannot find him. With the help of this miraculous old man, the soldier succeeds in evading the princess's attack and in this way is able to redeem her. He marries her and becomes the king.[31]

The old zither player who is really God himself, expressed in psychological language, is a symbol of the Self. He helps the soldier, that is, the ego, to overcome the destructive anima figure and even to redeem it.

In a woman, as we have said, the Self takes on a feminine form. The following Eskimo tale may serve as an example:[32]

A solitary maiden, who has been disappointed in matters of love, is carried off to heaven by a sorcerer who travels about in a copper boat. He is actually the spirit of the moon, to whom men are accustomed to pray for success in the hunt. Once, when the moon spirit has gone out, the maiden visits a little house that stands next to that of the moon sorcerer, and in it she finds a "little woman," who wears bizarre clothing made of "the sewed-together guts of the bearded seal." This little woman, who also still has a little daughter living with her, warns the heroine of the story about the moon spirit, saying that his real intention is to kill her. She says he is a wife murderer, a kind of Bluebeard. In order to save her, the little woman weaves a long rope, on which the maiden will be able to climb back down from heaven to earth. This she does on the new moon when the little woman is able to make the moon spirit unconscious. The maiden lets herself down on the rope, but when she reaches the earth, she does not reopen her eyes fast enough, although the little woman has explicitly told her to. As a result she is turned into a spider and can never become a human being again.

The "old zither player who is the Lord God" in the first tale is a typical manifestation of the Self as the "wise old man" as he appears in the psyche of a man. The sorcerer Merlin appears in similar fashion in ancient stories, as does the god Hermes among the Greeks. The "little woman" with the gut-skin clothes in the above story is something similar, a figure of the Self in a woman. The old musician saved the hero from his destructive anima, and the little woman here saves the heroine from an Eskimo Blue-beard animus in the form of the spirit of the moon. However, afterward, through the fault of the maiden, things still manage to go wrong. We will discuss this later.

A Self figure may appear in dreams not only as a wise old man or a wise woman, but just as frequently as a young, even childlike figure, for the Self is something relatively timeless that is at once young and old.[33]

The following dream of a man provides an example of the Self as a youthful figure:

> From across the road, a boy came riding down into our garden. (There were no fence and bushes there as in reality. The boundary lay open.) I couldn't be sure whether he came on purpose or whether the horse brought him here against his will. Standing on the path to the studio, I watched his arrival with great pleasure and feasted my eyes on the sight of the boy on his beautiful beast. It was a very small but extremely powerful wild horse, the very soul of energy (it resembled a boar). It had a thick, silver gray, long-haired, bristly coat. The boy rode by me past the space between the house and the studio, and then dismounted to lead his animal carefully past the new flower border to keep it from treading on any of the red and yellow tulips that bloomed there in glorious profusion. In my dream this bed had just been newly put in by my wife.

This youth stands for the Self and the potentiality for a renewal of life, for the creative élan and fresh mental orientation that his appearance produces, in which everything is once more full of life and a spirit of enterprise. Turning to the unconscious can in fact really give this to a person. Suddenly a life that up to that point seemed boring and unfree becomes a rich adventure that never seems to want to end, rich with potential for new directions.

For a woman, this same figure often takes the form of a miraculous girl. An example is the following dream of a forty-eight-year-old woman:

> I was standing in front of a church and cleaning the pavement with a broom. Then I suddenly had to cross a river, across which a heavy plank had been laid. A student was there, and I wanted him to help me. But then I saw that all he wanted was to make

things hard for me by making the plank sway. Then suddenly on the other bank there was a little girl who reached out her hand to me. I thought she would never have the strength to support me, but when I took hold of her hand, she smilingly pulled me to the other bank, effortlessly, with supernatural force.

This dreamer was a religiously inclined person. In the dream, however, she is obviously no longer able to remain in the Protestant church. She has lost access to it, but she is still making an effort to keep the way to the church clean. However, it seems she now has to cross a river instead. This is a common symbol for a fundamental change of attitude. The motif of the student was associated by the dreamer herself with the fact that the evening before she had been thinking that perhaps she could satisfy her inner spiritual search through some course of study—something that the dream clearly advised against. She dares to try to cross the river by herself, and a Self figure, the little girl, comes miraculously to her aid. She is little, but supernaturally strong.

However, this mode of appearance as a human being, old or young, is only one among many possible ways in which the Self might manifest in dreams and visions. The different ages show not only that the Self is present in all situations of life, but also that it extends into a realm beyond that grasped by our conscious sense of time.

In fact the Self is not fully contained within our conscious domain and its temporality. It has a quality of timelessness and ubiquity. Thus it is often symbolized by a "great man," who encompasses the entire cosmos. When such a symbol crops up in the dream of an individual, usually one may hope for a creative solution of his conflicts, for at that point his psychic core has been activated and a unity of his inner being has been achieved, which is capable of overcoming even major difficulties.

It is no wonder then that the figure of a cosmic person appears in many myths and religions and for the most part plays a very positive role. Such a figure appears in our culture, for example, in Adam; in Persia, as Gayomart; or in India, as Purusha. It is often described as the fundamental principle of the universe. The Chinese, for example, believed that, at the first, before the world existed, a divine man, P'an Ku, existed who gave form to heaven and earth. When he cried, the Yellow River and the Yangtse Kiang originated. When he breathed, the wind blew. When he spoke, the thunder rolled. When he cast his gaze about, lightning occurred. If he was in a good mood, the weather was good; when he was out of sorts, it was cloudy. When he died, he fell into pieces, and from his body, the five sacred mountains of China arose: his head became Mount T'ai in the east; his trunk became Mount Sung in the center; his right arm became Heng Mountain in the north; and his left arm became Heng Mountain in the south; and both his feet formed Hua Mountain in the west. His eyes became the sun and the moon.[34]

As we already saw earlier, the symbolic images related to the individuation process show a tendency to appear in fourfold structures—for example, as the four functions of consciousness or as the four stages of anima or animus development. Thus this quaternity also appears here in connection with P'an Ku. Only under special circumstances does a symbol of the Self manifest in other numeric structures. It manifests naturally as four or further multiples of four: 8, 12, 16, 32, and so on. The motif of sixteen—four times four—is particularly important.

In our Western civilization similar ideas about the "cosmic man" have developed surrounding the figure of Adam as the primordial man. A Jewish legend, for example, relates that God, in order to create Adam, gathered red, black, white, and yellow dust from the four corners of the world and that, as a result, Adam reached from one end of the world to the other. When he bent over, his head touched the east and his feet the west. According to another Jewish legend, the souls of the whole human race were contained in Adam from the beginning. His soul was "like the wick of a lamp, wound with countless threads." This image clearly contains the notion of a unity of all human existence beyond all of the individual components. In this image, the "social" aspect of the Self, which we will speak of later, is also hinted at.

The cosmic nature of this "great man" seems to provide a further indication that the inner core of the human soul, that is, the Self, extends far beyond the dimensions of the individual ego, and in truth, we find in observing the unconscious and its manifestations that it possesses dimensions that are impossible to delimit.

In ancient Persia, the corresponding primordial man, Gayomart, is described as a gigantic shining figure. When he died, the metals flowed from his body, and from his soul gold originated. His seed fell to earth and produced the first human couple in the form of two rhubarb plants. Curiously enough, the Chinese P'an Ku is also depicted covered with leaves like a plant. He is a unity that arises as a living growth, that simply exists, without any animal-like movement, that is, without any manifestation of self-will. Among a group of Mandaeans still living today on the banks of the Tigris, Adam is worshiped as the secret "oversoul" or protecting spirit of the whole of humanity. According to their legend, too, he sprouted from a date palm (the plant motif again!).

We have seen that the process of individuation is symbolized by the unconscious as a tree, and here we also see a hint of the cosmic man appearing as a plant. The plant represents a lawful process of growth in accordance with a fixed pattern, as well as something that develops directly out of inorganic matter. In a similar fashion, the Self also appears as something that grows objectively in the human psyche, beyond all impulses and instincts, as the psychic element in us that stands for continuity and pure being. The plant always has a part of itself hidden in the earth, and the image of the plant in the human psyche points to the fact that we too have a part of us that participates in life as a whole that remains hidden from us.

In many Gnostic circles and in the East, the great man was already recognized as an inner psychic image rather than described as a concrete reality. According to the Hindu view, the Purusha, for example, was something dwelling in every human individual, the only part of him that is immortal. This inner great man is also capable of redeeming the individual by guiding him out of creation and its suffering back to the eternal origin; yet he can only do that if the individual recognizes him and is inwardly alert for his guidance. In the symbolic world of the Indians, this figure is called Purusha, which means "person." He exists externally in the cosmos and also at the same time as something inner and invisible in each individual human being.[35]

According to many myths, this cosmic man is not only the beginning but also the ultimate goal of the world and its life.[36] The inner nature of all grain means wheat; and of all metal, gold; and of all birth, man," the medieval sage Meister Eckhart says in this sense.[37] Seen from a psychological point of view, this is actually the case. The inner psychic reality in every person ultimately contains a hidden goal—to realize the Self. Practically, this means that we will never be able to explain the existence of the individual human being purely in terms of utilitarian mechanisms such as survival, perpetuation of the species, sexuality, hunger, the death urge, and so on; rather, beyond all those, it serves the self-representation of the essence of humanness, which can be expressed only through a symbol, to wit, the image of the cosmic man.[38]

In the West the cosmic man is to a great extent identified with Christ and in the East with Krishna and Buddha. In the Old Testament, this same figure appears as the "son of man," and in later Jewish mysticism as Adam Kadmon.[39] Certain religious movements of antiquity simply called him Anthropos (the Greek word for man). All these symbolic figures point to the same mystery: the unknown meaning of human existence.

Certain traditions assert that this great man is the goal of creation; yet this is definitely not to be understood in an external sense, but rather as an inner goal. Hinduism, for example, assures us that though the real universe will not dissolve into the primordial man, at some point our perception of this material reality will indeed pass away, giving place to this "person."

As the rivers that flow into the sea, when they reach it, are absorbed into it and their own names and forms pass away so that one speaks then only of the sea, so the components of the watcher (the ego), when they come to the Purusha, are absorbed by him, and their name and form disappear. And then men speak only of the Purusha, and he (the Purusha) becomes indivisible and immortal.

The ego's orientation toward the external world and its ideas, which rush from theme to theme, and its desires, which seek object after object, disappear into the realization of the "great man."

These examples, taken from different civilizations and times, show how widespread the symbol of the cosmic man is as an image of the mystery of the wholeness of the human being. Because the symbol refers to something complete and whole, the great man is often represented as hermaphroditic. In this form he unites in himself the most important psychic opposites, male and female. This unity is often also symbolized as a divine royal, or otherwise distinguished, couple.[40] The following dream of a forty-seven-year-old man shows this aspect of the Self with particular clarity:

I am standing in an elevated place and see below me a magnificent, black female bear with a shaggy but groomed coat. She is standing on her hind legs, and on a slab she is polishing a flat, oval black stone, which is becoming increasingly shiny. Not far away, a lioness and a small lion are doing the same thing, except that the stone they are polishing is somewhat bigger and rounder. After a while, the female bear turns into a white naked woman of corpulent build, with long dark hair and dark, fiery eyes. I behave toward her in an erotically arousing way, whereupon she comes at me trying to catch me; but then I get frightened and escape back onto the building (or scaffold) where I was standing before. Later I find myself in the midst of many women, of which about half are primitive women with luxuriant black hair, and the other half are our (the dreamer's nation) women, with blond or chestnut brown hair. The primitive women (more young girls) sing a song in a very sentimental and melancholy fashion with high soprano voices. Then, atop a high coach, magnificently clothed, there appears a young blond man who wears on his head a royal crown of gold adorned with shining rubies. Next to him sits a young blond woman, who must be his wife but has no crown. It seems as though this couple arose through a transformation of the lioness and the small lion; they belong to the primitive group. Now all the women (the primitive ones and others) intone a solemn song, and the royal coach slowly moves off into the distance.

Here the Self, the dreamer's psychic core, first appears as a passing vision of a royal couple, which arises out of the depths of animal nature and of the primitive psychic level of the unconscious and then disappears again. The female bear represents the animal aspect of the mother goddess (Artemis, for example, was worshiped by the Greeks as a female bear). And the dark, egg-shaped stone she is rubbing symbolizes the true personality of the dreamer.[41] Polishing and rubbing stones is a well-known, quite primeval human activity. In Europe, "sacred" stones, wrapped in bark, have been found in caves in many places. These were obviously preserved by Stone Age people as containers of divine power. In Australia, there are still aborigines who believe that their dead ancestors dwell as benevolent divine powers in stones. By rubbing these stones, one imbues them—and oneself—with fresh force, as though one were charging them electrically.

The dreamer had not been inclined, up to this point in his life, to accept the earth-related feminine principle. He did not want to be tied down by marriage. He was afraid of being caught by this aspect of life, and in the dream, too, he escapes into a role of passive observation. The she-bear's rubbing of the stone was to show him that he should become involved in this aspect of life, because the very "friction" (marriage!) that arises in this manner would polish his own being.

When the stone becomes shiny, it becomes *like a mirror*, in which the bear-woman can see herself. Only by taking on earthly suffering can the human psyche be properly polished into a mirror of divine power. The dreamer, however, takes flight upward, that is, into all kinds of reflections, through which he may seek to evade the task of life. But the dream shows him that if he does this, his psyche, his anima, will remain undifferentiated. This is represented by the many impersonal women, who moreover remain split between a primitive faction and a higher-status one.

The lioness and her son, who now appear, embody the mystery of individuation, for they are trying to shape *round stones* (!), which are an image of the Self, and in fact they too are a royal couple and as such an image of inner wholeness. In medieval symbolism, for instance, the philosopher's stone—a well-known symbol of inner wholeness—is often represented by a pair of lions or a human couple riding on lions. The inner urge toward individuation often first comes into play concealed behind the passion of love for another person. The aspect of this that goes beyond the natural attachment to the opposite sex is ultimately directed toward the mystery or one's own realization of wholeness. For this reason, when one has fallen passionately in love, one also feels that becoming one with the beloved is the only worthy goal in life.

So long as the inner wholeness appears as a pair of lions, this means that the Self remains hidden in an overpowering passion.[42] Only when the lions have become a king and his queen has the urge toward individuation reached the stage of human consciousness, and then it appears as the dreamer's distant goal in life.

Before the lions had been transformed, the primitive women alone sang in a sentimental fashion; that is, the dreamer's feeling is still primitive and at the same time, sentimental. By contrast, in honor of the lions who have become human, the civilized and the primitive women join together in a song of praise. In an expression of acknowledgment on the feeling level, all the women together sing *one* song; that is, the inner split has been transformed into harmony.

Still another form in which the Self manifests is illustrated by the following so-called active imagination of a woman, which I will recount. By "active imagination" is meant a particular kind of meditation on fantasies, in which one relates to the unconscious as to a real partner.[43] This form of meditation can in many regards be compared to certain Eastern meditation techniques, such as those of Zen Buddhism or tantra yoga, or to the Western technique of the Jesuit *exercitia*, but with the fundamental difference that the meditator has no conscious goal or program whatever. In this way active imagination remains the solitary experiment of a free individual with himself or herself, devoid of any tendency to steer the unconscious. But we cannot go into this subject further here. I must refer the reader to Jung's essay "The Transcendent Function."

In this woman's meditation, a deer appeared, which spoke to her and said, "I am your child and your mother at once and am called the 'bond animal,' because I establish a bond between people, animals, plants, and stones, when I enter into them. I am your fate or the 'objective I,'" it continued. "My appearance redeems you from the meaningless arbitrariness of life. I establish a bond between the mind and the body and between life and death. The fire that burns within me burns in all of nature. When a human being loses this, he becomes lonely, egotistical, directionless, and without strength."

The Self is often symbolized as an animal, which represents our instinctive nature and its connection with our natural surroundings. (That is why there are so many helpful animals in myths and fairy tales.) This relationship of symbols of the Self with the natural surroundings and even with the universe shows that this "atomic nucleus of the psyche" is somehow interwoven with the whole inner and outer world. All the higher organisms known to us are attuned to a specific environment in time and space. Animals, for example, have their territories, their building materials, their food types, to which their instincts are precisely attuned. One need only consider the fact that most grazing animals give birth to their young exactly at the time when grass is most abundant. A highly reputed zoologist therefore said that the inner nature of animals stretches far out into the world and imbues space and time with psyche.[44] The human unconscious, too, is attuned at an ungraspably profound level to its environment, its social group, and, beyond that, to space and time and the whole of nature. The "great man" referred to above as the psychic center of the Naskapi Indians not only reveals inner processes in dreams but also provides advice to the hunter, such as how and where he should hunt. The Naskapi also derive from dream motifs the magical songs that they use to attract game animals.

However, this seems to apply not only to people still living in nature, but as Jung discovered, to civilized people as well. Dreams also provide us with a total orientation to our inner and outer worlds.

Indeed, observation of our dreams often has the effect of making the outer world symbolically meaningful to us. The result is that we begin to live in a small "cosmos," because the little things in the world around us begin to acquire importance for us in a context of inner meaning. A tree in front of the window, a car, or a stone picked up while out on a walk, can attain symbolic meaning through our dreams. When we pay attention to our dreams, the cold, impersonal world around us loses its meaningless arbitrariness and becomes a realm full of individual, significant, mysteriously ordered events.

Nevertheless, our dreams are less concerned with external adaptation than those of primitives. They revolve for the most part around the "right" attitude of the ego to the Self, since this relationship, as a consequence of our modern way of thinking, is much more disturbed than with primitives. Primitives still live from their inner center, whereas we are often so entangled in outer matters that the messages of the Self do not get through to us. We live in the illusion of a clearly structured outer world, and this obscures our inner perceptions. Yet, precisely through our unconscious, we are still strangely bound up with our psychic and material environment.

As already mentioned, the image of a stone, jewel, or crystal appears with special frequency as a representation of the Self. We already saw this in the dream in which lions were polishing a round stone. In many dreams also, the stone is shaped like a crystal, for the mathematically precise conformation of the crystal evokes perhaps most strongly the feeling that a principle of order dwells as a living spirit even in "dead" matter. Thus the crystal is a symbol of the union of the most extreme opposites.

Perhaps the stone is also especially suitable as a symbol of the Self, because its nature is most completely expressed by its pure "suchness," its pure being-as-it-is. How many people are unable to resist bringing home and keeping unusual stones without having any idea why they do it? It is as though these stones contain some vital mystery for them. People seem to have done this from the earliest times, seeing in certains stones their own life force and mystery. The ancient Germans, for example, believed that the souls of the dead lived on in their gravestones, and our custom of putting up stones at graves derives in part from the symbolic idea that something eternal remains of the deceased that is best symbolized by a stone.[45]

Although human nature in one way differs perhaps more from a stone than from anything else, the reverse is also true: the unconscious core of a human being is perhaps most closely akin to the stone. The stone symbolizes a form of consciousness that is just pure being, beyond emotions, fantasies, feelings, and the current of thoughts that characterizes ego consciousness. It is a unity that merely exists, that was and is always there, unchanging. In this sense the stone symbolizes perhaps the simplest and at the same time most profound experience of the eternal and immutable that a person can have. We can observe a tendency in nearly every civilization to erect stone monuments to the memory of famous men and events. The stone that Jacob erected on the spot where he had his famous dream, like the stones people set up at the graves of local saints and heroes, shows this tendency in people to use a stone to symbolize an "eternal" experience. No wonder that in many religions the God image or at least the place where God is worshiped on earth is indicated by a stone. The most sacred of things for Muslims is the black stone in Mecca, the Kaaba, to which every man is to make a pilgrimage at least once in his life.

In the symbolism of the Church, Christ is "the stone which the builders rejected" (Luke 20:17), or the "spiritual Rock that followed them" (1 Corinthians 10:4). The medieval alchemists, who in a prescientific manner were seeking the "secret of matter," hoping to find in it God or God's actions, saw this secret embodied in the so-called philosopher's stone. They already sensed, however, that this stone they sought was a symbol for something that in reality is only to be found within the human psyche. An Arabic alchemist, Morienus, gives the following description: "This thing [the philosopher's stone] is extracted from you; you are its mineral, and you can find it in yourself, or to put it more clearly, they [the alchemists] take it out of you. If you recognize this, the love and veneration you have for the stone will grow within you. Know that this is the indubitable truth."[46] The alchemical stone, the *lapis*, symbolizes something in us that can never be lost and can never dissolve, something eternal, which for this reason is equated by many with the experience of "God within us."

It usually takes periods of great suffering to clean away all the inessential psychic elements covering the inner stone;[47] but there is no human life in which an experience of the Self does not break through at least once. A religious attitude toward life would be one in which one sought to recover this unique experience and gradually to get a firm hold on it (after all, the stone is precisely a thing that lasts) in such a way that it gradually becomes something to which one can relate continually.

The fact that the highest and most frequent symbol of the Self is a thing made of inorganic matter, however, points to a further problem that awaits exploration—the still unclarified relationship of the unconscious psyche to matter. This is an issue with which psychosomatic medicine in particular is struggling.[48] It may, however, well be that what we call psyche and matter represent the same unknown reality seen from the inside and the outside. Jung introduced a new concept into this problematical area, which he called synchronicity. This refers to a "significant temporal coincidence" of an inner with an outer occurrence where the two are not causally dependent on one another. The emphasis is on the word "meaningful," for obviously there are lots of meaningless coincidences. If an airplane crashes in front of me just as I'm wiping my nose, that is a coincidence without the slightest meaning, but if I order a blue dress in a shop and they send me a black one by mistake just on the day that one of my close relatives dies, that strikes me as a meaningful coincidence. The two occurrences are not causally related; they are connected only by the meaning that the color black has in our society.

Whenever Jung observed such meaningful coincidences in the life of a person, he also saw by his or her dreams that at that very time an archetype was activated in the unconscious. In the example above, it was the theme of death that expressed itself simultaneously in the two events. The common denominator is a symbol, a message of death.

When we begin to note that certain type of events seem to "like" to cluster together at certain times, then we begin to understand the ancient Chinese, who based their entire medicine, philosophy, and even architecture and statecraft on the science of coincidence. The ancient Chinese texts do not ask how to do things in terms of cause and effect, rather they ask what is attracted to coincide with what. The same idea is encountered in astrology as well as in the divination techniques of the most varied cultures.[49]

By introducing the concept of synchronicity, Jung opened the door to a new way of understanding the relationship between psyche and matter, and it is to this relationship that the symbol of the stone seems to point. But this is still a completely unresearched area of reality, which awaits the investigations of future generations of physicists and psychologists. The discussion of synchronicity may seem a digression from our theme, but synchronicity had to be mentioned briefly, because it is a theme full of creative possibilities for the future. Moreover, synchronicity phenomena almost always occur during the most important phases of the process of individuation. They are often paid no heed, because the individual of today has not learned to watch for such coincidences and make them meaningful in relation to the symbolism of his dreams.

The Relationship with the Self

Today more and more people, especially those forced to stay in the cities because of their jobs, suffer from a sense of emptiness and boredom. It is like perpetually waiting for something that never comes. Movies, sports events, and political enthusiasms may distract us for a while, but time and again we come back from them to the wasteland of our own apartments, tired and disenchanted once more.

The only worthwhile adventure for the people of today is the adventure within. Realizing this dimly, many are turning to yoga and other Eastern teachings; but that is really no adventure, for there we do no more than adopt the knowledge already acquired by the Indians and Chinese, without having a *direct* encounter with our *own* inner center.[50] There is, it is true, the same concentration on the inner psyche that is found in Jungian psychology, with the difference that Jung has shown a way for us to come into contact with our own inner being alone and free, without preconceived rules.

When one gives daily attention to the reality of the Self, it is as though one has to live on two levels. As before, one devotes one's attention to one's duties in the external world, but at the same time one heeds all the messages and signs in dreams and events through which the Self makes known its intentions and shows the direction in which the stream of life is tending. Old Chinese texts that depict this type of approach make use of the image of a cat waiting in front of a mousehole. Attention, it is said, must be neither too tense nor too slack. "When one practices in this manner . . . , with time it will bear fruit, and when the right moment comes, it is like a ripe melon falling—something happens that triggers the inner awakening of the individual. Then the meditator is like someone drinking water: only he knows whether it is cold or warm. All doubts disappear, and he will feel happy like a person meeting his own father at a crossroads."[51]

Thus, in the midst of ordinary life, we are suddenly involved in an exciting inner adventure, and since it is unique for each person, it can neither be imitated nor stolen.

When a person loses contact with the regulating center of his psyche, it usually happens for the following reasons. A single instinctive drive or emotion can carry him away into a one-sided state of mind. This can also happen to animals. A sexually aroused stag often forgets all safety precautions and even its hunger. Being carried away in this manner is something primitive peoples greatly fear; they call it "loss of soul." Another form of this kind of disturbance is excessive daydreaming that keeps secretly circling around certain complexes. This is a threat to the ability of consciousness to concentrate.

The other reason is opposite in nature. It consists in excessive consolidation of ego consciousness. Although a disciplined consciousness is a requisite for nearly all civilized activities (everybody knows what happens when a railway switchman gives way to daydreaming), it also has the unfortunate aspect of helping to repress impulses and messages from the Self. For this reason the dreams of a great many civilized persons revolve around the restoration of contact with the unconscious and its core, the Self.

In the representations of the Self in myth, we may note a repeated emphasis on the four cardinal directions, and in many images, the "great man" occupies the center of a four-part circle—a structure that Jung referred to using the Indian term *mandala* (magic circle). This symbolizes the "atomic nucleus" of the psyche, about whose structure and significance ultimately we know nothing. Interestingly enough, the Naskapi often represent their great man not as a person but as a mandala figure.

In Eastern cultures, mandala images are primarily used meditatively to restore inner balance. A traditionally structured mandala prepared by an artist is placed in front of the student for his contemplation. As with all preconceived religious rites, this can become a purely external gesture. But to his astonishment, Jung discovered that such mandala images can also appear spontaneously out of the unconscious in people who have no idea of such meditation practices. This happens with particular frequency in situations in which people feel confused, unhappy, and "in a mess." The appearance of this symbol usually brings with it an overwhelming experience of inner peace, a sense of the meaningfulness of life and of inner order. This is true even when it appears spontaneously in the dreams of modern people who have no knowledge of the religious traditions mentioned above; in fact, it may perhaps have an even stronger effect then, because tradition and knowledge cannot block or weaken the primordial experience.

The following dream of a sixty-year-old woman, which ushered in a new phase of intellectual productivity in her life, provides an example of this.

> I see a landscape in darkened light, and in the background the crest of a hill sloping gently upward and then continuing on the same level. On the rising line of the horizon moves *a square pane that shines like gold*. In the foreground is dark, unplowed earth, which is beginning to sprout. Then suddenly I see *a round table with a gray stone slab top*. At the moment I become aware of the table, the gold-gleaming square pane is on it. It has disappeared from the hill. Why and how it suddenly changed location, I don't know.

Landscapes in dreams (as often in art) symbolize ineffable unconscious "moods." Here the darkened light of this dream landscape indicates that the brightness of the sun, that is, of daytime consciousness, has been dimmed and that now the inner nature begins to appear by the light it reflects itself. Until now, the symbol of the Self was no more than a hint of something longed for on the dreamer's mental horizon, but now it shifts and becomes the center of her psychic landscape. At the same time, seed sown long ago begins to sprout, for the dreamer had already been making an effort over a long period to follow her dreams, and this was now bearing fruit (a reminder of the relationship of the cosmic man to plants!). Now the gold pane is suddenly situated on the right, that is, in the place where we consciously recognize things. The right usually symbolizes skillful, conscious; left symbolizes unskillful, unconscious, "sinister." The golden pane is now situated on a round stone table and is no longer moving around; this means it has found a lasting foundation.

The motif of roundness (the mandala) generally represents natural wholeness. The square, on the other hand, symbolizes its conscious realization. In this dream the rectangular pane and the round table come together. Thus a conscious insight takes place within the nature of the Self. Round stone tables play a major role in myths. An example is King Arthur's Round Table, which is an image derived from the table of the Last Supper.

Whenever a person turns sincerely to his unconscious psyche and its knowledge (not, however, when he dwells on subjective thoughts and feelings) by considering its objective expressions, such as dreams and spontaneous fantasies, sooner or later the image of the Self will appear and confer upon the ego the potential for a renewal of its life. Now the most difficult problem that arises in this context has to do with the fact that all the modes of manifestation of the unconscious we have mentioned—the shadow, the animus, the anima, the Self—possess a light and a dark side. As we have seen, the shadow can be something base, a reprehensible instinctive drive that should be overcome, but it can also be a vital aspect of one's being that is pressing to be realized. In the same way, animus and anima can also play a dual role. They can bring about vital further development and creativity or rigidification and death. And even the Self, this most all-embracing symbol of the unconscious or of wholeness, has a dual aspect as well. This can be seen, for example, in the Eskimo tale given earlier, in which the "little woman," although she tries to help the heroine on the moon, actually ends up turning her into a spider.

Indeed we could even say that the danger of the dark side of the Self is the greatest, because the Self also represents the greatest inner power. The danger consists literally in becoming a spider, that is, that one might begin to "spin" grand delusions and become possessed by them. In such cases, a person might believe he has grasped the meaning of the most profound of cosmic enigmas, with the result that he loses all ability to communicate with his fellow human beings. A sure sign of this is the loss of one's sense of humor and sociability. Grand delusions, such as believing one is Julius Caesar or Jesus Christ, come about through identification with the Self. But the opposite can also occur—that one is unable to establish contact with the Self, because it is covered over and masked by too many unconscious impulses or conventional prejudices. On this account, the image of the Self often appears in myths as "a precious treasure, difficult to obtain."

The emergence of the Self can also place the conscious ego in serious danger. This dual aspect of the Self is especially well depicted in the following tale from ancient Iran, entitled "The Mystery of the Badgerd Bath."[52]

The noble prince Hātim Tāi received from his king the command to investigate the mystery of the Badgerd [which means "Castle of the Nonexistent"] Bath. In the course of his quest he must face many dangerous adventures, from which no one has ever before emerged alive. Finally he reaches a round edifice, to which he is admitted by a barber with a mirror in his hand. But as soon as he gets into the water inside, he hears a thunder clap, darkness shrouds everything, the barber disappears, and the water begins to rise relentlessly. Hātim swims desperately in circles. The water continues to rise, reaching the ceiling, and he believes he is lost. Then he prays to God and reaches for the round stone that seals the dome. Once again there is a clap of thunder, everything is transformed, and Hātim is suddenly standing alone in the desert. After more laborious wandering, he comes to a magnificent garden, in the middle of which is a circle of stone statues. In the center he sees a parrot in a cage, and a divine voice speaks to him: "O hero, there is almost no chance you will escape this bath alive. Once Gayomart [the primordial man] found a gigantic diamond which shone more brilliantly than the sun and the moon. He

343

decided to hide it so it could not be found and therefore built this enchanted bath to protect it. The parrot here is a part of the spell. At his feet lie a golden bow and arrow. You may try to hit the bird with them three times. If you hit him, the spell will be lifted. If not, you will be turned to stone, like these others here."

Hātim tries the first time and misses the target. His legs turn to stone. He misses the second time and turns to stone up to the chest. Then he closes his eyes and shouts," God is great!" He shoots blind and hits the mark! There are claps of thunder and clouds of dust. When these subside, where the parrot was he sees an immense glittering diamond, and all the statues turn into living people, who thank him for saving them.

The symbols of the Self here are easy to recognize: the primordial man Gayomart, the round, mandala-shaped bath, the stone in the middle of the roof, and the diamond. But the last is surrounded by danger. The demonic parrot is the embodiment of an evil spirit of imitation, which causes people to miss the target and which turns them psychically to stone. For as was pointed out before, the process of individuation precludes mimicry of other people. People are constantly trying, through "external" technical copying, to imitate the inner experience of their great religious leaders, Christ, Buddha, and others, and thus rigidify psychically into tiresome formalism. What imitation ought to consist of is pursuing one's own inner way as those great leaders did, with courage and sincerity similar to theirs.

The barber with the mirror who disappeared symbolizes the gift of reflection, which Hātim loses when he needs it the most— the rising water represents the danger of being absorbed by the unconscious and losing oneself in one's own emotions. For in order to understand the message of the unconscious, one must not let oneself get carried away. The ego must maintain its composure, for only when I remain a conscious person can I realize the contents and messages of the unconscious. But how can a person undergo this supreme experience of being one with the universe and at the same time remain conscious that he is only a little ego? When I think of myself negatively as a mere statistical number, my life no longer has a meaning; and when I experience myself as a part of the cosmic whole, how can I then keep hold of my earthly standpoint? Reconciling these inner opposites within oneself is one of the most difficult things the process of individuation requires us to accomplish.

The Social Aspect of the Self

When we take in the impression of the tremendous overpopulation that exists today, especially in the cities, almost inevitably we feel oppressed and begin to think: "I am Mr. X or Ms. X, I live on X street, like thousands of others, and it really wouldn't make much difference if a few people like me got killed—there's more than enough of us anyway!"[53] And when we read in the newspaper about the death of endless numbers of people who do not mean anything to us, this feeling of the senseless insignificance of our life is reinforced. That is the point where turning to the unconscious can provide the greatest help, for dreams take the dreamer seriously in every detail of what he does and situate his life unexpectedly in meaningful larger frames of reference.

Something we know only theoretically—that everything comes down to the individual—here becomes clear *experientially*. Often we have a direct experience of something like the "great man" calling upon us quite personally, asking us to fulfill a specific task. This alone can give an individual the strength to swim against the current of the collective view and take his own psyche seriously.

Of course this can sometimes be unpleasant, because it goes against the intentions of ego. For example, you want to go out with friends, but a dream forbids this and demands that you undertake some creative work instead. Thus the task of individuation is often felt to be a heavy burden.

In connection with this aspect of individuation, the legend of Saint Christopher is an apt symbolic story. Because of his pride in his strength, Christopher wanted to serve only the strongest lord. First he took service with a king, but when he saw that the king was afraid of the devil, he served the devil. Then when he saw the devil was afraid of Christ, he decided to serve him, and waited for him for many years at a ford. One stormy night a child asked Christopher to carry him across the river. With ease he lifted the child to his shoulders, but with every step he took across the river, it became heavier, until he felt as though he was carrying the entire world. Then he saw that Christ was the burden he had taken on his shoulders. Thereupon Christ granted him forgiveness for his sins and eternal life.

The miraculous child is an image of the Self, which literally weighs on the natural man and yet at the same time is the only thing that can save him. In art it is often depicted as the globe of the world, which clearly shows its meaning, for the child and the sphere are widespread symbols of wholeness.

When a person attempts to follow his unconscious, not only can he no longer do just what pleases him, but he can also not always do what pleases the people around him. As a result, he must often take leave of his original group in order to come to himself. This fact causes many people to say that taking the unconscious seriously makes people asocial and egotistical. But this is not really the case, for there is another factor in play here—the collective or social aspect of the Self.

When a person pays attention to his dreams, he discovers that they are often concerned with his relations to the people around him. For instance, dreams can warn him not to trust a certain person too much. Or he might dream about a joyful encounter with a person he had perhaps completely overlooked until then in the outside world. In any case, there are then two types of possible interpretation. Either the dream content is a *projection*, that is, the dream image of the person is *a symbol for an inner aspect of the dreamer himself*. (This type of dream interpretation is called interpretation on the subjective level.)[54] But it is also often the case that dreams are communicating something to us about a real person out there, that is, the dream has a meaning on the "objective level." In this respect, the unconscious plays a role that is still far from understood in all its ramifications. For, like all the higher animals, the human being is unconsciously attuned to the manifestations of the other beings around him and instinctively perceives their problems quite independently of what his consciousness thinks about them.[55]

Our dream life gives us a glimpse into these subliminal processes, and also exercises an influence on us. When I have a dream that gives me happiness about a person in my environment, I will involuntarily take a greater interest in that hitherto overlooked person, even if I do not interpret the dream at all. In this, the dream image can blind me in its quality as a projection as well as convey objective information. To find out which of these is happening, a painstakingly circumspect attitude of consciousness is required. As in all inner processes, here too, the Self is the last and highest authority and thus the one that also regulates personal relationships. Through the influence of the Self, people who are spiritually in harmony with each other and who have similar outlooks often come together. This is a mode of group formation that often functions completely independent of outer social and organizational factors. The unifying element is not based on previously known relationships and common interests but on shared connectedness through the Self. An excess of social obligations arising from the mode of group formation is even quite harmful, because it gets in the way of this other hidden operation of the unconscious in bringing people together. Political manipulation of mass consciousness or advertising and propaganda that go beyond the bounds of purely communicating the truth are also harmful in this way, even when they are carried out on the basis of an idealistic outlook.

Here of course the question arises of whether the unconscious part of the human psyche can be influenced at all. It has been shown in practice that one cannot influence one's own dreams. True, there are people who claim they can, but a closer look shows that they are only doing what I do with my unruly dog—I order him to do what I know he is going to do anyhow. The unconscious can be altered only through a long process of working on it—in tandem with a change in the point of view of consciousness. When symbols are used by people in an attempt to influence public opinion, naturally—to the extent that they have a genuine symbolic content—they do initially make an impression on people; but whether people's unconscious and emotions will really finally be taken in is incalculable. Statistics about pop hits show that no producer can know in advance if his product is going to be a big hit or not. The unconscious, in the masses as well as in the individual, obviously retains its autonomy.

This point is often called into question by people who are not familiar with the unconscious, because dreams so frequently contain motifs the dreamer encountered the day before his dream. But when we take a closer look, we see that these "daytime remains," as they are called, have for the most part been changed or incorporated into entirely different frames of reference. Beyond that, we have to ask ourselves, why does the dream pick out these particular motifs and not a thousand others that I have also read about? The unconscious picks up only the images and events that fit in with its own significative frame of reference. For example, a person who represses his childlike spontaneity might read about a child being run over and then dream about this the following night. The external event is taken over by the unconscious in order to represent an inner state of affairs symbolically.

The same thing can happen with collective outer contents. Here too the unconscious often borrows images from the experience of the external world in order to express itself. Thus in modern dreams I have often encountered the image of divided Berlin as a symbol for the "sore spot" in one's own psyche, for the place of greatest conflict, which is for that reason also the place where the Self is most likely to turn up. Many dreams also come up relating to the film *Hiroshima, mon amour* which for the most part contain the message either that the two lovers (in the film) should come together—an image of the Self—or that an atomic explosion is going to take place, which is an image of madness and total dissolution. So although in such cases it may seem that the place or the film has influenced the unconscious, this is not actually true.

Only when specialists in manipulating public opinion use economic pressure or physical force are they able to influence the psyche of a people for a period of time. But this means only a suppression of the unconscious, which leads in the masses to the same consequences as in the individual—to mental illness. All attempts to suppress the unconscious over long periods of time are doomed to failure, since they run counter to instinct.[56]

We know from studies on the socialization of higher animals that small groups (from ten to fifty individuals) generally provide the best possible conditions of life, both for the individual animal and for the group; and the human being seems to be no exception in this respect. His physical life, his spiritual and psychic health and his ability to contribute to society all seem to thrive best at this level. As far as we can tell from our current understanding of the individuation process, the Self tends to bring about the formation of groups as well as a sense of connectedness with *all* human beings; and at the same time a clear-cut feeling of commitment toward specific other individuals. Only when the principle of group cohesion emanates from the Self can it be hoped that conflicts arising from ambition, envy, and negative projections will not cause the group to fall apart.

That of course does not mean that no differences of opinion and conflicts of duty can arise; but when they do, each individual should pull back emotionally from them and pay heed to his inner voice. This will enable him to find the approach that the Self requires of him.

Fanatic political partisanship (not the fulfillment of the duties of citizenship) therefore often seems to be incompatible with the process of individuation. For example, a man who was very politically active in an attempt to liberate his homeland from a foreign power had the following dream:

With compatriots of mine I am climbing the steps up to the attic of a museum where there is a hall resembling the cabin of a ship, painted black on the outside. From the inside, a distinguished woman in her middle years named X opens the door. (X is a historical hero of the dreamer's country associated with freedom, like Joan of Arc in France or William Tell in Switzerland.) Inside the hall hang the portraits of two aristocratic women in flower-pattern brocade gowns. As Ms. X explains these pictures, they come to life—first the eyes take on life, then the chests begin to breathe. Astounded, the people pass into a lecture hall where Ms. X is to speak. She says that the pictures came to life through her intuition and feeling. But the people are outraged; they say X is mad and even leave the hall.

The motif important for us in our present context is that the anima figure, Ms. X, is a figure entirely invented by the dream, but she bears the name of a great hero of national freedom (for example, like Wilhelmine Tell, William Tell's daughter). Through this the unconscious is expressing more than clearly that at present it is not important for this man to try to liberate his country externally, as X once did, but rather liberation through the anima, the psyche, will occur through bringing the pictures of the unconscious to life. That the museum room has the appearance of a black-painted ship's cabin is also significant. The color black suggests night, darkness, and turning inward, and the ship's cabin motif makes the museum of pictures into a ship also. If the terra firma of collective consciousness is inundated by unconsciousness and barbarity, this museum ship is capable of becoming a Noah's Ark for the resurrected images of the unconscious, is capable of carrying those who embark on it to another spiritual shore. Pictures in a museum are dead vestiges of the past, but through the attention given them by the anima, they are imbued with fresh living meaning.

The outraged people in the dream represent an aspect of the dreamer himself that is under the influence of the collective consciousness, which disapproves of bringing these psychic images to life. They embody his resistance to the unconscious. This resistance says something like: "This is all well and good, but if the atom bomb falls, this kind of thing will be of very little help." This aspect of the dreamer is incapable of divesting itself of statistical ideas and rational prejudices. The dream, by contrast, shows that today the true liberation of people can only proceed from a psychic transformation. What is the point in "liberating" his country when afterward there will be no psychic goal of life for the sake of which the freedom could be used? When people no longer see any meaning in life, then it also does not matter under what Eastern or Western regime it experiences its decline. Only when it can create something meaningful through freedom is freedom important. That is why finding an inner meaning to life is more important for the individual than any other concern.[57]

The ability to influence public opinion through the means that have become usual for us today is based on two factors: one is statistical surveys of collective trends and unconscious complexes—especially the power complex; the other is the projections of the manipulators of public opinion. Statistics, however, do not do justice to the individual. If the average size of stones in a pile is five cubic centimeters, one still may very well not find even one stone of this size in the whole pile! Thus even the most refined probability calculus is incapable of taking account of the unique individual; for probability presumes improbability, and the basis for the individual element in human beings and their destiny often lies in this very area of improbability. Only a philosophical point of view that leaves room for both the regular and probable *and* the exceptions to it can do justice to this fact.

It is thus clear that attempts to manipulate public opinion cannot produce much good. On the other hand, when an individual truly makes his way along his own path of individuation, this has a contagious effect, in a positive sense, on the people around him. It is like a spark leaping—something that usually occurs without a lot of verbiage and when no conscious manipulation is intended.

Virtually all the religions of the world contain symbols that illustrate the process of individuation or its most important aspects. The Self, in the Christian world, as we have already mentioned, is projected as the "second Adam," as Christ; in the East it is Krishna or Buddha.[58] These figures represent for the individual the model of a personality of greater amplitude, which he or she may attempt to emulate. And we also find that many people have dreams in which these figures appear as guiding counselors. On the whole, with people who are still contained by their religion, that is, who "believe" in its contents and doctrines, the psychic regulation of their lives takes place through religious symbols. Their dreams also often revolve around them. For example, a Catholic woman, right after the "Declaration of the Assumption of Mary," dreamed that she was a Catholic priest. Her unconscious extended the idea of the dogma in a manner something like this: "Now Mary is almost a goddess, so she should also have priestesses."

Another Catholic woman, who harbored certain criticisms about minor, secondary aspects of her faith, dreamed that the church in her home city had been torn down and a new one had been built; but the old tabernacle with the consecrated hosts and the statue of the Mother of God was to be brought from the old church to the new one. This dream shows that the man-made aspect of religion needed a renewal, but that the most profound images related to God becoming human and the Great Mother would survive the changes to the faith. Dreams like this are an indication of the vital interest of the unconscious in the religious thinking of an individual.[59]

This raises the question of whether it is possible to find any overall trend in the religious dreams of modern people. Jung noted with relative frequency a tendency in the dreams of contemporary Christians (Protestants and Catholics) to complete the trinitarian God image with a fourth element, which tended in the direction of the feminine, dark, material, or evil. For instance, we find dreams about the redemption of the devil or about Mary ascending to Heaven in the form of a naked black woman. A nun dreamed that the water mixed with the wine in the Eucharist—that is, the human nature of Christ—had to be better understood.[60]

Of course this fourth element that has been excluded from the

Trinity has always existed, but has remained separated from the God image in our conscious thinking; thus it has been seen more as an antithesis (for example, as the devil or the lord of this world). But today the unconscious seems to be trying to bring the two aspects of this split in the God image back together. Naturally, the central symbol in any religion, the God image or the mandala, is particularly exposed to these kinds of unconscious tendencies toward change.

A Lamaist abbot once explained to Jung that real mandalas are the ones created in the individual imagination (directed fantasy activity) when there is a disturbance of the psychic equilibrium of the group or when an idea cannot be found and must be looked for because it is missing from the sacred doctrine. Here, two fundamental aspects of the mandala symbol are being referred to at the same time. On the one hand the mandala serves a conservative purpose, restoration of the old order; and on the other hand, a creative purpose: providing form for something that does not yet exist. This latter aspect is not in conflict with the former, because in most cases a restoration of the old order cannot be achieved without simultaneously creating something new. It is as though the old returns on a higher level in the new. It is like a spiral, which returns again and again to the same point as it continues to grow in a particular direction.

A picture painted by an unsophisticated woman educated as a Protestant shows just such a spiral mandala. This woman was commanded in a dream to paint the Godhead, and in the dream she saw the image of it in a book. Of God, she saw only his cloak blowing in the wind, its movement setting it off from a spiral in the background. There was another figure on the cliff, whom she did not see clearly. When she woke up, she realized with a sudden shock that this was "God himself."

Usually Christian art depicts the Holy Spirit as a flame or a dove, but here it is shown as a spiral. This is an example of the spontaneous appearance out of the unconscious of a new idea that is not yet contained in the doctrine. It is not a new idea that the Holy Spirit constantly urges us toward innovation, but the depiction of this as a spiral is new.

The same woman subsequently painted a second picture, which was also derived from a dream. It sought to depict the dark wing of Satan sinking down over Jerusalem, the seat of Christ's work.

The wing was broken, recalling the cloak of God from the previous picture. The viewer of the first picture was situated somewhere high above in the air with an unhealable cleft between the two cliffs in front of her. The blowing cloak of God did not quite reach across to Christ. The second picture was seen from the earth. A form that appeared to be a dark variant of the cloak of God was coming down upon two onlookers (the woman and her positive animus). Thus seen from a higher viewpoint (in the first picture), the form spreading out as it fluttered in the wind was a part of the Godhead, above which rose the spiral, that is, an image of the potential for higher development. Seen from the level of human reality (in the second picture), the same thing blowing in the wind was the dark and eerie wing of the devil.

If we think out this hint of the unconscious to its conclusion, we see that the opposites of good and evil, light and dark, are moving closer together in the image of the Self as seen by our consciousness. But the images also have a significance transcending the personal level. They prophesy the sinking of a divine darkness over the Christian world, a darkness behind which, however, the potential for further development makes itself known. The axis of the spiral is not aimed upward, but in the direction of the picture's background. Through this the picture expresses the idea that the further development of the Self symbol is tending toward the depths and the background. It is leading neither into the heights of the spirit nor into the lower realm of material reality, but rather into a *further dimension*, that is, into the unconscious.

When such religious symbols emerge from the unconscious of an individual human being, it creates a profound malaise in many people. They become afraid that this could unsuitably change or relativize officially accepted religious symbols and teachings. This is even often the source of a rejection of analytical psychology and the entire unconscious.

From the psychological point of view, we may respond to this as follows: Today, as far as their relationship to religion is concerned, there are three kinds of people. The first group is composed of those people who still really believe in their own religion. Its images and doctrines are directly comprehensible to them, and in such an immediate and living way that no doubt can slip in at all. This is the case when there is relatively strong agreement between conscious views and the unconscious background. Such people can afford to look at the facts of psychology without prejudice, without having to be afraid of losing their faith. Even if their dream life happens to appear unorthodox in certain details, these details can be assimilated into their existing views without great difficulty.

A second group of people have lost their faith and replaced it with some conscious, reasonable outlook. For such people, the psychology of the unconscious is simply an introduction into a hitherto completely undiscovered realm, and such people should encounter no difficulty in becoming involved in exploring it. All the same, we find in practice quite frequently that these people, too, fend off an encounter with the unconscious. This is because their rationalism is secretly a fanatical faith, almost like a religious conviction. They behave as though theirs was a scientifically objective approach, but this is by no means the case. Instead such people belong to the group we shall mention next.

There is a third large group of people who, though they no longer believe in their inherited religion in their heads, in another part of their being, still do half "believe." An example is the French philosopher Voltaire, who railed in enlightened terms against the Catholic Church ("Écrasez l'infâme"), but who according to certain reports, before his death, amid fear and trembling, had himself given the last rites. His head was faithless, but his feeling was orthodox Catholic. Such people remind us of passengers stuck in the automatic doors on the bus who are unable either to get in or get out. Although their dreams, too, would have something to say about this very problem, they often find it difficult to turn to the unconscious because they are at odds within themselves about what they want and do not want. In the last analysis, paying serious heed to the unconscious, too, is a matter of the personal courage and integrity of the individual. The complicated plight of these people stuck in no-man's-land is in part conditioned by the fact that today the collective religious teachings are part of the collective consciousness (what Freud called the superego), though they formerly originated in the unconscious. Of course this is contested by many historians and theologians, who maintain that some sort of revelation took place. For many years, I have looked for something that would prove the Jungian point of view, but such evidence is hard to come by, because almost all religions are so old that their origin has been lost from view. However, the following example seems to me a relatively good indication of how rites originate.

A medicine man of the Ogalala Sioux Indians named Black Elk, who died not long ago, relates in his autobiography that when he was nine years old he became seriously ill, and in the midst of his fever he had an extraordinarily vivid vision. He saw four groups of magnificent horses spring forth from the four cardinal directions, and then he saw, enthroned on clouds, the six grandfathers of the world, the ancestral spirits of the tribe. They bestowed on him six healing symbols for his people and showed him a new way of life.[61]

When he was sixteen years old he suddenly developed a terrible fear of thunderstorms. Whenever it thundered, he heard voices that said, "Hurry, hurry!' It reminded him of the thundering of the hooves of the horses in his vision. An old medicine man helped him at this time by explaining that his fear came from having kept the vision to himself. He had to communicate it to his people. He did this, and the tribe translated the vision into reality as a ritual with horses. Black Elk and many of his people averred that the performance of this exercised a salutary influence. "Even the horses seemed to be happier and healthier than before."

The enactment of the dream was not repeated only because shortly thereafter the tribe was destroyed by the whites. But an Eskimo tribe living on the Colville River in Alaska recounts the origination of their "eagle ceremony" in these terms:

> Long ago a young hunter shot a beautiful eagle which made such an impression on him that he stuffed it and made offerings to it. One day when he had gone hunting in a snowstorm, two animal men suddenly appeared in front of him who said they were messengers from the eagle world and carried him off with them. Then he heard a kind of drumming, and they said to him: "That is the heart of a mother beating." Thereupon a woman dressed in black appeared, the eagle's mother, and demanded that in honor of her dead son he introduce an eagle ceremony among his people. After they had showed him how to perform the ceremony, he suddenly found himself lying exhausted in the snow in the place where he had first met the messengers. Then he showed his people how to perform the ceremony, which they still do to this day.[67]

These two examples show how a ritual or a religious custom can arise directly from an experience of the unconscious of an individual and can then shape the lives of an entire tribe. Such customs, when repeated, are continuously reshaped and refined over time until they become more or less fixed. But this process of crystallization also has a negative side, which is that as a result of it, more and more people forget the original experience and end up just believing what has been told them concerning the custom. Then they even consider further creations from the unconscious as blasphemy.

Nowadays this is to a large extent also true for us. Although Christianity seems to place an especially high value on the immortal soul of the individual human being, one is well advised not to understand this in too practical terms, because otherwise many people will react with shock. Sometimes theologians even defend their genuine religious symbols and symbolic doctrines *against* the religious function of the psyche, which they experience as threatening, forgetting that the heritage they are defending owes its existence to precisely this function; for without the human psyche, which has received and shaped "divine" inspirations, no religious symbol would ever have entered the reality we experience as human beings. (We need only think of the prophets or evangelists.[63])

If in response to this the claim is made that there is such a thing as a religious reality per se, independent of the human psyche, we can only inquire, "Who or what is making that statement if not a human psyche?" Our postulations can never leap beyond the bounds of the psyche, for it is our sole organ for grasping reality.

Thus the modern discovery of the unconscious shuts a door somewhere forever on the illusory spiritual reality "in itself" that our ego so blithely imagines. In modern physics this door has also simultaneously been shut, in this case on the illusion that a physical reality in itself could ever be apprehended.[64] But at the same time, the discovery of the unconscious opens the door to an imponderably multifaceted field of reality whose bounds cannot be set, in which objective research and the personal ethical adventure combine in the most unusual fashion. It is possible that the recognition of this fact will lead to an entirely new way of "doing science," for now feeling, the function of moral valuation, can no longer, as hitherto, be excluded. However, the possibility of communicating this way of proceeding in the new field is limited, because much that has to do with it is unique and is therefore not transferable without remainder from person to person through language. Here too a door is shut on an illusion—the illusion that one can completely understand another human being and prescribe for him or her what is "right." But here too, by way of compensation, the door opens on a new area, the discovery of the unifying function of the Self operating in a multitude of individuals. Thus in place of the intellectual word games prevailing today there appears a psychic action working on an essential level for the realization of the consciousness of the individual. What effect this will have in the realm of human spiritual and social development we do not know. But one thing strikes me as certain: future generations will have to pay heed to Jung's discovery of the process of individuation if they wish to avoid a situation of regressive stagnation.

Notes

1. Cf. C. G. Jung, cw 8, paras. 421, 443ff., 551ff.; cw 9/ii; and G. Adler, *Studies in Analytical Psychology* (London, 1948).

2. Cf. C. G. Jung, cw 9/ii, paras. 1ff.; and vol. 12, paras. 20, 44, 230.

3. Cf. F. G. Speck, *Naskapi: The Savage Hunter of the Labrador Peninsula* (University of Oklahoma Press, 1935).

4. Cf. C. G. Jung, cw 9/i, paras. 489ff., 525ff.; and 9/i, paras. 7ff. and 297ff.

5. Cf. R. Wilhelm, *Dschuang-Dsi, das wahre Buch vom südl. Blütenland* (Chuang-tse: The True Book of the Southern Land of Blossoms) (Jena, 1923).

6. Cf. C. G. Jung, "The Philosophical Tree," cw 13, paras. 304ff.

7. Cf. H. Maspéro, *La Chine antique* (Ancient China) (Paris, 1955), pp. 140f. My thanks to Mrs. Marianne Rump for this information.

8. Cf. C. G. Jung, cw 17, para. 306ff.

9. Cf. *Psychologische Interpretation von Kinderträumen* (Zurich, ETH, 1938/39). Cf. also C. G. Jung, *The Development of Personality*, cw 17; M. Fordham, *The Life of Childhood* (London, 1944), esp. p. 104; E. Neumann, *The Origins and History of Consciousness* (Princeton: Princeton University Press, Bollingen Foundation, 1970); F. Wickes, *The Inner World of Consciousness* (New York, 1927); and Eleanor Bertine, *Human Relationships* (London, 1958).

10. Cf. C. G. Jung, *The Development of Personality*, cw 17; Jung discusses the psychic core in paras. 300ff.

11. Cf. J. Bolte and G. Polivka, *Anmerkungen zu den Kinder- und Hausmärchen der Brüder Grimm*, vol. 1 (1913–1932), pp. 503ff.; this includes all the variations of the Grimm's fairy tale "The Golden Bird."

12. Cf. C. G. Jung, cw 9/ii; cw 12, paras. 36ff., "The Undiscovered Self (Past and Future)," in cw 10, paras. 488ff. Cf. also F. Wickes, *The Inner World of Man* (New York, 1938). A good example of the realization of the shadow is given in G. Schmalz, *Komplexe Psychologie und körperliches Symptom* (Complex Psychology and Physical Symptoms) (Stuttgart, 1955).

13. Cf. A. Piankoff, *The Tomb of Ramses VI*, parts 1 and 2 (Pantheon Books, Bollingen Series, 1954).

14. Cf. C. G. Jung, cw 6, paras. 470ff.; cw 8, paras. 517ff.

15. *The Koran*, trans. E. H. Palmer (Oxford University Press, 1949); C. G. Jung, cw 9/i, paras. 240ff.

16. Cf. Somadeva, *Vetalapanchavimsati*, trans. Tawney (Bombay, 1956); also Heinrich Zimmer, *The King and the Corpse* (New York, 1948).

17. Cf. *Der Ochs und sein Hirte* (The Ox and the Oxherder), trans. Koichi Tsujimura (Pfullingen, 1958), p. 95.

18. Cf. C. G. Jung, cw 9/i, paras 20ff. and ch. 3; cw 17, paras. 338ff.; cw 8, paras. 662 ff.; cw 11, paras. 46ff., 71ff., 759 ff.; cw 7, paras. 296ff.; E. Bertine, *Human Relationships* (London, 1958), pt. 2; Esther Harding, *Psychic Energy* (New York, 1948); and others.

19. Cf. K. Rasmussen, *Die Gabe des Adlers* (The Eagle's Gift) (Frankfurt, 1926), p. 172.

20. Cf. W. Hertz, "Die Sage vom Giftmädchen" (The Saga of the Poisonous Maiden), *Abhandlungen der königlichen Bayerischen Akademie der Wissenschaften* (Proceeds of the Royal Bavarian Academy of Sciences), XX, vol. 1 (Munich Division, 1893).

21. Cf. C. Hahn, "Der Jäger und der Spiegel, der alles sieht" (The Hunter and the Mirror That Sees Everything), in *Griechische und Albanesische Märchen* (Greek and Albanian Fairy Tales), vol. 1 (Munich and Berlin, 1918), p. 301.

22. Cf. Eleonor Bertine, *Human Relationships*.

23. Cf. C. G. Jung, cw 11, paras. 243 ff.; cw 9/ii, paras. 352ff.; cw 12, paras. 29ff., 141ff., 168ff.

24. On the four stages of the anima, see C. G. Jung, cw 16, paras. 361ff.

25. Linda Fierz-David, *Der Liebestraum des Poliphilo* (Poliphilo's Dream of Love) (Zurich, 1947).

26. Cf. Marie-Louise von Franz in *Aurora Consurgens,* translated by R. F. C. Hull and A. S. B. Glover (London: Routledge and Kegan Paul, 1966).

27. Jung examined the chivalric cult of the lady in cw 6. Cf. also Emma Jung and M.-L. von Franz, *The Grail Legend,* translated by Andrea Dykes (New York: Putnam, 1970).

28. Cf. C. G. Jung, *Two Essays on Analytical Psychology,* cw 7, paras. 207ff.; cw 9/ii, paras. 20ff. See also Emma Jung, *Animus und Anima,* passim; Esther Harding, *Woman's Mysteries* (New York, 1955); Cf. Eleonor Bertine, *Human Relationships,* pp. 128ff.; Toni Wolff, *Studien zu C. G. Jungs Psychologie* (Studies on C. G. Jung's Psychology) (Zurich, 1959), pp. 257ff.; Erich Neumann, *Amor and the Psyche: The Psychic Development of the Feminine* (Princeton: Princeton University Press, 1990).

29. Cf. "Der Tod als Geliebter" (Death as the Beloved), *Zigeunermärchen* (Gypsy Fairy Tales), in *Die Märchen der Weltliteratur,* pp. 117f.

30. Cf. C. G. Jung, cw 9/i, paras. 306f.; cw 7, paras. 374f.

31. Cf. "Die schwarze Königstochter" (The Black Princess), *Märchen aus dem Donaulande.*

32. Cf. "Von einer Frau, die zur Spinne wurde" (The Woman Who Turned Into a Spider), trans. K. Rasmussen, in *Die Gabe des Adlers,* pp. 121f.

33. Cf. C. G. Jung, cw 9/i, paras. 259ff.

34. H. Maspéro, *Le Taoisme* (Paris, 1950), p. 109. See also J. J. M. de Groot, *Universismus* (Cosmic Thought) (Berlin, 1918), p. 40; H. Koestler, *Symbolik des chinesischen Universismus* (Symbolism of Chinese Cosmic Thought) (Stuttgart, 1958); and C. G. Jung, *Mysterium Coniunctionis,* cw 14, para. 573.

35. Cf. A. Wünsche, *Schöpfung und Sündenfall des ersten Menschen* (Creation and the Fall into Sin of the First Man) (Leipzig, 1906), pp. 8f., 13; Hans Leisegang, *Die Gnosis* (Gnosis) (Leipzig: Kröner, 1924). See also C. G. Jung, *Mysterium Coniunctionis;* and cw 12, paras. 209ff., 447ff. There is a possibility of connections between Chinese P'an Ku, Persian Gayomart, and the legends concerning Adam; on this see S. S. Hartmann, *Gayomart* (Uppsala, 1953), pp. 46, 115.

36. Cf. E. S. Drower, *The Secret Adam: A Study of Nasorean Gnosis* (Oxford, 1960), pp. 23, 26f., 37.

37. Cf. F. Pfeiffer, *Meister Eckhart, Predigten* (Meister Eckhart, Sermons), trans. C. de B. Evans (London, 1924), vol. 2, p. 80.

38. Cf. C. G. Jung, cw 9/ii, paras. 68ff.; "Answer to Job," in cw 11; and cw 14, paras. 570ff.

39. Cf. G. Sholem, *Major Trends in Jewish Mysticism* (1941); and C. G. Jung, cw 14, paras. 585ff.

40. Cf. C. G. Jung, cw 16, paras. 410ff.; and cw 14, paras. 349ff., 532ff. One could also mention the round primordial man whom Plato described in the *Symposium* or the Gnostic God-man figure.

41. Cf. C. G. Jung, cw 13, paras. 126ff., 70ff., 308ff., 315ff.

42. Cf. C. G. Jung, cw 12, passim; cw 16, paras. 353ff.; and Toni Wolf, *Studien zu C. G. Jungs Psychologie*, p. 43.

43. Cf. C. G. Jung, cw 8, paras. 131ff.

44. Cf. A. Portmann, *Das Tier als soziales Wesen* (The Animal as a Social Being) (Zurich, 1953), p. 368.

45. Cf. Paul Herrmann, *Das altgermanische Priesterwesen* (Ancient German Priestcraft) (Jena, 1929), p. 52.

46. Cf. C. G. Jung, cw 12, para. 421, note 45.

47. Cf. C. G. Jung, cw 12, para. 404.

48. Cf. C. G. Jung, cw 7, paras. 230ff.

49. Cf. C. G. Jung, "Synchronicity: An Acausal Connecting Principle," cw 8, paras. 816ff.

50. Cf. C. G. Jung, "Concerning Mandala Symbolism," cw 9, part 1, paras. 627ff.

51. Cf. Lu Kuan Yü (Charles Luk), *Ch'an and Zen Teaching* (London), p. 27.

52. Cf. *Märchen aus Iran*, in *Die Märchen der Weltliteratur* (Jena, 1959), pp. 150f.

53. Cf. C. G. Jung, "The Undiscovered Self (Present and Future)," in cw 10, paras. 488ff.

54. Cf. C. G. Jung, cw 8, paras. 509ff.

55. Cf. A. Portmann, *Das Tier als soziales Wesen*, pp. 65ff. and passim. See also N. Tinbergen, *A Study of Instinct* (Oxford, 1955), pp. 151f. and 207f.

56. Cf. El. E. E. Hartley, *Fundamentals of Social Psychology* (New York, 1952); and T. Janwitz and R. Schulze, "Neue Richtungen in der Massenkommunikationsforschung" (New Directions in Mass Communication Research), in *Rundfunk und Fernsehen* (Radio and Television) (1960), pp. 7f., passim. Also ibid., pp. 1–20; and "Unterschwellige Kommunikation" (Subliminal Communication), ibid., Numbers 3/4, pp. 283, 306. (My thanks for this information to Mr. René Malamud.)

57. Cf. C. G. Jung, "The Undiscovered Self (Present and Future)," in CW 10, paras. 488ff.

58. Cf. C. G. Jung, CW 11, paras. 413ff., 243ff.

59. Cf. C. G. Jung, CW 12, paras. 169ff.

60. Ibid.

61. Cf. Black Elk, *Black Elk Speaks*, ed. J. G. Neihardt (New York, 1932). German edition: Schwarzer Hirsch, *Ich rufe mein Volk* (I Call My People) (Olten, 1955).

62. Cf. K. Rasmussen, *Die Gabe des Adlers*, pp. 23f., 29f.

63. Cf. C. G. Jung, CW 12, Introduction.

64. Cf. W. Pauli, "Die philosophische Bedeutung der Idee der Komplementarität" (The Philosophical Significance of the Idea of Complementarity), *Experientia*, vol. 6, no. 2, pp. 72f.; and "Wahrscheinlichkeit und Physik" (Probability and Physics), *Dialectica*, vol. 8, no. 2 (1954), p. 117.

JUNG'S DISCOVERY OF
THE SELF

■■

To me it seems to make sense to talk about the practical side of psychological work first, since in my experience misunderstandings between experts in different fields arise principally from their having too little down-to-earth contact with each other's specialized material. C. G. Jung's basic views on the discovery of the Self, which he called individuation, are taken as premises here: the first stage is the integration of the shadow; the second is the assimilation of the inner powers of the opposite sex, anima and animus; and finally, there is the discovery of the Self.

The shadow is a collective designation for the most varied characteristics of the ego personality—in our culture usually inferior, natural or instinctive, or even evil characteristics—that have been repressed through education or personal abhorrence. The anima comprises the positive and negative—for the most part also repressed—feminine characteristics in a man. In its positive aspect it is feminine empathy or sensitivity, sometimes also the sense of feeling, eros, artistic tendencies, love of nature, acceptance of the validity of the irrational. Negatively, it is moodiness, irritability, subjective judgment, whininess, hypochondria, sentimentality. The animus in a woman manifests positively as initiative, depth of thought, consistency, courage, sense of religious truth; negatively as rigid opinionatedness, brutality, exaggeratedly masculine behavior, and so on.

The main aspect of the Self is numinosity itself—that which is ultimately supreme, a revelation of "the meaning of life," the divine inner psychic center, the inner peace beyond all conflict, that which is experienced as the absolute inner truth.

Modes of Therapy

People who undergo Jungian analysis today are, generally speaking, either those who are compelled to seek treatment by a physical or psychosomatic symptom or an addiction, or—much more frequently—those who suffer psychically from a depression, a psychic conflict, or a sense of the meaningless of their existence, and who have come to feel, through reading Jung's writings or just on their own, that an inward journey might resolve these problems. The greater part of these no longer have genuine religious faith as part of their life—for after all, such a faith should be able to solve these problems or at least make them bearable. Many of them, however, are still really Christian believers who nonetheless are unable to find in their faith the answer to a specific problem in their lives.

What Jung attempted to reduce to order by using the classificatory concepts of the three stages of individuation comes down in reality to an endlessly ongoing process, which varies individually and takes on a different form for each analysand. Many require a long breaking-in period before—once they are liberated from rationalistic prejudices—they are able to take their dreams seriously at all. Others arrive at the beginning with highly significant dreams in which they sense their own solution to their problems; but they are unable to arrive at an adequate understanding of them. In many cases, dreams revolve for years around minor personal themes: corrections in analysands' attitudes toward the people around them, critical considerations relating to childhood fixations, arrogance, low self-esteem, pettiness, conventionality, deficient mastery of emotions, and so forth.

One category all by itself is that of people who have a so-called creativity problem, that is, who are obviously destined and impelled by their own psychic makeup to engage in creative work of an artistic or scientific nature, but are unable to find their way to doing it. This is frequently a result of arrogance: "If I can't be Leonardo da Vinci, then I won't try anything at all." Sometimes it is conventionality, because what they ought to be bringing up from their psychic depths runs against the prevailing collective fashion. Or else they do not see what form the actualization of the pressing creative contents within them could take and must first find this form by way of their dreams. On their long way, the analyst accompanies them as a "companion in suffering" and interpreter of their dreams.

If shadow problems are involved which according to the viewpoint of the dreams should be placed under conscious control or combated, then no moral conflicts with prevailing moral views (in our culture, Christian ones) arise. Sometimes, however, the dreams insist on the acceptance of unconventional features: the paragon of virtue is advised to be more of a naughty pleasure seeker, sexuality is praised as something beautiful, a well-aimed fit of anger is presented as the right way to deal with an obnoxious wife or unruly children. In this case there *may be* a clash with rigid moral views of consciousness, but only with rigid ones, for I have yet to see the unconscious make really profoundly immoral demands; however, it is a part of nature and cares little for petty social rules.

Greater difficulties come about on the next stage, the integration of animus and anima. To begin with people have to learn to see in practical terms what these are at all and how and where they are active in them. For in fact we are basically and to a very great extent *possessed* by these extremely powerful unconscious contents. In practice this means that whenever we are emotionally stirred up, we think that it is *our own* feelings and opinions we are defending with such holy conviction, with such great emotion. To confront a man as being anima-possessed (for the most part recognizable by the raised voice, the sentimental undertone of his words, the persistence in assertions of power based on insecurity) is hardly ever successful or advisable. Rather I believe in the roundabout approach and the patient detail work of dream interpretation. The same holds true for the animus-possessed woman. Discussing her "opinions" with her is like running into machine-gun fire.

Because these powers are more deeply unconscious for us than the shadow, they are most often only recognizable in projection—in a man's case in some overwhelming fascination with a woman or with a man in a woman's case—that is, in that disastrous and blissful condition usually called "being in love." In accordance with the overwhelming power of these contents, in earlier times they were always seen as deities. "*O mater saeva cupidinum, parce, precor, precor*" ("O cruel mother of passion, spare me, I pray you, I pray you"), cries Horace when he sees that, at an advanced age, he is on the verge of falling in love with the beautiful Chloë. Falling in love is "destiny," and the ego knows that even with good intentions and the like, it can do nothing about it. For this reason Jung says that the integration of the shadow is an apprentice's work, but the integration of the animus and anima is a masterpiece.

From Collective to Individual Experience

In the Middle Ages, the negative animus of women was embodied in the devil (the witch trials), the positive animus in Christ. The negative anima of men was projected onto pagan fairies, mermaids, or witches; the positive anima was seen in the Virgin Mary or in such soul guides as Dante's Beatrice. (The splitting apart of the dark and light aspects is specifically Christian; it is found far more rarely in other cultural spheres.) How naive equations of this sort of animus and anima with religious figures originally were is shown, for example, by the passion of the female martyr Perpetua, who once had a dream about a kindly old shepherd or another time about a helpful master of gladiators. When she awoke she immediately assumed that these figures must represent Christ. Any very powerful good spirit simply had to be Christ, even though the dream itself did not say so at all.

As long as animus and anima are experienced in this way, projected onto collective religious figures, the individual is to a great extent relieved of the problems they pose for consciousness. When, for example, a medieval knight chose Mary as the "lady of his heart," she caused him no individual difficulties of the sort a real woman nearly always causes a man. She did not stand in the way of an orderly marriage. The trade-off, however, was that he also was not able to become conscious of the individual features of his anima. Today the problem of projection of animus and anima onto collective religious figures has become much less acute, and thus these contents exert pressure directly and immediately on the individual. Hence the vulnerability of marriages.

But this crisis also has the advantage that now man and woman must confront each other psychologically in a much more serious fashion than ever before, rather than more or less living right past each other. And it is only in a serious relationship to a person of the opposite sex that it is possible to become conscious of the animus or anima. We should not, however, think that when we speak of animus and anima we are exhausting the subject. These are only classificatory concepts. The objectively existing factor they refer to is full of still unpenetrated psychic mysteries, wrapped up in the *mysterium coniunctionis*, about which Jung did not dare write until the end of his life, something that almost none of us understands in its full depth.

However, the analyst has to deal with the simpler aspects of these problems every day, wherever marital problems or anything to do with what is called "love" are concerned.

And finally, the Self. Jung used this notion to sum up a multitude of psychic images, all of which are characterized by their high degree of numinosity and their incisive personality-altering effect, mostly healing, sometime destructive. They possess the quality of holiness in the sense described by Rudolf Otto in his book *The Idea of the Holy*. Sometimes it is a pure "voice" that

speaks sublime words from above or from the beyond with absolutely convincing effect. Sometimes in the dreams of men it is a
personification, a supremely exalted old man, sometimes explicitly called God; or in the dreams of women the personification is
often that of a great nature-mother of ultimate authority and
power; or the Self appears as a holy and miraculous child, as a
luminous heavenly body, as a golden ball or crystal, or as a mandala, that is, as a circular or four-membered or square pattern.
When such a symbol appears in a dream, either a great crisis or
"inner peace" is in the offing, sometimes both at the same time.
The dreamer seldom hesitates to call such an experience divine,
for it has a profoundly moving and altering effect.

After having observed these great experiences of the Self in
himself and others, Jung then also saw them hinted at in more
minor dream motifs which do not have the same shocking imme-
diacy but always exhibit an inner-balance-restoring function. Let
us look, as an example, at the dream of a woman who suffered
from a depression brought about by external circumstances:

> She sees three elk in a forest at a crossroads, a male on the right,
> a female in front, and another female on the left. She herself is
> approaching from the fourth direction. A sublime voice from
> above says: "If you will only come here each time to this place,
> that will be good; for here the elk always know where you must
> go next."

This dream brought her significant relief.

When I am dealing with a person who is still rooted in his or
her faith, I never hesitate to interpret such a voice as the voice of
God. Jung only used the word "Self" for this, which he borrowed
from Eastern philosophy, to avoid having the idea laden with
historical associations. Thus it is better to say to an atheist, for
example, that it is the Self, because otherwise the word "God"
immediately constellates his hatred for the "conventional" God,
who has been spoiled for him by inappropriate education.

The Criticism of Relativism

The term "Self" is also appropriate, however, because it includes the god experience of other religions. The enlightenment of the Buddha, for example, would be an experience of the Self, just like the conversion experience of Augustine. Such views are repugnant to Christian theologians for two reasons: first, because they seem to express a certain relativism; and second, because they are seen as psychologism in the sense of a violation of certain boundaries by science.

In response to the first criticism, that of relativism, we can say the following: In one's practical work as a psychotherapist, one has to deal with people of the most various religions and cultures. I myself have encountered in my work not only Swiss people, but also German, French, English, and Italian people, a Ukrainian, Koreans, Japanese, North Americans, South Americans, Scandinavians, Indians, and so on, and I have worked with Protestants, Catholics, a rabbi, Shin Buddhists, a Sikh, and so forth. In order to understand people with such different cultural backgrounds, one must be as free as possible from the prejudices of one's own cultural viewpoint—one must be able to listen.

A little example: The dream of a Korean begins with the sentence, "I am standing in the hallway of my parents' house." Here one cannot apply our idea of hallway. Upon questioning, it emerges that the hallway is the place where a Korean family assembles for religious rites and thus roughly corresponds to a home chapel in our culture. Such realizations bring about a habit of restraint with regard to one's own temperamental and traditional bias. Thus in this sense it is true: we do intentionally make a great effort—to the extent that it is possible (which is unfortunately never enough)—to cultivate a certain relativism; and according to Jung's view it is sectarianism, to put the shoe on the other foot, that is one of the most harmful factors in religious life. In my experience, religious people can always understand one another. Much more difficult is the contact between religious people and rationalists.

But this is only half the truth. For whoever treads this inner path himself has inner experiences of the Self along the way that make a definitive mark on him. These experiences strike like a lightning bolt; they remain unforgettable one's entire life long, and one is never the same person as before. For oneself, they have a quality of absoluteness, indisputable truth, which no one else can ever dislodge. That is why Jung stressed again and again that the religious experience has a character of absolute evidence that is entirely self-validating. For one who goes through this inner experience, it is absolute, in no way relative or susceptible to being relativized, and in this same sense it is also morally binding. That is precisely the opposite of the opinion expressed in the criticism of relativism.

But it is true—and this seems to me to be one of the most advanced aspects of Jung's approach—that the help afforded by psychology is based on the premise that every person himself or herself harbors that divine One, the Self, in the ground of his own psyche, and that it can reveal itself to him at any time in his own language and in his own way. This conviction rests on the daily experience of the unpredictable autonomous intelligence and "genius" of dreams.

When one has, for decades, worked with the dreams of the most various people—I have estimated my own experience in this field at no less than forty thousand dreams, and Jung himself, according to his calculations, at over ninety thousand—one is impressed again every day by the uncanny, as it were, inhuman "cleverness" of the composition of dreams. Perhaps a person might come for consultation who is facing an imminent and problematic decision. He wants to get a divorce, for example, but not give up his children. And what do dreams do in such cases? They do not touch upon the burning issue at all, but they criticize the dreamer on account of his rationalism or obstinacy or other faults. To begin with there is disappointment, even shock, that the unconscious took so little notice of the current situation. Only later in retrospect does one discover that, eluding a confrontation with the rigid position of consciousness with ingenious subtlety, the unconscious was aiming at dismantling an unchanged basic approach of the dreamer's, at a "change of mind" that would result in the problem described above unexpectedly being solved in an entirely different way than foreseen.

However, even after the study of forty thousand dreams, today I would never be able to predict what a person's dream "should" be like regarding a given situation; each dream composition is always so creatively unique and ingenious. The intelligence of the dream can only be compared to the other miracles of nature, the ingenious organization of the hereditary codes, for example, or the biological molecular processes, or the development of higher organisms altogether. That is why, historically, dreams and waking vision have always played a role in all the various religions of the earth. That is also why the Old Testament recounts many dreams sent by God Himself. From this point of view, every person has within the depth of his psyche that which he needs, that is, his own access to the ultimate primordial ground of his being or—in our language—to an experience of God. He has an opening at the deepest level of his psyche where something eternal can flow in—always unpredictable and always deeply stirring whenever it happens.

All the same, by no means every person who undertakes a Jungian analysis is healed or even improves. Jung estimated the number of healed and improved patients in his own practice at 70 percent. The two greatest obstacles to this kind of healing that comes from within are, according to his view (and also according to my own experience), lying, especially in its worst form, self-deception, and the intellectualism that is akin to lying. The style of people who take this approach is incompatible with the basic premises of a Jungian analysis, and when such people do nevertheless undertake Jungian analysis, they do it for the most part only so they can find out how to make money by preaching their knowledge to others without being touched by it themselves. Such people, unfortunately, also exist, just as in nature there are bee flies, who look exactly like bees and try to destroy them so they can feed on the honey they have gathered. Why the Creator made such creatures is part of the *mysterium inquitatis*, which we do not understand.

The Criticism of Boundary Violation by Psychology

The second criticism, that of psychologism, requires closer consideration. To begin with, in treatment the psychotherapist does not try to engage religious questions, since what he does is always to try to connect with wherever the dreamer is in consciousness. But many analysands come up with these questions themselves, and when they do not, their dreams often do, quite unexpectedly. And this is not in some way induced by Jungian analysts. Twice people who were in the midst of Freudian analysis have come to me with a "big," that is, religious, dream. Their analysts had said, "You have to discuss that with a Jungian analyst"; this means that they themselves were so impressed that they did not dare interpret the dreams in terms of veiled sexual desire; but then they had no idea how they *could* understand it.

So if this is a case of boundary violation, then it is one committed by the unconscious of the patients, not by the analysts. But the analyst usually cannot send the patient on to a theologian, because as a rule patients resist this. They want to understand their dreams in the framework of the inner experience they have had up to this point. If there is a priest or minister with sufficient understanding, and if the patient is willing to seek him out, then of course one can refer the patient to him. And Jung in fact did this, mostly with Catholic patients. For the most part, however, theologians today are still too inexperienced to be able to help in any way. For instance, once a peasant woman came to me who from her earliest childhood had had vivid visions, primarily visions of light. She was completely normal. "I went to the minister with this," she told me, "but, you know, they don't understand anything about it. The minister even gave me a frightened look, as though I were crazy." And conversely, it also has happened not infrequently that priests and ministers have been very impressed by the religious visions of people who have consulted them, without realizing that they were dealing with a case of schizophrenia.

Since the unconscious of patients spontaneously produces religious symbols and since it is precisely in them that a potential for bringing about a cure lies, the therapist cannot leave them aside. As a result, he often finds himself, willy-nilly, suddenly deeply involved in discussing ultimate religious questions, which formerly were the province of priests and ministers.

But that is not all that is meant by the criticism of psychologism. It has another aspect. One repeatedly hears from theologians of both major denominations that in therapy God, Christ, and so on, are devalued into "merely psychological" contents. As Jung never tired of pointing out in his works, this criticism is based on an undervaluation of the psyche. After all, we do not know, and do not even pretend to know, what the psyche is in itself. It is an unplumbable mystery whose bounds we do not know. To speak of it as "merely psychic" is therefore nonsense. Moreover, this contradicts the view of the Christian tradition, which affirms that the *imago dei* is embedded in the depths of the psyche and is at work there.

Moreover, Jung pointed out that in speaking about God images as being based on an archetype, the word "archetype"—since it denotes something that has been shaped—directly presupposes something that has shaped it. He himself was convinced that God is something objective that transcends the psyche. But that was no more than a personal conviction not susceptible to empirical proof.

For that reason here is precisely where we find the boundary where psychology leaves off. It endeavors to speak only about that which is empirically provable. Thus it can observe and describe God images in the psyche and their overwhelming influence, but concerning God per se, it has nothing to say. Therefore, when somebody would like to make a statement about God per se, psychology has no response. Naturally, however, psychology can sometimes wonder what gives a person the right to make statements about God per se. Studying theology at some university by no means has such a transformative effect on the personality that the person who completes such a study thenceforth becomes the vehicle of metaphysically revealed truth. I at least would find this hard to believe. I have analyzed many theologians and in the course of doing so have seen that, thank God, they are also just human beings with a human psyche, in the depths of which a God image is at work.

The apparent contradictions that repeatedly come up these days between theology and Jungian psychology have a certain historical basis, which Jung, among other things, explained in his book *Aion*.[1] From time to time the metaphysical concepts and statements of theologians of all culturally more highly developed religions seem to lose touch with their experiential basis, and then they can no longer evoke the primal experience that is so charged with meaning. The words no longer have any living content; they have degenerated into sterile ideas. It is like people clinging to possessions that once meant wealth; the more ineffectual and incomprehensible and lifeless they become, the more obsessed with them people become. Through inner psychological experience, on the other hand, the words can once again be connected with the understanding of the ego and again become actual in the sense of active.

Psychoanalysis as an Aid to Faith?

Once a Japanese professor of Buddhism came to me, who was not only a scholar of theology, but also a man of faith who from the time of his early youth had had certain enlightening experiences. Nevertheless, he suffered from a stomach ulcer— presumably because of a difficult wife whose behavior he could not "digest." I said to him, "Try asking the inner light, the Buddha Mind, how you should deal practically with this problem, and perhaps also what you should eat." He looked at me with total amazement. Later he wrote to me that he had succeeded in this and that he was much better. "I see," he wrote, "what Jungian psychology does; it reconnects religious ideas with a dimension of reality as a substructure." The inner light, although he had experienced it, had become for him a theological idea in his head; thus (being also affected by the relatively passive attitude of Eastern people toward the "inner light") it never occurred to him to make it part of the whole sphere of his life. We may also note that Chinese and Japanese Buddhism, in contrast to Indian Buddhism, always stresses that the "world of illusion" and the world of "truth" are identical, that is, the latter also shines through in situations of everyday life.

If it were always so easy as it was with this Japanese man, Jungian psychology would be able to help the Christian denominations of today to fill up their churches once again. In other words, they could guide people for whom the metaphysical ideas of Christianity are no longer meaningful in gaining an experience of them, so they could once again believe in a genuine and whole fashion. And in fact that does happen again and again in individual cases, but not across the board. This is rooted in the fact that in the deepest constellations of the psychic ground, many people *develop*, and in consonance with very slow, century-spanning transformational processes, *they change*. The psychic formulation of yesterday's truth is no longer that of today. Ulrich Mann showed this in convincing fashion in his book *Theologische Tage* (Theological Days). The unconscious cares little for official views, and therefore many people's dreams frequently contain forms of the Christian symbols that are not orthodox. Thus I have sometimes seen the idea of priestesses of Mary cropping up in the dreams of Catholic women, or in the dreams of other people, Christ as a living statue of metal speaking to the dreamer.

Sometimes also, the dream images are not unorthodox, but they portray in a strange concrete form truths that were familiar to us only as abstract ideas. For example, I remember a dream that I had myself about thirty years ago, after the death of my father. He came to me and said, "The resurrection of the flesh is something that really exists; come with me, I'll show it to you." He took me to the cemetery and, after a little looking around, to a grave (which was not his), where with horror I suddenly saw that the ground was moving. As I looked on in terror, expecting a half-rotted corpse to appear, a golden crucifix about sixty centimeters high, with a golden crucified figure *that was actually alive* on it, worked its way out of the earth with jerky movements. My father cried: "Look! That is the resurrection of the flesh!" It's true that we use the formula "resurrected in Christ," but I had never been able to connect anything with this, and as strong an impression as this dream made on me, if I were unacquainted with Jung's work on the symbolism of alchemy, I would, even today, have no idea how to work with it.

The unorthodoxy of many of the symbols produced by the unconscious is immensely various. For this reason, Jung never proposed *his* personal faith, which was based on *his* experiences of the unconscious, as generally valid. When, in other periods of history, a man had deep religious experiences, as was the case with Jung, he always founded a religious sect or movement; and it is, in my opinion, one of the most extraordinary aspects of Jung's personality that he did *not* do that. He said: "If we are convinced that we know the ultimate truth concerning metaphysical things, this means nothing more than that archetypal images have taken possession of our powers of thought and feeling. . . . In the face of possession or violent emotion reason is abrogated. . . . In view of this extremely uncertain situation it seems to me very much more cautious and reasonable to take cognizance of the fact that there is not only a psychic but also a psychoid unconscious, before presuming to pronounce metaphysical judgments which are incommensurable with human reason. There is no need to fear that the inner experience will thereby be deprived of its reality and vitality. No experience is prevented from happening by a somewhat more cautious and modest attitude—on the contrary. That a psychological approach to these matters draws man more into the centre of the picture as the measure of all things cannot be denied. But this gives him a significance which is not without justification. The two great world religions, Buddhism and Christianity, have, each in its own way, accorded man a central place, and Christianity has stressed this tendency still further by the dogma that God became very man. No psychology in the world could vie with the dignity that God himself has accorded to him."[2]

Jung's Personal Confession of Faith

For these reasons, Jung did not declare any of his knowledge—in the manner of the founder of a sect—as religious truth, but only in the form of an open subjective confession. He even often fought against his students adopting his inner discoveries as their view rather than seeking their own. When a female student of his, well advanced in years, asked him before his death if he thought there was a life after death and how he saw it, he answered, "It will be of little help to you on your deathbed to think about what I believed. You have to look for an answer to this question within yourself." With other students he liberally discussed his convictions on this subject, but in the case of this woman, it was to be feared that she would convert it to an "animus opinion," that is, to a rigid formula, rather than relating to it as a genuine insight. Thus he refused to tell her.

Jung described himself as on the furthest left wing of Protestantism, in a place where the individual stands alone and unprotected before the inner experience of God without any intermediary institution or collective teaching. Because extremes touch, Jung, with this approach, was also close to the furthest right wing of Catholicism, to great mystics like Saint John of the Cross, Teresa of Ávila, and especially Meister Eckhart. In another context Jung once described Protestantism as a "spiritual catastrophe," a catastrophe, which when lived consistently to its conclusion, however, leads to a kind of "spiritual poverty" that favors an inward turning toward the primal religious experience.

He put his own personal, subjective confession of faith, which, as we said, made no claim to general validity, down on paper in the "Answer to Job" and in the "Late Thoughts" written by him in his *Memories, Dreams, Reflections*. Therefore, I shall present these thoughts of his from the latter work in précis form.[3]

"What is remarkable about Christianity," he begins his remarks, "is that in its system of dogma it anticipates a metamorphosis in the divinity, a process of historic change on the 'other side.'" This begins in the form of a new myth after the Creation, namely, the rebellion and fall of Satan and the Fall of Man, that is, as a split in the hitherto harmonious, integral Godhead and world. The next key stage is the self-realization of God in human form, in Christ—an idea that further developed into the idea of *Christus in nobis*, Christ within us. In this way, the previously only metaphysical image of God entered into the psychic realm of inner experience. At the same time, however, the originally ambivalent God image cast off its darkness and was extolled as *summum bonum*.

Starting about in the eleventh century of our era, more and more symbols of unrest and doubt appeared, coupled with the fantasy of a coming world catastrophe—psychologically interpreted, a threat to consciousness. The problem of evil, the not-yet-incarnated other side of the divine image, became acute. "The Christian world is now truly confronted by the principle of evil, by naked injustice, tyranny, lies, slavery, and coercion of consciousness. . . . That outpouring of evil revealed to what extent Christianity has been undermined in the twentieth century. . . . Evil has become a determinant reality. . . . We must learn how to handle it, since it is here to stay. How we can live with it without terrible consequences cannot for the present be conceived."

Thus we are in need of an inward turning. "Touching evil brings with it the grave peril of succumbing to it. We must, therefore, no longer succumb to anything at all, not even good. A so-called good to which we succumb loses its ethical character." Ultimately, after all, on a practical level, both good and evil are measured by human judgment and, therefore, are never finally sure. This practical relativity of good and evil, however, certainly does not mean that these categories are invalid. For all time, the wrong we have done, thought, or intended will wreak its vengeance on our souls. But since we can no longer blindly believe in the conventional rules, every ethical decision becomes a creative act of the individual in the here and now.

The psychological situation in the world today is described by Jung as follows: "Some call themselves Christians and imagine that they can trample so-called evil underfoot by merely willing to; others have succumbed to it and no longer see the good. Evil today has become a visible Great Power. One half of humanity battens and grows strong on a doctrine fabricated by human ratiocination [Marxism]; the other half sickens from the lack of a myth commensurate with the situation." Those among today's youth who want nihilistically to smash to pieces everything that exists, without a constructive countersuggestion or plan for the future, who thus want destruction and only destruction, are in reality in the grip of the dark evil side of God; they are possessed, and there are many of them. If they were to come to power, not only would there be a catastrophe but also this would once again mean a psychic split, rather than a healing of the "metaphysical rift" that characterizes Christianity. Christianity, Jung goes on, is asleep and has refused a hearing to the dark stirrings of growth in the mythical ideas of the collective unconscious.

The further development of the myth should begin with the "outpouring of the Holy Spirit on the Apostles, by which they were made into sons of God, and not only they, but all others who through them and after them received the *filiatio*—sonship of God—" for their invisible inner man has its origin and future in the primordial image of the wholeness of God. "The *complexio oppositorum* of the God-image thus enters into man, and not as a unity but as a *conflict*, the dark half of the image coming into opposition with the accepted view that God is 'Light.' "

So today we are gradually becoming conscious of a deep inner split. Prompted by this, today the unconscious is producing more and more symbols of the uniting of opposites, either in the form of mandalas, an image for the one divine inner whole, for the *complexio oppositorum*; or else the same content appears personified in a figure like the *lapis philosophorum* of alchemy or in a

Christ image, which in contrast to the offical view also includes the dark side and material nature, and is thus truly whole. The crucifix of living gold from the dream described above would be an example of this.

Jung sums up his remarks as follows:

> The myth must ultimately take monotheism seriously and put aside its dualism, which, however much repudiated officially, has persisted until now and enthroned an eternal dark antagonist alongside the omnipotent Good. . . . Only thus can the One God be granted the wholeness and the synthesis of opposites which should be His. It is a fact that symbols, by their very nature can so unite the opposites that these no longer diverge or clash, but mutually supplement one another and give meaningful shape to life. Once that has been experienced, the ambivalence in the image of a nature-god or Creator-god ceases to present difficulties. On the contrary, the myth of the necessary incarnation of God—the essence of the Christian message—can then be understood as man's creative confrontation with the opposites and their synthesis in the self, the wholeness of his personality. The unavoidable internal contradictions in the image of a Creator-god can be reconciled in the unity and wholeness of the self as the *coniunctio oppositorum* of the alchemist or as a *unio mystica*. In the experience of the self it is no longer the opposites "God" and "man" that are reconciled, as it was before, but rather the opposites within the God-image itself. That is the meaning of the divine service, of the service which man can render to God, that light may emerge from the darkness, that the Creator may become conscious of His creation, and man conscious of himself.[4]

In the industrial quarter of Zurich, the church was nearly empty until a Jakob Böhme specialist, the minister Dr. Richard Weiss, came there, and in accordance with the ideas of Jakob Böhme, took up the problem of the dark side of the God image in his sermons. Thereupon the church began to fill up noticeably again, more and more. That shows that even the masses, who would hardly understand these thoughts of Jung's, are tormented by the same problem and are seeking an answer to it.

But it is not only the unanswered question about evil that has led to the erosion of Christianity. To a much greater extent, it is the natural sciences, with their predominantly materialistic and deterministic premises, that have brought this about. It is true that even in the sciences sometimes the religious problem crops up in the very background. When, for example, Albert Einstein heatedly responded to Niels Bohr's presentation of his idea of complementarity, "God doesn't play with dice"; or when Wolfgang Pauli, when he heard about the parity-principle breakthrough, shouted, "Then God is left-handed"—at such times one senses that the physicists also, at least the more important modern researchers, are still looking somewhere behind supposedly "dead" matter for traces of the hand of the Creator, seeking to become conscious of a new image of God.

Psychology and Alchemy

The split between the natural sciences and the Christian churches has been gradually developing since about the sixteenth century. Before that the chemists and physicists attempted to understand their findings within the context of faith, but from the beginning their emphasis lay more on *experience*, and indeed, the personal experience of the individual. In addition, at that time the split between observer and object, which is being overcome again in our time, was not so profound. Many "introverted" observers even paid more attention to their psychic processes during their researches than to the external object. That is the reason that the symbolism of alchemy is of such enormous importance. Not only did it include nature—all too neglected by Christianity—more in its picture of the world, especially matter and sexuality and the physical human being, but it also provided an expressive outlet for individual formation of symbols in the unconscious. Thus we can observe in the admittedly hard-to-understand, dreamlike symbolism of alchemy all those further developments of the

Christian myth that the official doctrine so thoroughly over-looked.

So it is no wonder that the symbols that arise in the individuation processes of modern people, and especially those whose consciousness is marked by natural science's view of the world, particularly resemble the fantasies of the alchemists. For this reason, Jung, in his *Psychology and Alchemy*, published and interpreted a dream series of a modern physicist that exhibits this phenomenon. The God image appears there especially frequently in a nonpersonified form, in mandala form, because the modern person senses and seeks God for the most part in the mysterious and shockingly wondrous, meaning-filled order of being, more there initially than in dialog with an inner humanlike partner. But even the symbol of the inner partner is not absent from this dream series, be it in the form of a voice or an "unknown companion."

The symbol of matter, which had not yet been abstracted into a mathematical formula, often appears in its primordial form—in the archetypal image of a great world-mother, and points to another deficiency in the wholeness of the Christian myth, namely, the need to complete its one-sided patriarchal God image with a feminine component. Movements in this direction existed already at the beginning in the idea of the secret androgyny of Christ and in the often very vividly personified feminine figure of the Sapientia Dei. It was for this reason that Jung as we know, greeted the *Declaratio Assumptionis Mariae* of Pius XII as an act of major significance. This not only cut the ground out from under anti-Christian materialism, as the pope seemed consciously to perceive, but was also a further step toward reconciling the opposites within the Christian image of God, since according to what is stated in the text of the *Declaratio*, Mary ascended to the heavenly *thalamos*, or bridal chamber.

The consequences of this symbolic statement of course have not been thought out to their conclusion and will surely take a few centuries to become more generally conscious. For example, what do a man and woman do when they enter a "bridal chamber" together? And who will the child be who is produced by their union? These were questions that the ancient alchemists asked themselves.

The symbolism of alchemy is ultimately not anti-Christian, as some might think, but, as Jung points out, "is rather like an undercurrent to the Christianity that ruled on the surface. It is to this surface as the dream is to consciousness, and just as the dream compensates the conflicts of the conscious mind, so alchemy endeavors to fill in the gaps left open by the Christian tension of opposites. . . . The historical shift in the world's consciousness towards the masculine is compensated at first by the chthonic femininity of the unconscious." The alchemical myth, however, is not a mother-daughter myth corresponding to a father-son myth, but rather a mother-son myth. "This goes to show that the unconscious does not simply act *contrary* to the conscious mind but *modifies* it more in the manner of an opponent or partner." As the spiritual God descended into the world of man in order to beget the incarnated son, in the same way the world of the mother of the unconscious produced, "with the aid of the human spirit," a son, "not the antithesis of Christ but rather his chthonic counterpart." Jung is referring here to the central figure of alchemical symbolism, Mercurius, or the *lapis philosophorum*, which was considered the redeemer of the macrocosm. What this psychic occurrence "evidently amounted to was an attempt to bridge the gulf separating the two worlds as compensation for the open conflict between them."

"This answer of the mother-world shows that the gulf between it and the father-world is not unbridgeable, seeing that the unconscious holds the seed of the unity of both. . . . In nature the opposites seek one another—*les extrêmes se touchent*—and so it is in the unconscious, and particularly in the archetype of unity, the self."[5] The symbolism of the individuation process revolves around this center, the Self, which as the goal of development actually has a redemptive significance, that is, it has a psychically healing effect. The central Christian ideas were originally based on perception of the symbols of the unconscious process of individuation and were then, with the *consensus gentium*, declared as a generally binding truth.

A New Relationship between Conscious and Unconscious

Any person for whom the principal Christian ideas have fallen apart must, as the early alchemists did, once again seek out their roots, primordial inner experience. Thus Jung says, "When, therefore, modern psychotherapy once more meets with the activated archetypes of the collective unconscious, it is merely the repetition of a phenomenon that has often been observed at moments of great religious crisis, although it can also occur in individuals for whom the ruling ideas have lost their meaning. An example of this is the *descensus ad inferos* depicted in *Faust*, which consciously or unconsciously, is an *opus alchymicum*."[6] It is the merit of the new book by Rolf Christian Zimmermann, *Das Weltbild des jungen Goethes* (The Philosophy of the Young Goethe)[7] to have shown not only that Goethe's "private religion" and "secret beloved" was "chymics," but also that strong impulses of it remained alive into the eighteenth century in South German Pietism, for example, in the work of Oetinger.

No wonder Jung, as a student in the *Gymnasium*, was so deeply impressed by *Faust*, since there he came in contact for the first time with that undercurrent of Christianity whose symbolism profoundly occupied him in the second half of his life up to the time of his death. That undercurrent continues to manifest in the unconscious of many modern people, where it strives toward an expansion of the Christian myth through which the rift between the natural sciences and religion could be healed. If the physicists cited above were consciously or unconsciously ultimately looking for the way God works in matter, then this would reflect the alchemical myth according to which, in the form of a preconscious projection, the God image plummeted into the inorganic world and now is thrusting its way up from there into human consciousness.

One cannot speak of alchemical symbolism without referring to Jung's important—if not most important—discovery of the synchronicity principle, that is, his discovery that symbols produced sporadically and spontaneously by the unconscious through the action of the archetypes tend to coincide in a meaningful way with material occurrences in the external world, constituting an exception to the causal determinism of all natural processes still widely espoused by natural science. This points empirically to an unobservable cosmic background, which imparts order to psyche and matter at once.

What we call synchronicity phenomena today, the naive understanding of past times interpreted as miracles or as divine intervention in the world. Amusingly, in the English-speaking countries, in the legal language related to matters of insurance, an unpredictable and rare accident is today still called an "act of God." Such events cannot be accounted for even through the best computer-generated probability calculus. As a result no one can be insured against them. In any case, acts of God are often not particularly pleasant.

Ethnology and history teach us that a people whose religion is destroyed or has declined and rigidified loses its potential to survive. That is why today it has become a question of life or death for us whether or not the principal ideas of Christianity can once again be related with the spontaneous and autonomous life of the unconscious psyche. Toward the end of his life Jung was wont to say that he had been too optimistic in his life; it was the stifling stupidity and unconsciousness of people more than the evil in them that seemed to be steering us toward a worldwide catastrophe. Here Jung was more concerned over the population explosion than over the danger of war (although the latter is often made more acute by the former).

Thus we are gradually nearing a state that has been entered upon by many individuals before us, a state in which our best intellectual tools and theories are inadequate in solving our problem. We have reached a point where we can rely only on an "act of God," about which we cannot know for sure whether it will appear to our shortsighted human vision as "good" or not. But instead of helplessly waiting for something to happen, it seems to me at least to make more sense to work on joining the life of the unconscious psyche once again with consciousness so that it can convey to us its meaning-charged messages. But this is work that only the individual can do, and he has to begin with himself.

Notes

1. C. G. Jung, *Aion*, cw 9/ii.

2. C. G. Jung, *Mysterium Coniunctionis*, cw 14, paras. 787f., pp. 404f.

3. The following remarks are drawn from C. G. Jung, *Memories, Dreams, Reflections*, pp. 327ff.

4. Ibid., p. 338.

5. Introduction to C. G. Jung, *Psychology and Alchemy*, cw 12, paras. 26, 27, 30, pp. 24f.

6. Ibid., para. 42, p. 36.

7. Munich: Fink-Verlag, 1969.

BIBLIOGRAPHY

Adler, Gerhard. *Studies in Analytical Psychology.* London, 1948.

Adolf, Helen. *Visio Pacis: Holy City and Grail.* Pennsylvania State University Press, 1960.

————. "New Light or Oriental Sources of Wolfram's Parzival." Publication of the Modern Language Association of America, Vol. 42 (1947).

————. "The Esplumeor Merlin." *Speculum* 21 (1946).

Adso, Montier-en-Der von. "Libellus de ortu et de tempore Antichristi." In *Sibyllinische Texte und Forschungen.* Ed. E. Sackur. Halle, 1898.

Aelian. *De natura animalium.* (Quoted in R. Onians, *The Origin of European Thought.*)

Allendy, R. *Le Symbolisme des nombres.* Paris, 1948.

Baudrillart, Alfred. *Les divinités de la victoire d'après les textes et monuments figurés.* Paris, 1874.

Beit, H. von. *Symbolik des Märchens.* 3 volumes. Berne, 1952, 1956, 1957.

Berefeldt, Gunnar. *A Study on the Winged Angel.* Uppsala, 1968.

Berthelot, M. *Collections des anciens alchimistes grecs.* Paris, 1887/88.

Bertine, Eleonor. *Human Relationships.* London, 1958.

Bhagavadgita. Tr. Kashinath Trimbak Telang. Oxford: Clarendon Press, 1908.

Black Elk. *Black Elk Speaks.* Ed. John G. Neidhardt. New York, 1932.

Boltke, G., and J. Polivka. *Anmerkungen zu den Kinder- und Hausmärchen der Brüder Grimm.* Leipzig, 1913, 1932.

Bousset, W. *Der Antichrist.* Göttingen, 1895.

———. *Die Apokalypse Johannis.* Göttingen, 1906 (reprint 1966).

Brhadaranyaka-Upanishad. See *Thirteen Principal Upanishads.*

Bruno, Père de Jésus-Marie. "Elie le prophète." *Etudes Carmélitaines, Desclée de Brouwer 156,* Vol. II.

Chinesische Märchen. Ed. Richard Wilhelm.

Corbin, Henry. *Creative Imagination in the Sufism of Ibn Arabi.* Princeton: Princeton University Press, 1969.

———. "Terre céleste et corps de résurrection." *Eranos-Jahrbuch* XXII (1953).

Das Böse. Zurich, Stuttgart: Rascher, 1965.

Deussen, P. *Sechzig Upanishads des Veda.* Darmstadt, 1963.

Die Edda. Tr. Genzmer. Jena, 1933.

Diels, H. *Fragmente der Vorsokratiker.* 6th ed. Ed. W. Kranz. Berlin: Weidmann, 1951.

Die Märchen der Weltliteratur. Jena, Köln, Düsseldorf: Diederichs.

Dietrich, A. *Mutter Erde.* 2nd ed. Berlin, 1913.

Drower, E. S.. *The Secret Adam.* Oxford, 1960.

Dschuang-Dsi, Das wahre Buch vom südlichen Blütenland. Tr. Richard Wilhelm. Jena, 1923.

Eckhardt, Meister. *Schriften.* Ed. H. Büttner. Jena, 1934.

Eluard, Paul. Ed. L. Perrot and J. Marcenac. Paris, 1964.

Eyik. *Harzmärchen oder Sagen und Märchen aus dem Oberharz.* Stade, 1862.

Fierz-David, Linda. *Der Liebestraum des Poliphilo.* Zurich, 1947.

Fordham, Michael. *The Life of Childhood.* London, 1944.

Forstner, D. *The World of Symbols.*

Frazer, James George. *The Golden Bough.* 6 vols. London: Macmillan, 1923.

Frobenius, L. *Das Zeitalter des Sonnengottes.* Berlin, 1904.

———. *Erythräa: Länder und Zeiten des heiligen Königsmordes.* Berlin, Zurich, 1931.

Gadamer, Hans Georg. *Wahrheit und Methode: Grundzüge einer philosophischen Hermeneutik.* 4th ed. Tübingen, 1960–75.

Gehrts, Heino. *Das Märchen und das Opfer.* Bonn: Bouvier, 1967.

Geoffrey of Monmouth. *See* Zumthor, Paul.

Green, Patricia Dale. *Cult of the Cat.* London: Heinemann, 1963.

Gressmann, Hugo. *Die Lade Jabwehs und das Allerheiligste des salomonischen Tempels.* 1920.

Grimms. *Kinder- und Hausmärchen,* Vol. 2, No. 123. In *Die Märchen der Weltliteratur.*

Grimms' Fairy Tales for Young and Old, Tr. Ralph Manheim, New York: Garden City, 1977.

Groot, J. J. M. de. *Universismus.* Berlin, 1918.

Grünbaum, M. *Neue Beiträge zur semitischen Sagenkunde.* Leiden, 1893.

Gubernatis, A. de. *Die Thiere in der indogermanischen Mythologie.* Leipzig, 1874.

Güntert, H. *Der arische Weltenkönig und Heiland.* Halle a. S., 1923.

Handwörterbuch des deutschen Aberglaubens. Ed. Hoffmann-Kreyer. Berlin, 1918–41.

Harding, Esther. *Psychic Energy.* New York, 1948.

———. *Journey into Self.* London, 1956.

———. *Woman's Mysteries.* New York, 1955.

Hartley, El. E. E. *Fundamentals of Social Psychology.* New York, 1952.

Hartmann, S. *Gayomart.* Uppsala, 1953.

———. *Gayômart: étude sur le syncrétisme de l'ancien Iran.* Uppsala, 1953.

Hermann, Paul. *Das altgermanische Priesterwesen.* Jena, 1929.

Herz, W. *Die Sage vom Giftmädchen.* Abhandlungen der königlich bayrischen Akademie der Wissenschaften ICI. Vol. XX, 1. Abteilung. München, 1893.

Hohmann, Josef. *Friede, Wirkungsgeschichte und kollektives Unbewurtes.* Frankfurt/M.: Europäische Hochschulschriften, 1984.

I Ching, or Book of Change. The Richard Wilhelm translation rendered into English by Cary F. Baynes. 3rd ed. Princeton: Princeton University Press, 1967.

Jakobsohn, Helmuth. "Das Gegensatzproblem im altägyptischen Mythos." In *Studien zur Analytischen Psychologie C. G. Jungs.* Zurich, 1955.

Janwitz, T., and R. Schulze. "Neue Richtungen in der Massenkommunikationsforschung." In *Rundfunk und Fernsehen.* 1960.

Jarmann, A. O. H. *The Legend of Merlin.* Cardiff, 1960.

Jolles, André. *Einfache Formen.* 2nd ed. Darmstadt, 1958.

Jonas, Hans. *Gnosis und spätantiker Geist.* 2nd ed. Göttingen, 1964.

Jung, Carl Gustav. *Collected Works* (=CW). Ed. Gerhard Adler et al. Bollingen Series XX. Princeton: Princeton University Press, 1954ff.

———. *Aion.* cw 9/ii.

———. "Analytical Psychology and Education." In cw 17.

———. "Answer to Job." In cw 11.

———. "Essays on Contemporary Events." In cw 10.

———. "Flying Saucers: A Modern Myth." In cw 10.

———. "Foreword to Harding: 'Psychic Energy.'" In cw 18.

———. *Memories, Dreams, Reflections.* Ed. Aniela Jaffé. New York: Vintage, 1989.

———. *Mysterium Coniunctionis.* cw 14.

———. "On the Psychology of the Trickster Figure." In cw 9/i.

———. *Psychological Types.* cw 6.

———. *Psychology of Alchemy.* cw 12.

———. "The Psychology of the Transference." In cw 16.

———. "The State of Psychotherapy." In cw 10.

———. *Symbols of Transformation.* cw 5.

———. "Synchronicity: An Acausal Connecting Principle." In cw 8.

Jung, Emma. "On the Nature of the Animus." Tr. Cary F. Baynes. In *Spring,* 1945. New York: Analytical Psychology Club of New York, 1957.

Jung, Emma, and Marie-Louise von Franz. *The Grail Legend*. Tr. Andrea Dykes. New York: Putnam's Sons, 1970.

Kerényi, Karl. *Gods of the Greeks*. Tr. Norman Cameron. London, New York: Thames & Hudson, 1951.

Kirfel, W. *Die dreiköpfige Gottheit*. Bonn, 1948.

Koestler, H. *Symbolik des chinesischen Universums*. Stuttgart, 1958.

The Koran. Tr. E. H. Palmer. Oxford University Press, 1949.

Lehner, E., and J. Lehner. *Folklore and Symbolism of Flowers, Plants, and Trees*. Tudor, N.Y., 1960.

Leisegang, Hans. *Die Gnosis*. Leipzig: Kröner, 1924.

Löpfe, A. *Russische Märchen*. Olten, 1941.

Lorenz, Konrad. *Wie der Mensch auf den Hund kam*. Hamburg: Deutscher Taschenbuch Verlag, 1966.

Luk, Charles. *Ch'an and Zen Teaching*. 3 volumes. London, 1960–62.

Lüthi, Max. *Das europäische Volksmärchen*. Bern, 1947.

Marko, K. *Evolution wider Willen*. Graz, Vienna, Cologne, 1968.

Maspero, H. *La Chine antique*. Paris, 1955.

———. *Le Taoisme*. Paris, 1950.

Meier, "Moderne Physik—Moderne Psychologie." In *Die kulturelle Bedeutung der Komplexen Psychologie,* 1935.

Morgenstern, Julian. *The Ark, the Ephod and the "Tent of Meeting,"* Cincinnati, 1945. (Quoted in *Kulturgeschichte des Alten Orients,* ed. H. Schmökel, Stuttgart, 1961.)

Müller, E. *Der Sohar*. Zurich, 1959.

Müller, Max. *The Upanishads*. Oxford University Press, 1926.

Neumann, Erich. *Amor and the Psyche: The Psychic Development of the Feminine*. Princeton University Press, 1990.

———. *The Origins and History of Consciousness*. Princeton: Princeton University Press, 1970.

Nielsen, D. *Der dreieinige Gott*. Berlin, London, 1922.

Ninck, Martin. *Die Bedeutung des Wassers im Kult und Leben der Alten*. Repr. Darmstadt: Wissenschaftliche Buchgesellschaft, 1960.

————. *Götter und Jenseitsglauben der Germanen.* Jena, 1937.

————. *Wodan und germanischer Schicksalsglaube.* Jena, 1933.

Onians, Richard Braxton. *The Origins of European Thought.* Cambridge University Press, 1954.

Pauli, Wolfgang. "Die philosophische Bedeutung der Idee der Komplementarität." In *Experientia,* Vol. VI, No. 2. Basel.

————. *Naturerklärung und Psyche.* Zurich, 1952.

Piankoff, A. *The Tomb of Rameses VI.* Bollingen Series XL, Part 1 and 2. New York: Pantheon, 1954.

Plutarch. *Über Isis und Osiris: Text und Kommentar* by Theodor Hopfner. Prague, 1940.

Portmann, Adolf. *Das Tier als soziales Wesen.* Zurich, 1953.

Post, Laurens van der. *The Heart of the Hunter.* London, 1961.

Preisendanz, K. *Papyri Graecae magicae.* 2 volumes. Leipzig, 1928.

Przywara, E., S.J. *Deus semper maior: Theologie der Exerzitien.* Freiburg i. Br., 1938.

Quispel, G. "Der gnostische Anthropos und die jüdische Tradition." In *Eranos-Jahrbuch* XXII (1953).

Rauh, H. D. *Das Bild des Antichrist im Mittelalter.* Münster, 1973.

Reitzenstein, R., und H. Schraeder. *Studien zum antiken Synkretismus aus Iran und Griechenland.* Repr. Darmstadt, 1965.

Renner, E. *Goldener Ring über Uri.* Zurich, 1941.

Sachs, Hans. *Fabeln und Schwänke.* Ed. Goetze und Drescher.

Sälzle, K. *Tier und Mensch, Gott und Dämon.* Munich, Basel, Vienna.

Sarasin, P. *Helios und Keraunos.* Innsbruck, 1924.

Schärf-Kluger, R. *Saul und der Geist Gottes. Studien zur analytischen Psychologie C. G. Jungs.* Zurich: Rascher, 1955.

Schmalz, G. *Komplexe Psychologie und körperliches Symptom.* Stuttgart, 1955.

Scholem, Gershom. *Major Trends in Jewish Mysticism.* 1941.

————. *Von der mystischen Gestalt der Gottheit.* Zurich, 1962.

————. *Zur Kabbala und ihrer Symbolik.* Zurich, 1960.

Somadeva. *Vetalapanchavimsati.* Tr. Tawney. Bombay, 1956.

Speck, F. G. *Naskapi: The Savage Hunter of the Labrador Peninsula.* University of Oklahoma Press, 1935.

Ta Tiung Shu. *Das Buch von der Großen Gemeinschaft.* Cologne, Düsseldorf, 1974.

The Thirteen Principal Upanishads. Tr. Robert Ernest Hume. Oxford University Press, 1921.

Tinbergen, N. *A Study of Instinct.* Oxford, 1955.

Tsujimura, Koichi. *Der Ochs und sein Hirte.* Pfullingen, 1958.

Tucker, Robert. *Karl Marx: Die Entwicklung seines Denkens von der Philosophie zum Mythos.* Munich, 1963.

Usener, H. *Götternamen.* Repr. Frankfurt/M., 1948.

Vielhauer, J. *Das Leben des Zauberers Merlin.* Amsterdam, 1978.

von Franz, Marie-Louise. *Aurora Consurgens.* Tr. R. F. C. Hull and A. S. B. Glover. London: Routledge & Keagan Paul, 1966.

———. *C. G. Jung: His Myth in Our Time.* Tr. Andrea Dykes. Evanston, Ill.: Northwestern University Press, 1974.

———. *Number and Time.*

———. "Über religiöse Hintergründe des Puer-Aeternus-Problems." In *Der Archetyp.* Basel, New York, 1964.

———. *Zeit: Strömen und Stille.* Frankfurt/M.: Insel, 1961.

Wickes, Frances. *The Inner World of Consciousness.* New York, London, 1927.

———. *The Inner World of Man.* New York, Toronto, 1938.

Wilhelm, Richard, and Carl Gustav Jung. *The Secret of the Golden Flower: A Chinese Book of Life.* San Diego: Harcourt Brace Jovanovich, 1970.

Wolff, Toni. *Studien zu C. G. Jungs Psychologie.* Zurich, 1981.

A. Wünsche. *Der Sagenkreis vom geprellten Teufel.* 1905.

———. *Schöpfung und Sündenfall des ersten Menschenpaares.* Leipzig, 1906.

Wyss, A. *Die Milch im Kultus der Griechen und Römer: Religionsgeschichtliche Versuche und Vorarbeiten.* Gießen, 1914.

Zimmer, Heinrich. *The King and the Corpse*. New York, 1914.

————. "Merlin." In *Corona* 9, book 2. Oldenburg, Munich, Berlin, 1939.

Zimmermann, R. C. *Das Weltbild des jungen Goethe*. Munich: Fink, 1969.

Zumthor, Paul. *Merlin le prophète*. Lausanne, 1943.

Index

■■

groups
center of, 257
masses versus, 258
See also relationships
guilt, 114
primal, 158–159

heroes
collective unconscious and, 45
as ego, 174–175
frivolous, 79–80
simple man, 12, 194
historical periods
psychotherapy and, 2
unconscious and, 3
historical-spiritual roots, 7
history
collective unconscious and, 23
dreams, collective and, 12
hidden current of events and, 263
psychology and, 8
Hypnerotomachia (Colonna),
317–318

I Ching, 200, 278, 282
Idea of the Holy, The, (Otto), 368–369
illusions of objectivity, 358
Incarnation, 91
individuation, 21, 364
beginning of, 300
collective responsibility and, 55
decreases in distance between people
and, 53
dreams and, 222, 292, 293
dream symbols and, 309
fourfold structures and, 328
impulse towards, 163
mandala and, 134
midlife period, conflicts and, 224
natural process of, 261
phases of, 134–135
process, 32, 133
questions about, 135
religion and, 240
Self and, 324
shadow, consciousness of, 246
shadow, insight into and, 301–302
spiral process of, 135
symbolism of, 384–385
unconscious and, 295–296

instincts, 6, 114–115
human social behavior and, 244
inheritance of, 245
magical ideas around, 9–10
religion and, 10–11, 252
isolation, human behavior and, 251

Jakobsohn, Helmuth, 139, 199, 255
Jesus. *See* Christ, Jesus.
Jolles, André, 76–77
Judaism
Adam legend and, 255
cosmic man (Adam) and, 138–139
warlike Messiah and, 47
Jung, C.G.
Aion, 12, 23, 46, 263
animals, God and, 90
"Answer to Job", 12, 47
collective unconscious and, 6
Eros and, 51–52
fairy tales and, 174
horse sacrifice and, 92
humanity's state today, 153
individuation, 133
Klaus's vision and, 42–43, 422–423
love, understanding and, 50–51
malice of objects and, 129
"Man and His Symbols", 292
Memories, Dreams, Reflections,
379–381
mythical tales, unconscious psyche
and, 111–112
personal confession of faith, 378–382
primal guilt, sexes and, 158–159
psyche, human relationships and,
256
psychological rules, contradictions
in, 84–85
Psychological Types, 203
Psychology and Alchemy, 134
"Relations between the Ego and the
Unconscious, The," 238
rose-colored blood and, 49–50
serpent, 287–288
the significance of consciousness, 118
stages of psychological treatment,
221–222
synchronicity principle, 386
unconscious atmosphere of family
and, 1–2

C. G. JUNG FOUNDATION BOOKS

Absent Fathers, Lost Sons: The Search for Masculine Identity, by Guy Corneau.

*Archetypal Dimensions of the Psyche, by Marie-Louise von Franz.

Creation Myths, revised edition, by Marie-Louise von Franz.

Ego and Archetype: Individuation and the Religious Function of the Psyche, by Edward F. Edinger.

The Feminine in Fairy Tales, revised edition, by Marie-Louise von Franz.

Gathering the Light: A Psychology of Meditation, by V. Walter Odajnyk.

A Guided Tour of the Collected Works of C. G. Jung, by Robert H. Hopcke. Foreword by Aryeh Maidenbaum.

In Her Image: The Unhealed Daughter's Search for Her Mother, by Kathie Carlson.

The Interpretation of Fairy Tales, revised edition, by Marie-Louise von Franz.

Knowing Woman: A Feminine Psychology, by Irene Claremont de Castillejo.

Masculinity: Identity, Conflict, and Transformation, by Warren Steinberg.

*Psyche and Matter, by Marie-Louise von Franz.

*Psychotherapy, by Marie-Louise von Franz.

Shadow and Evil in Fairy Tales, revised edition, by Marie-Louise von Franz.

Transforming Sexuality: The Archetypal World of Anima and Animus, by Ann Belford Ulanov and Barry Ulanov.

*Published in association with Daimon Verlag, Einsiedeln, Switzerland.